A POETIC FOR SOCIOLOGY

A POETIC FOR SOCIOLOGY

Toward a logic of discovery for the human sciences

RICHARD HARVEY BROWN

The University of Chicago Press
Chicago and London

The University of Chicago Press, Chicago 60637
The University of Chicago Press, Ltd., London

© Cambridge University Press 1977
All rights reserved. Originally published 1977
University of Chicago Press edition 1989
Printed in the United States of America

98 97 96 95 94 93 92 91 90 89   5 4 3 2 1

Library of Congress Cataloging in Publication Data

Brown, Richard Harvey.
   A poetic for sociology : toward a logic of discovery for the human sciences /
Richard Harvey Brown. — University of Chicago Press ed.
      p.   cm.
   Reprint. Originally published: Cambridge, England ; New York :
Cambridge University Press, 1977.
   Bibliography: p.
   Includes index.
   1. Social sciences—Methodology.   2. Humanities—Methodology.
3. Aesthetics.   4. Sociology—Methodology.   I. Title.
[H61.B679   1989]   88-38839
300′.18—dc 19   CIP
   ISBN 0-226-07619-9 (alk. paper)

For my wife, NATHALIE BABEL

My poetic
draws much from her poetic insight
My thought on the morality of thought
draws much from her moral courage

Contents

Preface

Personal knowledge and interests are inevitably expressed in theoretical formulations. As my case is no exception, a cautionary note may be proper at the outset. After receiving a statistical functionalist version of sociology at Berkeley and Columbia, I spent a number of years "applying" this knowledge in programs of intentional social change – economic development planning in Latin America, antipoverty activities in New York City, stints with think tanks and consulting firms. What struck me most in this work was the dissonance between social theory as I had learned it and political reality as I was experiencing it. Social theory *was* relevant to practice as a rhetoric for legitimating political proposals as "scientific." It was used instrumentally despite its weakness as explanation or reflection.

On this practical level there seemed to be affinities between a positivist theory of knowledge, a functional statistical theory of society, and a linear, objectivistic approach to institutional change. In the hands of conservatives the social systems models encouraged efforts to control society much in the manner that experiments are controlled. When liberals were in charge their reluctance to exercise such control insured that programs simply failed. In either case the intention of helping people was vitiated by the manipulativeness of the helping techniques; the increasing demand for experts to run larger and more complex organizations violated the increasing need for nonalienating forms of work and of governance.

While I was out in the field there had emerged in America a "new" sociology that promised to be true to the data as existentially enacted. As I came to understand them, existential, phenomenological, and other such sociologies did indeed capture the negotiated nature of social process. To understand how consciousness is shaped in interaction, how a persona gets enacted, or how professionals define a situation so as to control their clients, it was to such theories that one had to turn. Yet the problems that interested me most were still the old-fashioned ones – class conflict, social mobility, and institutional change. I wanted a macrotheory of action but instead found microtheories of consciousness.

In trying to bridge these two realms, I discovered that the conflicts between schools are not so much a war of armies as an anarchy in the streets. Moreover, each major theoretical group bases its work on a different theory of knowledge. Thus, no bridge could carry the weight I wanted to put on it unless its foundations were set in the deeper, epistemological substrata that underlies the conflicts between sociological schools. To be adequate no theory can do without some of the things possessed by alien camps. Yet each camp assumes a definition of knowledge that either excludes its rivals, or asks of them only "What's in it for me?" Most sociology imitates physics and justifies itself in terms of positivist epistemology. In contrast, the more humanistic sociologies are truer to the data, yet they appear to operate in the realm of intuition, to be a matter of interpretation rather than of truth.

Thus, I set out to find a conceptual vocabulary that could justify interpretive procedures as a rigorous way of knowing and under which, at the same time, the epistemology of positive sociology could be subsumed. Cognitive aesthetics, or what might be called a critical poetic, provided the beginnings of such a vocabulary.

This book is a translation of sociology into such a poetic. The work has taken me a long way from the initial questions of the relation between theory and practice, between consciousness and action. Although I have not addressed these questions directly, it is toward such a confrontation that this book has been written.

College Park, Maryland
November, 1976

Richard Harvey Brown

Acknowledgements

An earlier version of this manuscript was submitted as a Ph.D. thesis and special thanks go to my dissertation committee, which included Stanford Lyman, Randall Collins, Jack Douglas, Rudolf Makkreel, and Fredric Jameson. Dr. Lyman served as chairman and intellectual guide. He extended innumerable hours of "idle talk" through which I was able to clarify the problem I wanted to address. His advice on how to organize my materials has been invaluable. Randall Collins was my severest critic from a scientific and historical sociological perspective, and any merits this book may have in this regard are due to his good counsel. Jack Douglas offered much advice on the politics of social research and on alternative strategies for addressing my intended audience. Rudolf Makkreel was unstinting in both his demands for conceptual rigor and his generosity in guiding me into alien philosophic domains. Fredric Jameson suggested the basic idea of demonstrating my theses through literary critical examinations of seminal sociological texts.

While at the University of California at San Diego I had the good fortune to work in an environment of intense intellectual avidity, much of which was inspired by Aaron Cicourel, Joseph Gusfield, Cesar Graña, Fred Davis, and Trutz von Trotha. Herbert Marcuse, Louis Marin, and the late Robert Levine also helped me. Though encountered late in the course of this work, Kingsley Widmer nurtured me by personal example and substantive remarks. Also during this period I came to know Manfred Stanley, who has been a witness to the power of ideas as well as a critic and companion.

Each of these scholars was helpful in many more ways than those mentioned and, although varied in their particular gifts, their common commitment to the life of the mind has been a mainstay and inspiration. The same applies to Benjamin Nelson, Sigmund Diamond, Herbert Passin, and the late Raymond Sontag, all of whom conveyed a passion for ideas and encouraged me during struggles toward self-definition.

The governing spirit of this book also was influenced by Amrit Baruah, John Clark, Elizabeth Durbin, Robert Fishman, Walter Jonas, George Peabody, Sam Scheele, Philip Waring, and Laszlo Zukmann, all of whom helped me toward a stance of moral and political reflection. Stanford Lyman deserves thanks in these connections too, as friend and confrère as well as mentor. My brother Jason Brown, a scientist, enlightened me on relations between my own work and current theories of the structure of mind. My parents, Samuel R. Brown and Sylvia Brown, supported this project in many indirect but important ways. My appreciation of them will be expressed in the dedication of future works. Throughout the years of work on this project Colleen Carpenter provided much encouragement. Her personal kindness is matched only by her professionalism in preparing this manuscript for press.

In addition to these persons, certain authors have strongly influenced this work. I therefore wish to affirm my debt to Laurence Foss and Nelson Goodman, whose lucid writings inspired my discussion of symbolic realism in Chapter 2 and in the Coda, respectively. For Chapter 4 on metaphor, Mary Hesse's *Models and Analogies in Science*, C.M. Turbayne's *The Myth of Metaphor*, and Douglas Berggren's essays in the *Review of Metaphysics* were of central importance as sources for many basic ideas, analytic categories, and examples. Paul Diesling's *Patterns of Discovery in the Social Sciences* also provided important insights and examples. George Lundberg, the positivist, was accidentally rebaptized as Ferdinand Lundberg, the Marxist!

Chapter 5 on irony also draws on a wide range of works by authors from several disciplines. In particular, Louis Schneider's admirable essays inspired my comparison of Goffman and Sorokin, as well as many substantive comments on the ironic nature of Sorokin's thought. Also of fundamental importance for this chapter is the seminal work of Douglas Colin Muecke, whose brilliant book, *The Compass of Irony*, must be a starting point for any student of this subject. Materials from Muecke's work entered my text variously in the form of quotations, instances, paraphrases, and examples. Indeed, my introductory and some analytic remarks on irony reflect a thorough assimilation—and refocusing—of Professor Muecke's thought. Also influencing this chapter are the writings of David Worcester, Bert States, and Kenneth Burke, who has continued to be an inspiration since the completion of this work.

A POETIC FOR SOCIOLOGY

1
Poetics and sociology: an invitation

Tell me where is fancy bred,
Or in the heart or in the head?
How begot, how nourishèd?
  Reply, reply?
Shakespeare (*Merchant of Venice*, III, 2)

Our thesis is that an aesthetical view of sociological knowledge
– a poetic for sociology – can contribute greatly to resolving
methodological (and, implicitly, praxiological) contradictions
confronting the human studies today. These contradictions are
visible in the divergent epistemologies of various schools of
contemporary social science. For example, the study of speech
may be either Chomskyian or Skinnerian; political science may
invoke statistics on voting behavior, or it may be largely interpretive in the manner of Arendt or Aron; history may follow
the positivism of "Cliometricians," or it may be inspired by
Collingwood or Hegel. A similar pluralism of methods is seen
in sociology per se. Functionalism, in its purer forms, grounds
itself in a realistic metaphysics of a priori principles and logical
deductions; experimental empiricism takes a logical positivist
approach; symbolic interactionist and existential thinking oppose both these schools, insisting that sociological understanding is yielded by interpretive procedures that focus on meanings
that actors give to their own situations.

While all such approaches may attain consistency with their
own principles, the epistemology of each contains assumptions
that contradict those of the others. Moreover, given the inef-
fability of lived experience, any attempt to compare competing
criteria of knowledge with an "objective standard" merely results – as with the sorcerer's broomstick – in yet another concept of social reality and sociological knowledge. Nonethe-

less, adequate social theory seems to require contributions from each of these schools. It thus appears that any criteria of adequacy for theory in the human studies must include at least the following:

1. That theory be phenomenologically true to the data; that it be resonant with social reality as intended in the consciousness of the actors themselves.

2. That theory be hermeneutically self-conscious; that it be dialectically self-reflective of its own methods and interests.

3. That theory be explanatory in terms of controlled comparisons; that it yield "if X, then Y" statements and, as such, inform us of probable futures and provide a guide for societal actions.

4. That theory be general theory; that it be able to comprehend social reality at any level of abstraction or any range of data.

In this essay we advance "cognitive aesthetics" as a framework for developing such a method of logic. Cognitive aesthetics, we argue, has four principal advantages. First, it permits us to move beyond copy theories of truth in both art and in science. Second, it provides a framework within which the pioneering artist and the pioneering scientist are both seen as involved in essentially the same activity: making paradigms through which experience becomes intelligible. These two advantages give birth to a third and fourth; for if art and science are seen to have an essential affinity, then the possibility is opened for a fusion of the two principal ideals of sociological knowledge: the scientific or positivist one, stressing logical deductions and controlled research, and the artistic or intuitive one, stressing insights and subjective understanding. Finally, insofar as such a fusion is possible, cognitive aesthetics provides a source of metacategories for assessing sociological theory from any methodological perspective.

One implication of such an aesthetic view is that no given symbol system – whether it be astrology, baroque iconography, or quantum physics – has ontological priority over any other. All are equally "real." Given this, our choice of symbol systems, in some ultimate sense, becomes a matter of taste (Feyerabend, 1970:90–91). However, it does not become "merely" a matter of taste. Instead, we can discern *canons* of aesthetic judgment that may be used as criteria of adequacy for theories or representations from any symbol system.

Conventionally, however, aesthetic concepts often refer to

purely *noncognitive* experience. "Where science stops," it is said, "there art begins." "Art" is associated in popular conceptions with emotions and feelings, with the unique, particular, and unpredictable, with creativity and genius; "science," on the other hand, is thought of as the province of rationality, ordered and disciplined thought, clearly defined problems, and carefully tested solutions. The battle over which is superior – science versus art, truth versus beauty, knowledge versus intuition – has raged since the followers of St. Simon fought those of Rousseau, and it continues today in the conflict of positivistic scientists, technocrats, and cold warriors, against "soft" sociologists, counterculturists, and participants in the human development movement.

The most striking aspect of this debate is that both parties share the same definition of rationality, the same divisions between means and ends, facts and opinions, and objectivity and subjectivity. Both accept similar assumptions about the separation of science and rationality (the objective, cognitive) as against feeling and art (the subjective, sensual). The difference between the two camps is that positivists take facts and objectivity to be the grounding of their work while their opponents believe that ideas and subjectivity constitute a "higher science." Given this situation, intellectual "statesmen" come to be those who articulate a more moderate stand – for example those who point to the role of inspiration behind scientific finds or to the descriptive properties of art.

In contrast to both these views, this essay takes an *aesthetical* view of rationality. Just as scientific theories require *aesthetic* adequacy, works of art present a kind of *knowledge*. For cognitive aesthetics, both science *and* art are rational in that they both presuppose various criteria of economy, congruence and consistency, elegance, originality, and scope. Such criteria are those by which we organize experience into formal structures of which "knowing" is constituted. As they are expressed in "coherence systems" such as art, science, or sociology, these criteria are determinate as well as freely created. They are determinate in that they are culturally embedded and hence historically inherited, and also because they can be articulated in terms of normative paradigms. But they also can be invented or transformed; Hence we do not invest them with an absolute ontological status.

Such an aesthetic of knowledge undercuts both scientific *and* sensual absolutism: It presupposes that the practice of science itself constitutes a commitment to values such as fitness and economy and that the practice and appreciation of art become nonsense unless conducted in terms of aesthetic criteria of rationality. The coherence systems of art and science obviously are different enough to justify distinction. To borrow the example of languages, French is not Spanish, and even less is it Chinese. Yet linguistics may reveal commonalities between all three and even show how the particular "genius" of each lies in the way it solves problems common to all languages. Similarly, from the viewpoint of a cognitive aesthetic, sociology is neither a natural science nor a fine art. Yet as a coherence system or symbolic form, it shares features with both. And with the fall of absolute distinctions between science and art, a possibility is opened for creating social theory that is at once "objective" *and* "subjective," at once valid scientifically and significantly humane.

ASSUMPTIONS AND METHODS OF APPROACH

"Every science secretes an ontology," says Merleau-Ponty, "every ontology anticipates a body of knowledge" (1964:98).[1] Just as each school of sociological thought implies some logic of inquiry, so *our* study of these logics presupposes some method of approach. Paul Diesing (1971) has identified four ways in which philosophers talk about social science, and his typology may help us specify our own rules of discourse. The first of Diesing's types is "conceptual analysis," examples of which include Winch (1958), Peters (1960), Taylor (1964), and Anderson (1964). By this method the investigator selects some core concept – say, intention or action – and then analyzes it in terms of its ordinary use within the language game of some discipline.[2] From such analysis the informal logic of that domain is made explicit and self-contradictions are eliminated. For example, distinctions may be made between the use of "action" as "the making sharable of intentions" or as the "spatiotemporal movement of persons." Similarly, "thinking" may mean one thing when used with reference to people, another with reference to computers.

A second approach to the study of logics of inquiry is "rational reconstruction" or, more commonly, logical positivism or logical empiricism. By this approach a "pure" language and method of science is posited and then used as a standard against which to criticize the "errors" of practitioners in various disciplines. A statement by Helmer and Rescher (1958) serves as an example: "But once a new fact or a new idea has been conjectured . . . it must be capable of objective test and confirmation by anyone." Physics is the model here and, standing above physics, some axiological science like geometry. Also implied is a strict separation of fact from theory, of conjecture from proof, of discovery from verification. It also is worth noting what Helmer and Rescher *omit*: They never tell us what "objective test" or "confirmation by anyone" means to a field anthropologist, a historian, or a symbolic interactionist.

A third approach to analyzing logics of inquiry is the "typological method," in which the investigator classifies sociological writings according to certain tentative procedural criteria. As more and more works are examined, the criteria – and the resultant typology – tend to become more and more complex. This approach usually does not focus on historical development – the categories are assumed to have existed logically prior to examples of them, even if examples can not be found. The typological method differs from conceptual analysis and rational reconstruction in that it does not focus on language use per se, nor does it necessarily presuppose one type to be preferable to others. Examples are Briefs (1960), Martindale (1960), McKeon (1951), Sacksteder (1963, 1964), Schwab (1960), and Wallace (1971).

A fourth way of exploring logics of inquiry is that of the participant-observer. In this approach the investigator treats sociological methods as ongoing activities. His focus, however, is not on the techniques of research but on the "logic in use" of sociologists, who are seen as members of a subculture with its own rituals, language, and myths. This is philosophy in the spirit of Peirce, James, and Dewey; it is practiced today by Hanson (1958, 1961), Abraham Kaplan (1964), Diesing (1971), Kuhn (1962), and Toulmin (1961). Following Dewey, these writers understand "logic" as the procedures scientists use when they are doing well as scientists. This may be different from what philosophers, or even sociologists themselves, say is the "ideal" or "correct" logic of inquiry.

As in social research, the participant-observer of methods must immerse himself in the methodological discourse and activities of the members, coming to understand the meanings they themselves invest in their language and practice. A variety of materials may be used as sources: firsthand involvement in research work of various types; sociologists' autobiographies and personal reports; direct observation of interactions between colleagues; socialization in graduate training; social control as exercised by tenure committees, journal editors, and foundation officers; and arcane rituals and myths such as Ph.D. orals, meetings of professional associations, apocryphal anecdotes, and idealized accounts of the purposes, values, or methods of the profession. In this spirit, articles by sociologists on method may be treated as informants' reports, journal articles as cultural artifacts, and methodology courses as cooption techniques. Polemical articles are especially useful as indicators of intra-tribal conflicts.

Implicit in such an approach is the assumption that "logics" develop in time. They neither preexist transcendentally nor are they posited a priori by the investigator. Moreover, it is assumed that there is no absolutely correct doctrine: The fruits of each method must be assessed in terms of the meanings and goals of its practitioners. Although the participant-observer may tend to overemphasize the internal cogency and systemic aspects of various schools, this same tendency encourages a dialectical playing off of one school against the others. The emergence of this process, hopefully, is not that one abandons inquiry in the face of the impossibility of absolute knowledge, but that one comes to understand the postulational and socially embedded character of all claims to truth. Such "truth systems," "institutional epistemologies," or "standardized hermeneutics" (Turner, 1969:9), are absolute only in the sense that they govern propositions advanced under their auspices. Outside their particular domains these systems may make no sense at all. Thus, for example, to say "That's an efficient painting" is, on the surface at least, an absurd statement, for it assumes that the domain of engineering governs aesthetic objects. Similarly, to say "That's a divine social theory" is to be either gushy or irrelevant, for here one is confusing social science and theology.

In this introductory chapter we take a participant-observer approach, with touches of the typological method. In comparing principal schools of sociological thought, we argue that no one form of sociological theory is adequate by itself. Instead, each approach requires the others for completeness. At the same time, however, the underlying epistemologies of each approach are, in many ways, logically incompatible with those of the others. Without some resolution of these underlying contradictions, attempts to unify various approaches remain fragile and superficial at best. Yet each of the implicit epistemologies presents itself as a fairly complete – if not a closed – system, and thus the possibilities of resolution on this deeper, logically antecedent level, are discouraging.

Such a predicament suggests that we may have been asking the wrong question. That is, instead of choosing one paradigm and banishing all the rest, or dissolving all paradigms into one, we might be wiser to "let one hundred flowers bloom." By doing this, however, we do not abdicate our responsibility for specifying what constitutes an adequate explanation. On the contrary, we seek what might be called "canopy concepts," by which the adequacy of all proposed approaches might be judged.

In so doing, in the body of the essay we move from the participant-observer and typological methods closer to the methods of conceptual analysis and rational reconstruction. In conceptual analysis, however, the focus is on clarifying the uses of terms within the ordinary discourse of sociologists, which does not imply the "meta-" categories we seek. On the other hand, in rational reconstruction, a metasystem *is* posited, but it is posited a priori and absolutely; moreover, rational reconstruction has assumed physics, geometry, and symbolic logic as paradigmatic expressions of pure science, against which the human studies inevitably fall short.

In contrast to all these approaches, then, we attempt to analyze various sociological writings from an aesthetic viewpoint as though they were novelistic, poetic, or dramatic texts. The choice of verbal rather than plastic arts such as painting or music is significant. There are three major categories generally used in aesthetic analysis: "form," "content," and "surface" (Hospers, 1964). Surface refers to the tonal qualities of music or color, for example, not what they represent (content) or the way they are arranged (form). The verbal arts have little of this surface quality. Consider, for example, how much of an aesthetic experience one could have reading a poem in unknown language, or whether anything is lost if a poem is printed or handwritten. With the verbal arts the physical qualities – that is, the immediate auditory or visual surface – are largely irrelevant. It is meaning and structure that count. Sociology, like the verbal arts, also lacks this surface quality, but it can, like them, be judged in terms of its formal and mimetic power. For these reasons the critical concepts associated with the novel, poetry, and drama – that is, "poetics" – provide a privileged vocabulary for the aesthetic consideration of sociological theory.

Having borrowed our aesthetic criteria from the arts, however, we will not then posit them for sociology a priori. Instead, each concept is redefined in terms of its special applicabilities in this new context. The result, hopefully, will contribute not only to the clarification of sociological method and theory but also to cognitive aesthetics, itself part of a general theory of signs.

A metaphor may help crystallize this point: that of the five blind men feeling an elephant. By extension, one blind man, say the functionalist, feels the tusks; another, the statistical sociologist, feels the legs, and so on, each thinking that it is *he* who knows what the elephant "really" is like. A sighted person, coming on such a scene, might put together all the partial views to form a picture of the "true" elephant. In this essay we make no claim to have such sight. Ultimate, fundamental knowledge is as inaccessible to us as it is to the blind men. Indeed, we claim that any assertion as to what the true elephant is like is still another view, a picture from *some* perspective. Metaperspectives may be more comprehensive and precisely cogent, but they are no more absolute than the perspectives that they hope to embrace.

When we speak of canopy categories, then, we do not expect them to refer to "real" elephants, "real" knowledge, or the "real" social world, in the sense that any of these can be absolutely known. One lesson to be drawn from the multiplicity of competing approaches in our discipline is that social theory must be conducted in terms of *some* approach, but that none of these can justify ultimate claims. Thus our canopy categories represent neither a theory of society nor a method of doing such theory. Instead, they provide a vocabulary for talking about different methods and approaches, which is not contained within any one of them.

To deny claims of absolute knowledge is not, however, to say that knowledge is not possible or to accept an uncritical relativism. Instead, our view is that knowledge exists *as* knowledge only in terms of some universe of discourse, some system of meaning, some institutional epistemology. Those various symbol systems cannot be ultimately grounded themselves, yet any theory or method of approach derives its status as "knowledge" or "correct procedure" in terms of one or another of them.

In this broad sense, the "poetics" we use is very close to what is meant by "semiotics," as a theory or method for comparing symbol systems and the types of knowledge derivable from them

(Gadamer, 1965; Mayenowa, 1967). In its narrower usage, however, poetics refers specifically to the symbology of the verbal arts. We have drawn on this usage for the basic terms of our analysis. Thus Chapter 3, "Point of View," uses concepts associated with the novel; Chapter 4, "Metaphor," draws on analyses of poems; Chapter 5, "Irony," employs terms taken from criticism of drama. Poetics also is used to refer not to specific verbal arts, nor to symbol systems in general, but to the *verbal* arts as opposed to the plastic arts, the sciences, and so on. Our use of poetics on this level implies that sociology is such an art, but also that art is something of a science. These implications will be explored in Chapter 2, "Cognitive Aesthetics."

CONTEMPORARY SOCIOLOGY: A BUDGET OF CRISES

It is now generally acknowledged that sociology is experiencing a profound crisis, out of which, presumably, will come a new paradigm for the study of conduct. There is much less agreement, however, on the precise nature of this crisis, or on the character of the underlying philosophic views that are at stake. Daniel Bell, for example (1960), pictures a struggle between American functionalism and Soviet Marxism. Other writers, such as Hannah Arendt, Herbert Marcuse, and Jürgen Habermas, blend the dialectical humanism of Marx with concerns about language, embodiment, and intersubjectivity, and oppose this amalgam to American *and* Soviet positivisms. Still other writers, such as Robert Merton, see the great split to be between macro- and microsociologies. Jack Douglas refers to absolutist approaches and Peter Manning to functionalism, which, they say, must give way to a new existential model. Thomas P. Wilson (1969) speaks of normative versus interpretive paradigms, and Trent Schroyer of objectivistic versus subjectivistic theories (1973), each in his own way echoing the historicist debate between nomothetic and ideographic explanation or, more recently, between explanation by cause and explanation by reason.

Not only is our cake cut at different angles; each cutting makes of it a different cake. Moreover, many of those with knives in hand are what might be called paradigm imperialists.[3] For example, Kingsley Davis declares that all sociological analysis is functional analysis, whereas Howard Becker argues that all social theories commit the "sin" of subjective interpretation. Thus, despite important differences within each theoretical and methodological approach, in each there is an underlying unity of perspective that sees *that* approach as the most significant type of scientific inquiry. Writers within each camp may assent verbally to the truism that the other approaches have something to contribute, but their practice often is to exclude enemies and incorporate additional turf. As Abraham Kaplan says,

> Each of the methods does assign a place to the others; their function is to serve its own needs. For the experimenter, theory is of no concern except as it suggests experiments or guides their design and interpretation; the theoretician returns the compliment; and so for the rest. None of the methods is appreciated by the others in terms of its own problems and interests; each asks only, "What's in it for me?" (1964:276)

Our purpose in this essay is to suggest a poetic for sociology which could provide a common language for assessing all approaches. Before launching that project it may be best to array some of the dominant "crises" in the discipline. Among these are high-level theory versus low-level description, nomothetic explanation by causal laws versus ideographic interpretation of unique situations, neopositivism versus neo-Marxism, and functionalism versus phenomenology. These pairs are by no means mutually exclusive; within each pair the dichotomies may share common attributes or in part be defined in terms of each other. Orderliness in our exposition, therefore, should not be taken to mean that in practice these schools are either wholly homogeneous or entirely discrete.[4]

Nomothetic versus ideographic

The oldest and most frequently recurring debate on sociological approaches is between explanation by cause or universal law against hermeneutic understanding of particular wholes, usually by means of interpretation of rules or motives. This conflict can be traced to Vico's reply (1948) to Descartes (1912). Descartes argued that knowledge of history and the social world was uncertain if not impossible, because it could never be objective in the manner of mathematical physics. Vico took this very argument and turned it on its head: *Because* history and society are created by persons, we can understand them better than the physical world, which is alien to us. This debate was revived in the nineteenth century as a conflict between science and history. Science was defined in terms of hypothetical-deductive or experimental-causal knowledge, whereas history was thought of as the study of the structures of intention underlying unique events (Rickert, 1962; Windelband, 1961). Whereas scientists claimed that only their approach constituted knowledge, historians insisted that what they did either was "really like" science or, conversely, that its very differentness yielded a higher truth.

In contemporary sociology, the nomothetic-ideographic debate takes the form of experimental-statistical methodology as opposed to participant-observer or clinical methods. The experimental approach takes "variables" as its subject matter – that is, events that exhibit measurable variations in rates of occurrence. Its basic objective is to identify variables that behave in lawlike regularities and then to codify these regularities into general theories. Originally variables were studied in pairs, but with the development of more sophisticated statistical techniques (Bartlett, 1962; Rao, 1965), sociologists were able to control statistically for many variables at once. This possibility has led many theorists to believe that causal analysis of discrete variables can eventually be built up into analyses of whole systems (Buckley, 1967, 1968; Merton, 1957; von Bertalanffy, 1968; J. Sutherland, 1973). From the interpretative viewpoint, however, the aggregation of causes into systems, even if successful, would overlook the questions of the geneses, boundaries, and structures of systems, which are seen as more than the sum of (the causal linkages of) the parts. On the other hand, to *posit* the existence of systemic properties is to beg one of the central questions that causal explanations were intended to solve.

The holistic, historicist approach was first used in the social sciences by anthropologists, then later by sociologists, social psychologists, and political scientists. Its primary subject is not discrete variables but whole systems – a primitive tribe, a gang or neighborhood, a business firm.[5] In each case the emphasis is on the essential defining characteristics of that particular system, its cohesion (*zusammenhang*), its boundedness, the ways in which parts and whole reciprocally define and delimit each other, and the ways it achieves and maintains its individuality. The focus is not on general laws but on the implicit *rules* emergent in that particular system. Procedurally, instead of setting up controlled experiments, the researcher himself becomes partially socialized into the system. This can be done either imaginatively through documentary analysis (history), directly through membership (field research), or through a combination of both these methods, as in clinical or life histories where the analyst has a direct relation with his subject, but must reconstruct the subject's *other* relationships on the basis of his reports. The researcher, through participation in the normal rules and expectations of the members, gradually turns himself into an analog of the system (Diesing, 1971:6). When something happens he can imagine with accuracy its consequences to and for members in various social locations. Or he can imagine both the occurrence *and* its consequences. In contrast to objective experimental findings, this *personal* knowledge (Polanyi, 1958), or *verstehen*, is "from the inside" (Weber, 1951; Abel, 1948; Bergstraesser, 1947; Parsons, 1949:510ff, 1954).

High-level abstraction versus low-level description

For about twenty-five years prior to the middle 1950s it was widely held in America that sociology was rapidly becoming a true science. More and more specialized research projects were being undertaken, and grand theory on the European model was being revived by Talcott Parsons. These two enterprises soon would converge, it was felt, to produce a comprehensive science of society (Parsons, 1954:366–367; Lundberg, 1955:191–202).

One of the earliest and most influential critics of these assumptions was Robert K. Merton. Merton argues that it is inappropriate to assume that "Because a discipline called physics and a discipline called sociology are both identifiable in the mid-twentieth century, ... the one must be the measure of the other." Between these disciplines, he notes, "stand billions of man hours of sustained, disciplined, and cumulative research" (1957:6–7). On one hand, data has not been sufficiently accumulated to support general theory; on the other hand "a large part of what is now called sociological theory consists of *general orientations toward data, suggesting types of variables which need somehow to be taken into account, rather than clear, verifiable statements of relationships between specified variables*" (1957:9, Merton's italics).

Facing this gap between high-level abstractions and low-level data, Merton recommended the development of "theories of the middle range."[6]

> The recent history of sociological theory can in large measure be written in terms of an alternation between two contrasting emphases. On the one hand, we observe those sociologists who seek above all to generalize, to find their way as rapidly as possible to the formulation of sociological laws. . . . At the other extreme stands a hardy

band who do not hunt too closely the implications of their research but who remain confident and assured that what they report is so. . . . For the first group the identifying motto would at times seem to be: "We do not know whether what we say is true, but it is at least significant." And for the radical empiricist the motto may read: "This is demonstrably so, but we cannot indicate its significance." (1957:85)

To counter this predicament we need "theories intermediate to the minor working hypotheses evolved in abundance during the day-to-day routines of research and the all-inclusive speculations comprising a master conceptual scheme" (1957:5–6).

Merton's definition of the crisis in sociology has been questioned, as has his proposed solution to it. Instead, it has been argued (Willner, 1967) that grand theory and microscopic statistical research are not end points on a single continuum; each "pole" in fact represents different epistemic assumptions, and each implies a different methodology that can be applied at *any* scale or range of data.

When we look more closely at the underlying logic of the grand theory to which Merton refers, it turns out to be the telic, holistic, idealistic realism that, in fact, has been applied to micro- – as well as middle and macro- – ranges of data. For example, Parson's work on *The Social System* is broad gauge, but Merton's functional analysis of "The Role of the Intellectual in Public Bureaucracy" is midrange, while Goffman's *Encounters* is a kind of microfunctionalism.[7] On the other hand, if we look at what Merton calls "radical empiricism," it appears that the applicability of this nominalistic, aggregative, statistical approach is epistemologically grounded in logical positivism. Moreover, like functionalist theory, it has little to do with scale or range. Although the vast majority of quantitative surveys or experiments have been conducted on a narrow range of data, we can also look at the works of Durkheim, Stouffer, Kinsey, and the U.S. Bureau of the Census for examples of broad-gauged research.

What Merton seems to be getting at, of course, is that middle-range theories should be *testable* theories. Unfortunately this is confused with "middleness," which is a separate question. Cogency and precision cannot be equated with high, middle, or low levels of generality. The problem with the general theories to which Merton refers is not that they are general, but that they are inexact; similarly, small-scale problems are not a privileged domain of exactitude (Willner, 1967:xv). The question of testability refers not to scale but to cogency, precision, and the like. And the meanings of these terms arise from the epistemologies implicit in the methods or schools in which particular theories are couched.

Neo-Marxism and neopositivism: a dialectic of methods[8]

C. Wright Mills confronted the same gap between theory and research that troubled Robert Merton. But Mills proposed a different solution. Whereas Merton sees sociology as needing a new focus in order to develop as a science, Mills views it as a humanistic study that should avoid all "efforts to restate and adopt *philosophies of natural science.* . . . To limit in the name of natural science the problems upon which we shall work . . . is a curious timidity" (1959:57, 120, Mills' italics). In the place of positive science, Mills calls for the revival of a sociological imagination that would be self-reflective instead of pseudo-objective, and that would ground itself in praxis instead of grand theory or abstracted empiricism.

Largely inspired by Mills' work – and given additional impetus by the Vietnam war, the black and student movements, and the use of applied behavioral science as an instrument of established power in these conflicts – there has arisen in America a "new sociology" (Horowitz, 1964). Under this rubric is a rejection of both systems theory and survey research. However, instead of replacing them with studies of the middle range, these new sociologists stress the use of knowledge for social and political criticism, the analysis of institutionalized power, and the assumption of conflict, not harmony, as a basic model.

The revival of radical sociology in America also has been nourished by the influx of European Marxist thought, chiefly through the Frankfort school, which flourished in the 1920s in Germany and which largely migrated to the United States in the 1930s. In the decade following the Russian Revolution, the Frankfort school's philosophic critique of bourgeois science was seen as a political as well as an intellectual struggle, for the proletariat was thought to be ready for battle. By the time of Hitler's rise to power, however, these hopes were thoroughly disappointed. The later extensions of critical theory by Horkheimer, Adorno, and Marcuse forego mention of philosophy or of the proletariat as a modern revolutionary force. Instead, as Wellmer puts it, "critical theory conceives itself as a protest, but as a protest impotent in practice" (1971:52).

Critical theory thus found itself in a kind of double isolation. Revolutionary praxis was betrayed by the authoritarian bureaucracies of the East, and preempted by economic success in the West. The relative satisfaction and growing prosperity of workers under capitalism seemed contrary to the Marxist thesis of their progressive impoverishment, while the alienation of workers under Soviet socialism violated the thesis of their progressive liberation. In response to these conundrums, critical theorists left the economic arena and began to attack industrial society and instrumental reason in general. Their focus became the cultural or ideational superstructure rather than the base. An extreme example of this is Adorno's musical and literary essays – they reflect critical theory's alienation not only from praxis, East and West, but also from science itself.

These forfeitures, in both theory and in practice, underlie recent efforts of contemporary Marxists in both Europe and America to renew critical theory on a methodological foundation that is at once scientific *and* ideological, as a prelude to formal theory that can also be a guide to humanizing action. The goal of these thinkers is not only an ideological critique of industrial society, but also the building of a sociology that is *critical* in both the Kantian sense of self-reflection on the presuppositions of knowledge, as well as in the Marxian sense of unmasking the myths of society. The method of neo-Marxist sociology is thus dialectical *self*-criticism; its function is dialectical criticism of society – "to name that which secretly keeps society going ... [to] lift the rock under which evil broods" (Adorno, quoted by Schroyer, 1971:132).

In contrast to the neo-Marxist approach, one basic assumption of positivism is the ideal of knowledge without a point of view. Biases are thought to be controllable through operationalization of concepts and experimental controls. The lenses of such an apparatus remove the tints of our personal vision but are colorless themselves. Various social scientists may not always adhere to this ideal, either individually or as a group. Yet insofar as they deviate from the methods of value-free objectivity, they are thought to be unscientific.

Yet is it not possible, ask Marxists, that this positivistic method itself constitutes a point of view, containing its own interests and biases? For if positive science seeks predictability and control, would it not seem to have a vested interest in those conditions that provide the possibility for this type of knowledge – a stable, technically manipulable sociopolitical order? Indeed, the content of theories derived from this method tends to be technocratic, suggesting elitest management of society or, at their most generous, participation through top-down liberal reform.

Such an unacknowledged affinity between positive science and technical control of society suggests that science itself is an ideology in just the sense noted by Mannheim:

> The concept "ideology" reflects the one discovery which emerged from political conflict, namely, that ruling groups can in their thinking become so intensively interest-bound to a situation that they are no longer able to see certain facts which would undermine their sense of domination. There is implicit in the word "ideology" the insight that in certain situations the collective unconscious of certain groups obscures the real condition of society both to itself and to others and thereby stabilizes it. (1960:36)

Thus, in the Marxist view, the political use of behavioral science has resulted in positivism having become the legitimizing ideology of the ruling class. Despite the opposition of many behavioral scientists themselves,[9] their logic of method has been used as "the doctrine that social order can be consciously adapted to the requirements of contemporary science and technology" (Habermas, quoted in *TLS*, 1970:271). Ironically, value-freedom itself has come to provide an ethic for bureaucratic control.

In response to such assertions positivists make several claims, which Manfred Stanley calls the déjà vu, the messianic, and the nominalist arguments (1972:275). The first dismisses concern with the political implications of social science by saying that such fears have been voiced for generations, yet we continue to prosper. The second, messianic, argument counters the fears of technicism with an inventory of its blessings and future hopes. The social indicators movement (R. A. Bauer, 1966) and the Year 2000 studies (Kahn and Weiner, 1967; Bell, 1967, 1973) are of this sort.[10] The third, nominalist, position insists that radicals' fears, like truths, are just names. Moreover, because the social whole, like knowledge, is made up of individuals, rational controls are necessary if these individuals are to optimize their satisfactions.[11]

None of these arguments is surprising given empiricist assumptions. Yet it is precisely these assumptions that the dialecticians attack. In terms of these assumptions, all our values are private and subjective, and technical rationality becomes the sole canon for public – that is, scientific – decisions. What becomes of such a society, left with no criteria for choosing between life and death? What becomes of freedom of thought – let alone scientific freedom – when formal rationality becomes a "factor of production" subject to oligarchic control?[12] In such a circumstance, say Marxists, a sociology that, in the name of objectivity, excludes every kind of transcendence must inevitably become an apologia for the status quo.

From the positivist viewpoint, however, such criticisms are little more than metaphysics or opinion, a "practically oriented philosophy of history dressed up as science" (Albert, quoted in *TLS*, 1970:271). If the sociologist insists on playing the moral philosopher – of the Left *or* the Right – he does so in his *private* capacity; he expresses his personal taste, not publicly verifiable knowledge. Without such moral abstinence, science will be unable to perform its basic task of exact empirical description. The point is not to change society, but to explain it. The irony, answer Marxists, is that the positivist vision of knowledge and reality is now close to fulfillment. Rationality, once a heuristic analytic model, has been largely realized, either normatively or factually, through the rationalization of relations in industrial society. At the same time, science – by virtue of the success of its value-free mode of inquiry – has become an instrument of social domination. But on what principles and for what values? By its own admission, cultural meanings and forms of consciousness – including freedom – are not accessible to positive science. The very ascendancy of such a science thus has engendered a crisis that science itself is not capable of solving.[13]

Functionalism versus humanism versus positivism
The above discussion brings us to still another crisis in contemporary sociology: that between functionalism and the "humanistic" theories inspired by existential phenomenology and pragmatism. These humanistic theories share the basic assumption that people are or can be agents, that they create meaning in their worlds.[14] From such a perspective, functionalism – whether macro- or micro-, Parsonian or Marxist – is seen as having passed the point of marginal utility: Further cultivation bears less and less fruit. At the same time that functionalism seems beyond repair, sociology faces a new requirement brought about by its own success. Having begun by disenchanting the world, sociology has come to disenchant its

own deterministic mystique, thus forcing on its members a new self-consciousness as a prerequisite to any further scientific activity.

Briefly, this is the humanists' critique: Functionalism has made several unanalyzed assumptions about social reality, chief of which is that society is like an organism (see Ch. 4, 130ff.). Yet this presupposition begs the very questions that sociology seeks to answer. It not only prevents finding out how society is possible, it also lends itself to the absolutist contention of a determined world inhabited by creatures who are, for the most part, unaware of the forces that move them (Wrong, 1961). Functionalism further assumes a priori the interdependence of societal parts – that is, institutions, roles, and the like – contributing to the dynamic equilibrium of the whole. Moreover, human cooperation – a basic element to be accounted for by sociology – is presumed to be the natural outcome of socialization within a common value system; yet the nature of the socialization process remains almost as much a mystery as the explanation of its effects on human association. Since socialized individuals are presumed to be actors unwittingly manipulated by invisible social forces, functionalists put little stock in these actors' theories of knowledge and action, preferring to rely on their own "objective" observations and interpretations. Finally, functionalism's theory of social change is rooted in a teleology of dynamic equilibrium, the "proof" of which is attained by dividing observations into those that reflect the posited natural processes, and those that are deviant, dysfunctional, or accidental.

For the humanistic sociologist, another aspect of the functionalist dilemma is the unresolved relationship of social theory to the problems of value and social policy. The functionalist paradigm left both the investigator and the objects of his investigation in a state of fatalistic determinism, proposed a sterile neutrality toward social values, and thought of policies either as rationally facilitating the given system or as "ideological" and hence scientifically unsound. Thus even sociologists who were dissatisfied with contemporary policies and culture found that their theories stressed the logical "necessity" of the status quo, and labeled as deviant those activities that were not officially sanctioned.[15] Although many establishment sociologists espoused reform, the epistemology underpinning their position indicated an acquiescence to the existent value system. A clear and unambiguous commitment to values seemed necessary if sociology was to be made a resource for societal change. But how could this be achieved without violating the canons of functionalist thought?

The humanistic sociology that seeks to answer these questions is by no means fully developed. Incomplete in its theory and epistemology, and only partially represented in empirical studies, nevertheless it can be presented in the form of certain critical assumptions and applications.

Among its most basic assumptions is that any science must, in its orientations and methods, be faithful to the nature of its subject matter (Blumer, 1969). The subject matter of humanist sociology is intentional action and existential states; that is, conduct meaningfully oriented toward others and ways of being in the world. This definition of its subject distinguishes humanistic sociology from deterministic functionalism, as well as from structuralist, systemic, comparative, or statistical-hypothetical sociologies, insofar as these are not grounded in the observation and interpretation of meaningfully intended everyday action.

A second feature of humanistic sociology is its new understanding and radical inversion of the basic question of sociology. Traditional functionalism presupposes a system of socially shared symbols, expectations, and protocols and then explains items of behavior in terms of this already posited system. But in the humanist paradigm, any particular norm or role is not assumed to have an exact unambiguous meaning to each actor; instead, it is taken to be a problematic onto which he must impose meaning and action. This perspective radically reorganizes an age-old question. No longer do we search for the noumenal (i.e., the out-there-to-be-discovered) reality. Instead of asking, "What is the structure of social reality?" the humanist sociologist inquires, "How is reality socially constructed?" Interaction becomes not the reciprocity of roles and norms, or a situation where hapless actors serve as media of social forces, but instead a situated process of inference and interpretation.

These perspectives permit a further probing of functionalism's presuppositions. Such a priori conceptions as role, status, or class, and the claim of unambiguous clarity involved in employing such terms as crime rates, suicide rates, or marital rates, also are seen as social constructions built on presuppositions that now become available for inspection. One such presupposition is *shareability*, a concept that requires careful scrutiny from the humanist perspective. Shareability, instead of being assumed as a property of any social situation, may be treated as a problematic feature for actors to create and realize. This problematic applies not only to actors vis à vis one another, but also to relations between social actors and the sociologist. By treating shareability as a topic for sociological investigation, instead of a resource for sociological explanation, humanistic sociology returns to questions originally posited by Hobbes and by Marx: How is society possible? and What are the dialectics of sociological knowledge?

The humanist critique of functionalism thus rests on two main points:

1. To the extent that functionalism adheres to the data it is positivistic – that is, it assumes that meanings of conduct are given and are objectively knowable to observers. This, in the critics' view, begs the central question for social research: How is reality constructed interactionally?

2. By presupposing a social system, functionalism reifies concepts such as "function," "systems maintenance," and the like, that are not explanations at all but only redundant descriptions of the data in question.

While this critique uproots functionalism's stakes from much sociological turf, at times it also has clouded important logical issues. First, the critique tends to overlook basic differences between functionalism and positivism as distinct logics of method. Second, it often does not provide general criteria for knowing when an abstraction is a reification and when it is not. The result is that many phenomenological theorists criticize only functionalism's positivist side and then – armed with the techniques of participant observation and member test verification – go on to develop descriptive-explanatory models which, in terms of their logical structure, are hard to distinguish from traditional functionalist ones (e.g., see note 7).

Both functionalism *and* phenomenological sociologies are interpretive procedures based on a concept of human consciousness and intentionality ("ultimately" for functionalists, "directly" for phenomenologists). Hence, in both these approaches theoretical formulations at some point must be justified in terms of motivational plausibility and verisimilitude. Even for a sociological realist like Durkheim, the functional side of his book, *Suicide*, has to explain the positivist side (the statistical correlations) in terms of variables that would make no sense except for their motivational insight. For example, "altruism" can be understood only if we imaginatively recreate, say, a soldier's feeling of loyalty to his comrades or to his code of honor. What, however, is the relationship between the elegant statistical logic and the logic of intentionality? Comparative statistical analysis has become familiar to the scientific mind, but it is not clear that Durkheim's *interpretation* of his causal correlations follows the same logic. On the contrary, it has been argued that Durkheim ceases to be a positivist at exactly this point and becomes instead a functionalist (Lukes, 1973; La Capra, 1973). By assuming a kind of psychosocial economy, he seems to be saying that when one has died socially – when the self one valued is no longer tenable socially – one simply kills the body that houses that self. By what method of analysis was this idea extrapolated from the data? Whatever the nature of such an interpretive logic, it seems clear that it is not the same as the positivist logic used in generating statistical covariance or testing hypotheses.

To return to our original question concerning the crises in contemporary sociology, these appear to be more complex than a simple opposition of two schools. In the present instance, functional and humanist sociologies both provide telic interpretations, one the functions of society, the other the intentions of persons. As interpretations, however, both these procedures differ from the causal logic of positive science. Functionalists worry over this difference; phenomenologists try to go beyond it; but it is acknowledged by both.[16]

THE CENTRAL PROBLEMATIC

The foregoing, we believe, leaves us with a paradox: No one school of sociology can generate satisfactory theories without using methods of opposing schools. Yet each school denies the epistemological validity of its opponents. In instances where one school has refused to borrow from others, it either has narrowed the definition of sociology to fit its method or, in expanding its methods, has incorporated just those "errors" of which it accused its rivals.

For example, the concept of praxis is used by Marxists to launch an attack on bourgeois sociology. Yet praxis remains a difficulty for Marxist theoreticians themselves. Similarly, their criticisms of the objectivist pretensions of positive sociology have served to heighten their own embarrassment with the objectivism of orthodox Marxists. Even for neo-Marxists, historical directionality has not yet been fitted with historicist construction. The dialectic between personal freedom and culture has not been reconciled with that between impersonal forces *within* culture. Moreover, to view Marxist theory as an aspect of praxis is no guarantee that it will be part of the *right* praxis. Again, to say that the criteria of "rightness" are contained in and justified by Marxist theory itself is to commit the same fallacy of which bourgeois sociology is accused (Birnbaum, 1968:130).

Much the same can be said of an equally radical theoretical innovation – ethnomethodology – a "final solution" that, like Marxism, reincorporates many of the old problems. In their studies of the creation of meaning through interaction, ethnomethodologists observed that, although words may hold the same meaning in different situations, they also have separate meanings that relate only to the situations in which they are being used. The words index – or stand for – features of *that* particular situation. Yet – and here is the paradox – if meaning is context specific, how can meanings be rendered shareable across contexts? Moreover, isn't such shareability presupposed in the possibility of communication in any given context in the first place? This contradiction has been evaded by identifying certain "invariant processes" that lie not in the content of what is communicated, but in the method *by which* people communicate it. Earlier symbolic interactionists took meaning as pure product; they could use it as a resource for explanation, but they could not explain its coming to be. In contrast, ethnomethodologists take meaning as pure *process*. Yet this process is then understood in terms of certain situationally invariant properties, thereby avoiding the initial question of how understanding emerges historically. Moreover, the very effort to get at invariant procedures beneath the content of language smacks of just that positivism against which interactionists initially fought. Language is "purified" of the actors' meanings in order to get at underlying "laws." Our point, of course, is that the old dramas are being enacted by new performers. In this case, the ideographic versus nomothetic debate is being replayed under the rubrics of unique meanings and invariant properties.

A broader example can be drawn from humanist and functionalist sociologies, both of which contradict yet require each other. The first treats the creation of social reality, the second explains action in terms of that reality taken as given. These certainly are complementary aims. In Marxian terms, one could understand the creation of social meanings as the more or less intentional work of free individuals; the deterministic func-

tioning of society then could be seen as reflecting the concretization of this meaning content into rigid and alienating forms.
Humanist sociology may be prior in a logical sense, since it
yields understanding of the shared meanings which functionalism takes as its starting point; but it is not prior in the sense of
offering a better analysis of the *same* phenomena, for each defines its subject matter in a different way. Any adequate theory
of society must respond to both these definitions; hence neither
approach is adequate when used to the exclusion of the other.
Yet, these approaches have very different ideas about what
constitutes *knowledge* of social reality. Thus we are left with
a choice between a theory that is incomplete but epistemologically consistent or a theory that is complete – dealing with both
meaning creation *and* social causation – but that stands, epistemologically, with one foot in cotton and the other in mud.[17]

This inventory of dilemmas is not presented for love of
perversity, though we admit to that, too. Instead, it is a way of
summing up the central problematic of this essay, and setting
the stage for the arguments that follow. Unreflective thought im-
agines itself to be a subjectivity at work on its object. Yet by
raising thought to a higher power through an aesthetic self-consciousness, this initial subject-object dualism may be dissolved in
the realization that the methods of any form of thought are the
source of its objectivity. Thus, the dilemmas of one level of
analysis may become the subject matter of analysis from another, dialectically higher level. If this is true of all thought, it
must be especially true of the sciences of man, who both creates
his world and is yet created by it. Thus the apparatus for solving
sociological problems that we have discussed above may be
turned into the problem to be solved with the apparatus of
aesthetics. Our interest is not in aesthetics per se, but as an
instrument by which sociology may be lifted to a new self-
consciousness. Insofar as we are able to place the old problem-
solving *methods* in this larger context, it may become possible
to restate the old *problems* in such a way that they provide their
own solution. Instead of trying to deal with our dilemmas head
on, according to their own terms, we hope to understand the
dilemmas as themselves marks of the deeper contradictions
latent in the very ways in which sociologists have defined their
own enterprise.

With this as a prelude, we now seek to define our basic framework – cognitive aesthetics – and then try to demonstrate the
utility of a poetic for sociology through discussions of point
of view, metaphor, and irony in sociological theory.

2
Cognitive aesthetics: symbolic realism, and perspectival knowledge

[Among the Wintu there is a] recurring . . . attitude of humility and
respect toward reality, toward nature and society. I cannot find an
adequate English term to apply to a habit of thought that is so alien
to our culture. We are aggressive toward reality. We say, This is
bread; we do not say, as the Wintu, *I call this bread* or *I feel* or *taste*
or *see it to be bread*. The Wintu never says starkly *this is*; if he
speaks of reality that is not within his own restricting experience, he
does not affirm it, he only implies it. If he speaks of his experience
he does not express it as categorically true.
Dorothy Lee (1959:129)

Correspondence theories of science and art focus on ways in
which these symbolic forms copy or resemble some reality external to them. Formalist or cogency theories, in contrast, tend
to deal with the internal properties of the scientific theory or
work of art. Both these views are transcended yet integrated in
symbolic realism. In this chapter we first give a brief account
of correspondence theories and make explicit their assumption
concerning an independent, copyable, external reality. We then
argue that, despite great differences, major schools of modern
philosophy tend to agree that all ways of knowing the world
are both symbolic and perspectival. One implication of this view
is that both science and art are symbolic forms that frame or
create their own domains of application. Such a position makes
possible a reinterpretation of both correspondence and cogency
theories. In this view one does not speak of internal versus external properties. Instead, when the scientific theory or art object
is successful, both the internal and external come to be seen as
elements of a single structural system. Just as science affects
perceptual and cognitive transformations by changing our
models of the world as a natural order, art similarly affects
paradigm-induced expectations. Instead of taking science as
the measure of all things – scientific realism – we argue that
there is no fundamental difference in the way in which science
and art empower us to articulate the world; this is the view of
symbolic realism.

Within this framework sociology, which previously has had to choose between science or art as a model, can now move beyond this dichotomy. As a discipline that concerns itself chiefly with structured symbol systems, aesthetics is a privileged language for discourse about such a freshly conceived science of conduct.

POSITIVE SCIENCE AGAINST ROMANTIC ART

Much of contemporary disputes in the social sciences over theoretical paradigms, moral and political values, and "hard" versus "soft" research techniques, is part of a larger and older debate: that between positivism and romanticism.

Positivism draws sustenance from the practical experiments of Bacon and the mathematical deductions of Descartes. It takes physical science as its model and assumes a natural standpoint from which "reality" is strictly distinguished from the "symbols" that represent it. From this position the meaning of a word or expression is the thing or behavior to which it refers. Statements that are true are those that correspond to objectively verified events or conditions "out there." Statements that cannot be so verified are either false, nonsensical, or emotive. An example of the verifiable or "correct" use of the word "temperature" would be to refer to readings on measuring instruments that take advantage of two critical events in nature, the freezing and boiling points of water. To report the facts objectively, the voice of science ideally must correspond to its objects in this one-to-one fashion, with no connotative meanings slipped in to the expression. Thus, in addition to such pointer-reader measures as thermometer temperatures, mathematics also presents itself as a language of science. The part of communication that cannot be reduced to pointer readings or mathematics is declared to be subjective and hence epistemologically invalid – a kind of symbol cloak beneath which "reality" remains hidden. To the extent that common speech must be used at all, it should be expunged of " 'fictitious entities' so that its primary function of stating objective truth might be most completely achieved" (Abrams, 1953:300. See Richards, 1936; Ogden and Richards, 1946; Carnap, 1942; and Osborne, 1970:97).

Metaphor and personal meaning – which are explicitly "symbolic" and "subjective" – are thus consigned to poetry, which in the positivist view is nothing more than "a kind of ingenious nonsense" (Newton, quoted by Bush, 1950:40), "to be accounted rather as a pleasure or play of wit than a science" (Bacon,

1864:IX, 62). As Jeremy Bentham said, "All poetry is misrepresentation. Indeed, between poetry and truth there stands a natural opposition: false morals, fictitious nature. The poet always stands in need of something false. . . . His business consists in stimulating our passions, and exciting our prejudices. Truth, exactitude of every kind, is fatal to poetry" (1962:II, 253–254).

In contrast to this view, romanticism crystalized as an opposition ideology in the nineteenth century. Inspired by Vico and Hegel, philosophers and poets defended art as representing various "higher" truths: the subjective response of the artist to the thing represented, the inner feelings of the artist upon the act of creation, and the artist's vision, philosophy, or personality in general. "We have Beauty," as Nietzsche put it, "in order to preserve us from Truth."

This romantic view was a radical turning point in aesthetic theory. Traditionally art was assumed to represent reality either in its phenomenal or its ideal manifestations – the Platonic and neo-Platonic theories. But in the early modern period this representational function was thought more and more to be the privileged area of science, in the form either of Bacon's phenomenal empiricism or Descartes' mathematical idealism. In reaction to this view, but at the same time accepting its assumptions about the nature of the scientific enterprise, defenders of art turned inward for the "that which" that art represents. There developed a strict dichotomy between "reality" and "symbols," between "truth" and "beauty." Positivists tried to eliminate the use of symbols in science, whereas critics and aestheticians tried to find a home for art outside of nature.

These paired views may be summarized as follows:

Science	*Art*
truth	beauty
reality	symbols
things and events	feelings and meanings
"out-there"	"in-here"
objective	subjective
explanation	interpretation
proof	insight
determinism	freedom

As this thinking found its way into the human studies, there arose a methical dualism, "two orders . . . separate but unequal" (Gouldner, 1962:210). Seeking to be true to what they conceived of as science, many sociologists strictly distinguished their "subjective" sensations from the "objective" properties of that which they studied. It was thought that the personal feelings, interpretations, and point of view of the analyst must not enter into his account of the "out-there" structure of social action. Other sociologists took the opposite view, asserting that personal empathy was required in order to enter the actors' consciousness, and hence to discover sociological truth. Thus in the positivist view sociology was to imitate physics, while in the romantic view sociology was to be not a science but an art.

PHILOSOPHIC BACKGROUND TO SYMBOLIC REALISM

As it is reenacted today, the debate between positivists and romantics is increasingly sterile. Adequate social theory must be both objective *and* subjectively meaningful; it must yield understanding of persons' consciousness and agency as well as explanations of social forces beyond their immediate control. Yet in terms of the positivist-romantic debate such theory would appear to be methodologically impossible, in that each side cherishes different assumptions concerning the nature of social reality and how we can know it. It is thus necessary that both positivism *and* romanticism be reformulated, and that an ontology and epistemology be developed that encompasses sociology's scientific *and* artistic modes. As Randall Collins puts it, "Positivism needs to be purged. Romanticism needs to be borrowed from ... It is the combination of determinism and freedom, after all, that constitutes the greatest art; advances in scientific sociology can move its aesthetics beyond a tired romanticism, hopefully into something greater" (1957:28, 34).

Some clues to just such a postromantic, *cognitive* aesthetic for sociology are found in principal schools of modern philosophy: pragmatism, analytic and ordinary language theories, existential phenomenology, and *neo*positivism itself. The perspective that emerges from an examination of these schools might be called symbolic realism, which transvalues and transcends both scientific realism and romantic idealism.

The most striking resemblance of modern philosophic schools is a negative one: their revolt against Bacon and Descartes. In his articles of 1868,[1] for example, Charles Saunders Peirce launches a systematic attack on the basic tenets of this positivist framework: the ontological duality of mind and body, the subjectivism implicit in the ultimate appeal to direct personal

verification, the belief that language is a mere vehicle or ornament of thought, the doctrine of clear and distinct ideas and the
unreality of that which is vague, the belief that language can be
sidestepped in favor of a direct intuition of objects, and the
method of doubt and the elimination of bias as a path to an
absolute foundation of knowledge.

An attack on intuitionism, subjectivism, and the giveness
of facts also is found in Wittgenstein's *Philosophic Investigations*. Indeed, Wittgenstein's very idea of "language games"
presupposes that meaning and truth are relational to rules,
intentional action, and intersubjectivity; by contrast, in the
Cartesian framework knowledge is wholly contemplative,
grounded in logical absolutes, and knowable only through personal intuition.

A critique of positivism is likewise a main theme in existential phenomenology. The primacy of either ideas or perception
is challenged by Kant's notion of knowledge as mediated by the
categories of the mind. Fichte and Hegel made inquiry dialectical, showing how truth and reality, subject and object, are two
moments in the same process. Then Marx, Dilthey, Kierkegaard,
Heidegger, Merleau-Ponty, and Sartre grounded knowledge and
understanding in the praxis of lived experience.

*Neo*positivism also lends its voice to critics of *naive* positivism, while at the same time reformulating itself so as to avoid
the weaknesses of its genitors. Indeed, positivism can best to be
seen to have two components: the naive, materialist "objectivist"
side, and a highly critical component deriving from Berkeley
and Hume that actually issues into a new basis for science.[2] In
examining and reformulating the premises of earlier positivist
thought, neopositivist philosophers such as Austin, Polanyi, and
Kuhn have drawn on this critical component to open the way to
a social conventionalism and a sociology of science (à la Hume
and Peirce), to a language analytic philosophic sociology (à la
Winch and Harré), and to the close examination of the empirical workings of intersubjective worlds (à la Garfinkel, Cicourel,
and Sacks).

Ironically, the earlier positivists' program to reduce our
vague language to instant-by-instant experience, is precisely the
problem of setting sociological abstractions on an experiential
basis. Today, however, this empiricism is neither objective nor
subjective, but intersubjective and mediated. In the sophisticated
neopositivists' view one's own subjective states can be an analogic instrument for observing the subjective states of others.

Such observations differ only in degree, not in kind, from so-called "objective" observations; both types of observations are mediated by the "instrument" of observation, and both are subject in principle to validation by their coherence with a larger body of data and theory.[3]

Beyond this shared critical bent, there are overlaps in the ideas advanced by neopositivists, pragmatists, existential phenomenologists, and ordinary language philosophers to replace the earlier positivist and romantic models. For example, pragmatists speak of *conduct*; analytic philosophers have recently shown great interest in *action*; existential phenomenologists use the term *praxis*; neopositivists allow that objectivity is relative to rules of observation and verification and that these conventions are essentially social and experiential in nature. Although such terms as conduct, action, or praxis have different histories and nuances, each presupposes the person to be a conscious and intentional actor. Moreover, each major school sees the world or worlds as constituted of, or knowable only through, symbolic constructs. Finally, each school sees formal knowledge – whether in the sciences or the arts – as presupposing consciousness and understanding in everyday social life.

In philosophers as diverse as James, Dewey, Dilthey, Husserl, and Wittgenstein we find agreement that the commonsense understanding of experience is the framework within which all inquiry must begin. Dewey speaks of this framework as the social matrix within which emerge unclarified situations that may then be transformed by science into justifiable assertions. Wittgenstein refers to ways of knowledge as "forms of life." Husserl speaks of the "life-world" within which all scientific and even logical concepts originate. Alfred Schutz, in "The Basic Subject Matter of Sociology," says:

> Any knowledge of the world, in common-sense thinking as well as in science [or in art], involves mental constructs, syntheses, generalizations, formalizations, idealizations specific to the respective level of thought organization. The concept of Nature, for instance, with which the natural sciences have to deal is, as Husserl has shown, an idealizing abstraction from the *Lebenswelt*, an abstraction which, on principle and of course legitimately, excludes persons with their personal life and all objects of culture which originate as such in practical human activity.[4]

Major contributions to this general argument also are found in the writings of Charles Peirce. "The very origin of the conception of reality," says Peirce, "shows that this conception essentially involves the notion of a COMMUNITY" (Peirce, 1960: V:311). This community, or collective world of life and action, is constituted of symbolic interaction. Peirce makes this clear by linking sign processes with processes that involve mediation (thirdness), that is, social processes between persons. One example of such a relationship is "giving," which does not occur unless the event of transfer of an object from one hand to another is mediated by the intentions of both parties (1960:V: 484). Peirce then develops this formulation to show that reality, mind, and indeed persons themselves are symbolic (see Morris, 1932:284). Instead of the sign for a person, "the word or sign which man uses *is* the man himself." Man *is* no more than he intends.

> Man makes the word, and the word means nothing which
> the man has not made it mean, and that only to some man.
> But since man can think only by means of words or other
> external symbols, these might turn around and say: "You
> mean nothing which we have not taught you, and then
> only so far as you address some words as the interpretant
> of your thought." In fact, therefore, men and words
> reciprocally educate each other; each increase in man's
> information involves and is involved by, a corresponding
> increase of a word's information. (V:313) . . . That every
> thought is an external sign, proves that *man* is an external
> sign. (II:156, our italics)

This idea that all knowledge – whether formal or common-sensical – is symbolic construction, brings with it the possibility of multiple realities, each with its own mode of articulation. Alfred Shutz, in his article "On Multiple Realities" (1945: 533–576), provides a phenomenological framework for the philosophic examination of such worlds. Similarly William James, in his psychological investigations, speaks of the "sub-universe of sense, or of physical 'things' as we instinctively apprehend them." James notes "the world of science," of "ideal relations, or abstract truths," "the world of 'idols of the tribe,' illusions or prejudices common to the race," "the various super-natural worlds, the Christian heaven and hell, the world of Hindoo mythology," "the various worlds of individual opinion," and "the worlds of sheer madness and vagary" (1893:II:Ch. 11).

Ordinary language philosophers, working from a very dif-ferent direction than Schutz or James, have arrived at similar conclusions. Like Schutz, these thinkers also focus on the clash between the positivist image of the person and the image that is manifested in everyday life (Sellars, 1963; Urmson, 1956; C. Taylor, 1964; R. S. Peters, 1960). Some ordinary language philosophers argue that the very subject matter of sociology – human conduct – far from being objectlike, can be understood only in terms of such concepts as rules, meanings, and intentionality and, hence, that a social science on the model of the physical sciences may be impossible (Winch, 1958; Louch, 1966; Skinner, 1953:14–32). Richard Bernstein (1971) and Charles Taylor (1964) carry this line of analysis still further, up to its dialectical turning point. Even granting that the person *conceived as agent* cannot be reduced to the positivist model, this does not prove that the model of intentional person is the only appropriate one. To illustrate: let us allow a massive conceptual structure to everyday life in which the category of the person as agent is fundamental. Let us also suppose that concepts such as intention, action, and so on cannot be adequately translated to some more basic nonteleological framework. Granting all this, what have we demonstrated? For even if we have elucidated the irreducible structure of ordinary language and understanding, we still have not shown that this is the only legitimate or correct view of man. That is to say, as Bernstein has noted, the entire "manifest" view of conduct, though perhaps not *reducible*, can instead be sidestepped and simply *replaced*. The model of intentionality may be the only model suitable for explaining the person *conceived as agent*; but this in itself is no demonstration that that is the only legitimate or possible conception or the only model of explanation.

By a similar reasoning, Charles Taylor argues against absolutisms of both the deterministic *or* the humanistic approach. Taylor first attacks the bias that scientific explanation must take a causal form. He also argues that teleological explanations are not necessarily mentalistic or exclusive to individual actions; instead, they are empirical and can refer to any actions or movements that occur "for the sake of" something else. The question for Taylor then is not the possibility of developing a single, all-inclusive theory of behavior, but which models and forms of explanation will be most fruitful for various definitions or ranges of experience. Thus, although he is critical of behaviorism and feels that teleological explanations offer a more hopeful approach, Taylor does not exclude the possibility that some form of mechanistic theory may replace the teleological model.

The concept of multiple realities thus can be critically directed toward the "realities" of theories themselves. For if no single approach can claim ultimate validity, then all theories in a fundamental sense must be metaphoric. Just because they are instruments of perspective and organization, they must treat their subject matter *as* something; but in so doing they forego any claim to describe their subject matter as it "really is." Instead, all representations of human nature are symbolically mediated; none of them can claim to give us ultimately truths. Thus implicit in ordinary language analyses is the (logical) possibility of dualistic or even multiple systems for accounting for what we are, what we think, and what we do.

Instead of excluding one or another form of sociological thought, ordinary language philosophy suggests that various forms may have an equal validity. Such a covalence, and complementarity, may be illustrated by comparing Mead, Wittgenstein, and Heidegger. In Mead we find a seminal model of the construction of mind, self, and social structure through symbolic gestures in interaction. Yet elsewhere in his writings Mead seems crudely behavioristic and evolutionistic. In contrast, Wittgenstein's later work offers the concept of language games as a model of meaning creation and interaction. The structure and function of such forms as commanding, questioning, recounting, or chatting, when properly understood, can be seen as a key to the structure and function of play, commerce, or war. Yet this last analogy between language and other human activities is not developed by Wittgenstein: His model remains largely ahistorical and hermetic, instead of being elaborated to include *conduct* as itself a kind of language. Finally, in Heidegger, we find just the ontology of historical being that is needed in Wittgenstein and Mead. Yet Heidegger does not apply this ontology systematically to an analysis of language games or interaction, which are the key areas of Wittgenstein's and Mead's thought. Each writer thus compensates for limitations in the others, and together they provide the possibility of a theory of conduct by which to represent the structure and construction of social-historical expressions.

Symbolic realism emerges from the schools we have discussed. It has roots in the skeptical, conventionalist component of pragmatism and neopositivism, it borrows from recent German and French philosophic thought, and it is enriched by British linguistic philosophy. Peirce's pragmatism, for example, gave birth to a sophisticated neopositivism based on a consensual model of truth. Similarly, post-Wittgensteinian philosophers are now finding that their emphasis on (verbal) rules and intentions need not go together with their antibehaviorist program, thus opening a way back to an empirical, transverbal yet nonmechanical sociology. Also defying neat categorization, and illustrating the borrowing and convergence between schools, is Husserl – the phenomenologist as crisis positivist – whose "followers" in fact repudiated his search for presuppositionless, absolute knowledge. Instead they favored a coherence model of truth tied to an action image of man (with implicit criticism of the purely linguistic model of the analytic approach).

Joined under the canopy of symbolic realism, all these schools resist the absolutisms of both naive positivism and romantic idealism; instead they seek to borrow from yet transcend the limits of both sides of the old debate. The schools do not deny a distinction between appearance and reality; yet rather than seeking to eliminate "appearance" in favor of "objective" representations, they offer remarkable methodological tools for probing the duality itself. All these schools posit the lived world as the framework out of which formal cognition must emerge, and all of them understand "knowledge" to be relational to an intersubjective community of discourse. Thus each school, with its own particular voice, urges us to attend to the tensions between the given and the constructed and, in so doing, to remain true to the dialectical mediations through which structure, consciousness, and history achieve expression (Natanson, 1962:211).

In sum, then, on one side are the old-fashioned positivists who want not only explanatory laws to which everyone must agree, but laws that assume a purely material world and deny all subjective reality, including even that of the theorist. Opposing this are romantic subjectivists who want not laws but experience and intuitions that, they claim, are a kind of higher science. Transcending both these views is that which seeks generalized explanations of the natural as well as the human world, including subjectivity, without a materialist bias. This view finds its justification in a postpositivist, postromantic, dialectical, symbolic realist theory of knowledge. In such a view all knowledge is symbolic construction: Causal, lawlike explanation is itself an interpretive procedure, and interpretation itself can be a rigorous way of knowing.

TOWARD A COGNITIVE AESTHETICS

They said, "You have a blue guitar,
You do not play things as they are,"
The man replied, "Things as they are
Are changed upon the blue guitar."
Wallace Stevens (1967)

Playing the blue guitar is a figure for what pioneering artists, scientists, and other makers of paradigms do when they create new ways of expressing "things as they are." What we know as reality is constituted of such symbolization. As Nelson Goodman says, "The making of a picture commonly participates in making what is to be pictured. The object and its aspects depend upon organization; and labels of all sorts are tools of organization. ... A representation or description, by virtue of how it classifies and is classified, may make or mark connections, analyze objects, and organize the world" (Goodman, 1968:32). If we take this seriously, the idea of both artist and scientist as *makers* is reinforced, not merely as craftsmen but now in a cognitive and ontological sense. Further, the use of resemblance or imitation as a criterion of either truth or beauty is shown to be misleading. Finally, the strict separation between art and science is rendered null.[5]

Before going any further with these points, we should distinguish the pioneer from the merely competent artist or scientist – the persons who invent new languages from those who simply use existing idioms well. The first create the world, the second discover it. As Nisbet puts it, "There is more in common between Picasso and Einstein – in objective, in inspiration, and mode of fulfillment – than there is between Picasso and, say, Norman Rockwell or between Einstein and any of the stolid practitioners of what A. N. Whitehead once called 'dustbowl empiricism'" (1962:69). The stolid practitioner is the person who does not question the paradigm within which he works. Instead of creating new framework assumptions he duplicates or extends the inherited ones. In this sense the conventional artist or scientist may be said to *imitate*. What he imitates is not "reality," however, but the standard mode of representation. His net catches only those fish that are already dead.

In contrast the pioneer symbol maker forges new frames of vision that, he implicitly claims, are more comprehensive, perspicuous, and succinct than the previous ones. Thus, for example, Rodin invented a new way of showing (and, hence, of knowing) motion. Rodin displays each part of the body at a different instant of what would be, in linear time, a continuous action. The head of *John the Baptist* is at the beginning of a gesture while the hand is completing it. Yet just this mutual confrontation of incompossibles imposes a fictive unity through which motion assumes *durée* and action is realized in bronze (Rodin, 1911). But the first viewers of Rodin's sculptures considered them "unrealistic," just as those first to see Cezanne's drawings could not recognize the figures in them. Likewise, to the complaint that his portrait of Gertrude Stein did not look like her, Picasso is said to have replied, "Never mind, it will." Gloss: Once we have come to accept Picasso's (or Rodin's or Cezanne's) "grammar" or "rules of projection" we will see Miss Stein as Picasso drew her; we will "interpret" her accordingly.[6]

As in plastic and pictoral arts, so are there conventional and pioneering authors. For example, the naturalistic writer today can assume a shared framework with the reader. But because he sees further, thinks more, and writes better than we do, he acts as our delegate, naming events and emotions. Contemporary writers may be better or worse at this but, even at their best, once having chosen this conventional relation to their reader, they have locked themselves within a static framework. By contrast, major writers are those who have succeeded in finding Joyce's "ideal reader suffering from an ideal insomnia," an insomnia akin to that of the author himself. Such a writer is also a "reader," constructing a new code for the universe much as his readers must decode the meanings of his text. The conventional writer puts images into an existing code; the pioneer writer is an inventor of codes – his language creates space for the act of ciphering, surface for the enactment of transformations. With such writers we do not merely collaborate imaginatively – that is necessary to properly read even conventional fiction. With the pioneering writer a further commitment is involved: To realize his fictional world, he requires us to de-realize our own realities and hence to test ourselves against the world he has created.

Pioneering artists and scientists show us that the world is composed of facts – *facta*, things made. Different codes or sets of categories, different facts. To recognize the old data in new forms requires that we re-*cognize* the data itself. Nature does not merely imitate art. It is rather a *product* of pioneering description and discourse. If we subtract from his world the facts that are given to a man by previous frameworks, we get that man's net contribution – the measure of his conceptual sovereignty and the extent to which he can be said to be a pioneer. Science and art are not so much Cook's Tours as they are expeditions led by Lewis and Clark.

This takes us to a second point: the nullification of resemblance as a criterion of representation. "Unlike the conventional artist, the pioneer is conspicuously uninterested in how a subject is normally represented, and conspicuously interested in how the subject might look in relative isolation from those normal patterns" (Foss, 1971:237). The pioneer wishes to impose new conventions to supersede the old. In Platonic terms, he is an institutor of forms. Norman Rockwell fulfills what we might call forms or paradigm-induced expectations; Picasso breaks through what exists and establishes successor paradigms that mobilize new expectations. In these terms, realism or literal truth – as in representational art or accurate description – is not an absolute relationship between a picture and its object. It is, instead, a relationship between the system of representation employed in the picture and the system that everyone takes for granted. When new rules of projection come to dominate, the definitions of realism are thereby adjusted.[7] Our sense of the concreteness of reality depends on the concretization of our points of view. As a way of seeing becomes sedimented, habitual, or mummified (to use Gurvitch's term, 1962), we forget that our viewpoint is *a way* of seeing, not necessarily *the* (only correct) way. We tend to omit specifying the frame of reference when it is our own. At that point it is the pioneering artist or scientist who must unravel our mummified perceptions and make them live again.

In "The Way the World Is," Nelson Goodman makes some interesting remarks on this point (1960:48–56). Goodman argues that the world is as many ways as it can be credently described, seen, or pictured, and that it makes no sense to speak of *the* way things are. Ryle takes a similar position (1954:75–77) when he compares a table seen as a solid object or as a swarm of atoms and a library according to the catalogue and according to the accountant.

This is all to say that in the representational systems of both science and art, what is there is known only in terms of some frame of reference. We cannot see an object except against a ground. Yet the scientific realist has traditionally taken this frame for granted and thus, by implication, has uncritically assumed his frame to be *the* frame, an optimally sufficient one. In such a fashion, "realism" is used as the name for the currently dominant style or system of representation. Accordingly, as we adopt one particular system, certain paintings, for example, those of the Renaissance, furnished the most realistic rendition conceivable. *Given a different system*, Manet, Braque, or Picasso "tell it like it is." But how *is* it, really? (Foss, 1971:237). "For a Fifth-Dynasty Egyptian the straightforward way of representing something is not the same as for an eighteenth-century Japanese; and neither way is the same as for an early twentieth-century Englishman. Each would to some extent have to learn how to read a picture in either of the other styles" (Goodman, 1968:37).

Scientific realists have proposed, of course, that each such way of seeing is a partial perspective, and that *the* way the world is may be arrived at by combining these views while at the same time canceling out the biases of each. Such attempts are useful when conducted *within* the same domain of discourse – indeed, this is a method of elaborating and building up a consistent theoretical frame. But insofar as this is possible we are not talking about different ways the world is, for particular points of view within the same domain are better understood as aspects of the same *frame* of view.

The difficulty with the scientific realists' proposal comes when we deal with basically different frames of vision, different paradigms or symbolic languages that, of their nature, are incommensurable. How do we conjoin a picture with a polygraph, a myth poem with a regression analysis? As Goodman says,

> Any attempted combination of all the ways would be itself only one – and a peculiarly indigestible one – of the ways the world is. But what is *the world* that is in so many ways? To speak of the ways the world is, or ways of describing or picturing the world, is to speak of world descriptions or world-pictures, and does not imply there is a unique thing – or indeed anything – that is described or pictured. Of course, none of this implies, either, that nothing is described or pictured. (1968:6–7,n.4)

Rules governing "the real world" vary across personal, class, historical, and civilizational lines. We thus ought not ask with the scientific realist, "Does Ptolemy, or Luther, or Einstein represent it as it is?" We should rather ask with the *symbolic* realist, "Is the system of representation to which Ptolemy, or the others implicitly subscribes an adequate one, given such and such intentions?"

The analogy we have drawn between invention of theories in the sciences and breakthroughs of style in the arts, coupled with the critique of correspondence as a criterion of representation, underlines the fundamentally *cognitive* character of aesthetic experience. Says Foss,

> This is the sense in which the dichotomy of cognitive and emotive, truth and beauty – at least so far as it is used to measure the difference between the scientific and the aesthetic – is wrongheaded. Or, it is so by the margin that we fail to allow for the emotions, if these are what generate the artistic act, as capable of functioning cognitively. What is being said is the different symbol systems, whether artistic or scientific, are deployed to the same end: intelligibility. This is obviously not intended as a statement about the psychological motivations of the individual artist, but rather about the impact of the work of art on our subsequent ways of thinking, feeling, and seeing. It is therefore meant as a descriptive rather than dogmatic claim. Shakespeare, no less than Newton, affects our ways of construing experience. (Foss, 1971:241)

What Thomas Kuhn says about major turning points in science might be equally well applied to the arts. In a literal sense, the ways in which Giotto, Ucello, Rembrandt, or Matisse changed their worlds – to speak only of pictorial art – is much like the ways in which Copernicus, Newton, Lavoisier, or Einstein changed theirs:

> Each produced a consequent shift in the problem available for scientific [read: artistic] scrutiny and in the standards by which the profession determined what should count as an admissible problem or as a legitimate problem-solution. And each transformed the scientific [artistic] imagination in ways that we shall ultimately need to describe as a transformation of the world within which scientific [artistic] work was done. (Kuhn, 1962:6)

Such breakthroughs, in one domain or the other, constitute "tradition shattering complements to the tradition bound activity of *normal* science [or art]" (Kuhn, 1962:6).[8]

Symbolization, then, regardless of its particular mode of expression, must be judged by how well it enhances our perception and our understanding. "Truth and its aesthetic counterpart amount to appropriateness under different names" (Goodman,

1968:264). Differences in the impact of breakthroughs associated with art or science reflect differences in the way our culture evaluates these activities, more than intrinsic differences in the natures of these symbolic forms.

Let us now hear objections: If the picture or description is not and cannot be taken as a description of "reality," what then is it? If we abandon the scientific realists' classical canons for relating sentence to the thing signified, are we not left with a vain swirl of signs, a solipsistic paralysis of expression? Is there then no scientific or artistic progress, no accumulation of knowledge? Is this the high point of our reasoning, to realize that the world is only "as if," to unmask "research" as a plodding in circles, to accept that human history is in some sense stationary?

Rather than answer these questions directly, we may take them as the *Angst* of a scientific realist on the brink of paradigm change. This distress reflects a presumption of the possibility of absolute knowledge on an ultimate ground; it is the regret of one who has overinvested in the promisory notes of terminal categories, a world redeemable only when "all the data are in."

If we have put aside some of the old questions, however, this does not mean our tongues are blind. Instead of ending discourse, the assumption of symbolic realism opens new paths to travel. For although we no longer speak of scientific progress in the sense of linear accumulation, or of an evolutionary hierarchy of cultures, we do have a new way of seeing each theory and each culture. If science can no longer properly claim to falsify all other languages of Being, we now are able to listen to each with a new attention. As Merleau-Ponty tells us,

> If no painting comes to be *the* painting, if no work is ever
> absolutely completed and done with, still each creation
> changes, alters, enlightens, deepens, confirms, exalts,
> re-creates, or creates in advance of all the others. If
> creations are not a possession, it is not only that, like all
> things, they pass away; it is also that they have almost all
> their life still before them. (1964:190)

There is thus a special kind of "progress" in the reading of culture and conduct as symbol scripts of Being: Reality becomes richer and more varied in the multiplication of the forms of its symbolic expression. This is not progress, gradually encompassing more and more reality until, at some distant time, Being has been encircled and conquered. It is rather progress in the respect of progressive revelation, in which each theory, each world view reveals another immanence in our own world, in which each vision of reality provides an additional perspective into our capacity for objectification. Symbolization not only makes things clear – the discovery of reality. It also makes things *real* – the creation of reality. Science, art, and other symbolic forms give existence to what, for us, otherwise would not be. "Thought can bring forth and make what did not yet exist into an object of experience, that is, into reality" (Jaspers, 1959:27). As Cassirer tells us:

> Myth, art, language and science appear as symbols; not
> in the sense of mere figures which refer to some given
> reality by means of suggestion and allegorical renderings,
> but in the sense of forces each of which produces and posits
> a world of its own. . . . Thus the special symbolic forms
> are not imitations, but *organs* of reality, since it is solely
> by their agency that anything real becomes an object for
> intellectual apprehension, and as such is made visible to us.
> The question as to what reality is apart from these forms,
> and what are its independent attributes, becomes irrelevant
> here. For the mind, only that can be visible which has some
> definite form; but every form of existence has its source
> in some peculiar way of seeing, some intellectual formu-
> lation and intuition of meaning. Once language, myth, art,
> and science are recognized as such forms, the basic
> philosophical question is . . . that of their mutual
> limitations and supplementation. (1946:8–9)

Cassirer reminds us that under the management of symbolic realism a number of new questions are placed at the center of the philosophic stage: What are the relations between the ways of representing the world and their respective domains of application – the forms and the contents of symbol systems? How do the various symbol systems limit and supplement each other? What vocabularies can we use to describe or compare various modes of expression? Even if we no longer talk about absolute primacy, are there criteria for judging the relative adequacy of symbolic expressions? These are the questions we touch on now.

FORM AND CONTENT

The dualism of positivism are many: form versus content, intrinsic versus extrinsic, knowledge versus experience. But recently we have become aware that each term in these pairs implicates and depends on the other, that, instead of positing opposition, it is more useful to speak of the "structurings of content" or "embodiments of form." This point is illustrated by the reciprocal limits of either purely formalist or purely representational theories of art. Mondrian's work, for example, appears to be purely formal; nevertheless he intends it to convey a content from nature:

> Impressed by the vastness of nature, I was trying to express
> its expansion, rest, and unity. At the same time, I was
> fully aware that the visible expansion of nature is at the
> same time its limitation; vertical and horizontal lines are
> the expression of two opposing forces; these exist every-
> where and dominate everything; their reciprocal action
> constitutes "life." (quoted by Hospers, 1964:101)

Similarly, Marc Chagall, whose work seems to be crammed with representational content, insists that his concerns are purely formal:

> But please defend me against people who speak of
> "anecdote" and "fairy tales" in my work. A cow and
> a woman to me are the same – in a picture both are
> merely elements of a composition. . . . I feel myself more
> "abstract" than Mondrian or Kandinsky. . . . In the case of
> the decapitated woman with the milk pails, I was first led
> to separating her head from her body merely because I
> happened to need an empty space there. In the large cow's
> head in *Moi et le Village* I made a small cow and a woman
> milking visible through its muzzle because I needed that
> sort of form, there, for my composition. (Sweeney,
> 1944:90)

The difficulty, and ultimately the fruitlessness, of strictly separating form and content, "intrinsic" and "extrinsic," also is illustrated by the development of literary criticism since Taine (1913). In the nineteenth century criticism was largely positivistic, seeking in "race, milieu, and moment" the causes of literary effects, much as scientists looked for the causes of physical motion. To understand literature was to understand the external forces of which it was the product. In reaction to this, there arose in twentieth-century America a New Criticism that focused on the work itself. To explain the inner devices by which an author had made a novel the particular novel that it was, the New Critics undertook studies of such "internal" formal properties as metaphor, symbolism, and plot structure. Independently, a somewhat parallel movement, Formalism, arose in Central Europe. Thus the present generation of literary scholars received with one hand a method that focused on sociological, psychological, and historical "contents," and with the other hand an approach that focused on inner form. The recent "Structuralist Controversy" (Macksey and Donato, 1972; Lane, 1970) in the cultural sciences can be seen as an attempt to overcome this bifurcation of method. In this new model, the forces at work on the author, the material he draws into his novel from life, the generally accepted interpretations made by his audience, or the strictly formal devices within the work itself "are viewed not as absolute yardsticks or impassable barriers beyond which the interpreter should not go, but as no more than elements in a total picture, and these elements can always be reinterpreted according to the requirements of the totalization" (Girard, 1972:19). Rather than structure *versus* correspondence, here one speaks of the structure *of* correspondences both *within* the work and *between* the work and its external referents.

Much of what has been discovered in the criticism of the pictorial and narrative arts is equally true of scientific formulations. Here, however, the vocabulary in use is one of data and theory and not of contents and form. On this point we may turn to Polanyi's discussion of the relation between formal theories of lung disease and the X rays that constitute evidence "belonging to" those theories:

> Think of a medical student attending a course in X-ray diagnosis of pulmonary diseases. . . . At first the student is completely puzzled. . . . Then as he goes on listening for a few weeks, looking carefully at ever new pictures of different cases, a tentative understanding will dawn on him. . . . And eventually a rich panorama of significant details will be revealed. . . . He has entered a new world.
> . . . Thus, at the very moment when he has learned the language of pulmonary radiology, the student will also have learned to understand pulmonary radiograms. The two can only happen together. Both halves of the problem set to us by an unintelligible text, referring to an unintelligible subject, jointly guide our efforts to solve them, and they are solved eventually together by discovering a conception which comprises a joint understanding of both the words and the things [both the theory and its data]. (1958:101)[9]

In contrast, in the scientific realist view we have theories *about* a certain set of data, just as we have pictures *of* certain objects. From this viewpoint the development of theory is a two-phase process: First we have the objects—we hold them in consciousness and understand what they are; second, we propound a theory that encompasses them. Now for conventional science, or conventional art, such a view is a useful, if limited, account. Conventional practice *is* conventional just because its objects have already been defined by a given theoretical frame, and the "propounding of a theory" really consists of elaborating or qualifying a theory that we already have in mind. But when we speak of pioneering science, the scientific realist's view breaks down. For example, in the wave-particle theory of light, we know what we mean when we speak of photons because we depend on a fairly adequate analogy to molecules. We thus can hold some picture of photons before we have a theory about them, and to this extent the image of a two-phase separation of data and theory holds up. Yet even here much of our understanding of what the objects are awaits the second phase. When we speak of *wavicles* however, there is virtually no separation between data and theory. Explanation becomes description. As Quine says, "Our coming to understand what the objects are *is* for the most part just our mastery of what the theory says about them. We do not learn first what to talk about and then what to say about it" (1960:16). Statements or X rays or other representations are significant only in relation to a surrounding body of theory. The fact that such theories are justified only by supplemental scientific observation does not matter; for the definition of what *constitutes* such observation is also made from the point of view of a surrounding body of theory.

To commit ourselves to a paradigm is thus to submit to a double uncertainty. We must rely on the formalism of our theory or art work in order to apprehend its contents, yet this formalism is always subject to reformulation in light of our experience with these contents. This paradox is inevitable for the questioning mind. Just because it *is* formal, the theory, plot, or composition can never represent all that we know of its contents; yet because this knowledge is knowledge of the *contents*, we have articulate access to it only through its form. As form we see the relationships as important; as content we stress the entities without focal awareness of the unformed spaces between them. Both of these are legitimate and necessary ways of seeing. Though logically incompatible, they combine in aesthetic vision for their mutual enrichment.

Chekhov tells us that if a shotgun hangs on the wall in the first act, it must go off in the last. This suggests a relation between

form and content, element and plot, in which each makes us
more aware of the other. To the dramatically sophisticated
audience, the gun prefigures the developing logic of the action.
Yet the detail becomes a significant one only from this more
comprehensive viewpoint. Similarly, when we hold in aesthetic
attention a work of art or a scientific theory, we are more sensitive to both configurational properties as well as to salient details. In light of the broader expressive pattern, failures of fit,
minute "false notes," and subtle relations of harmony and
contrast are more readily perceived. As Osborne says,

> When we take up the synoptic attitude of attention to a
> work of art [or a scientific theory] . . . our percipience is
> more not less acute in such cases. . . . When we perceive
> the configurations in ordinary life and attend to them for
> the practical purpose of recognition only, it is the over-all
> structure that we notice, not the details. . . . But aesthetic
> vision is not for the practical purpose of recognition, and
> when a work of art [or a theory] is fixed in contemplation,
> both detail and general properties receive their due, neither
> obscuring the other. (Osborne, 1970:190–191)

"SUBJECTIVE" SYMBOLS VERSUS "OBJECTIVE" SCIENCE

What are the implications of these views for a hermeneutic
of cultural forms? How can we now speak of the relationships
among various scientific disciplines, and between various symbolic forms such as art, science, religion or ordinary language?
An exchange between Robert Bellah and Benjamin Nelson on
the sociology of religion is illuminating on just these points.
Bellah first insists that

> Noncognitive and nonscientific symbols are constitutive of
> human personality and society – are *real* in the fullest
> sense of the word. . . . What this signals is a shift away
> from the mechanical model of early natural science in
> which reality was seen as residing in the object, the
> function of the observer was simply to find out the laws in
> accordance with which the object behaves, and "subjective"
> was synonymous with "unreal," "untrue," "fallacious.". . .
> [In contrast to this view] I am prepared to claim that . . .
> religion is a reality sui generis. To put it bluntly, religion
> is true. (1970:93)

Most studies of religion, says Bellah, have not recognized
this religious truth of religion but instead have treated religion
as scientific error, as functionally consequential, as a childlike

fantasy or as false consciousness. In contrast, if we wish to respect the nature of our subject matter as a symbolic reality in its
own right, we

> must have a kind of double vision – at the same time that
> we try to study religious systems as objects we need also to
> apprehend them as religious subjects ourselves. . . . The
> canons of scientific objectivity or value neutrality . . . do
> not relieve us of the obligation to study our subject as
> whole persons – which means in part as religious persons.
> (1970:96)

Benjamin Nelson – no naive realist but himself a student of
cognitive systems – vigorously attacks Bellah's position as an
antiintellectual and reductive subjectivism:

> The academic study of religion must continue to be
> scientific or in fact it will not be *a study* of anything. It
> saddens me that Professor Bellah now seems to be offering
> his support to an ill-founded claim . . . one which asserts that
> there is no ground whatever for a separation between
> subject and object. What this claim overlooks is that the
> *subject* involved in scientific utterance is not the individual
> person – whether the scientist or the ordinary man. . . . The
> *subject* is actually the *logical subject*, a sentence, a sign, a
> proposition. . . . A logical subject is simply an utterance.
> . . . From the viewpoint of the scientific study of religion,
> . . . the critical fact is the relationship between a sentence
> and some state of affairs. (1970:109)

Despite Nelson's being "saddened" by Bellah, and Bellah's
"dismay" at Nelson (1970:112), it seems to us that the gentlemen are speaking past each other. For Bellah, what is real is in
some sense true. For Nelson what is true is in some sense real.
Bellah speaks of the subjective status of religious *apprehensions*;
Nelson speaks of the logical status of scientific *propositions*.
Yet given symbolic realism there is little *necessary* conflict between their views. For, in the symbolic realist perspective, not
only must we respect the integrity of religion as a symbol
system, we must also understand that science too is a symbol
system.[10] Symbolic realism does not assert the priority of one
over the other – in fact, it is specifically against such hubris.
Yet this by no means excludes the possibility of studying one
symbol system from the viewpoint of another. Thus Bellah partly
misleads us in suggesting that while both religion and science
are symbolic forms, the mode of awareness of science is cognitive while that of religion is subjective. In addition to studying

religious systems scientifically, he says, "we need also to apprehend them as religious subjects ourselves." The implications here are (1) that such apprehension as religious subjects is subjective in a noncognitive sense and (2) that conversely, the proper apprehension of scientific systems would be objective.

Bellah's argument should be amended on these points. *Any* apprehending we do must be "as subjects ourselves" or it is not an apprehension. But subjective here must mean personal and tacit, preobjective rather than noncognitive.[11] And this is no less true of science than of religion. To apprehend science we must do so as scientific subjects ourselves. That is, we must immerse ourselves – either directly or imaginatively – in the praxis of science or we will never fully understand it. Just as we cannot know what a "hammer" is without interiorizing the intention that such an object embodies, so we cannot know what a hypothesis or an experiment is without a similar entering into the meaning of such terms as they are understood by those "on the inside" of scientific practices; for example, medical students must immerse themselves personally in an experience with X rays in order to apprehend both the X rays and the theory of pulmonary disease of which they are the evidence.

Subjective thus means a personal and tacit apprehension of both the symbol system *under* study and the symbol system *from which* it is studied. Such subjectivity is *cognitive*. It is informed by, or is a search for, paradigmatic understanding. Benjamin Nelson is thus correct in insisting on the importance of the *logical* subject in scientific understanding. But we would be wrong to believe that this is the whole of science, to assume that the logical procedures of science do not go hand in hand with a tacit and personal apprehension of that which is being defined and analyzed in formal logical terms. At the center of scientific practice are persons, out of whose life worlds science grows as a mode of perception and expression. Symbolic realism does not require a sacrifice of cognitive rationality either in science *or* religion, but it does insist that both science *and* religion are symbolic constructs, the understanding and use of which must grow out of preobjective apprehensions. Neither science nor religion is an epiphenomena of the other or of anything else.

One conclusion to be drawn from this is that any inquiry – whether scientific or religious or artistic – must be based in part on a personal and, in a sense, nonrational belief. This is true not only in relation to that existential reality which must be experienced before it can be formally known. The paradox for the paradigm maker is also that he must posit the autonomy of a reality that he in fact creates. "The point of the creative act of expression," says Albert Hofstadter, "is *to arrive at a target that is not there*: once the target is there, the expression has been accomplished" (1965:35, Hofstadter's italics). Similarly Polanyi tells us that even

> The most daring feats of originality . . . must be performed on the assumption that they originate nothing, but merely reveal what is there. And their triumph confirms this assumption, for what has been found bears the mark of reality in being pregnant with yet unforeseeable implications. . . . The whole process of discovery and confirmation ultimately relies on our own accrediting of our own vision of reality. (1958:130)

Many others have said about the same. Note Polya's comment that "When you have satisfied yourself that the theorem is true, you start proving it" (1954:II, 76), or St. Augustine's dictum *"nisi credideritis, non intelligitis"* – unless ye believe, ye shall not understand. Believing is seeing.

A second point is that the study of anything is always the study of it from the viewpoint of something else, and that that study, if properly conducted, must not be a reduction but rather a "transcoding" into another symbol system. The scientific realist would strip off the "symbols" in order to expose the underlying "scientific reality"; transcoding is, instead, an interpretation in which meanings are extravasated while the symbols keep their blood. Rather than draining the symbol, such a mode of interpretation gives it new life. The interpretation itself becomes part of the symbol, just as an interpretation of a poem becomes, on the next reading, a part of what the poem says. The interpretation – the study – becomes a metaphor for the symbolic expressions studied. Each is deepened. Quine's warning to linguists thus applies to poets, anthropologists, and other transcoders – to all, in effect, who wish to articulate and to understand one reality in terms of another: "Wanton translation can make natives sound as queer as one pleases," but it also can make them sound familiar and banal (1953:47–64). Neither are distortions of some true meaning of the native's symbols, so much as they are a loss of aesthetic distance, that distance – a simultaneous nearness and farness – needed to avoid vulgarizing the language of both the linguist *and* the native whom he studies.

Modes of interpretation, then, may be judged by whether they build a wall of explanation between us and their objects, or whether they make their subject matter newly accessible. As Paul Ricoeur says, "If we can no longer live the great symbolisms . . . in accordance with the original belief in them, we can, we modern men, aim at a second naiveté in and through criticism. In short, it is by *interpreting* that we can *hear* again" (1967:351). To transcode symbolic vocabularies is to assume that existential reality may speak to us through any number of symbolic forms. But each of these vocabularies may be rearticulated by using any one of them as the code for representing the others.[12] "Meaning," as Greimas puts it, "is nothing but the possibility of such *transcoding*" (1970:13). A literary motif can be reexpressed in the form of sociology, the lived truth of ordinary language can be reexpressed in drama or in a computer model of syntax, the vocabulary of moral intentions can be reexpressed in the vocabulary of political praxis. Each symbolic form is privileged only for expressing its own special domain and purposes.

There is perhaps something unsettling in this notion that not only theories within a scientific discipline, but the very subject matter of these disciplines, and indeed the disciplines themselves, are "merely" symbolic constructs. Yet a cognitive aesthetic – a dialectical hermeneutic that recaptures the fuller meaning of a thesis by transcoding it and thereby transcending its partiality – may be an appropriate way of knowledge in a world where we have abandoned fixed objective realities. To transcode the vocabularies of Being is to recognize that all of our world is objectification – at once an expression and an alienation of reality. To accept the necessity of such disguises, of such a "tragedy of culture," is not to make oneself at home in our world. But it is a step toward building a science through which we can understand it.

3
Point of view

I am like a spy in a higher service, the service of the idea.... I do
not go to work straightforwardly but with indirect cunning; ... in
short, I am a spy who in his spying in learning to know all about
questionable conduct and illusions and suspicious characters, all the
while he is making inspection is himself under the closest inspection.
Kierkegaard (1962:87)

The concept of aesthetic perception or the aesthetic point of view
allows us to step outside the dreary debate between the "objectivity" of measurement and causal explanation and the "subjectivity" of understanding. Aesthetic perception is neither pure
reflection nor ordinary awareness. Instead, it combines the
detachment of the former with the intuitive immediacy of the
latter, though each is heightened and focused. Aesthetic perception may also be understood as a contemplative representation of the world in the imagination; the *con-* of contemplation
expresses the simultaneity and wholeness of aesthetic perception,
the *re-* of representation expresses the imaginative interioriza-
tion of the aesthetic object.

The aesthetic point of view does not seek to remove the actor
from the perceptual act, so that he can "objectively" know its
object. Nor does it require a "subjective" commitment to the
predefinitions and categories of the everyday world. Instead,
aesthetic awareness requires that one stand outside both ones
own attachments, *as well as* outside the naturalistic categoriza-
tions of that which one apprehends.

Primary to any aesthetics is this question of the nature of
aesthetic apprehension. In this chapter we briefly define the
"aesthetic point of view" as this concept is widely understood
by contemporary aestheticians. We then explore three areas of
sociological theory that can be informed by this concept. These
are (1) the proper point of view for doing sociology, (2) the

use of point of view as a resource within sociological analyses, and (3) point of view as a method by which sociologists may reflect on their own points of view.

POINT OF VIEW

The modern conception of aesthetic perception emerged from moral and religious debates of the seventeenth and eighteenth centuries. Central to this conception is "distinterested appreciation," a concept first articulated by Lord Shaftesbury in opposition to the "intelligent egoism" of Hobbes. Actions done from fear of consequences or in hopes of reward – that is, "interested" actions – can have no moral value, insisted Shaftesbury, no matter how enlightened the self-interest might be. Shaftesbury contrasted disinterested appreciation to any desire to possess or use the object of attention. Aesthetic interest terminates in the object on which attention is directed. A paradigm of this attitude, said Shaftesbury, is the enjoyment of mathematics, where perception does not relate to any "private interest of the creature, nor has it for its object any self-good or advantage" (quoted by Osborne, 1968:154).

Religious experience also was used as a source of definition of the aesthetic attitude. The notion of a disinterested love of God – for himself and not from hopes of salvation or fears of hell – arose out of controversies between Jesuits and Jansenists. In a letter to the Scottish savant Burnet, written in 1697, Leibniz defined disinterested love as "finding one's pleasure in the happiness of another." A year later in his *Lettre à Nicoise* Leibniz refers to a concern for the *existence* of things standing apart from our interest in their use.[1] Similarly, in his *Enquiry*, Edmund Burke defined beauty as "that quality . . . in bodies by which they cause love," a *disinterested* love unlike "desire or lust, which . . . hurries us on to the possession of certain objects." Kant carried the concept of disinterested appreciation a step further, focusing specifically on the aesthetic experience as such. Kant excludes from the aesthetic attitude not merely considerations of advantage, possession or use, but also concern even for the existence of the object. To reach a pure aesthetic experience, he says, "one must not be in the least prepossessed in favor of the real existence of the thing, but must preserve complete indifference in this respect in order to play the part of the judge in matters of taste" (quoted by Osborne, 1968: 179).

This belief that the appreciation of aesthetic properties requires an attitude of disinterested attention has become a commonplace of modern aesthetic theory.[2] Edward Bullough has this concept in mind when he contrasts aesthetic and mundane perception:

> This contrast, often emerging with startling suddenness, is
> like a momentary switching on of some new current, or
> the passing ray of a brighter light, illuminating the outlook
> upon perhaps the most ordinary and familiar objects – an
> impression which we experience sometimes in instants of
> direst extremity, when our practical interest snaps like a
> wire from sheer overtension, and we watch the
> consummation of some impending catastrophe with the
> marvelling unconcern of a mere spectator. (1969:398)

Given the exigencies of everyday life, such an attitude of disinterested yet heightened attention is obviously not the most common one. Indeed, for most of us aesthetic perception occurs only rarely, by accident, as it were, or in specifically defined situations such as museums. For example, we may be stranded for two hours at the train station with nothing to read and nothing to do. At such a moment our practical intentions may be forced into abeyance and we may see the "station" as a composition of volumes and colors. Similarly, although we may rise at dawn every morning to go to work, it may be only on a vacation cruise that we perceive the sunrise aesthetically.[3]

In such a mode of awareness the taken-for-granted world is disconnected or "distanced." Perceptual and compositional activity increase and predominate over classificatory thinking. In naive consciousness, we see what we expect or think we will see – the category or the project is embedded in what is perceived. *This* experience is not seen in and for itself as a structural unity, but as an experience of this *type* for this *use*. In aesthetic consciousness these relationships are reversed: We think with our eyes. What in mundane experience is grasped only prepredicatively now comes more fully to consciousness. The vague perceptual qualities that habitually go unnoticed or are taken only as clues to categories or to conduct, are now seen as precise and determinate. In this attention a new object is constituted and made articulate.

Through aesthetic perception we refashion original objects out of mundane ones, and we suddenly recognize our mundane surroundings *as* mundane. Such an attitude, of course, is much akin to phenomenological suspension, which can occur at those "odd moments in our lives when we are aware of ourselves *as*

attending a lecture, performing a duty, witnessing an event"
(Natanson, 1970:10).[4] "Distance" or "disinterested attention"
is at the heart of the aesthetic attitude. But distance here means
psychical rather than physical distance. It refers to *di-stance*, a
two-dimensioned mode of perception, an ontological standing
apart from conventional categories, and an ontological standing
near to the phenomena as given. Everything is at once infinitely
close and infinitely remote. The closeness lends perspecuity and
"presence," the remoteness permits synoptic and reflective
awareness.[5] Such a transformation by the action of distance, as
Bullough puts it,

> is produced in the first instance by putting the phenomenon,
> so to speak, out of gear with our practical, actual self; by
> allowing it to stand outside the context of our personal
> needs and ends – in short, by looking at it "objectively," as
> it has often been called, by permitting only such reactions
> on our part as emphasize the "objective" features of the
> experience, and by interpreting even our "subjective"
> affections not as modes of *our* being but rather as
> characteristics of the phenomenon. (1969:399)

As long as one clings to the positivist ideal of the absolute
spectator, of knowledge with no point of view, then one's personal situation and responses can be seen only as a source of
error (Merleau-Ponty, 1969:109). Yet such a distinction between the purely cognitive and the purely emotional, between
strict objectivity and strict subjectivity, are put aside in aesthetic
perception. Instead, through aesthetic distance both ideas *and*
feelings become ways of knowing and expressing the world.[6]

Interpreted in this fashion, aesthetic perception, distance, or
point of view are general concepts, having no necessary relation
to any particular genre or even to what is conventionally known
as art. As such, they are especially useful for illuminating the
nature and processes of nonartistic modes of creation and discovery. Within the domain of sociology, distance or point of
view may shed light on at least three areas:

1. The point of view of the sociologist *as* sociologist.
2. Point of view as a resource for sociological reporting and
analysis.
3. Point of view as a method of dialectical self-reflection.

Each of these areas has its counterpart in art theory and in
the conceptual richness to be expected of a long critical tradition. While point of view is often used effectively in sociological
writings, in art and literary circles it has received far greater

attention as an element of discourse. Perhaps a greater awareness of the artist's options, and of the critical vocabularies that
have risen to accompany them, will aid sociologists toward a
similar self-reflective sophistication. This hope, in any case,
informs the following discussion.

SOCIOLOGICAL DISTANCE

Distance, defamiliarization, dispassionate engagement,
seeing the reality behind the mask, appreciating the intrinsic
qualities of the mask itself, disinterested interest, idle curiosity
(Veblen) – all these terms have been used to describe an optimal
perspective for apprehending social reality. Each term implies
a stance similar to what Simmel describes in his classic essay,
"The Stranger."

> The stranger is . . . being discussed here not . . . as the
> wanderer who comes today and goes tomorrow, but rather
> as the person who comes today and stays tomorrow. He is,
> so to speak, the *potential* wanderer. . . . The unity of
> nearness and remoteness involved in every human relation
> is organized, in the phenomenon of the stranger, in a way
> which may be most briefly formulated by saying that in the
> relationship to him, distance means that he, who is close
> by, is far, and strangeness means that he, who also is far,
> is actually near.

> Another expression of this constellation lies in the
> objectivity of the stranger. He is not radically committed to
> the unique ingredients and peculiar tendencies of the
> group, and therefore approaches them with the specific
> attitude of "objectivity." But objectivity does not simply
> involve passivity and detachment; it is a particular
> structure composed of distance and nearness, indifference
> and involvement. . . . Objectivity is by no means
> non-participation (which is altogether outside both
> subjective and objective interaction), but a positive and
> specific kind of participation (1950:402, 404; cf. Schutz,
> 1944).

Simmel used the concept of the stranger to refer not to the
sociologist himself, but to persons who were precariously situated in the social order. Carrying on in that tradition, Park
and Stonequist developed the idea of the marginal man, perceiving him largely as an unfortunate product of the contact and

mergence of one civilization with another. What we suggest, however, is that rather than viewing such an aesthetic di-stance as dysfunctional to the individual, instead it be reconstituted as having positive functions for social science and for society as a whole: for society, as a way of being in the world, a critical consciousness not only for the outsider or marginal man, but also for any responsible citizen; for social science, as a means of adjudicating the farness of positivism with the nearness of personal interpretation, as a way of transcending the totalizing power of positive thinking and yet reincorporating it with its antithesis – the power of *negative*, personal, and dialectical thought.

Simmel's distinction between form and content in intimate relationships also is helpful in making our point:

> Intimacy is not based on the *content* of the relationship. . . .
> Inversely, certain external situations or moods may move
> us to make very personal statements and confessions,
> usually reserved for our closest friends only, to relatively
> strange people. But in such cases we nevertheless feel that
> this "intimate" *content* does not yet make the relation an
> intimate one. For in its basic significance, the whole
> relation to these people is based only on its general,
> unindividual ingredients. That "intimate" content,
> although we have perhaps never revealed it before and
> thus limit it entirely to this particular relationship, does
> nevertheless not become the basis of its form, and thus
> leaves it outside the sphere of intimacy. (1950:127)

Using the aesthetic notion of point of view as a code, we can now translate Simmel's sociological *insight* into a sociological *policy* and *method*, a stance for social research. To illustrate: The field-worker in his participant-observer role seeks to bring his relationships with informants to the point of trust and openness. While this may avoid the ethnocentricism of the over-distanced "pure" observer, it also contains risks of cooption, overrapport, or "going native" characteristic of the under-distanced pure participant. However, if intimate *content* can be combined with *non*intimate *form*, both nearness and farness may be simultaneously achieved. If content is intimate "secrets may be shared without either of the interactors feeling compelled to maintain the relationship for more than a short time" (Gold, 1969:35). If the form of the interaction remains *non*-intimate, the sociologist can avoid greater commitment to the viewpoint of his informant than to his own professional stance.

The participant side of participant-observation thus affords nearness, while the observer side lends farness. The two combine through aesthetic di-stance in a relationship between intimate sociological strangers. "Whenever pretense becomes too challenging, the participant-as-observer leaves the field to re-clarify his self-conceptions and his role-relationships. . . . [He needs] cooling-off periods during and after complete participation, at which times he can 'be himself' and look back on his field behavior dispassionately and sociologically" (Gold, 1969:36, 34). Psychical distance failing, the sociologist can reestablish it by distancing himself in time and space.[7]

Although these functions of aesthetic distance are rarely mentioned by sociologists, they have long been acknowledged by more literary students of conduct. It is significant, for example, that Machiavelli wrote *The Prince* while removed from the daily struggles for power. In exile from Florence, he reflected on his own point of view:

As those who wish to delineate countries place themselves
low in the plain to observe the form and character of
mountains and high places, and for the purpose of studying
the nature of the low country place themselves high upon
an eminence, so one must be a prince to know well the
character of the people, and to understand well the nature
of a prince one must be of the people. (1963:xxxvi)

Similarly, Tocqueville knew that optimum distance will vary with the purposes of the observer:

My present object is to embrace the whole from one point
of view. . . . A traveller, who has just left the vast city,
climbs the neighboring hill; as he goes farther off he loses
sight of the men whom he has just quitted; . . . but his eye
has less difficulty in following the boundaries of the city,
and for the first time he sees the shape of the whole. Such
is the future destiny of the British race in North America to
my eye; the details of the immense picture are lost in the
shade, but I conceive a clear idea of the entire subject.
(1956:138)

Tocqueville was "distanced" not only in his generalizing theoretical stance; he also had the built-in psychic distance of an outsider. He was an aristocrat in an age of egalitarianism, yet he was marginal to the aristocracy itself. He was at once a scholar and a man of practical affairs. Most important, he was a Frenchman in a foreign land.

Aesthetic perception of *artistic illusions* requires a suspen-

sion of *dis*belief. A similar perception of *social reality* requires
a suspension of *belief*. For example, by disbelieving that
equality and freedom must necessarily be conjoined, Tocqueville was able to see the demagogic features of the former and
the fragility of the latter. At the same time, he also provided an
implicit commentary on France while writing of Americans,
much as anthropologists express the complexity of their own
societies in their studies of "primitive" cultures.[8] In each case
the analyst gains new insights into his own society for being
outside it, and greater insight into his hosts' culture for not being fully a member. Thus the most enduring studies of America
were written by a French aristocrat and an English gentle-
woman, Harriet Martineau (1962), while the classic examination of our caste system was done by a Swede, Gunnar Myrdal
(1944), from one of the most homogeneous of cultures.[9]

One technique for achieving distance in poetry is what Victor
Shklovsky calls "roughening," as when the surface flow of
poetic language is purposely broken so that the reader becomes
aware of the words themselves as they act to construct the poem
(1965:22). A counterpart of this technique in sociological research is to artificially break the flow of interaction in order to
reveal the underlying work by which a social exchange
is accomplished. For example, in one of their experiments,
Garfinkel and his students assumed a manner of naive incom-
prehension, in order to force their subjects to explicate the
background rules of the situation and to show what conduct is required to maintain them:[10]

Subject:
    Hi Ray. How is your girl friend feeling?
Experimenter:
    What do you mean, "How is she feeling?" Do you mean
    physical or mental?
S: I mean how is she feeling? What's the matter with you?
    (He looked peeved.)
E: Nothing. Just explain a little clearer what do you mean?
S: Skip it. How are your school applications coming?
E: What do you mean, "How are they?"
S: You know what I mean.
E: I really don't.
S: What's the matter with you? Are you sick? (1967:42–43)

In like manner, one of Kenneth Clark's tactics for establishing
distance from the placid surface of social interactions was "to
plan confrontations and conflicts among individuals within

groups and between groups in order to draw forth deep feelings and ambivalences, and to see how these individuals responded to and interpreted and resolved those conflicts" (Clark, 1965:xix).

In addition to *being* a stranger, as with the visiting anthropologist, or *estranging* the subject matter, as do Garfinkel and Clark, sociologists also can achieve distance by taking the point of view of strangers, by studying persons who themselves are "within" but not "of" their situations.[11] "In almost any society ... the observer is likely to find persons with a penchant for seeing themselves objectively in relation to their society, such as the traveled Pacific Islander or the small-town 'intellectual' " (Vidich, 1955:358). Such persons may be used as informants, or they may be examined as subjects for the light that their lives casts on the larger society. Thus the study of persons who have just changed status or who find themselves at the interstices of conflicting roles has yielded important insights into identity management, rule construction (and evasion), social control, and institutionalization. Likewise, by understanding the worlds of villagers newly arrived in the city, or of Negro intellectuals, children of mixed marriages, bisexuals, factory foremen, professional women, spies, criminals, military chaplains, or persons who "pass," we come to better understand the workings of society in general (Shibutani, 1955; Stonequist, 1937; Seward, 1958).[12] As Erving Goffman says,

> The important thing about criminals – and other
> desperados such as children, comics, saboteurs, and the
> certified insane – is not what they do or why they do it.
> Nor is it necessary to look into the darkness of their souls
> in order to learn about the darkness of our own. .... The
> importance of these strays is not in the cue they provide as
> to what, in our heart of hearts we do also, but rather in the
> contrastive light their situation throws on what, in doing
> what we do, we are doing. A radical ethnography must take
> ordinary persons doing ordinary things as the central
> issue. (1971:260)

Bronislaw Malinowski uses all three of the above methods of distance in his efforts to discover "what natives really think": "Children were perceived to look like their father but not at all like their mother. Furthermore, siblings, children of the same father, did not look like each other. Thus two brothers might each be said to look just like their father; yet it would be vigorously denied that they looked like each other" (Segall, *et al.*, 1966:26; Malinowski, 1924, 1927, 1929).

Yet the question remained as to whether Trobrianders "actually did not see" these similarities, or whether they simply were "refusing to report them." Malinowski resolved this issue with essentially negative reasoning. First, he became aware that there was something that needed explaining because he was an outsider or negative of that culture. Then, by violating rules of conduct, he discovered that it was taboo to mention that two brothers looked alike. Furthermore, in estimating the probity of his respondents' reports, he gave deciding valence to reports from persons who on other occasions had expressed culturally dissident beliefs. Thus Malinowski came as a stranger, estranged the host culture by violating its rules, and studied strangers (dissidents) in order to resolve the paradoxes that emerged.[13]

POINT OF VIEW AS A RESOURCE

We have argued that aesthetic distance or point of view provides a means of transcending the objectivity-subjectivity debate and of characterizing the stance that is appropriate to sociological inquiry. At the same time, however, point of view can be an organizing principle *within* sociological analysis itself. If a goal of sociological explanation is to give a fuller and more cogent vision of the world, then all the partial perspectives or points of view *within* the analysis must be ordered and arranged so as to achieve the picture or perspective of the work as a whole.[14]

The chief materials for this structuring activity are the relationships between the observer's point of view and those of the people on whom he reports. In a novel, for example, the author's command of his characters' thoughts and actions allows him to create material suitable to the manner in which he desires to report it. The characters can be shaped to fit the author's style and genre. But for the sociologist, the characters have much more a life of their own and, hence, a greater tension exists between what is observed and the manner in which it will be conveyed.

Jean Pouillon's comments in *Time and the Novel* may help us on this point. Pouillon distinguishes three types of discourse or reporting according to the position the author assumes in relation to his subjects: the author as superior, as equal, or as inferior. Balzac, for example, assumes authorial omniscience; he is the god whose creatures act out his novel. In contrast, Proust incorporates himself into his novels as Marcel, becoming one character among others. The third position, in which the author is inferior to the characters, is illustrated by the "new novel"

of Robbe-Grillet, where incomplete and perplexing actors seem
to dodge even the most generous attempts to account for their
use of the novel's time.[15]

Oscar Lewis's *Five Families* (1959) suggests itself for examination in terms of this literary model, not only because of
its adroit use of novelistic techniques, but also because Lewis
claims that his method of reporting can yield "objective"
knowledge.[16] In this work Lewis uses "the Rashomon-like technique of seeing the family through the eyes of each of its members . . . through long, intensive autobiographies of each member of the family." Yet how does Lewis's use of *multiple* points
of view *within* the narrative contribute to forming the story
which eventually gets told? Such a question also touches on the
problem of objectivity versus subjectivity, of course, in that the
author's interaction with his characters will inevitably be revealed in his building their discourse into a single narrative.

Lewis does not intervene openly as the narrator, but the
presence of an observer-reporter is felt from the opening lines.
The authorial point of view is present but not accounted for.
While the point of view of each member of the family is carried
by spoken "autobiographies" that have been transcoded by the
author-anthropologist into a "realistic" text, the author's voice
enters the work indirectly, sometimes as an attribution of motive, sometimes as a statement of the actors' interior thoughts;
for example, "She did not want to use a match to light the fire
for a box of matches cost five centavos and was still a luxury"
(p. 24). "Well, her daughter Machrina could sleep a little
longer" (p. 25).

In such cases it is impossible to separate the transcoded elements of the character's speech from the commentary of the author. By guessing, however, we might imagine the following distinctions: "I did not want to use a match to light the fire" – Why
not? – "Because a box of matches costs five centavos" – And then
comes the commentary: "It was *still* a luxury." By breaking
apart the sentence we become aware that Lewis' original version
draws the reader unwittingly into the author's point of view.
"It was still a luxury" could pass as a thought expressed by
Esperanza Martinez. Her very name suggests a trusting hope
that villagers one day will be able to afford matches. More
likely, however, the author-anthropologist has mixed his own
language with that of his character. A perspective of continuous
progress and achievement is implied, as well as a comparison
with American farmers' standard of living. The anthropologist's

commentary is therefore available at the reader's discretion. Because the style is indirect, the reader and the author can have it both ways. If the reader is sympathetic with the implicit ideology, he will ease himself into the author's chair and impute a "rightness" to the mixture of author's comments and characters' thoughts. But if the reader is unsympathetic, he will accuse the anthropologist of lacking "objectivity," of mixing commentary and text.

Such a criticism, translated into a novelistic point of view, mandates that the character and the author speak with separate voices. Stated more strongly, this suggests that there is one point of view that is the privileged one for "objective" observation, a point of view that somehow stands entirely above the action and reflects it the way a mirror reflects an image. As applied to our Mexican peasants, this assumes that there is a describable truth about the characters that they themselves may not understand but that a superior author can directly observe and report. A box of matches cost five centavos. Matches are used by so many people with such and such a frequency. The *real* reasons for their behavior are such and such. These are the facts, whether the actors are aware of them or not.

In contrast to such extreme objectivism, Lewis's way of reporting suggests an equality between the author and his character. "Although I was a foreigner and a 'norte-Americano,' I encountered no hostility and very little antigringoism among these families" (p. 5). The assumption is that even if the characters do not always speak directly, rapport and friendship will ensure likeness between their voices and that of the author. Given this, it matters little whether comments such as "it was still a luxury" belong to Esperanza's style or the narrator's (both of which in any case are Lewis's). Flaubert once said that the illusion of truth in his work was achieved through the objectivity of his style. This proposition may be reversed with reference to Lewis: His objectivity is an illusion yielded by the truth-giving equality of his point of view.[17]

If Lewis's work shows the author as equal, statistical, experimental, and macrofunctional, theorists represent the author as superior to the persons under study. Both the field researcher and the macroanalyst act and are acted on by their subjects; but they meet this encounter in opposite ways. The experimenter or social systems analyst does most of the acting, and then restricts the ways he may be acted on to highly controlled limits. He defines his subject matter in advance, specifies the conditions under which it may be said to occur, applies the appropriate stimuli, and generally controls the subject matter so that it may finally either: (1) act; or (2) not act, in the predicted manner. This last action, or rather *re*action, is the unique contribution of the subject matter to the process of observation. Neither perceptual bias nor poetic license may be allowed to distort it.

The question of superiority of the author through greater knowledge may not be only a matter of a stance or heuristic assumption, but also one of *actual* control and manipulation. In clinical or field work, deception generally is seen as a harmful barrier to communication; it usually is felt and reciprocated, resulting in too distant a relationship and untrustworthy data (Wax, 1960). But, for experiments, deception is often considered necessary to avoid contaminating the data. Indeed, the experience of Kelman (1965) in his attempts to avoid manipulating subjects, suggests that it is often impossible to conduct controlled experiments with full disclosure to those being studied.

A third relationship the author may assume toward his subjects is that of *inferior*. Carlos Castañeda, for example, not only took the role of acolyte to an Indian *brujo*; he also used this perspective to describe his master's nonordinary world (1968). Similarly, Harold Garfinkel, in his study of an "intersexed" person, describes his growing understanding of the management of sexual identity from the viewpoint of someone who is being successfully conned by the person he is studying (1967:116).

Most sociological writing, like most modern fiction, assumes authorial omniscience as a basic stance. But then, after having taken full command of the narrative, the author may invoke a variety of other representational techniques:

1. He can make selective use of a number of individual points of view, borrowing a specific character's angle of vision when it suits his purpose.
2. He can use the theatre of 'showing not telling,' for the moment presenting a quite objective look at things.
3. He can analyze anything about the story by use of critical comment and generalization. . . .
4. He can take a panoramic view of events, giving an account of simultaneous happenings or disassociated scenes that a narrator-agent could cover only by the use of most improbable devices.
5. He can discover multiple traits and facets of the characters [or cultures] under study readily and plausibly without

having to work things around to bring any single point of view within discovery range. (Macauley and Lanning, 1964:111–112)

In *Talley's Corner*, for example, Elliot Liebow begins by presenting the slum as viewed by a white employer, but then moves to the "inside" and "over-" views that dominate the rest of the book:

> A pickup truck drives slowly down the street. The truck stops as it comes abreast of a man sitting on a cast-iron porch and the white driver calls out, asking if the man wants a day's work. The man shakes his head and the truck moves on up the block, stopping again whenever idling men come within calling distance of the driver. At the Carry-out corner, five men debate the question briefly and shake their heads no to the truck. The truck turns the corner and repeats the same performance up the next street. In the distance, one can see one man, then another, climb into the back of the truck and sit down. In starts and stops, the truck finally disappears.

> What is it we have witnessed here? A labor scavenger rebuffed by his would-be prey? Lazy, irresponsible men turning down an honest day's pay for an honest day's work? Or a more complex phenomenon marking the intersection of economic forces, social values, and individual states of mind and body? (1967:29–30)

Liebow's contrast of perspectives is used mainly to highlight the viewpoint of his principal subjects: unemployed ghetto men. More extensive use of contrasts is seen in Thomas Scheff's work on conflicts between doctors and attendants in a mental hospital (1961, 1966), or in Scott and Lyman's study of the student revolt (1970). In these works conflicting points of view are not merely expository devices; instead, they are the substance of the social reality that is described.

The transcoding of observation into report is thus a highly problematic art, laden with choices which the sociologist ignores at his peril. A different use of even one word can transform the reality that gets conveyed. Consider, for example, the care with which Radcliffe-Brown (1948) tries to express the concept of *ot-kimil* from the viewpoint of the Andamanese, or the way Malinowski struggles with the Trobrianders' concept of *mana*. In contrast, the survey researcher, taking a stance superior to his subjects, develops logically exhaustive and mutually exclusive categories and scales. These are objective in that they are not particularized to any special group (as is *ot-kimil*) and thus permit comparison, generalization, and formalization; they may be applied in numerous settings regardless of the actors' conceptions of their own action.

If extreme objectivist writers may be thought of as over-distanced, other sociologists can be seen as having gotten too close to their subject matter (see Miller, 1952:97–99). The Chicago School, for example, so stressed the uniqueness of their subjects' worlds that they were unable to adequately articulate the linkages and interdependencies of these groups and the larger social system. Compare, for instance, the overdistancing of Talcott Parsons to the underdistancing of Anderson or Zorbaugh. First Parsons:

> There is a certain relatively in the conceptions of conformity and deviance. . . . It is not possible to make a judgment of deviance . . . without specific reference to the system . . . to which it applies. The structure of normative patterns in any but the simplest sub-system is always intricate and usually far from fully integrated; hence singling out one such pattern without reference to its interconnections in a system of patterns can be very misleading. (1951:250–251)

The "structure of normative patterns" and the "interconnections within a system" are defined by the sociologist rather than the actors. The actors, operating as they do within discrete situations, are almost always bound to be "misled." The level of discourse of the reporter is "superior" to the speech of any possible subjects (except perhaps other sociologists). As a reduction of language into strictly denotative meanings, the words are weak in the contextual embeddedness that would create nearness to what is actually observed.

In contrast, consider Chicago sociology of the 1920s:

> Jungle populations are ever changing. . . . Here is one place where every man's past is his own secret. . . . The hobo is his own housewife. He not only cooks . . . but has invented dishes that are peculiar to jungle life. Chief among these is "mulligan stew." Moreover the art of telling a story is diligently cultivated by the "bos" in the assemblies about the fire. (Anderson, 1923:18–20)

> The rooming house which has replaced the boardinghouse is a very different sort of place to live. One comes and goes

as one wishes, does very much as one pleases, and as long
as one disturbs no one else, no questions are asked. . . . It
was at the "Y" that I had my first acquaintance with that
most pitiful figure of the rooming house – the old and
unmarried woman who works. They were conspicuous in
either the cafeteria or the upstairs sittingroom, because of
their loneliness – eating lunch at the solitary table, sitting
by themselves knitting, with shabby and unbecoming
clothes, care-worn faces, and toil-worn hands. I was to
learn later some of the tragedies their mute lips harbored
(Zorbaugh, 1929:73, 75, 77). One may be ill and die
without producing a ripple on the surface of the common
life. (Hayner, 1929:113)

In these examples the reporter-observer has become too involved with his subjects. These devices – the focus on the here
and now ("here is one place . . ."), the situational embeddedness ("the cafeteria," "the solitary table,") the use of member
speech ("bos," "Y"),[18] the graphic, sentimental images "care-
worn faces," "toil-worn hands"), the first-person shock of recognition ("I had my first acquaintance . . ."), and the placing of
the reader in the midst of the action ("One comes and goes . . .,"
"One may be ill and die . . .") – all make it virtually impossible
to "distance" what is observed from one's reactions to it. The
artistic equivalent would be for us to put ourselves in a state
of pathological jealousy while watching *Othello*. Our own
jealousy would make us incapable of dispassionately appreciating the quality of *Othello's* jealousy, or of perceiving its structural function in the play as a whole. In contrast, the artistic
cognate of overdistanced sociology would be the observer who
– because of saintliness or an incapacity to love – would be
unable to enter into Othello's state of feeling. From this distance
Othello's conduct would simply appear irrational and, in the
absence of credible motives, the play either would make no
sense or would be seen not as tragedy but as farce.

V. N. Volosinov makes some points that might further illuminate the above works. In his essay "Reported Speech," Volosinov distinguishes this category of linguistic expression from
either narrative exposition or direct quotation: "Reported
speech is speech within speech, message within message, and at
the same time also speech about speech, message about message"
(1971:149). Volosinov then discusses the "dynamic inter-
relationship of these two factors, the speech being reported (the

other person's speech) and the speech doing the reporting (the author's speech). This dynamism [of linguistic interrelation] reflects the dynamism of social interorientation in verbal-ideological communication between people" (1971:153).

Our main interest in these relationships is the distance, or level of *author*-ity that the author assumes toward his subjects. For example, an author who presumes total control might keep his subjects silent or, insofar as they are allowed expression, they might be made to use the language of the author, however foreign it may be. For example, the textual existence of persons studied by a statistical positivist is at the discretion of their author – he may not acknowledge them at all, instead insisting that his study is of forces, attitudes, or variables. Even if he gives them voice, it may be audible only through the screens of chi-squares and standard deviations; that is, as a way of illustrating the method by which the subjects' "naive" voices were coded into the authoritative statistical voice of the author.

In contrast to this is direct dialogue or soliloquy, as represented by more literary approaches to fieldwork such as the autobiographies by Sutherland or Thomas and Znaniecki. In such cases the author-sociologist makes himself the vehicle for transmitting the subject's intentions. Conversely, in the statistical or experimental mode, it is the subjects of the experiment who are passive; they become vehicles for actions initiated by the author.

Unlike either statistical reports or ethnobiographies, most ethnographies consist neither of discourse that is totally commanded by the author, nor of the direct speech of the characters – that is, they contain much "reported speech." Yet even within this domain it is possible to distinguish tendencies toward "superior," "equal" or "inferior" stances in the author's relation to his subjects. But what, exactly, are the stylistic means by which these distances are achieved?

As implied above, one key dimension for affecting distance is the freedom with which the subjects' speech is allowed to enter the text. At one extreme the subjects' speech may be embalmed and dressed in a tuxedo, at the other extreme it may enter in shabby clothes still smelling of the street. Goffman's distinction between "backstage" and "frontstage" is useful here. Aristocrats – the overclass – can be virtually all *front*stage in their conduct, for the backstage of reality has been screened out of their world through structural and stylistic devices. In contrast, proletarians – the underclass – may be virtually all *back*stage; they lack the stylistic and structural powers for preserving in

their worlds a sphere of good form. Parallel to this, in aristo-
cratic or formal writing, subjects' speech must conform to the
rules of frontstage or it will not be admitted into the text (note the
revulsion of the French court dramatists to the appearance of
gravediggers in Shakespeare's plays). In proletarian writing
(e.g., Gorky or his approximations in sociology, such as
Polsky), the backstage takes over, and not only the speech but
also the scene or context of the speech enters the narrative; for
example, the poolroom or jailhouse. In the first type of reporting, the authorial context is dominant; in the second, this authorial context is absorbed into the reported speech. In terms of this
imagery, most sociological writing is "middle class"; it has both
a backstage *and* frontstage, both authorial context as well as
subjects' reported speech.

Another distinction is not the relative dominance or space
allotted to authorial context or to reported speech, but the relative *firmness of the boundaries between them.* Where the
authorial stance is to be superior, strict boundaries must be
forged. Generally, the more authoritative the stance of the
author, the less the leeway between truth and falsehood, between
good and bad, will remain in the reported speech. The "what"
of speech will be separated from its qualifying "why" and
"how" – at least as they might be understood by the speaker.
Equivocality of the speaker's context will be prohibited from the
text, and the author's context will have been purged of ambiguity
before the reported speech is placed within it. Given that evaluative responses have been preempted or screened out, there is
little space for an observant attitude toward these factors that
give the speakers' utterances their individual characters.

The superior style of speech reporting is most employed by
sociologists of a positivist bent. It is similar to what Wölfflin
called the "linear" style of painting, in that the entire context
displays a complete stylistic homogeneity – that is, the author
and his subjects speak the same language, and the grammatical
and compositional manipulation of the reported speech achieves
a maximal compactness and plastic relief. It has a flat surface
and geometric depth. The linear style of speech reporting thus
has a built-in tendency to thematicize the speakers' utterances,
not so much in constructional terms as in terms of meaning. The
results are achieved, however, only at the price of depersonalization.

The opposite of the linear or positivist style may be called
"pictorial" or "humanistic," of which Oscar Lewis' works pro-

vide an excellent example. Here the reported speech is infiltrated in subtle ways by authorial comments. The precise external contours of the reported speech are broken down, yet the speech is individualized to a much greater extent – it is made more palpable by introducing the subjects' context along with their speech. Hence a greater range of the subjects' language contextual peculiarities may be reflected through inclusion of various nonverbal facets of their verbal performance.

If the pictorial style allows for greater wholeness, verisimilitude, and individuality, the very weakening of boundaries through which this is effected also permits the author's commentary to permeate the subjects' talk. On the ideological level, this represents a departure from the value neutrality and authoritarian rationality of the linear style. Instead, the pictorial approach tends to relativize values, and then to extend a sympathetic reception to individualized verbal nuances of thought, conduct, or feeling, leaving more textual space both for the speakers to express themselves and for the audience to decipher their meaning. Carried to its extreme, this might entail a neglect of the denotative meaning of an utterance – its "what" – in favor of its color and context. That is, not only is discrete interpretation suspended by the author, but the very assumption that there is a meaning distinguishable from the speech act itself is suspended as well. Instead, the subject's speech may be thought of as wholly self-referential, relating only to their own world and understandable only when one has entered that world. Such an entry is facilitated first by allowing much of the subject's context into the text, and second by breaking the barriers between the author's context and the subject's speech. If the reader refuses this invitation, however, the text appears opaque, and the reported speech can be comprehended only as part of the decor, on a par with clothing or furnishings, in the sense that these would be seen as "mere objects" having no communicative or connotational significance.

In general, then, the more sharply defined the boundaries between authorial context and reported speech, the stronger will be the feeling of hierarchy and distance between the sociologist and his subjects. In the linear or positivist style the speaker's individuality is a factor only as it occupies some specific position in a schema pregiven by the authorial context, and beyond that position it has no existence for the author. The interest and devices are such that the speaker's individuality cannot congeal into an image. But the opposite is true of the pictorial or humanistic style. Here the speaker's individuality is presented through his subjective manner of being and speaking, either individually or typologically. Instead of being screened by a formalistic style, here the author's evaluations enter the text through such stylistic tactics as those noted in our comments on Chicago sociology.

We may now summarize the above in terms of our earlier discussion of level or distance of the authorial voice: To the extent that the author's speech rather than the reported speech occupies the space of the text, and to the extent that the boundaries between authorial context and reported speech are rigid, there will be greater superiority in the stance of the author. Conversely, to the extent that there is more reported speech and more permeable boundaries, there will be less distance and hierarchy between the author and the subjects. This is represented in Figure 1.

Having come this far, it is now easier to see where different sociological styles might be located in such a model. The positivist style of sociology clearly would go in the upper-left quadrant (*a*), while much of descriptive ethnography probably would fit comfortably in quadrant (*b*). The lower-right quadrant (*c*) is represented in sociology by what we call novelistic ethnography,

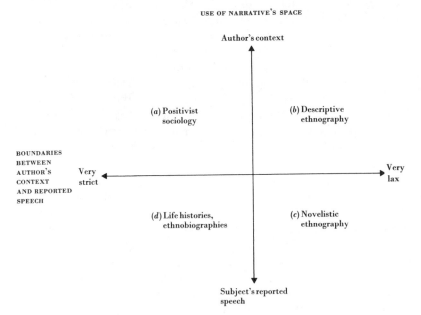

Figure 1

while the lower left (d) might hold life histories and ethno-biographies.

Whether superior, inferior, or equal, however, the sociologist must choose his language with care. The "objectivity" of a report depends on the adequacy with which certain stylistic devices are employed within the sociologist's text. Just as the speech of the subjects is not a neutral carrier of meanings independent of that speech, so the language of the sociologist must reflect an awareness of the peculiarities of the linguistic phenomena under scrutiny. Stylistic self-consciousness is a precondition of reportorial accuracy – whether it be accuracy in the sense of the text reporting pointer-reader responses of the subjects, or accuracy in the sense of representing authentically the subjects' world. Rhetoric requires cognizance of the boundaries and devices for reporting speech. Words have property rights that must be respected.

The above remarks have concerned the point of view of the observer-reporter in relation to those whom he studies. But point of view can be a resource of analysis not only *within* a single study, but also *between* the observations of different researchers or informants. An implicit understanding of this is reflected in the actual practice of much social research, although it is not often acknowledged in textbooks on method. Instead the literature on methodology is rife with suggestions on how to eliminate "biases" of point of view (e.g., Llewellyn and Hoebel, 1941; Churchman, 1957). Knowledge is seen ideally to exist independently of the knower. To approximate this ideal, the investigator must eliminate his subjectivity – the source of bias – and instead make his methods a litmus of the society under study.

In contrast to this approach we have argued that knowledge is possible only through the interpretive processes which the knower enacts in his encounter with the subjects in question. In this view, objectivity is not depersonalization, but a mastery of passion. Through such an attitude, the inquirer is presumed to be able to "accept the other's illusions as real money," and then to ask how such "illusions" are possible. The "bias," rather than being suppressed, is used as a source of understanding. The various voices do not cancel each other out, nor is truth limited to those points on which they agree; instead, much as characters in a play, each voice enriches the others, each contributes to the dialectical construction of more and more comprehensive *meta*-perspectives. These metaperspectives are not objective in that they have eliminated bias but in that they organize the "biases" of various actors into a structured mimesis of the domain of experience to be explained.

A well-known instance of such a structuring of perspectives has grown out of the conflict between Robert Redfield's study of Tepoztlan, Mexico, and that made there twenty years later by Oscar Lewis.[19] Redfield (1930) discovered a community that was family oriented, close knit, cooperative, and deeply religious. Lewis (1951) found suspicion, factions, materialism, and isolation. The time difference could not entirely explain such disparities, nor could the research techniques of the two investigators. After much reflection, many anthropologists concluded that *both* these accounts are correct: Redfield had obtained the "official" version of the culture, the way people like to think of themselves and the ideals against which they interpret their conduct. On the other hand, Lewis drew a picture of the underbelly of the beast, the day-to-day pettiness and striving. At the same time that both versions are correct, however, each is incorrect in its incompleteness.

Despite such a happy resolution, the Redfield-Lewis debate remained troublesome (Foster, 1960–1961). For if anthropology must to some extent be autobiography, how could one get an objective account? One appears to be confronted on one side by a dogmatic and self-contradictory objectivism (Lewis, 1970) and, on the other, by a solipsistic relativism. Yet Redfield himself seems to provide a way out of this dilemma by abandoning the image of the researcher as a mechanical recorder:

> It seems to me that with the recognition of the influence of
> personal choices on the resulting description we arrive at
> the possibility of combining two contrasting viewpoints
> into a combined viewpoint of the protean and unattainable
> absolute reality. I think we may well conceive of the
> process by which understanding of human wholes is
> advanced as a kind of dialectic of viewpoint, a dialogue of
> characterizations. (1955:137)

Such a view, we believe, expands and deepens our understanding of objectivity and clarifies the nature of the research act. C. Wright Mills states this even more strongly:

> The sociological imagination, I remind you, in considerable
> part consists of the capacity to shift from one perspective
> to another, and in the process to build up an adequate view
> of a total society and its components. It is this imagnation,
> of course, that sets off the social scientist from the mere

technician. . . . There is a playfulness of mind back of such combining as well as a truly fierce drive to make sense of the world, which the technician as such usually lacks. (1959:211–212)

Despite their continued use of a positivist vocabulary of methods, even statistical researchers seem to share Redfield's sentiments – at least at a gut level – for their formal, highly distanced, "objective" findings are regularly "adjusted" in light of near-range reports by persons "in the know." Moreover, even statistical sociologists have tried to build a dialectic of viewpoints into their official method of research. In a limited way this is effected by the use of multiple operations of measurement. As Webb *et al.* put it, "The operational implication of the inevitable theoretical complexity of every measure . . . calls for a multiple operationalism, that is, for multiple measures which are hypothesized to share in the theoretically relevant components but have different patterns of irrelevant components" (1972:3; see, for example, Garner, 1954; Garner, Hake, and Eriksen, 1955; Campbell and Fiske, 1959; Campbell, 1960; and Humphreys, 1960).

Of course, it is no news that characteristics of the sociologist can substantially affect a set of findings (Hyman *et al.*, 1954; Kahn and Cannell, 1957). Indeed, much of the literature on methodology is devoted to identifying these biases and finding ways to eliminate them, to screen out the connotative subcommunications so that the subjects' responses will be only to the denotative questions. Thus the works of Katz (1942), Cantril (1944), and Athey (1960) demonstrate the differential effect of the race of the interviewer. Similarly, Riesman and Ehrlich (1961) report that the age of the interviewer produces a bias, with the number of "unacceptable" answers higher when questions were posed by younger interviewers. The religion of the interviewer also has been found to "contaminate" the data (Robinson and Rohde, 1946; Hyman, *et al.*, 1954) as has his social class (Riesman, 1956; Lenski and Leggett, 1960). Similarly, in their study of age and sex variables, Benney, Riesman, and Star report that "Male interviewers obtain fewer responses than female, and fewest of all from males, while female interviewers obtain their highest responses from men, except for young women talking to young men" (1956:143).

All of these writers are seeking, in effect, a stereoscopic vision on their subject matter through multiple operations. The assumption and language, of course, is that ideally the bias can be removed, and that measures can be found that are truly non-reactive (Webb, *et al.*, 1972). Yet other scholars, rather than seeing differences between interviewers' findings as evidence of distortion or contamination, have instead taken each as an expression of the view from a certain social location. For example, Melville Dalton does not dismiss company records as biased and, hence, inadmissible evidence; instead he took their pattern of falsification as management's official definition of the world and as an instrument in its political bargaining (Dalton, 1964:77–78, 81). One could carry such thinking further and reinterpret most checks for reliability as a means not merely of "canceling out error" but rather of getting additional points of view, each a representation of that particular encounter between researcher and subject.[20] Such a translation of reliability into the aesthetic vocabulary of point of view suggests a similar reformulation of conventional notions of validity. Truth becomes not a correspondence between statement and object, but instead an artistic "truth to," in which the concinnity and perspicuity of the representation makes it an emblem for the world that it signifies.

POINT OF VIEW AS AN INSTRUMENT OF SELF-REFLECTION
The concept of distance or estrangement has yet a third advantage: it permits us a new conception of the history and social location of sociological theory itself. Once distance is seen as crucial to the doing of sociology, the growth of the discipline is best thought of not as a steady aggregation of insights and facts but as a series of leaps by which pioneering scholars distanced themselves from their own profession. Instead of evolutionary progress, the history of sociology is reconceived as one of alternating ruptures and placidity, in which each new sociological "present" is a break with the dominant paradigms of preceding generations. Without such a distancing, fundamental discoveries cannot occur.

It is the present where the past is made "the past," where the sociology of our masters is made "their" sociology in contrast to the sociology that we are creating today. Theoretical metaphors of society, which originally *were* understood to be metaphoric, for later generations become taken-for-granted descriptions of what society "really is." Through such definitions of reality we become adjusted to the *previous* environment (McLuhan, 1968: 12). Intellectual and institutional arrangements, which initially may have served the creative spirit, instead tend to calcify and oppose it. The critical use of inherited concepts thus requires a redefinition of present reality with new terms and, in so doing, a distancing from the web of interest in which dominant paradigms tend to become entangled. In such a project of paradigm renewal sociologists must bracket their own world along with everything else. For only from such a transcendental point of view can sociologists examine the bases of their own claims to knowledge, the degree to which their own paradigms have stagnated, and whether their habitual perspective has become that of powers that be.

These points also help dissolve the debate between reflexive and objective sociologies; now both can be seen as points of view, each with its own uses and limits. Self-reflection cannot replace social observation, nor can the use of objectivist techniques free one from the moral and scientific obligation to be methodologically and politically self-aware in ones own research process. Self-reflection is not romantic introspection; it can instead be a rigorous way of knowing; objective social research, even while being objective, also is inevitably a rhetoric of persuasion, a key device of which is point of view (see Gusfield, 1974).

In much this spirit, Max Weber understood that value-freedom constituted a commitment and an obligation, with its own existential imperatives as well as its potential for paralysis. Weber saw value-freedom as a *tool* for certain kinds of work, a heuristic means of stepping outside prevailing ideological debates (Weber, 1946). The scholarly world *can* be a different world than the political one; yet on a higher level, the choice of either world had its own ethical implications. Thus, although Weber defended science from traditionalism and from politics, he also sought to limit its influence in the realm of personal and social values. His god, ultimately, was not science but individual conscience.

Weber's sense of calling is harder to maintain in an age of establishment-sponsored research where personal morality can no longer be divorced from professional, institutional acts. In response to these difficulties, Alvin Gouldner suggests that today sociological self-reflection must rest "upon an awareness of the fundamental paradox: namely that *those who supply the greatest resources for the institutional development of sociology are precisely those who most distort its quest for knowledge*" (1970:498, cf. 1962), Gouldner's italics).

Jürgen Habermas pursues this point further, arguing that

the quest for knowledge is compromised not only by "selling out" but, more profoundly, by remaining un-self-conscious of its own presuppositions:

> From everyday experience we know that ideas serve often enough to furnish our actions with justifying motives in place of the real ones. What is called rationalization at this level is called ideology at the level of collective action. In both cases the manifest content of statements is falsified by consciousness' unreflected tie to interests, despite its illusion of autonomy. The discipline of trained thought thus correctly aims at excluding such interests. In all the sciences routines have been developed that guard against the subjectivity of opinion, and a new discipline, the sociology of knowledge, has emerged to counter the uncontrolled influence of interests on a deeper level, which derive less from the individual than from the objective situation of social groups. But this accounts for only one side of the problem. Because science must secure the objectivity of its statements against the pressure and seduction of particular interests, it deludes itself about the fundamental interests to which it owes not only its impetus but *the conditions of possible objectivity* themselves ... If knowledge could ever outwit its innate human interest, it would be by comprehending ... this natural basis reflexively. (1968:311–312)

Such self-reflectiveness implies, as we have seen, a dialectic within and between a number of shifting levels of vision. At their simplest, these would include the level of the constitution of that which is to be treated as fact; the level at which the explicit analytic frame of the study clashes with or closes off contrary frameworks; and the level at which the investigator's own implicit historical, social, and political-moral points of view are made explicit and reincorporated into the analysis. Each of these levels has its own inner dynamics as well as dynamic relations with the others. What is most important, however, is that concepts such as levels or spheres should not be allowed to sediment into a kind of solid-state methodological chemistry. Instead, point of view may be used as a strategy for dealing with levels that are essentially fluid and interpenetrating.

Drawing an example from literature for sociology, we know that great novels are dominated by some point of view; but in modern times there has emerged a "point of view of point of

view," by which the writer incorporates into the text his awareness of his own awareness. Thus, in *The Counterfeiters*, Gide's
hero, a novelist who is writing the book as the action proceeds,
speaks of his purpose:[21]

> What I want is to represent reality on the one hand, and
> on the other that effort to stylize it into art. . . . I invent the
> character of the novelist whom I make my central figure;
> and the subject of the book, if you must have one, is just
> that very struggle between what reality offers him and
> what he himself desires to make of it. (1955:207)

A similar strategy, properly adapted, seems required of any
sociology that seeks to represent not only the formation and conflict of multiple social worlds, but also its own methodological
presuppositions and political intents. As Gouldner says, "Insofar
as social reality is seen as contingent in part on the effort, the
character, and the position of the knower, the search for knowledge about social worlds is also contingent upon the knower's
self-awareness. To know others he cannot simply study *them*,
but must also listen to and confront *himself* . . ." (1970:493).
The voice and standpoint of the author must be understood as
itself a commentary which, if not brought to explicit awareness,
is of necessity "bootlegged" into the consciousness of the reader.
This applies not only to the subjective biases of the author or to
conflicts within his data; it also, and more importantly, refers
to the methods of his scientific praxis and to the objective social
transformation that, at least implicitly, his work is intended to
serve. Just as the literary use of point of view helps integrate
diverse elements into an artistic whole, so the reflective use of
point of view in sociology can integrate into a consistent structure the irrationalities of the world, *yet without having to deny
their irrationality*.

Sociologists have tended to disclaim this structuring process;
yet to eschew point of view as an instrument of presentation
and analysis is to assume that the order of theory lies in the
objects themselves. This is to make utopias of theories (cf.
Dahrendorf, 1958). Our naming objectivist theories as "uto-
pian," however, is not an act of dismissal but an effort at
self-transformation. Through such an effort the dialectic of
point of view would be made to operate both within sociology and between social theory and political action. Thus the
subjective introspection implicit in Gouldner's recommendation as well as the scientism and social engineering of the positivism that he attacks would both be transcended. To use point of

view reflectively in this fashion would be to achieve what Kierkegaard called the "mastered moment" (1965), the moment when
aesthetic distancing overcomes its nihilistic and idealistic
tendencies, when the sociologist achieves in his theory an authentic representation of lived experience itself.

4
Metaphor

Concepts, like individuals, have their histories and are just as
incapable of withstanding the ravages of time as are individuals. But
in and through all this they retain a kind of homesickness for the
scenes of their childhood.
Kierkegaard (1965:47)

In Chapter 2, "Cognitive Aesthetics," we argued that what
we know is known through paradigms. Apprehension is through
some frame of vision. In this fashion we see the world *as* one
thing or another – simultaneous and static as in the medieval
projection, for example, or linear and progressive as in modern
vision. The rules of baseball define what will be seen as a
"ball" or a "strike," much as the rules of psychoanalysis define
what is to be apprehended as a "repetition compulsion."
Physics, too, creates its "forces" and "vectors," much as
sociology brings "role conflicts" or "trained incapacity" to
consciousness.

To say this is to say that all knowledge is perspectival: Anything we know is known *as* something; it is construed from some
point of view. Some implications of this conception of knowledge with reference to sociology were discussed in Chapter
3, "Point of View." In this chapter we carry our inquiry
further by systematically treating metaphor in sociological
theory.

In the broadest sense, metaphor is seeing something from
the viewpoint of something else, which means, in terms of the
arguments presented so far, that all knowledge is metaphoric. If
this is true, then the rich tradition of critical poetics suddenly
becomes available as an epistemic resource. This vocabulary
does not provide criteria for judging the accuracy of a repre-

sentation to that which it presumes to represent. But it does offer criteria for judging what makes a good metaphor, what are the varieties of metaphor, and how metaphors may be most effectively used.

In the narrowest sense, metaphor can be understood as an illustrative device whereby a term from one level or frame of reference is used within a different level or frame. For example, Robert Park says, "Our great cities, as those who have studied them have learned, are full of junk, much of it human. . . ." This use of the term "junk" with reference to humans – seeing people as junk – conveys an impact and connotative richness not achievable by conventional description.

Metaphor also is the key to model building; indeed, a model may be thought of as a metaphor whose implications have been spelled out. Metaphors as models are of two sorts: analogic and iconic. *Analogic* models, as with the illustrative use of metaphor, take a meaning unit from one context and employ it in another as, for example, in Glazer and Strass' model of "awareness" in which dying patients are seen as undercover agents trying to gain secret information. In contrast, *iconic* models create new objects of inquiry through the intersection of apparently disparate frames. Durkheim's model of Arunta religion as the ritual enactment of society is of this type.

A third type of metaphor may be called "root metaphor," a fundamental image of the world from which models and illustrative metaphors may be derived. In sociology there are five principal root metaphors: society seen as an organism or as a machine, and social conduct viewed as language, the drama, or a game.

In this chapter we examine the cognitive status of metaphor, discuss its use in science and in art, and address the objections of our scientific critics. We then outline criteria of adequacy for metaphors in sociological theory. In seeking to show how the representation of social reality is through and through metaphoric, we discuss three principal uses of metaphor:

1. As a didactic or illustrative device.
2. As elaborated into a model.
3. As a paradigm or root metaphor from which many models may be generated.

Such an awareness of metaphor hopefully will yield greater *self*-awareness in the construction of sociological reports and the making of sociological theory.

THE COGNITIVE STATUS OF METAPHORS

The question of the cognitive status of metaphors tends to appear whenever philosophers discuss the fundamental questions of similarity, identity, and difference. This is not only because metaphors are employed in every realm of knowledge; it is also because metaphors are our principal instruments for integrating diverse phenomena and viewpoints without destroying their differences.

Despite its apparent centrality, however, until modern times metaphor was not acknowledged to have an explicitly cognitive function. Aristotle, for example, divided the uses of speech into three categories: logic, poetic, and rhetoric. Given this division – and the assumption behind it that language plays no part in creating that which it describes – metaphor may be used to illustrate a point or sway a crowd or as an ornament of poetic style. Yet, as he put it, "All such arts are fanciful and meant to charm the hearer. Nobody uses fine language when teaching geometry" (*Rhetoric*, *III*:1404a).[1] This view of metaphor prevailed for many centuries. Indeed, under the joint influence of plain-speaking Protestants and early positive scientists, the function of metaphor – along with "fine language" in general – was further demoted.

Yet beginning with Vico, this traditional view has been challenged by philosophers such as Nietzsche, Coleridge, and Croce. Instead of seeing metaphor as an embroidery of the facts, such thinkers viewed it as a way of *experiencing* facts and, by making them objects of experience, giving life or reality to them. In their view, poetic imagination stretches the mind *and* reality – the word *and* the thing – through metaphor. By revealing the concrete physiognomy of the experienced world, metaphor was thought to precede historically or logically the concretized meanings of literal or scientific discourse. Still, by stressing the emotional and precognitive nature of poetic revelation, the romantics reinforced the traditional dichotomy between metaphor and scientific thought. Moreover, by so energetically distancing themselves from scientists, they placed themselves in the company of schizophrenics, aphasiacs, and children whose utterances, by the romantics' own criteria, could not be distinguished from poetic metaphor.

Another view of metaphor is the cognitive aesthetic or, more commonly, the tension theory, which appeared recently among philosophers and literary critics. Borrowing the romantics' insight that creative thought is metaphoric, this school – if it can as yet so be called – has extended the idea of metaphor as a logic of discovery to include science as well as art and has distinguished creative activity in both these fields from the normal science or art that goes on in each. Such a theory has profound implications for the philosophy of science and for logic of method in the human studies, for it suggests that both the deductive and the inductive models of scientific explanation be reformulated by the view that formal representations – whether in science or in art – be understood as a metaphoric redescription (or creation) of the domain of the explanandum.

Much recent literature holds that the traditional accounts of scientific explanation are in trouble (Feyerabend, 1957:143, 1962; Kuhn, 1962; Sellars, 1961). In this chapter we propose that a cognitive aesthetic theory of metaphor be considered as an alternative logic of discovery. A first step in this must be to outline this theory in its principal tenets (see Berggren, 1962, 1963; Black, 1962; Brooks, 1965; Hesse, 1970; McCloskey, 1964; MacCormac, 1971; Ricoeur, 1972; Schon, 1963; and Turbayne, 1962). They are briefly as follows.

Metaphor involves a transfer (*metaphora*, carrying over) of one term from one system or level of meaning to another; for example, Dante's "Hell is a lake of ice" or the *corpuscular* theory of light or *kinetic* theory of gases.

For this basic aspect we retain Aristotle's definition of metaphor as "the transference of a word to a sense different from its proper signification," or as "giving the thing a name that belongs to something else" (*Poetic*, XXI; *Rhetoric*, III:x). But for our purposes we extend Aristotle's definition and see the term "name" to mean not merely a word but any sign or group of signs.[2] By this extension a sculpture or painting may be metaphoric, as can theories, hobby horses (Gombrich, 1965), or gestural signals in interactions (Birdwhistell, 1970; Scheflen, 1972). We also extend metaphor to include the other tropes. Synecdoche and metonymy – using a part for the whole and using one word for another of which it is an attribute – are potential metaphors between closely related terms. Irony is a metaphor of opposites. In all these cases, however, the metaphor has at least two systems of reference – although usually focal interest is only in one of them; for example, when we say "man is a wolf," we wish to discover something about men even though we may also learn something about wolves. The partial

exception to this would be "iconic" or self-referential metaphors. For example, a map is a metaphor for the town it represents, but clearly a cartographer could map out a city that does
not exist in space or time. Formalist art shares this property
with formal mathematical theories, in that much of the referents
of both are immanent within the system of representation itself.

By transferring the ideas and associations of one system or
level of discourse to another, metaphor allows each system to
be perceived anew from the viewpoint of the other. Certain
aspects of each are illuminated, others shadowed over. Moreover, because even literal expressions are understood in terms
of their implicit connotations, if the elements of the metaphor
are translated back into "plain prose" they may retain the enriched meanings gained through metaphoric association. For
example, the "nature" of tortoises and hares is changed by
the fable that makes their race a metaphor for human fates;
similarly, concrete machines are seen more as embodiments of
abstract mass and motion once the machine metaphor has become
our model for theoretical physics. Our understanding of the
"meaning" of a representation thus involves more than the ability
to recognize its referent, or even to use it correctly. Understanding also requires the ability "to call to mind the ideas, both
linguistic and empirical, that are commonly held to be associated with the referent in the given language community. Thus
a shift of meaning may result from a change in the set of associated ideas as well as a change of reference or use" (Hesse,
1970:160). Metaphor drives its points home on a two-way
street.

If taken literally, the metaphor must be patently absurd; for
example, men are not literally wolves, gases are not in the usual
sense collections of massive particles. To state this point conversely, by taking our first criteria only, the statement "Joan
is a girl" would be a metaphor, since the term "Joan" is a
member of the species "girl" – that is, "Joan" and "girl" are
on different levels. Yet this is excluded as a metaphor by our
second criteria, since "Joan is a girl" makes sense literally in
a way that "Joan is a dust mop" does not. The logical, empirical,
or psychological absurdity of metaphor thus has a specifically
cognitive function: It makes us stop in our tracks and examine
it. It offers us a new awareness (McCormac, 1971:241). The
arresting vividness and tensions set off by the conjunction of
contraries forces us to make our own interpretation, to see for
ourselves.

Metaphors are intended to be understood; they are category errors with a purpose, linguistic madness with a method. The significance of the "absurdity" is largely a function of the distance of the two (or more) systems of inference involved. For example, to speak of "the sweet innocence of the child" has little power to instruct us because we already know that "sweet innocence" has affinities with children; that is, the systems are too close for much that is new to appear in the space created by their juxtaposition. At the other extreme, to say "the sweet innocence of the hypotenuse" is similarly vapid, but here it is because the systems to which the key terms refer are too distant for one to be illuminated by the other. In contrast to both these examples, "the sweet innocence of the *hangman*," though literally contradictory, intimates some principle of assimilation between the two systems. Though we do not know at the outset how far the comparison extends – or even exactly what the common genus *is* – the metaphor does provide us with a program for exploration, a potential agenda that might be susceptible of elaboration into a formal theory.

Another test of the significance of absurdities – unlike the word salad or paralogic of speech disorders – is that, because metaphors are intended to be understood, they also may be *mis*-understood. With our hangman, for example, we might be speaking ironically, intending to highlight the real evil of the hangman's task; *or* we might mean that as an instrument of blind justice the hangman is not personally culpable of ending lives.

To hold that metaphors are meant to convey intelligible meanings is to reject the view that they are merely a decorative or emotive use of language; or conversely, it is to suggest that style and emotions themselves convey cognitive content. This applies to poetic metaphors as well as to scientific models, which are nothing less than metaphors elaborated. Thus, as we have tried to show, although many philosophers of science believe that models are purely subjective or illustrative, having no cognitive status of their own, this view is based on a misconception of both metaphoric *and* literal or scientific language. The scientist who develops a theory in terms of a model cannot with consistency dispense with the model as though it were a ladder to be kicked away once the new theoretical plateau has been reached. The model is an ingredient of the theory, for the theorist cannot, and need not, make explicit all the implications of the model he is exploiting; other workers in the field "catch on" to the model's intended associations. Indeed, they may elaborate the model further than the original theorist had foreseen, or they may find the theory unsatisfactory because some of the implications of the model that its originator did not investigate, or even think of, turn out to be empirically false. Yet none of this would be possible unless the model functioned cognitively as part of the commonly understood theoretical language of that scientific community (Hesse, 1970:165).

Metaphors and models are not only creations that can lead to formal mathematical theories, and that cannot entirely be divorced from such theories. It also is the case that such theories are themselves metaphoric, monumentally so in fact, in that they assume that the chaotic processes of the world have the purely formal properties of mathematics. Insofar as scientists are not aware of the absurdity of this – that is, to the extent that they believe the world really *is* mathematically organized – they have turned their metaphor into a myth; they have accepted as true what in literal terms is absurd.

Metaphors must be consciously "as if" (cf. Vaihinger, 1924). This point may be shown by a negative example. Most students consider as metaphor those substitutions that give an old name to something new, even if they have become so buried in our language that it takes an etymologist to dig them out. When geometricians speak of the leg of an angle, or plumbers the elbow of a pipe, we sense that the part of the angle or pipe referred to really is a leg or an elbow in the *new* meaning of these terms. Similarly, "lousy" or "skyscraper" are often called "frozen metaphors," because they are taken to be directly descriptive rather than analogs from lice in one's hair or a giant scraping the heavens. Just because pungent and connotatively rich metaphors stick in our minds when first encountered, a process of sedimentation tends to occur until the metaphor is no longer seen as a creation of the imagination. It becomes instead simply a name or description.

For our purposes, however, metaphors (or at least "living" metaphors) must not only *in*tend to be significant, they also must *pre*tend they are not literally absurd. They must be what Vico called "credible impossibilities." In this sense metaphors are like counterfactual statements (Weiss, 1961:164); e.g., to say that "heat flows" is to pretend that, if heat were a fluid, it would flow. As an antidote to what Blake called "single vision and Newton's sleep," metaphoric thinking requires a "double vision" that can hold an object in attention simultaneously from two (or more) points of view and, in so doing, *create* it as *that* particular object of experience. In such a "stereoscopic vision" (Stanford, 1936:105) we can maintain the interchange between two systems or levels of discourse. But this vision itself requires us to suspend commitments to literal reality and to take seriously (though not literally) our poetic or theoretical fictions. This interaction of both sets of referents – the two systems or levels, and the literal and pretended – is precisely what makes it impossible to collapse the cognitive import of metaphor to a literal, univisioned, nontensional statement. To *believe* the metaphor literally is to accept an absurdity as truth, to make of metaphor a myth; but to *reduce* metaphor to a literal statement is to destroy what cannot survive except at the intersection of juxtaposed perspectives. In metaphors a logical or empirical absurdity stands in tension with a fictive truth, yet this counterfactual truth itself depends on a creative confrontation of perspectives that cannot be literalized or disengaged without destroying the insight which metaphor provides (Berggren, 1962:240).

That metaphor retain its consciously "as if" quality is thus a pivotal point, for on it turns the difference between using metaphors and being used by them. Awareness of our use of metaphor provides an escape hatch from the prison house of language, or at least lets us know we are confined. Such an awareness is two sided: It enables us to see the metaphoric in what is taken as literal and also to make believe that metaphors are literally true. The first is an act of unmasking as when, for example, we come to understand Descartes's "machine of nature" as Descartes himself appears to have done: "I have described the Earth and the whole visible universe *as if it were* a machine, having regard only to the shape and movement of its parts." There is a universe of difference between such an awareness and the view that the world actually *is* a machine.[3]

To unmask metaphors that have become myths requires negative insight and circumspection; to create *new* metaphors is a leap of the imagination. It not only demands that we say "No" to the organization of experience as it is given to us in preordained categories; it also requires us to rearrange cognition into new forms and associations. The new metaphor, then, is not *merely* a substitution of a term from one frame to another. Quite beyond this, metaphor can create a new amalgam in our understanding. New metaphors, especially when elaborated into models and theories, are not merely new ways of looking at the facts, nor are they a revelation of what the facts really are. Instead, the metaphor in a fundamental way creates the facts and provides a definition of what the essential quality of an experience must be. And for this new reality to be entered into and comprehended – from the inside as it were – the metaphor must be taken *as if* it literally were the case. Thus metaphors do not exist per se. Rather, they require circumspection and imagination, an attitude of "as if" in which we suspend what is taken literally, and take as literal what we know to be absurd.

Iconic and analogic metaphors. What we have said above applies to all metaphors. But we now are in a position to make a further distinction between two basic types of metaphors: iconic and analogic. An *iconic* metaphor creates the object or image as a unique entity. It shows what a thing *is*. An *analogic* metaphor creates an image by contrast or comparison – it shows what a thing *is like*. The first is holistic or systemic, the second is relational between systems or elements. For example, "when the poet calls old age 'stubble,' he produces in us learning and knowledge by means of the common genus, for both old age and stubble are past their prime" (Aristotle, *Rhetoric*, III:x). This is an analogic metaphor: as life is to old age, so the harvest is to stubble. Such an illumination by means of comparison is even more explicit when the metaphor "admits of paying back" its gift to the original context of the borrowed term as, for example, in the saying attributed to Pericles that "the youth which had perished in the war had vanished from the city as if one had taken the spring from the year" (Aristotle, *Rhetoric*, III:x).

In contrast, iconic metaphors tend to be auto-referential within a single frame. In this broad sense, a statue is an icon of the person portrayed, at least in terms of certain features. A photograph may be an icon of even greater abstraction, for it translates spatial relations into two dimensions, and color into black and white. Organization charts are even more abstracted because they represent fewer dimensions, and what they do represent – organizational process – is conveyed in static form. Likewise sociograms. Mathematical representations of sets of phenomena are probably the most abstract iconic metaphors in that they represent synthetic, contextually embedded statements about conduct in terms of wholly tautological analytic or logical truths about numbers.

Where the analogic metaphor lets us *com*prehend the particular in its likeness or relatedness to other particulars that have been newly classified in a common group, the iconic metaphor allows us to *a*pprehend what the particular is in its uniqueness. This executive meeting, election, coffee date, society, or whatever, has a just-so-ness that distinguishes it from any other event or type. Yet conventional attempts to describe this uniqueness dissolve into words that cover many similar situations. To convey this uniqueness, then, instead of arranging words or frames in a linear series, iconic metaphors *juxtapose* universals so that a unique and unparaphrasable image emerges.[4] Wallace Stevens's poem "Thirteen Ways of Looking at a Blackbird" provides examples:

i

Among twenty snowy mountains
The only moving thing
Was the eye of the blackbird.

iii

It was evening all afternoon
It was snowing
And it was going to snow.
The blackbird sat
In the cedar limbs.

Here the metaphors appear not to refer to anything outside themselves. The images in the first three lines, for instance, may be a metaphor for "infinite stillness," "winter," "death" or the like. But exactly which one of these or other possible referents is the correct one is not made clear in the lines themselves. What *is* clear, however, is the immediate – but untranslatable – impact of *these* lines. In this sense they are, like Kafka's tales, a metaphor for themselves. The opposition of terms creates a new emergent, but that new emergent *is that* poem, and cannot quite be put in any other words. What is going on here is the formation of a new whole out of apparently unrelated and irrelevant elements.[5] As Eliot remarks:

> When a poet's mind is perfectly equipped for his work, it
> is consistently amalgamating disparate experiences; the
> ordinary man's experience is chaotic, irregular,
> fragmentary. The latter falls in love, or reads Spinoza, and
> these two experiences have nothing to do with each other,
> or with the noise of the typewriter or the smell of cooking;
> in the mind of the poet these experiences are already
> forming new wholes. (1960:247)

Neitzsche also discusses this question in his essay "On Truth and Lie in an Extra-Moral Sense."[6] Metaphor had been seen as the origin of language by Vico, Herder, and Max Müller. But in this essay Nietzsche puts the question of origins in an epistemological rather than historical frame. His basic question is how the data of sensual perception may be articulated, that is, in what way they may be translated into language. Here metaphor as the transfer of an idiom of one frame or level to another refers to transfers between the idioms of feeling and those of speech. The human mind's first use of metaphor, says Nietzsche, is in the act of cognition itself – the translation of sensual perception into an image. Only through another metaphor can this image be translated into language. For Nietzsche both these metaphors are "leaps out of the original sphere into a radically different and new one." The transfer, or leap, takes place at a prepredicative level, even before the word is articulated. Nietzsche notes that we are hardly ever aware that we use nothing but metaphors when we speak. But this is because the original metaphors have worn out in the course of time. Scientific terms represent the last stage of this mummification of language. They merely *seem* to express their objects exactly and completely while, in fact, even scientific terms are "residua of metaphors" (1960:315; see Alleman, 1967).

This analysis of the language of science as basically metaphoric still leaves the question as to what distinguishes the language of the poem. Unlike science, says Nietzsche, poetry deliberately reactivates the metaphorical quality of language. The frozen metaphors of the natural standpoint are replaced by original metaphors that have intense iconic power. Poetry (like *pioneering* science) uses metaphor in a free, playful, ironic manner, as a kind of serious make believe. Poetry thus is *deliberate* deception, a betrayal of conventional definitions of reality. But precisely through this "deception" poetry corresponds to the basically illusionary character of language. The poet finds himself in a peculiarly ambiguous relation to reality. He must be a liar in the service of truth. That is, by lying deliberately, by using self-consciously metaphoric language to create new frames of vision, the poet achieves a greater capacity for perception and understanding. He makes, or "poets," a world.

This distinction reveals another. Nietzsche's discussion of poetic and scientific language is couched in terms of the positivist versus romantic debate. In contrast, if we distinguish pioneering science *and* art from conventional science and art, we see that the free or playful use of metaphor is that of the maker, while the use of frozen metaphor is typical of those who reproduce or elaborate existing paradigms. What makes metaphors frozen, or mere residua of metaphors, is not that they are scientific but that they are conventional. They emphasize linguistic or sequential relations to other *words*, which limits their simultaneous, connotative, multidimensional relation to other signs with a single referent (see Pribram, 1971: IV).

No effective metaphor, however, can be entirely iconic or analogic: Were it wholly iconic it would be incomprehensible; were it wholly analogic it would tell us nothing new about the things compared. Indeed, the most powerful metaphors are just those that are both (1) that which they express and no other (*sameness*) as well as (2) *like* other unexpected things. In both cases the meaning of the metaphor is not in its correspondence to an external referent; rather, the meanings lie in a kind of electric field of potential elaborations, the sparks of which would cease to fly if a central pole absorbed all the energy. Metaphor concentrates our attention on what is patently *not* there in the language, but which emerges in the interplay of juxtaposed associations.[7]

METAPHOR IN ART, SCIENCE, AND SOCIAL THEORY

Science and art both are metaphoric, but they are metaphoric in different ways. Let us first consider verbal metaphor in poetry as, for example, in John Clare's description of a primrose, "with its crimp and curdled leaf/ and its little brimming eye." Since this line has been much quoted by theorists of metaphor, it is a good place to examine where they go wrong. John Middleton Murray, for example, maintained that this "is surely an accurate description, but with an accuracy unknown to and unachievable by science" (Wheelwright, 1954:34–5). Then I. A. Richards argued that Murray fails to distinguish whether he takes Clare's lines "as a description of an object (the primrose) or the experience of seeing one"; and Richards concluded that the description applies not to the actual primrose, but to our experience of seeing or imagining one. Then Wheelwright answered Richards, insisting that "it is not my experience that is crimp and curdled; but the *primrose as experienced*" (see Wheelwright, 1954:34–5 and for citations above).

From the symbolic realists' perspective, however, the fallacies of the above positions are not merely that they have projected onto an object certain textures of feeling (Murray) or the reverse (Richards); there is the further criticism that the strict disjunction between objective and subjective presupposes a faulty conception of how we know. That is, the subjectivist/objectivist debate is not only irrelevant from a phenomenological viewpoint; it is also incorrect in assuming that "the inner meaning of things" (Wheelwright, 1954:133) is directly available through an intuition unmediated by objects, and that "external facts" are directly perceivable without the mediation of some point of view.

Thus, the entire debate is founded in error and, in fact, makes it impossible to distinguish poetry from fantasies of children, dogmatists, and madmen. There is a crucial difference, for example, between the complusive's concern that the water will be hurt as it falls on the rocks, and Hölderlin's reference to the "joyous undulation of the waves." The compulsive presumably believes the water to be capable of feeling; hence, in his view, he is speaking literally or, as we would say, mythically. In contrast Hölderlin, as accomplished poet, must appreciate the literal absurdity of the statement that the waves feel joy. Yet by making such a statement Hölderlin draws our attention to the feel *of*, not *in*, the waves. Unlike the child or madman, "the poet does not mythically confuse the textural feeling-of-things with actual things-of-feeling" (Berggren, 1963:255). For him the joy is neither in the waves nor in our apprehension of them. Indeed, if it may be said to be in anything, we should place the joy in the metaphoric tensions set off by the juxtaposition of sentiential and inanimate referents. And it is just such metaphoric juxtaposition that allows us to liberate the poetic feel of things from the prosaic things of feeling.

In the above example a form of consciousness (joy) is used to illuminate a visible focal referent (the waves), resulting in a feeling-of-the-waves. But as we have seen, metaphor can function in the opposite direction, making some visualizable phenomenon a vehicle for expressing our interior life. Whereas the first usage conveys feelings for tangible entities, the second gives embodiments for forms of feeling. Mallarmé's faun and Hart Crane's bridge, the nude as Kenneth Clark describes it, and the allegorical import of Baroque music and Byzantine art are examples of this second usage. Also of this type are metaphors of the mind, as in Plato's image of reason as a charioteer guiding two horses, one the will, the other appetite; or

Descartes' construing of mind as a pilot of a ship that is the body.

Metaphor is just as vital to natural science as it is to poetry or to discourse on our interior life, and in science the metaphoric tension also is between a form of consciousness and a visualizable phenomenon. In science, however, the referents are of very special sorts: the form of consciousness must be a purely formal (ideally, mathematical) theory or model, while the visualizable phenomenon ideally must be observable through controlled and calibrated methods. But even this difference fades when we speak of the "root metaphors" or paradigms of science. For here metaphors serve to define the boundaries of a given domain of discourse and to set limits for subtheories that can with consistency be extrapolated in it. For example, Aristotle's paradigm of motion was rest, a balance between force and resistance, while for Galileo uniform motion was just as natural as rest. But for Newton, a body's motion was to be taken for granted only when at uniform speed in a Euclidean straight line, free from all forces, including its own weight. Consequently, given their different foundational assumptions about the nature of motion, Newton had to introduce the theory of gravity to explain why, in the absence of resistance, an imaginary ship would not sail off into space along a Euclidean straight line. But, on the basis of different root metaphors, "Galileo would have considered the circular motion of such a ship around the earth entirely natural and self-explanatory, while Aristotle would have denounced the entire idea" (Berggren, 1963:461; Toulmin, 1961:79).[8]

Sociology, like science and the arts, also must re-present its world with metaphors. Sociologists, however, have not understood scientific theorizing to be through and through metaphoric and, hence, they generally have felt compelled to choose between a literalistic, reductive scientific positivism, or else abandon themselves to what they take to be the airy realms of creative intuition. Yet, as we have tried to show, this forced choice is based on erroneous assumptions about the natures of scientific and artistic knowledge. The choice for sociology is not between scientific rigor as against poetic insight. The choice is rather between more or less fruitful metaphors, and between using metaphors or being their victims. The root metaphors in sociology, for example, include the organism and the machine – images borrowed mainly from science. But sociologists also have elaborated general theories by construing conduct as drama, as language, or as a game. Yet, if what we have argued above is accepted, none of these metaphors may claim ultimate priority over the others – not, in any case, by asserting that it is a direct representation of reality. The metaphoric nature of theories precludes their being tested, in any ultimate sense, by "the facts." If we have no such tests of correspondence, however, we do have criteria for judging what constitutes a metaphor that works. These questions are discussed in the sections that follow.[9]

OBJECTIONS OF OUR SCIENTIFIC CRITICS

Modern science may be seen as the child of a marriage between Bacon's empiricism and the mathematical formalism of Descartes. The problem for science has been to propitiate both its genitors – to avoid a mythic or absurd equation of mathematics with Bacon's fact-world on one side, and to stay the absorption of theory into Descartes's pure mathematics on the other. The "solutions" to this dilemma, understandably, have tended to consist in either a lopsided monism of deduction or induction, or in a self-contradictory dualism that tries to keep both sides separate but equal. We have either two flies in the bottle, or one inside it and the other buzzing over our heads.

Raphael put this more elegantly. In his *School of Athens*, Plato is seen pointing upward, while next to him Aristotle indicates we should look down. From Raphael's pictorial metaphor, and from the perspective of metaphor outlined above, we can now group the objections of our scientific critics into three broad types: those of logicodeductive formalists who "point upward" to the primacy of mathematics, those of empiricists or operationalists who "point downward" to the primacy of the extensional world, and those whom we may call dualists who raise both hands in accommodation and perplexity.

To the command "Speak plainly, formalize, *deduce!*" we rejoin that deductive mathematics, if used scientifically, also is metaphoric for some domain of application, and that to overlook this is to inhibit paradigm innovation and to make metaphors into myths. Yet just such a logicodeductive view of science, articulated strongly by Pierre Duhem in 1914, continues to dominate methodological thinking on science today. Duhem contrasted two types of scientific minds: the Continental and the English. The first was thought to be abstract, systematizing, logical, and deductive; the other pictorial, gadget oriented, and mired in empirical images. In Duhem's view science should confine itself to mathematically stating the formal logical properties of its domain of application. Given this purpose, metaphors and models appear redundant. For example, in the billiard ball model of molecular activity, were we to focus on the positive analogies between billiard balls and molecules, and exclude the negative or nonanalogous aspects, then these shared formal properties could be restated in purely mathematical terms, thus rendering the model unnecessary and possibly misleading. Hence, if models are to be admitted at all, they must enter scientific discourse only as an illustrative device, a kind of psychological crutch for the scientifically feeble.

Six years later, in 1920, an English physicist, N. R. Campbell, took issue with his French compeer. Campbell argued that Duhem's view failed to account for the *dynamic* character of theories – their invention of and extension to new domains. In the billiards-molecules analogy, for example, instead of merely stating positive and excluding negative analogies, Campbell urged that we leave our formulations open to *neutral* analogies – those yet-to-be-discovered properties that the two referential systems may have in common (Hesse, 1970:8). Indeed, for Campbell and his followers, to lose this openness was to close off a principal avenue of scientific progress.

Another difficulty with Duhem's view lies in the relationship of formal theoretical explanans and experimental explicandum. Hypotheses are supposed to link the two. Yet if the hypothesis refers only to the theory that defines it, it remains merely an abstract mathematical or relational structure "which has no relevance whatsoever to the explicandum in question" (Berggren, 1963:459). Thus, to be testable the law or hypothesis must be conjoined with the observational domain of discourse; without this, science would remain a purely aprioristic system with no necessary connections to empirical phenomena. Formal theories, though possibly valid in a purely logical sense, do not establish their own empirical truth, nor do they provide the empirically specified hypotheses by which they could be tested. Were we to remain consistent with Duhem's reasoning, then, we would be forced to admit that theoretical and empirical truths have nothing whatever to do with each other. Instead of either taking or rejecting this absurdity literally, however, we suggest that scientific theory and practice consist in inventing and elaborating metaphors between formal nonspatial realities and empirically observable ones.

Thus, in response to the formalists' problematic, we propose the view of theory as metaphor, that is, that scientific theory is a nonspatial mimesis for (not *of*) the extensional world. A literal or univocal language may be possible for spatial reality, just as some form of Russellian language is at least conceivable for nonspatial reality. But scientific theories are neither of these. They rather are constituted of vital metaphors that provide the "nonspatial space" within which the interconnections between these two realms exist in dialectical tension. Scientific creativity depends on the ability to play two language games at once, to speak formal deduction while hearing one's own words translated into induction, to see the empirical data while simultaneously visualizing their purely formal relations, and to understand the "is" of experiment and the "must" of deduction as metaphors for each other, each retaining its autonomy while at the same time insinuating itself into the other. Whenever the tension between these two forms of reality breaks down the result is a myth. The mind, for example, *becomes* the brain, or motives collapse into behavior, much as if God literally (nonmiraculously) were to become Jesus, or equal justice were to materialize one day and picket on the courthouse steps. Yet the mind, motives, god, justice, formal mathematical theories, or other nonspatial realities can never themselves become spatial entities; they can only be made *visualizable* through the stereoscopic vision of metaphor.

A second enjoinder of our critics might be "Speak plainly, operationalize, *induce!*" To this also we must point out that the instruction itself asks us to be metaphoric – to restate what we have said above as if it were something else, to translate our aesthetic concepts into positivistic ones. But the elaboration of metaphors differs from the operationalization of concepts. In the latter there is, ideally, a one-to-one relationship between the operation of measurement and the concept measured. Indeed, the concept is collapsed into its measures. Yet such reduction loses the "as if" quality that is central to self-aware metaphoric thought. Thus animal experimenters who study human psychology and the behavior of rats often wind up studying human psychology *as* the behavior of rats, or human psychology *reduced to* the behavior of rats. In a similar fashion, one may "reduce" a subject matter upward, in the manner, for example, of a study on juvenile delinquency and the social system in which the conduct of juveniles becomes an epiphenomena of certain properties of the system (Burke, 1969a:97). Such reductive literalness is inimical to the spirit of discovery in science. But it should not be confused with the make-believe or ironic literalness of critics who wish to unmask the *naive* literalness of their opponents.

Plain language, as well as objective scientific language, is also metaphoric, at least in Nietzsche's sense. Yet the self-conscious, playful use of metaphor offers something that literal or frozen metaphors do not. Most statements in "plain language" can be paraphrased or translated into other words without sacrificing cognitive content, much the same way that machines can be used to translate technical texts. But effective metaphors, when created anew, cannot be translated literally without substantial loss of meaning. The suggestive power of metaphor lies precisely in the strangeness of a word when it is taken from one realm or level and placed within or alongside of another. The new context extends the original meaning of the focal word, just as the transferred word modifies its new context. There is, as Richards puts it, "a borrowing between and intercourse of thoughts, a transaction between contexts" in which two ideas "cooperate in an inclusive meaning" (1936:94, 119). The meaning of the metaphor is thus an emergent that lurks, as it were, in the silence between the metaphor's terms (see Allentuck, 1967). Obviously *this* meaning cannot be translated literally. Instead, the artlessness of plain language and everyday experience can be re-presented formally only through the *apparent* artlessness of accomplished theory or art.

What is lost by translating a strong metaphor into literal prose is not merely a grace of style or the charm of piquant associations. Instead, the loss is *cognitive*. First, there is a decrease in economy of expression. Second, the system of mutual implications is collapsed into a closed and static list of shared attributes; judgments as to their relative weight in relation to the principal metaphor are preempted through leveling, and potential further elaborations are closed off. Paraphrasing may properly be done, of course, *after* the original metaphor has been elaborated, for then the paraphrases will be seen either as submetaphors or iconic representations. The mimetic power of the original metaphor will be enhanced in proportion to the variety of perspectives from which it can with justice be perceived. Thus we could say that metaphors about the "nature of man" potentially have greater power than those about "the nature of stones" because the former focal term can be justly perceived from perspectives that are not literally relevant to the latter. Properly used, then, paraphrasing is not a paraphrasing into literalness, but into another metaphoric transfer. It does not reduce the borrowed term, but establishes mutual illuminations with it. The difference might be compared to that between translating the paintings of Monet into a spectograph, and translating them into the music of Debussy. In the former case, to quote Max Black in a similar connection, "The relevant weakness of the literal paraphrase is not that it may be tiresomely prolix or boringly explicit – or deficient in qualities of style; it fails to be a translation because it fails to give the *insight* that the metaphor did" (1968:229).

To defend metaphor in this fashion also is to criticize implicitly a more basic assumption lying under the concept of operationalization itself. This is the belief that the test of adequacy of a model is its correspondence to the facts, and that to perform this test one must specify one's variables into observables, that is, operationalize them. This seems to be presupposed in Merton's call to build bridges between microfacts, which are true but not significant, and macrotheory, which is significant but not validated (1957:85). Such a view is also expressed by Fred Kerlinger, who insists that the proper criterion of measurement is that it be "isomorphic to reality. . . . Is the measurement game we are playing tied to 'reality'? Do the measurement procedures being used have some rational and empircal correspondence with 'reality'?" (1973:416–418).

This type of thinking is incorrect and futile: First, it misses the nature of metaphoric thinking, which is at the heart of scientific (or any other cognitive) discovery; second, it misrepresents the nature of verification, in that it assumes that a fact-world is directly available without the mediation of language for comparison with the model and its extrapolations (predictions).

Numerous analysts have warned of the danger of equating a model or theory with the phenomena comprehended by its domain of application (Willner, 1967:24; Black, 1968:238; Toulmin, 1953:165; Hutten, 1954:285). The extensive discussions of "isomorphism" in the literature on models (Braithwaite, 1962) make it clear that the term has nothing whatever to do with surface similarities between the model and that which it represents. Instead, the model is an expression of certain aspects, generally formal ones, of that for which it has been constructed. Indeed, it is more accurate to speak of a metaphor or model *for* something rather than *of* something, because the model is intended to serve some conceptual purpose, not to be an imitation of a thing's appearance. Indeed, to be persuasive as a candidate idea structure for describing a given subject matter, a model *must* differ from the subject matter. Were this not so the original structure itself would be either as obvious as that of the model, or would be obvious to no one, including the model builder. As Norwood Hanson puts it,

> Models are . . . a way of presenting structures that might *possibly* enforce subject matters. They do so in ways . . . more compelling (i.e., simpler and more focused) than would just another confrontation with the subject matter itself. . . . Reproducing perplexities exactly is not the same as highlighting their structures. . . . By completely eliminating *all* differences between the model and the original state of affairs one ends up destroying the very thing the model [or theory, or science, or art] was meant to achieve – namely, the provision of an "awareness of structure" absent from the original confrontation with a complex phenomena. (Hanson, 1971:79–81)

Not only is the copy theory epistemologically weak; it also inhibits the construction of useful models. If the simulation of appearance were the purpose of models, the models would be constructed in terms of pregiven, conventional categories. But at the center of every discovery, of the eye or of the mind, is some novel method of representation that helps us apprehend the phenomena in a new and more fitting manner (Toulmin, 1953:165). Thus the most telling innovations in all the sciences, when examined in the historical context of the moment of their formulation, generally violate common sense in that they seem not to represent the world as it "really is" (Willner, 1967:24).

What we suggest, then, is that the rule of correspondence be turned on its head. Seeking correspondence between measures and reality is fruitless, because "reality" is knowable only through some set of measures. What we can achieve, however, is correspondence between two sets of concepts – that is, between our nominal and our operational definitions. But seen from the perspective of metaphor, this means isomorphism between the two realms of discourse that in positivist terms are called "data" and "theory." To be useful for building theories, then, concepts must be translatable into measures. But the key word here is translation – not identity – and, in the terms of our discussion, this means that theoretically useful metaphors are ones that can be elaborated into submetaphors or that have points of connection with other metaphors.

Merton's notion of a gap between macrotheory and micro-research can be reformulated in these terms. The macrotheories are metaphors that have not been elaborated into models that include specific empirical domains as their submetaphors. Similarly, if what Merton calls "research findings" are seen as metaphors, the problem becomes that of our not knowing which theories or models they are metaphors *for*. One without the other won't do.

Even if we recognize that models cannot present the world as it really is, however, it still might be argued that the "really is" world is nonetheless obdurately *there*. Here we have something of a compromise: a relativism of models alongside an absolutism of phenomena. Such a position is implicit in W. I. Thomas's dictum that what men take to be real is real in its consequences – suggesting a distinction between real consequences or actions and unreal models of reality. Similarly, Robert Merton, in his discussion of the codification of laws (1957:49) refers to Benjamin Whorf's observation that people react to their conceptions of states of affairs rather than to what the states of affairs are in fact. For example, in the presence of empty gasoline cans people behave carelessly, lighting cigarettes, freely tossing about lighted stubs, and so on, although in fact the "empty" drums are at least as hazardous as the filled ones because they contain highly explosive vapor. "Empty" is ambiguous: It means null and void, and it also means devoid of gasoline. To the uninitiated it means the former; to the technical staff it means the latter. Merton's point is that sociological conceptualization determines an investigator's response to data in a similar way. Other sociologists have made similar use of the parable of the five blind men, each of whom "sees" a different part of the elephant because of his perspective.

Such metaphors are misleading because they presuppose that there are consequences, facts, or elephants that are somehow knowable independently of *some* perspective. Moreover, the criteria of correspondence are useless for distinguishing what is merely another perspectival view and what is the "real" elephant. As behaviorists themselves have demonstrated (for summaries see Bruner, 1973; Segal *et al.*, 1966; and Merleau-Ponty, 1967), the medium of perception – in this case the metaphor – does not merely select, but rather creates or constitutes its own data; that is, it makes of them objects of experience.

The compromise thus collapses, and we are confronted with a paradox. Either all perspectives must be equally absolute, which is a contradiction of terms, or all claims to absoluteness are perspectival, which appears to leave us with no criteria of knowledge. The fear of such solipsistic relativism has forced many analysts to remain loyal to an epistemology that, deep down, they no longer trust. We are arguing, of course, that the paradox is a false one and can be overcome by a poetic for sociological knowledge.

Central to any such aesthetic is the idea that the metaphor defines its own domain of application and, as it were, summons it into existence. A salt shaker marked "DDT" is no longer a salt shaker. A killing called "euthanasia" is no longer a killing. *The Student-Physician* is a different subject than *Boys in White*. The representation "Bacon-Descartes-Mach" makes of Descartes something different from "Descartes-Husserl-Sartre." The new allocation of terms first changes our attitude toward Descartes, then Descartes. A shift of name, as effected through a metaphoric concept transfer, changes one's assessment of the facts. And, if the new attitude becomes generally accepted, the metaphor can change the facts themselves. Because of its economy and punch the striking metaphor tends to become widely adopted; and as this happens it is transformed into a literal description of "the way things really are" (Turbayne, 1962:22; Goodman, 1960:48–56). Metaphors lose vivacity as they gain veracity.

To say that metaphors should always be taken "as if" is not to suggest that they are fictions, however, but only that they are expressions for phenomena that cannot be directly conveyed. That is, the aesthetic view neither affirms nor denies the existence of an unmediated world of things. Instead, it *suspends* any such ontological judgments and instead examines the forms in which that-whereof-we-cannot-speak gives itself up to us. The relativism implicit in such an aesthetic suspension is a question of method, not a matter of belief. To assume that a model must be either "real" or "fictional" is to judge the representation as though it were a copy of surface appearance. But the function of metaphor is neither to copy "reality" nor to be an unbounded product of the romantic imagination. Rather, it provides a new way of understanding that which we already know, and in so doing it reconstitutes from these materials new domains of perception and new languages of thought.

All this is anathema to positivists who claim that any metaphoric use of language is simply bad science, in that it extends description beyond those precisely observable phenomena that constitute the experimental evidence at hand. But carried one step further, the restriction of description to the immediate data prohibits the scientist from claiming to speak "scientifically" about any phenomenon not already observed. Even in its limited form the restriction forbids the scientist to rely upon a theory in his own research whenever that research enters an area or seeks a degree of precision for which past practice with the theory offers no precedent. These prohibitions are logically unexceptional, which is what makes them so useful in unmasking the positivist's metaphor. For to accept the implications of this metaphor – of the concept *as* its operations – would be to prohibit just that research through which science develops (Kuhn, 1962:106).[10]

It is thus a mistake to talk about stubborn irreducible facts. New metaphors not only represent appearances, they change them and even create new ones. New metaphors lie at the heart of new theories. To take a metaphor as purely fictional is to miss a possible occasion to elaborate it into a model. Likewise to take models as literal is to overlook their possible rivals (Diesing, 1971:122). For example, the literalness of the perfect competition model of economic conduct often precludes consideration of such alternatives as the *n*-person prisoner's dilemma model of industry; or Shubik's games of economic ruin, K-R stability, and other ideas for oligopoly (1959, 1964); or Boulding's theory of viability; or the various behavioral models growing out of Newell and Simon's General Problem Solver; or Leontief's input-output model (Cyert and March, 1963). And even these are mainly changes in dialect; really new languages for representing the running of a firm or an economy could include capitalism as welfare for the rich, as racketeering, as a day at the races, and the like. The point is that the choice between rival metaphors becomes apparent only when we preserve the "as if" quality of our metaphoric thinking. There are no criteria for comparing metaphors with some absolute reality; but, as we shall see, there are criteria for choosing between metaphors.

CRITERIA OF ADEQUACY FOR METAPHORS IN SOCIOLOGY

Though all theories are metaphoric, this does not mean that all metaphors are of equal value, or that traditional criteria of scientific adequacy cannot be reinterpreted in metaphoric terms. On the contrary, in this section we try to show why some metaphors are preferable to others and how traditional tests of adequacy can be modified or enlarged.

Empirical tests?

The classical way of determining the adequacy of a model or proposition in sociology is to compare it with experience. Between several propositions, the one that corresponds most closely with reality is to be preferred. Implicit here is the assumption that the material objects, objectively observed, will themselves determine the accuracy and extent of their correspondence to model or hypothesis. The scientist and his language are not seen as mediators; instead, the scientist removes his subjective self from the encounter with the data and, ideally, employs language that has a one-to-one correspondence with the things to which it refers.

From the viewpoint of *symbolic* realism, however, such an approach is logically circular and behaviorally impossible. This is because correspondence criteria of truth presuppose that we have knowledge of the objects of our test independently of our theoretical conceptions of them. We are assumed to be able to identify a "sexual neuroses" independently of the theories of Freud, or to be able to observe "role conflicts" apart from the theories of James, Cooley, or Mead. We are expected to discover whether an exchange is an economic or a military one by consulting the exchange itself, while at the same time holding no conception of it as economic or military. The data themselves are thought of as sending out their own self-identifying signals; as researchers, all we must do is tune our receiving instruments to the right channel and screen out subjective noise. Similarities between secret societies in Africa, Chinatown tongs, and the FBI (Little, 1965; Lyman, 1961; Navasky, 1971), or differences between attitudes toward death in the middle ages and today (Ariès, 1974), all are thought to be discoverable by letting the data speak for themselves, imprinting their stamp on minds freed from preconceptions (McHugh, 1970:326).

From such a separation of fact from theory, it follows that one may select preferable theories or propositions on the basis of their degree of correspondence with the data. These data, however, are not gathered willy nilly. Instead, ideally, they are observed in carefully controlled experiments. The data that are generated by an experiment are the data that count. Data observed without such controls may be interesting as illustrations, but they do not contribute to a proof. But, given this proviso, our original question about the preferability of models is reduced to one of the preferability of sets of observations. So we must now ask, why are experiments the privileged and legitimate situs for observation, yielding data that are acceptable as evidence? Why do noncontrolled observations *not* count? Moreover, what makes one experiment preferable to others?

Isomorphism and originality
The positivist criteria of adequacy for metaphors have to do with their correspondence to experimental evidence. But, as we have seen, this answer takes us back where we began, for we now must ask why one set of experimental data is preferable to others. We now try to show that this question is a restatement of the one we put to ourselves originally. That is, we argue that the criteria of acceptability of experimental data are much the same as the criteria of acceptability of metaphors. This should not be surprising, however, if one understands that experiments are themselves metaphors, or submetaphors, of the model or theory to which they relate. (We are not revolutionaries, seeking to overthrow the experimental method; instead, we wish to reinterpret it in terms of metaphoric thinking.)

At this point Kenneth Burke's distinction between informative and representative anecdotes is helpful. "The behaviorist," says Burke, "uses his experiment with the conditioned reflex as the anecdote about which to form his vocabulary for the discussion of human motives; but this anecdote, though notably informative, is not representative, since one cannot find a representative case of human motivation in animals, if only because animals lack that property of linguistic rationalization which is so typical of human motives. A representative case of human motivation must have a strongly linguistic bias, whereas animal experimentation necessarily neglects this" (1969a:59, 510).[11] This may be accepted with the proviso, of course, that what we are interested in about man is the *symbolic* dimension of his behavior. If, in contrast, the physiological psychologist is *not* interested in this, his anecdote may serve him well.

Isomorphism, then, means sameness in terms of the dimensions in which we are interested. An iceberg is more like a ship in scale and tonnage, but a toy model may be more useful for theories. The problem obviously becomes crucial when inferences are made to other levels or realms of action, which, of course, is what building theory is all about. The inference, like operationalization and experimentation, also is a carrying over, a metaphor or transfer of terminology of one realm into another. Where isomorphism is perfect, it is unlikely that *new* information will be yielded. Conversely, where metaphors yield the greatest insight, they are unlikely to be very isomorphic.

This paradox is illustrated in a story by Luis Borges about a country where cartography was pursued with passion (1966). To ensure greater accuracy the maps were constantly enlarged. Eventually a map was made that was exact in all respects. When put in place it stretched from border to border of the kingdom, a perfect fit. Such a map would be a reliable guard against nasty surprises. At the same time, however, it would preclude the possibility of *delightful* surprises. In contrast, metaphors characteristically employed in poetry are illuminating precisely because of their originality. But the very estranging that such metaphors accomplish in order to make us see freshly requires that the domains that are fused or compared be very distant. Hence, such metaphors generally do not permit extensive development. The great discoveries, in science and the arts, are just those metaphors that have this poetic originality, but that also are isomorphic enough to be elaborated by normal science (or by normal art).

Economy, cogency, and range

We have asked what makes facts relevant to a social theory. Putting the question differently, why do we feel that not having Tocqueville would be a greater loss than skipping last year's census? How is it that we learn more from Aristotle's *Politics* than from a shelf full of studies on the behavior of voters? Why do we find *The Polish Peasant in Europe and America* more instructive than the fact-filled reports of the Bureau of Immigration?

In each case, the great theorist *was* great because he saw how material that he researched directly could be metaphoric of a larger, more important domain.[12] Few political scientists are interested in the constitutional history of Athens, but all read Aristotle. Few are interested in Polish peasants, Arunta religion, Berkeley sorority girls, or German gymnasium students, but all read Thomas, Durkheim, Adorno, and Weber (Redfield, 1948). In each case the data, as raw data, are unimportant, one might even say unknowable or meaningless. But when the data are seen as an original iconic metaphor of the larger theoretical domain, they suddenly become significant. Indeed, it is in the discovery of just such metaphors that data become a "crucial experiment" or a "strategic research site."

Remember also that metaphoric transfer is a two-way street. The general theory can serve as a metaphor for a narrow range of data, as well as the reverse. Scientific genius lies in connecting the two extremes, thus satisfying in one stroke the criteria of economy and inclusiveness, of brevity and range. If we focus on the data as a metaphor for the theory, their special utility may lie in their brevity and simplicity, what might be called their practical and intellectual economy. Conversely, the special advantage of the larger theory, as a metaphor for the data, lies in its breadth and inclusiveness, its translatability to other domains.

With this in mind it is easier to understand the procedure of those sociologists who have not set out to test a theory but began with an anecdote and then discovered what larger domain it re-presented. This can be seen in the studies by the Lynds of *Middletown* (1929, 1937) and by Lloyd Warner of *Yankee City* (1959, 1963). Muncie, Indiana, as such, is largely irrelevant to what we learn from the Lynds's study about the *discrepancy* between economic myths and economic realities. On the other hand, if our interest shifts to the process of the *ritual enactment* of social myths, it is Newburyport as a particular place which becomes irrelevant. Instead, Warner's description of the parade on the Fourth of July, for example, becomes an emblem of this larger question (Bierstedt, 1949:590; Warner, 1959:107).

In the spirit of our own argument Lewontin notes "the experimental value of metaphors. It is easier to breed fruit flies than elephants, easier to put model airplanes in wind tunnels than jet bombers" (1964:280). Likewise, as Abraham Kaplan tells us, "A cognitive function is performed by the . . . models. . . . Because it is cheaper, safer, and faster, it allows for experimentation that would otherwise not be feasible. And by varying its construction or operation we can use it to trace out the consequences of alternate sets of assumptions, and so calculate an outcome or assess a theory" (1964:273).

Whereas Lewontin conceives of experiments as metaphors, Kaplan sees metaphors, or models, as experiments. This fits well with what we said above. In *scientific* realism, with its separation of theory and experience, reduction can go in only one direction: downward; the theory is reduced to the data or experiments that represent it. But from the perspective of *symbolic* realism, "theory" and "data" *both* are symbolic constructs and, hence, each can serve as an emblem for the other. Data can be reduced to theory as well as the reverse. Rats in mazes can serve as a behavioristic metaphor for men, just as, *mutatis mutandi*, men can serve as a mentalistic metaphor for rats. That the former is more common than the latter is not because of a difference in logic, but because we find humans of greater intrinsic significance than rodents.

One criterion of choice of metaphors, then, will be economy – ease of representation and manipulation, both conceptually and practically. And generally, the briefer, simpler, more economical the metaphor is, the greater will be our ease in handling it. As our discussion already has indicated, however, this criterion can not be unproblematically applied. Of the psychologist who says "It is easier practically to put rats into mazes than people," we must ask, "Yes, but at what conceptual cost?" Practical economy may lead to conceptual impoverishment, just as conceptual extravagance may bankrupt one's practical research.

Economy also serves as a criterion in a purely formal sense. But here economy is synonymous with coherence or concinnity – the precisely cogent, elegantly efficient integration of a broad range of diverse phenomena. What then makes a metaphor or model coherent, or conversely, what accounts for a metaphor's failure to illuminate our view of the principal subject? Mixed metaphors (Khatchadourian, 1968:240) illustrate congruence negatively, as a failure of fit. For example, some sociological writings draw their metaphors from two quite different sources: people and machines. In a *purely* mechanical model all we would have is the machine. But by mixing this metaphor with a human one, the social machine assumes additional characteristics. It comes to have purposes, goals, or functions; drives, forces, or needs. Thus society becomes a machine with ghosts both outside and within it. This double redundancy is further confused in that the functions, causes, or forces may be corporeal or incorporeal. In one version of this imagery, society is seen as a great clock; it is the job of the sociologist to take off the face of this clock and lay bare its inner workings. Again, what we have is a double view of reality: telic outcomes on the one hand, and underlying causes on the other. In contrast, a *purely* mechanical metaphor would not give ontological priority of one part of the machine over any other. Likewise, in a purely human imagery, both the face *and* the inner workings of society are symbolic constructs. Any event can become a sign; the movements on the face of society *suggest* its internal movements, but there is only one "clock," and both parts of it are examinable. In sum, then, lack of economy in the original conception – in this example through a mixing of metaphors – can result in redundancy, ambiguity, and contradiction (Turbayne, 1962:212ff).

The range of a metaphor refers to its power of incorporating other symbolic domains. The claim of universal range for a metaphor is thus a claim for its power to translate all other vocabularies into its own. Hence when we say that everything ultimately is psychological, biological, or political, we mean not so much that these are the essential raw materials of the world, but that "raw materials" as defined in various domains may be analyzed in the terms of the particular domain to which we give priority (Jameson, 1972:viii).

Expanding the range of an iconic metaphor generally pushes it in an analogic direction; elaborating or formalizing an analogic metaphor usually yields an icon. For example, the analog that "racism is a cancer in the body social" may be elaborated by asking "In what respect?" The more we ask this question, the more we identify those respects in which cancer is to the body as racism is to a society. If we are persistent and insightful enough, eventually we will exhaust the relevant points of comparison. At this moment one of two things has happened: We have learned everything about racism that medicine can teach us, and we abandon comparative analysis in this direction; or (in this case unlikely), we are led to develop a formal theory of, say, "systems breakdown," which explains *both* racism *and* cancer. In either instance, however, we at this point do not have an analogic model, but an iconic one.[13]

This process of elaborating metaphors can proceed either inductively or deductively. For example, we might build our metaphor upward piece by piece, from a narrow range into a general theory. Conversely, we might be able to deduce many submetaphors from a few general principles. To illustrate, suppose we pretend that "Rumors spread like diseases" (Rashevsky, 1951; Goffman and Newell, 1967).[14] In this case, we know quite a bit about epidemiology, and we can deduce an ample set of hypotheses concerning the transmission of rumor from our knowledge of the spread of disease.

Such deductive thinking is common among sociologists of a mathematical bent. Instead of seeing their formal models as a metaphor for formal properties in the flux of experience, they often tend to see experience as a metaphor of their equations. For such an analyst, a cafeteria line becomes a Markov chain, the closing of the Suez becomes a game of Prisoner's Dilemma, the myth of Oedipus becomes a twelvefold kinship table, and family squabbles become geometric bifurcation (Suppes and Atkinson, 1960). As with the metaphors of racism or rumors and disease, such models may be preformed and borrowed from another area of thought, rather than elaborated upward (see Glaser and Straus, 1967). Both cases, however, can be understood as the discovery of metaphors within metaphors. The primary metaphor has been analyzed into subordinate metaphors, much as a basic musical chord can be "filled in" with its appropriate overtones and harmonics. If the primary and subordinate metaphors belong to the same realm of discourse they will reinforce each other and strengthen the total system of inference and connotation. Indefinite elaboration will eventually exhaust the realm of discourse (the data as typified) and one will have closure (Garfinkel, 1967; Tarski, 1946:134).

On the other hand, elaboration may reveal that the metaphors and submetaphors are inconsistent. In this case one will have contradiction rather than closure. In ordinary discourse such contradictions are called mixed metaphor (Black, 1962:229). As we now see, the prohibition against mixing metaphors is not merely stylistic but logical.

In all these instances, the expansion of the metaphor can be viewed not so much as a testing of new hypotheses but more as the invention of a new language. The adequacy of this new language is measured by the amount of translation we are able to affect out of the older terminologies into the new. The language of politics is translated into the language of games, the language of religion is translated into the language of economics, the language of theology is translated into a psychological language of the self.

The last speaker of a near-dead language may be thought of as the bearer of history. Similarly, the discoverer of a new paradigm, that is, the progenitor of a scientific or artistic revolution, may be seen as the poet of a domain of discourse that is yet to be peopled with speakers. The new paradigm serves as a kind of code, but the overwhelming bulk of work of the revolution is in the sheer translation of all the old terms into the new. Numbed perceptions are awakened and mummified concepts unraveled, by forcing them through the hoops and hurdles of the new model. Yet the range and powers of absorption of the new paradigm also are not without limit. And when these limits are reached, proponents of still-other paradigms will claim that their models can absorb just those areas that are untranslatable by their rival (Kuhn, 1962:153; Jameson, 1972:132). In this situation, range, or the power of translation, emerges as a key criterion of adequacy. In this sense knowledge consists in the ability to reduce or elevate one type of reality to another. To reach the newer reality one must repudiate or suspend the conventional one only, as Lévi-Strauss puts it, "to reintegrate it later on in an objective synthesis from which all sentimentality has been banished" (1955:50).

ILLUSTRATIVE METAPHOR

Illustrative metaphor has been used since social theory began. Plato, for example, used myths, parables, legends, and allegories to make his points. *The Republic* as a whole is a metaphor in the form of a model, a point we shall look at later on. In *On Liberty*, John Stuart Mill uses an avian metaphor in a clearly rhetorical fashion:

To prevent the weaker members of the community from being preyed upon by innumerable vultures, it was needful that there should be an animal of prey stronger than the rest, commissioned to keep them down. But as the King of the vultures would be no less bent upon preying on the flock than any of the minor harpies, it was indispensable to be in a perpetual attitude of defense against his beak and claws. (1966)

We call such a passage illustrative for two reasons. First, Mill does not develop the comparison along multiple dimensions. The "flock:harpies, people:predators" comparisons are not elaborated in any detail and, in fact, do not lend themselves to such elaboration. (The terms of each pair do not quite fit with each other nor with the other pair.) The images are useful, however, in underlining the central point: Liberty requires a perpetual attitude of defense.

Second, Mill's *as if* use of the comparison is one-sided. He is only pretending to pretend. His make-believe has not also entailed a suspension of conventional belief. We and he know too well that his transfers are nothing but transfers, albeit not arbitrary ones. Even though the figures of speech are meant only illustratively, however, their appropriateness and fit is constituted of their *analytic* utility: They isolate and underline the central idea.

Freud also made extensive use of illustrative metaphor, often of a martial sort. The psyche is the battleground of conflicting armies, the ego fortifies itself or becomes weakened, the super-ego builds a wall around libidinal forces. As Harvey Nash notes:

[Freud compared] a temporary blockage of development . . . to an army held up for weeks by enemy resistance, on a stretch of country crossed quite rapidly in peace time. Regression was likened to troops giving ground in the face of enemy attack. Psychotherapy, on the other hand, was compared to the intervention of a foreign ally in a civil war . . . the therapist comes to the aid of the ego, which is under siege by the id. (1962:25–26; cf. Spector, 1972).

Such imagery is not merely decorative or stylistic; on a deeper level, it contributes to what story it is that gets told. Freud could have used other dominant metaphors, of course: a debate be-tween angels, instruments out of tune, and so on. But it is hard to see how he could have described newly conceived psychic processes except through *some* metaphor and, having chosen his images, how that description could avoid being shaped by them.

Illustrative metaphors also can operate in layers, as it were, with a surface metaphor being used to illustrate a deeper meta-phoric meaning. In such cases the author may be frank about his use of metaphors illustratively, while at the same time denying the metaphoric character of that which the surface metaphor is meant to evince. Daniel Bell provides a nice example of this in his discussion of America's two-party po-litical system: "Each party is like some huge bazaar, with hundreds of hucksters clamoring for attention. Life within the bazaars flows freely and licenses are easy to obtain; but all trading has to be conducted within the tents; the ones who hawk their wares outside are doomed to few sales" (1960:94). Bell's usage here is seductive. His use of simile (each party is *like* . . .) shows that the metaphor is not taken literally. Our parties are not huge bazaars. Yet the very denial of literalness on this surface level hides an even greater literalness on a deeper level. For in elaborating what Bell takes to be the empirical referent of this metaphor, he describes in quite literal fashion our political system as an arena in which benefits are optimized through rational competition between individuals and groups. Thus the bazaar is consciously used as a metaphor for rational political competition; yet Bell seems less conscious that "ra-tional political competition" is itself a transfer of economic man over into the political sphere. His underlying assumption is that citizens are consumers and that the polity is a series of marketlike relations between individuals. Economic rationality (which may be an inadequate metaphor even for economic conduct), becomes political rationality, and political conduct is seen as the efforts of discrete decision units to optimize their cost-benefit ratios in a marketlike political society.

Our point here is that the explicit use of illustrative metaphor often hides the more deeply metaphoric quality of that which it illustrates. One way to undress such imagery is to elaborate it beyond credible limits. We thus might ask, Who owns the bazaar? Are the shops merely front companies for larger, hidden interests? How are contracts enforced between buyers and sellers? And so on, much in the manner that both Durkheim and Marx, after their own fashions, attacked the utilitarian theory of society.

A more original use of metaphor can be found in the writings of Charles Horton Cooley: "A word is a vehicle, a boat floating down from the past laden with the thought of men we never saw; and in coming to understand it we enter not only into the minds of our contemporaries, but into the general mind of humanity continuous through time" (1909). The usage here is not merely decorative, as some sensualist theories of aesthetics would say. Instead, Cooley describes, in a highly condensed fashion, both the transmission of culture in history and the establishment of a common culture through language. Cooley's technique has a further subtlety, in that his metaphoric description (the first two lines), is immediately followed by a literal explication of the image (the last three lines). Yet his metaphor is at once so economical in expression and so rich in connotation that it stays more in our minds than the literal statement that follows it.

Cooley's best known metaphor is "the looking-glass self," which he and others eventually elaborated into a model of the self in social interaction:

A social self . . . might be called the reflected or looking-glass self:

"Each to each a looking-glass
Reflects the other that doth pass"

As we see our face, figure, and dress in the glass . . . so in imagination we perceive in another's mind some thought of our appearance, manners, aims, deeds, character, friends, and so on, and are variously affected by it. (1902:184)

Then Cooley elaborates and qualifies the image:

> A self-idea of this sort seems to have three principal
> elements: the imagination of our appearance to the other
> person; the imagination of his judgment of that
> appearance; and some sort of self-feeling, such as pride
> or mortification. The comparison with the looking-glass
> hardly suggests the second element, the imagined
> judgment, which is quite essential. The thing that moves us
> to pride or shame is not the mere mechanical reflection
> of ourselves, but an imputed sentiment, the imagined
> effect of this reflection upon another's mind. (1902:184)

The "as if" features of metaphor – as if the real thing were
metaphoric, as if the metaphor were real – are here in delicate
balance. The modesty of tone ("The comparison . . . hardly
suggests . . .") says that the metaphor is only a metaphor. But
in pointing out the limitation of the metaphor, Cooley actually
refines it, for we are shown that our response to the *mirror's*
reflection is in terms of what we think others would think of
that image. Hence the metaphor is shown to be more fitting than
we initially perceived; our selves really are looking-glass selves,
and not the sui generis entities we usually (literally) imagine
them to be.

Chicago sociology has been largely concerned with two problems: the development of a social self and the social psychology
of urban communities. The first of these interests has been seen
as an elaboration of Cooley's metaphor of the "looking-glass
self." The second interest can be viewed as an exploration of
a metaphor of Robert Park:

> Our great cities, as those who have studied them have
> learned, are full of junk, much of it human, i.e., men and
> women who, for some reason or other, have fallen out of
> line in the march of industrial progress and have been
> scrapped by the industrial organization of which they
> were once a part.

> A recent study by Nels Anderson of what he calls
> "Hobohemia" . . . which is almost wholly inhabited by
> homeless men, is a study of such a human junk heap. In
> fact, the slum areas that invariably grow up just on the
> edge of the business areas of great cities, areas of
> deteriorated houses, of poverty, vice, and crime, are areas
> of social junk.

I might add . . . that recent studies made in Chicago of boys' gangs seem to show that there are no playgrounds in the city in which a boy can find so much adventure, no place where he can find so much that may be called "real sport," as in these areas of general deterioration which we call the slums. (1952:60–61)

Like Cooley, Park first states the metaphor, then reminds us that it is only a metaphor (the "i.e." does this), then elaborates the analogs implicit in the initial comparison, and then closes not with the original metaphoric term – junk heap – but with a literal one – slum – in so unnoticed a fashion that the initial recognition that "junk" is merely a metaphor is negated, and we are made to see junk heaps and slums as isomorphic members of a common emergent genus. This isomorphism is not complete, of course, but it is made apparent on a number of dimensions, as seen in Figure 2.

By such formal elaboration metaphors become models and, as we shall see, though not all metaphors can be elaborated into models (at least not plausible or useful models), all models have their beginnings in metaphor. It could be argued, of course, that Cooley's and Park's metaphors were not elaborated into what became the social psychology and community sociology of the Chicago School. Instead, it might be said, the reverse is true, that we have merely used these two images as metaphors for the Chicago School's two main interests. It might even be argued that the essays, where the looking-glass and junk-heap images occur, were not widely read or were read *after* their supposed elaborations had already been written. In terms of the logic of inquiry,

(a) People, slums   (c) Junk, junk heaps

*	=	*

(b) Industrial   (d) Industrial
social organization   business organization

Common genus:

1. Geographic proximity.
2. Abandoned, thrown out, unclaimed by anyone as their own, homeless.
3. Waste product of a system.
4. Thought of as repulsive when not kept in its place.
5. A place for adventure. (Because it is not functional to the system that generated it, it provides the opposite of functional goal-directedness, that is, "real sport.")

Figure 2

however, such objections are moot. The fact that the Chicago School as a whole can be seen as an elaboration of these two metaphors, and that they in turn can be seen as metaphors for the entire school, only reinforces our point. For the very possibility of such an argument shows how brilliantly the two images use the double "as if" nature of metaphors, and this accounts exactly for their logical and mimetic power.

With these general properties in mind, we may now exemplify our earlier distinction between icon and analog with reference to illustrative metaphors. An essay by Georg Simmel – "The Ruin" – suits this purpose. To explain the peculiar evocative power of architectural ruins, Simmel begins by comparing architecture with other art forms. In painting or poetry "works of art" stand independently of the physical laws governing the materials from which they are made, the materials being used "only as a means of expressing spirit."

> Although architecture, too, uses and distributes the weight
> and carrying power of matter according to a plan
> conceivable only in the human soul, within this plan the
> matter works by means of its own nature, carrying out the
> plan, as it were, with its own forces. . . . This unique
> balance – between mechanical, inert matter which
> passively resists pressure, and informing spiritually which
> pushes upward – breaks, however, the instant a building
> crumbles. For this means nothing else than that merely
> natural forces begin to become master over the work of
> man: the balance between nature and spirit, which the
> building manifested, shifts in favor of nature. This shift
> becomes a cosmic targedy which, so we feel, makes every
> ruin an object infused with our nostalgia; for now the
> decay appears as nature's revenge for the spirit's having
> violated it by making a form in its own image. (1965:259)

Simmel obviously is speaking metaphorically. Yet we are per-plexed by the question "What is the ruin a metaphor for?" The special qualities of architecture are set off against the other arts, so here we have a negative comparison. But the other analogs – architecture, nature and spirit, our feeling in response to these – are all contained within the same closed orbit. Indeed, it appears that each is a metaphor for the others. But then if we seek to decode these analogies by asking "In what ways are they alike?" we again are stymied, for it becomes clear that each of the three terms are not merely "like" each other; they rather have become *embodiments* of each other, three expressions of the same thing. Architecture is an embodiment of the tension between spirit and nature as well as of our interiorized perception of this tension. Similarly, our feeling or perception incorporates both this tension between spirit and nature on the metaphysical level, as well as, or through, the tension in the concrete architectural expression. The analogs thus are not analogs at all in the strict sense of being "alike." They are iconic in that they are "the same."[15]

METAPHOR AS MODEL

Much of science is conducted through models, and models are nothing less than elaborated and determinate metaphors (Kaplan, 1964:265–288; Freudenthal, 1961:84).[16] Metaphoric statements, either iconic or analogic, may be elaborated into models by asking of them "In what respect?" (Sosensky, 1964:20). For example, in the iconic statement "America is stratified," the key term is taken from geology or archeology, but in our usage we don't mean layerings of the earth as, for example, one *might* mean when saying "Troy is stratified." By asking "In what respect?" we thus extend and make determinate the initial image. In this case we might say "America is stratified in the respect that it is characterized by persistent hierarchical divisions according to birth, education, occupation, income, privileges, and obligations." "In what respect?" "On the dimension of education, in the respect that . . . ," and so on.

The same logic applies when elaborating an analogic metaphor, such as "The Catholic Church is the General Motors of religion." The question "In what respect?" might be answered "In the respect that they both are rational organizations." Further elaboration might lead us to note that they both are characterized by fixed administrative regulations, hierarchic authority, written records, professional staffs, and so on. Each additional elaboration would require re-asking the question "In what respect?" Here, for example, one might answer, "They both have fixed administrative regulations in the respect that various functions are performed by (persons in) various positions as stipulated by rule; entrance into various positions is according to formal criteria, etc." Again, further answers to the question "In what respect?" would result in further elaboration. In this case we have elaborated the dimension "formal organization." Similar elaborations could be made on the dimensions of size, percentage of the market, esprit de corps, and the like. At a certain point the extension and intention of elaboration would be such that we could say the initial metaphor had become a model.

Generally the metaphors most susceptible to elaboration into models will be those borrowed from another frame within the same universe of discourse. For example, the above comparisons of people and birds, junk, or ruins all bring together terms from different universes. The images are striking just because of the extremity of opposition, but, for this reason, they cannot be elaborated in very many respects. Conversely, comparisons from frames within the same universe tend to be more readily elaborated into models. In the first case the "energy" flows in one direction only: Looking glasses say something about self-concepts but not the reverse. In the second case there is the mutual enrichment of a two-way flow. For example: "The overseas Chinese are the Puritans of Asia." "In what respect?" "In the respect that, like the Puritans, the Chinese have a strong family system, respect scholarly learning, and are inner-worldly ascetics. "In what respect?" "They are inner-worldly ascetics in the respect that they are disciplined in their work, frugal, disinclined to conspicuous worldly consumption, and achievement oriented." "In what respect?" "They are achievement oriented in the respect that . . ."

New metaphors appear when the initial one is dissected and the system of implications either is exhausted or begins to break down because of internal contradictions. If contradictions appear before an adequate model has been built, or if an old model gets "used up," the recourse is to find another metaphor. For example, instead of the overseas Chinese as the Puritans of Asia, we might imagine the overseas Chinese as Asia's *Jews*.

The elaboration of the new metaphor may be more consistent and also broader; for example, both Jews and overseas Chinese, unlike Puritans, were away from their native land. If the question "In what respect?" when asked of this new sub-metaphor calls forth the needed note to complete the principal metaphoric chord, then we would feel we have identified a salient variable. This enables us to return to and modify our original effort: Overseas Chinese are the early American Puritans (but not the British Puritans) of Asia. Depending on which group one is more interested in or more knowledgeable about, one may also reverse the metaphor: The Jews are the overseas Chinese of Europe, or General Motors is the Catholic Church of Detroit.

Iconic models

Most conceptual schemes in sociology are iconic. They picture what things are, rather than compare how things are alike. Studies on the nature of institutions, roles, statuses, organizations, functional prerequisites, class, power, norms, attitudes, values, and symbolic interaction all tend to be of this type. Weber's individual ideal types explicitly have an iconic function. His *The Protestant Ethic and the Spirit of Capitalism* presents an iconic model. It was only in his comparative studies of religion, through the instrument of *universal* ideal types, that Weber translates this into an analogic model. Durkheim's typology of mechanical and organic solidarity is also iconic, as are his anomic, fatalistic, egoistic, and altruistic suicides.

The vast majority of functional, structural, or systems analysis in sociology also is iconic (Davis, 1959). The notion of system, of course, can be elaborated into many submetaphors. Robert Redfield observed four distinct varieties of system during his work in Yucatan. One was the annual cycle of agricultural activities, a series of links in an endless means-end chain. A second subsystem was the maplike organization of human activity around four prominent geographical characteristics, which themselves were related like terms in a mathematical proportion. A third subsystem was radial, with corn in the center of human life and other things grouped around it and connected to it in different ways. A fourth, that of variations on basic themes, appeared in folklore and mythology. Still other patterns appeared as Redfield continued his work, often depending on the perspective he was taking: "[The patterns] do not connect themselves one to another by any rule or principle that I can see. And they crosscut or overlap one another; things seen in one systematic context are later seen again in another" (1941:24).

Iconic models not only describe; they also explain. But their mode of explanation is different from that of the analog. Where the analog focuses on species-species or genus-genus relationships, the iconic explanation is in terms of the interrelations of some genus and its particular species. The icon is a metaphor for selected dimensions of some *whole,* and any element of the model taken by itself becomes a submetaphor for some other part of the whole. To describe the relationships of the parts to each other and between all of them and the whole is to know what each of them *is*. As Radcliffe-Brown put it: "We have to explain why it is that the Andamanese think and act in certain ways. The explanation of each single custom is provided by showing what is its relation to the other customs of the Andamanese and to their general system of ideas and sentiments" (1922:230; see Beattie, 1968:118–121).

When all the subsystems are combined, the result is a model of the whole system under study. The chain, map, wheel, and music images of pattern become aspects of a single unity, the little community. Yet Redfield's model, by his own admission, is irregular and bulky. The metaphors are mixed; and so the system of implications creaks at its joints, in places even coming apart.

Something similar may be said of George Homans' model in his book *The Human Group*, in which he mixes such metaphors as bedsprings, a gasoline engine, vector analysis of physical forces, and an electrical circuit, in addition to the standard theatrical images of actor, role, and scene (Bruyn, 1966:134). Such variety serves a heuristic or exploratory function, for each metaphor paints the picture with a different brush. Yet to the extent that Homans wishes to present a logically cogent analytic model of the group, such mixing of metaphors prevents consistent elaboration. By contrast, the Kardiner-Linton models of personality and society are simple and clean: The two primary institutions of technology and family structure cause (and in our sense are metaphors for) basic personality, which expresses itself in secondary institutions. The absence of such primary metaphors to serve as the central loci of Redfield's and Homans' models is what makes their elaborations seem discordant or arbitrary. Consistency, economy, and elegance depend on the strength of the central metaphor at the heart of the model (Diesing, 1971:157).

Such a decoding of metaphors to elucidate the underlying logic of an argument can be done to virtually any theory, regardless of whether it is written in an artful or literary style. Thus, for example, in the turgid prose of Talcott Parsons we can distinguish at least five different metaphors for what he calls "dynamic equilibrium" (Sosensky, 1964:56):

1. Simple mechanical movement, expressed in the imagery of levers, inclined planes, and so on.

2. Celestial movement, where bodies change position but in fixed paths.

3. Thermodynamical movement, where the mean velocity of the molecules in various portions of a volume are the same.

4. Biological movement, where homeostasis is "sought" by an organism which changes in response to changes in external conditions.

5. Economic movement, where the individual terms – supply, demand, price – change but the character of their relationship remains constant.

One difficulty we have in integrating the various domains of Parsons's thought lies in his changing metaphors without telling us he is doing so. The same term – dynamic equilibrium or its equivalents – may be borrowed from or applied to two or more different realms or contexts, yielding lack of clarity and little integration.

One could, of course, move to a more abstract metaphor for human conduct that would make submetaphors of Parsons' various usages. Rapoport's definition of "system" is useful in this regard:[17]

> A fully rigorous definition of *system* would single out from all classes, aggregates, or phenomena those which can satisfy the following criteria:
> 1. One can specify a set of identifiable elements.
> 2. Among at least some of the elements, one can specify identifiable relations.
> 3. Certain relations imply others.
> 4. A certain complex relations at a given time implies a certain complex (or one of several possible complexes) at a later time.
>
> A complete specification of the elements and the relations among them defines a *state*. A dynamic theory of a system is therefore one which enables us to deduce certain future states from a given present state. (1966:129–190)

All of Parsons's usages would fall under this broader definition; yet, in moving to so high a level of abstraction, we are confronted with another problem: The metaphor "system" is now so broad that it does little to illuminate whatever specific subject matter we may have at hand. For example, we may say that a hospital is a "system" and a gay bar is a "system" because in each we can specify a set of elements, see certain relations that imply other relations, and so on. But as soon as we begin asking "In what respect?" the isomorphism between the various systems appears to be quite thin, and it becomes doubtful whether the salient aspects of either are brought into focus by the initial metaphor.

Other theorists have employed iconic thinking in an exactly opposite fashion. Instead of positing a highly abstract concept as a metaphor for some smaller domain, they begin with some telling detail, and then elaborate its implications so that it becomes a metaphor for the system as a whole. An example of this is provided by Becker and Geer:

> I first heard the word "crock" applied to a patient shortly after I began my field work. The patient in question, a fat, middle-aged woman, complained bitterly of pains in a number of widely separated locations.
>
> Over a period of several weeks . . . I finally arrived at an understanding of the term. Several students eventually explained their dislike in ways of which the following example is typical: "The true crock is a person who you do a great big workup for and who has all of these vague symptoms, and *you really can't find anything the matter with them.*"
>
> Further discussion made it clear that the students regarded patients primarily as objects from which they could learn those aspects of clinical medicine not easily acquired from textbooks and lectures; the crock took a great deal of time . . . and did not exhibit any interesting disease state from which something might be learned. This discovery in turn suggested that I might profitably investigate the general perspective toward medical school which led to such a basis for judgment of patients, and also suggested hypotheses regarding the value system of the hospital hierarchy at whose bottom the student stood. (1967:111–112, their italics)

What we have here are contexts within contexts, the contents of each being described through their relationship to each other and to the whole. Each context is a metaphor of the others. A new word used at bedside is a selective embodiment of the hospital's value system; the students' discussion of patients is a metaphor for their general perspective toward medical school. Each context has the quality of a hermetic language that can be decoded and known only through translation into another language that is equally hermetic. In the elaboration of this process, however, one builds up a sense that there are loan words, as well as a grammar, which, although differentially allocated, are largely shared. A description of these becomes the formal definition of the system.

Such a formal, holistic definition may be presented without reference to the process of elaboration or construction that is made explicit by Becker and Geer above. For example, Orrin Klapp outlines the conditions that determine how a person can become a fool and remain one:

> Because fool-making is a collective imputation it is not necessary, however, that a person actually have the traits or perform the role of the fool. A person is a fool when he is socially defined. . . . What makes a fool role stick? Among the factors responsible for permanent characterization as a fool we may particularly note (1) repeated performances or obvious personal traits which continually suggest the role of a fool; (2) a striking, conclusive, or colorful single exhibition which convinces the public that the person is irremediably a fool; (3) a story or epithet so "good" that it is continually repeated and remembered, making up an imperishable legend; and (4) failure to contradict a fool role by roles or stories of a different category. (1949: 159–160)

In this example Klapp says "it is not necessary . . . that a person actually have the traits or perform the role of the fool." Instead, there are certain factors responsible for his characterization as such. These prefatory remarks cloud what is otherwise a very "pure" iconic model. For, as we discussed earlier, the distinction between the "actual" and the "socially defined" is specious. Moreover, the term "factors responsible" suggests a causal relationship between the social definition and that which is done to enact it. But social definitions *exist* only in their enactment. Thus Klapp's model derives its strength, not from analogic or causal relations, as his language implies, but from the articulation of the mutual implications of the *elements* of role enactment in relation to the role as enacted as a whole.[18]

What we see in all these examples is that mimetic power of iconic models lies in their being amenable to indefinite *intention* – the deepening of inner metaphoric tension. As we elaborate and fill in the system of inferences it becomes richer and more refined; the model becomes an icon for more and more phenomena, each finding its place within the model, while the elements of the model themselves reallocate their significance within the larger whole (see Kaplan, 1964:335). As representations for wholes, however, iconic models must draw boundaries. The "lie" they tell is thus in their appearance of closure, which always is made in the face of elaborations that are incomplete. Awareness of this lie is preserved only so long as the model remains "as if." Building iconic models does not commit one to the a priori belief that everything is related to everything else. It is, instead, a methodological necessity imposed on us by our desire to make sense of what we have observed, to test the validity of our interpretations. Failure to reach closure compels us to expand our metaphors, to push our definitions of what is toward alien domains.

Analogic models
Analogic metaphors are not footprints in the forest that can be forgotten once our prey is caught; they are not mere heuristic devises we abandon when they have lead us to new theories. Instead, they are "an utterly essential part of theories, without which theories would be completely valueless and unworthy of the name" (Campbell, 1928; Feigl and Brodbeck, 1953:287). To elaborate an analogic metaphor is to engage in what is known as analytic induction (Lindesmith, 1968; Robinson, 1951; Cressy, 1950; Sutherland, 1960:66–67), or, more traditionally, the method of controlled comparison (Eggan, 1954; Hopkins and Wallerstein, 1967; Almond and Verba, 1963; Blau, 1965).[19] Collins asserts that the essence of this procedure "– and that is what science is – is to explain a phenomenon not by looking at it in isolation but by comparison and contrast to other things. To understand a thing we must compare where it occurs with where it does not occur and note the difference in the accompanying conditions" (1975:4).

In its simplest terms, the usual interpretation of controlled comparison is that it is the method of determining the cause(s) of a phenomenon from among a number of hypothesized factors. A factor is said to be the cause of a phenomenon insofar as it occurs or antecedes in all cases where the phenomenon is present, the phenomenon occurs or follows in all cases where the factor is present, and variations in one are accompanied by corresponding variations in the other (Mill, 1843).

All this is common knowledge; less commonly known is that this logic of controlled comparison is also the logic of elaborating analogic metaphors. An example might help. Suppose we are interested in the cause(s) of variations in high or low morale in different kinds of firms. We hypothesize a number of possible causal factors: average wages, company policy, size, type of technology, and so on. Let us say that we want to test for technology. Thus, to "cancel out" or control for the other possible factors, we would have to compare plants with the *same* wages, policy, and size and then see whether differences in levels of morale varied with the type of technology in use. We thus might select a bridge building company, a "think tank," a shipyard, a textile factory, an auto assembly plant, and a toy manufacturing firm. We would be careful to see that each firm had the same average wage, policies, and size and also were the same according to any other factor besides technology that might affect morale. We would then look at *differences* between the levels of morale and types of technologies of the six plants; that is, we would see which types of technology were associated with high or low morale. In this case, we might discover that the first three firms — the bridgebuilders, the think tank, and the shipyard — had very high morale, while in the textile, auto, and toy factories, morale was very low. Now this is not yet a theory, for a theory is a correlation with an explanation, and all we have here is a correlation. Moreover, we do not even know whether we have six different correlations — one for each firm, or two — one for each set of three plants. The technologies of the six firms seem to have little in common, nor is there any apparent difference between the technologies of each set of three. But then, on reflection, we may notice that bridgebuilders, think-tank employees, and shipmakers all make one unit of production at a time — there is one bridge, one research project, one ship, which must be completed before the next one is started and which in important ways is different from any other unit that will be produced. In contrast, the textile, auto, and toy plants are all assembly lines where the workers perform the same operations day in and day out. Instead of working on one unique product for a relatively long time, they work a short time on masses of identical products. In exploring this difference further, we may discover that mass production technology requires interchangeability of workers, rigid codes of procedure, and hierarchic authority, while single-unit production technology calls for teamlike work groups, loose rather than tight supervision, and greater individual autonomy and innovation — in other words, the very things that result in low or high morale. We now have a minitheory of technology and organizational morale.

This is an exemplary case of theory building through the

method of controlled comparison as it is usually conceived. It is, in fact, a simplified composite of experiments that have been conducted by a number of leading theorists in the field of formal organizations, all of whom are of a neopositivistic bent (Stinch-combe, 1959; Etzioni, 1961; Burns and Stalker, 1961; Blau, 1965; Woodward, 1965; Hage and Aiken, 1967). In interpreting their own method of controlled comparison, most neo-positivists would see it as a *testing of hypothesized factors* (Stinchcombe, 1968; Popper, 1963). In contrast, we now wish to turn our example inside out, as it were, and show that controlled comparison is more usefully viewed as a *discovery and elaboration of analogic metaphors*. In such a view we are focusing on the *logic* of inquiry, not its technique. Technique here refers to such questions as the choice between alternative measures of significance, the fineness of measuring instruments, the elimination of observer bias, and the like – in other words the problems that constitute the greatest part of most textbooks on methodology in the social sciences. Yet none of these treaties tell us how we know *which* factors are the ones we should test for, nor how to explain correlations that such tests may reveal. These questions – fundamental though they are in theory building – generally result in one of two suggestions. First, we are told that we should test for all possible factors and that the resulting statistically significant correlations *are* the explanation. Second, it is suggested that the formation of hypotheses and the interpretation of findings is the art of science – that is, mysterious, noncognitive, and so on. Thus, Nisbet (1962:74) speaks of "the wildness of logic" and the "twilight zone," while Popper (1963:192) tells us that theories are "the result of an almost poetic intuition. . . . We do not try to prove them. . . ." Instead, science is the effort "to *refute* them." Both types of responses avoid the basic question – the first by collapsing theory invention into a calculating machine, the second by vaporizing it into spirit.[20]

But let us return to our example. We are looking in formal organizations for metaphors for morale, high and low. What we need to find is diagrammed in Figure 3.

In pondering this out, we start with what we've got. That is, we begin by looking at some firms having high morale and others having low, and we try to figure out what the difference is between the two sets of firms, what each set has in common, and what explains their relationship to high and low morale. Such an explanation is represented by, and could be put into,

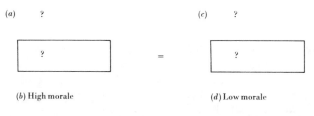

(a) ?

(c) ?

=

(b) High morale

(d) Low morale

Figure 3

two boxes – now blank. In our first set we have a bridge construction firm, a think tank, and a shipyard; in the second a firm that makes textiles, another that makes toys, and a third that assembles autos. All six plants are alike in wages, policy, and size, so these cannot be the attributes, differences, or explanation. Moreover, bridges, research projects, and ships seem to have no more in common with each other than they do with textiles, autos, and toys. Thus, the key cannot be found in similarities of surface appearance. Instead we must go deeper to find the common factors in each of the two sets. To do this we make metaphors, for example:

Shipyards are think tanks for vessels.

Textile makers are the auto assemblers of cloth.

Then we decode these metaphors, as in Figure 4.

To find the common genus we must ask "In what respect is the relation of $a:b$ like that of $c:d$?" Put this way it strikes us that, though the end product and the tools employed could hardly be more different, the organization of production that links shipyards to vessels, and think tanks to research reports, is very similar. Again, we ask "In what respect?" and find that each job is new and unique, that workers are not closely supervised, and so on. We also may reverse the metaphor – think tanks are the shipyards of research reports – to see if this generates additional "respects."

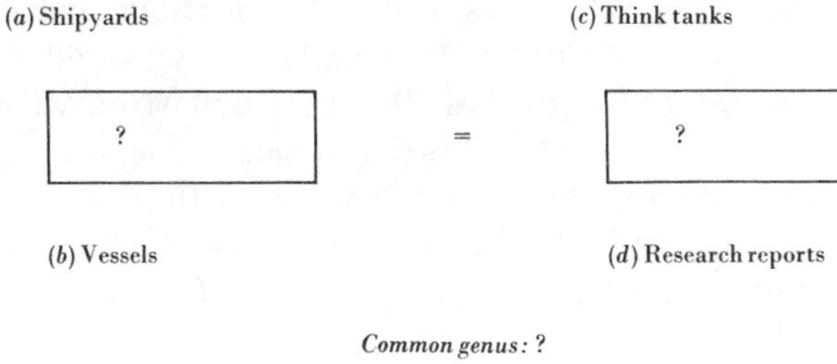

(a) Shipyards

(c) Think tanks

?

=

?

(b) Vessels

(d) Research reports

Common genus: ?

Figure 4

Once we have exhausted our store of submetaphors through elaboration, we may gather them back and then extend them to cover the entire domain which the emergent model was intended to serve:

(*a*) Certain features that   (*c*) Certain features that
        we call "single unit   we call "mass
        productions"   production"

(*b*) High morale   (*d*) Low morale

Common genus: require a social organization
that leads to . . .

With this core model in mind, we can now expand the metaphor further: The space program is the cathedral building of the twentieth century; heart surgeons run a boutique practice; Hilton hotels are factories for sleep. Having *in*tensified the metaphor with reference to the initial six plants, we now give it *ex*tension to other domains. What we now know a lot about – for example, factories – can become a means of informing us about the properties, structure, and processes of that about which we know little – for example, hotels. The factory becomes a metaphor for the hotel, and by this transfer the hotel comes to be redefined as a system of mass production technology and relations. The value of the analog, again, will be the degree to which it can be intensified within the new domain to which it was extended. That is, in asking "In what respects are Hilton hotels factories for sleep?" we should be able to portray in a simple yet comprehensive manner all the salient aspects of that domain.[21]

To cite a negative example of this, Aidan Southall notes that "The poor nations of Asia have become in a very real sense the slums of the rich Western nations. . . ." He then answers the question "In what respect?" this way: "A superficial but signal mark of this is their becoming the regular playground of the tourist, both official and unofficial. Whether tourist on vacation, economic advisor, or investor, his enjoyment of exotic places must be protected from insanitary contact with the ordinary people. Another aspect is the brain drain" (1972:137). Yet in other important respects, Southall admits, the isomorphism breaks down. Slums, he says, are contiguous to or enveloped by the dominant city, which makes it possible for them to export labor and to share in some degree in the institutional life of their oppressors. Third World nations, in contrast, are geographically too distant from the Western powers for this. Their situation thus is *worse* than the original metaphor suggested.

In a similar manner Malinowski (1927) shows the limits of the Oedipus complex, which Freud posited as universal. What Freud said about his Viennese patients is not a useful metaphor for the Trobrianders; in these islands personality formation is not a metaphor for sexual relations, but for relations of authority and power. Malinowski's model, then, might be further extended so that other areas of family life become domains of political theory. Thus, for example, ideals and taboos become embodiments of power relations, and exclusive sexual possession becomes a symbol of authority. In a similar fashion, the whole field of deviance could be reinterpreted as a submetaphor for the field of political sociology. (The opportunity model, white-collar crime, and labeling theory all suggest that deviance is a reflection of who has the power to legitimize or stigmatize certain types of conduct, who is able to evade sanctions, and so on.)

Analytic induction, controlled comparison, hypothesis testing, and inference can thus be seen as unselfconscious names for what may be understood as aspects of metaphoric thinking. This view, as we have seen, runs against the grain of conventional philosophy of science, which focuses on the falsification of propositions, rather than the generation and elaboration of models (Masterman, 1970:60). As such, however, the falsification theory of inquiry may be more a model for conducting neopositivist philosophy than for practicing the sciences of conduct.

THE ROOT METAPHORS OF SOCIOLOGICAL THOUGHT

Root metaphors are those sets of assumptions, usually implicit, about what sorts of things make up the world, how they act, how they hang together and, usually by implication, how they may be known. As such, root metaphors constitute the ultimate presuppositions or frame of reference for discourse on the world or on any domain within it. Thomas Kuhn has used the term "paradigm" to describe such ultimate frames and to distinguish between the normal science that is conducted within them and the scientific revolutions by which they are changed (1970). Max Black speaks of "conceptual archetypes" in a similar connection (1962:241); Paul Diesing uses the term "implicit ontology" (1971:124). Other closely related concepts include *"weltanschauung"* (Dilthey), *"habitus mentalis"* (Lukács; Panofsky), "eidos" (Bateson, 1941:32, 218–

256), "philosophy" or "world view" (Kluckhohn and Leighton, 1946; Krasnow and Merikallio, 1964:254), "dominant ontology" (Feibleman, 1956), "myth" (Bruyn, 1966:136–142), "domain assumptions" (Gouldner, 1970), "controlling assumptions" (Randall and Haines, 1946), "institutional epistemology" (McHugh, 1970:331), and "metaphysics" (Douglas, 1971a:3; Burtt, 1954).

Root metaphors differ from models or illustrative metaphors in two ways. First, they are characteristically below the level of conscious awareness. We spoke earlier of frozen metaphors; root metaphors are akin to frozen *models* – they are a kind of submerged or implicit model underlying the writer's thought (Black, 1962:239). Unlike models, however, root metaphors tend to be comprehensive in scope. They are, in a sense, the implicit metamodels in terms of which narrower range models are couched. We might say that root metaphors describe worlds, while models describe the contents of those worlds. Because of this root metaphors can only be iconic: For their users they *are* the world and contain everything in it; hence they cannot be analogically compared to anything else.

A number of philosophers have argued that such ordering schema are a prerequisite to any rational thought or, indeed, to the making sense of perception itself. In this sense the root metaphor is a basis and instrument of interpretation, a framework of meaning within which sensa become facts, in which facts become concepts, and in which concepts become discourse. This metaphoric basis of thought was discerned by Nietzsche, as we saw earlier, and it is noted again by Morris Abrams:

> Any area for investigation, so long as it lacks prior
> concepts to give it structure and an express terminology
> with which it can be managed, appears to the inquiring
> mind inchoate – either a blank, or an elusive and
> tantalizing confusion. Our usual recourse is, more or less
> deliberately, to cast about for objects which offer parallels
> to dimly sensed aspects of the new situation, to use the
> better known to elucidate the less known, to discuss the
> intangible in terms of the tangible. (1953:31)

In *World Hypotheses* Stephan Pepper suggests how the formation of root metaphors might take place:

> The method in principle seems to be this: A man desiring
> to understand the world looks about for a clue to its
> comprehension. He pitches upon some area of
> common-sense fact and tries if he cannot understand other

> areas in terms of this one. The original area becomes then
> his basic analogy or root metaphor. He describes as best
> he can the characteristics of this area, or, if you will,
> discriminates its structure. A list of its structural
> characteristics becomes his basic concepts of explanation
> and description. (1942:91)

Pepper is here speaking of philosophies of life or world views
more than root metaphors in the stricter sense of those paradigms which govern inquiry within any particular domain. Yet
other scholars who focus specifically on scientific inquiry have
said very similar things. Kuhn, for example, drawing on both
experimental psychology as well as the history of science,
suggests that "something like a paradigm is prerequisite to
perception itself. What a man sees depends both upon what he
looks at and also upon what his previous visual-conceptual
experience has taught him to see. In the absence of such training there can only be, in William James' phrase, "bloomin'
buzzin' confusion'."[22] Kuhn then extends this image of perception to refer to the paradigm as "a way of seeing," and the
switch from one paradigm to another as a "reseeing."

The illustrative metaphor that Kuhn uses in this connection
is the ambiguous Gestalt figure, or the experience of the subject when he suddenly "sees" the counterpossible figure.[23]
Kuhn's metaphor is a weak one, however, on several counts.
First, a paradigm is neither like one side of a Gestalt figure
nor the other, for each side taken as the whole of the figure
is simply a representation of a mundane object, which is much
less than a paradigm. Second, if we think of the figure as
ambiguous, this directs us away from the clarity, cogency, and
consistency that the paradigm brings to our inquiry. Third, the
Gestalt figure suggests that no deliberate effort is made on the
part of the perceiver and that the perception is not corrigible
to further reflection. This is truer of optical illusions than of
paradigm innovations. But in terms of Kuhn's Gestalt metaphor,
both are described as an equilibrium of stimuli within a comprehensive whole. This leaves no place for the intentional consciousness of the paradigm inventor. Finally, the Gestalt figure
of its nature is not susceptible to elaboration, which is one of
the hallmarks of a root metaphor; whereas extension and intensification of metaphor bring out hidden meanings and enrich
the system of implications, such action on a Gestalt figure inevitably tips it toward one interpretation or the other.

What Kuhn must be getting at then – or in any case what *we* mean by root metaphor or paradigm – is not its aspect as a psychic or physical entity, but *its use as a perspective from which to view something else.* The metaphor lies not in the thing seen, as the Gestalt analogy suggests, but in the stance of the see-er, his standing within one picture, so to speak, in order to attain a certain vision of another. A paradigm switch is thus similar to a switch in standpoints, although a word like "stand-frame" would be more correct.

This concept of root metaphor also tells us something about the difference between a problem and a mystery. To the extent that sociology is a problem-solving activity, the paradigm provides both the vocabulary for defining problems and the tools for solving them. That which falls outside of the paradigm is a mystery; a *reduction* to the terms of the paradigm can thus be a "profanation of the mystery" in a very real sense. The job of normal science, then, is to elaborate the root metaphor, to unravel its implications and apply it to each new domain it suggests, and to formulate its implications into broader and more economical theory. In scientific revolutions, on the other hand, new pradigms are found which de-mystify the mystery without profaning its character.

But mysteries also can arise from *within* a paradigm. As such they confront the investigator as an insolent guest: the un-welcomed finding, the all-too-true result, the awkward fact, the logical absurdity, the self-contradiction, the insoluable prob-lem of which the paradigm has guaranteed a solution. Such anomalies can be pushed back outside the scope of the metaphor, or they can be reduced to the metaphor's terms. But the further the metaphor is elaborated the more likely such anomalies will occur. This is the master irony of normal science, and to have pointed it out is Kuhn's most original contribution. As Master-man notes, all previous philosophers of science

> had blamed the gradual collapse of various scientific
> theories on the fact that they were eventually falsified in
> experience by, say, the emergence of new facts; i.e., on
> the non-cooperation, as it were, of nature. None had
> blamed it on the fact that theories, since they have to have
> concrete analogical paradigms at the heart of them to define
> their basic commitments, and since the effects of these
> paradigms is drastically to restrict their fields, collapse,
> when extended too far, by their own make-up; without any
> necessary accentuating irritation from nature at all.
> (1970:84)

Kuhn makes another point that, with some modification, is useful to us here. In the emergence and transformation of a science, he says, there is a preparadigm stage, then the crystallization of a dominant paradigm and with it the beginning of normal science and, finally, scientific revolutions in which the paradigm is overthrown. We amend this view with two qualifications. First, Kuhn's assertion that science begins with the emergence of a dominant paradigm also implies the reverse — that there are no dominant paradigms without the development of science. In sociology, at least, this is patently false. The organic, and later the mechanical, metaphor guided description of social phenomena long before the systematic empirical elaboration of this metaphor became institutionalized in what today is known as social science. Thus, it seems that the existence of a dominant paradigm is a necessary but not sufficient condition.

Second, while Kuhn shows how the agreement on a root metaphor can make its elaboration much more focused and efficient, he overstates the necessity of this for the emergence of science. Sociology (like other sciences) is, in fact, a multiparadigm enterprise, an arena in which a cluster of contrary or related metaphors compete for hegemony, each of them powerful, well articulated, and capable of translating most of the conceptual vocabulary of the others into its own. Such a state of affairs may go on indefinitely, but one may expect it to end with the metaphors declaring their autonomy of perspective, so to speak, and each establishing its own disciplinary domain. Conversely, a new metametaphor may emerge which incorporates the others, resolves their anomalies, takes over, and becomes for a time uniparadigm normal science.

The great archetypal metaphor in sociology is that society is, or is like, an organism. The following subsection is a treatment of that metaphor. But as one metaphor can be reinterpreted only from the perspective of another, so our critique of organicism in sociology is undertaken from the viewpoint of mechanism. Mechanism (or positivism), the metaphor of society as a machine, will then be dealt with in terms of still other root metaphors that have emerged under the inspiration of American pragmatism and European existentialism and phenomenology. These more contemporary metaphors, discussed in the final sections, are social conduct as language, as drama, and as a game. After treating all five of these root metaphors we will assess the chances for the last three to combine into a dominant paradigm for sociological thought.

Organicism

The education of the human race, represented by the people of God, has advanced, like that of an individual, through certain epochs, or, as it were, ages, so that it might gradually rise from earthly to heavenly things, and from the visible to the invisible.
Augustine

New, higher relations of production never appear before the material conditions of their existence have matured in the womb of the old society.
Marx

The thesis which I venture to sustain . . . is that the savage state in some measure represents an early condition of mankind, out of which the higher culture has gradually developed or evolved, by processes still in regular operation as of old.
Tylor

Everytime we undertake to explain something human, taken at a given moment in history – be it a religious belief, a moral precept, a legal principle, an esthetic style, or an economic system – it is necessary to go back to its most primitive and simple form, to try to account for the characterization by which it was marked at that time, and then to show how it developed and became complicated little by little, and how it became that which it is at the moment in question.
Durkheim

If one goes back to a primitive society, one finds the beginnings of the evolution of what we call "institutions." Now these institutions are, after all, the habits of individuals . . . handed down from one generation to another. And we can study the growth of these habits as we can study the growth and behavior of an animal.
Mead

Although spanning many centuries, these fundamental statements all express the idea that society is, or is like, an organism. Society is a bounded system, the telos of which is self-maintenance, or survival, and growth. The life of society is divided into stages; the characteristics of later stages are contained in the embryo of earlier stages; the process of unfolding is slow and gradual; contemporary "savages" represent in some measure an earlier stage of contemporary higher culture; the nature of anything human is imminent in the characteristics of its most primitive and simple form. In the dominant version of organicism, society is compared to the individual biological entity. However, in social Darwinism and some other conflict theories, the comparison is not to the single organism but to the biological species; here the imagery is one of competition between members and survival, or dominance, of the fittest.

This biological image of society is so deeply rooted that scholars often fail to recognize it as the central presupposition of their own social thought. But recognized or not, the metaphor can be seen in the substructure of the vast majority of Western theories of social order and change.[24] The seminal statement of this metaphor is Aristotle's and, as most later theorists borrowed from his formulation, we would do well to consider it first.[25]

In previous Greek speculation Aristotle could discern two poles: change and becoming; the material and efficient causes of the Ionians, versus the permanence, being, or form of Plato. Aristotle unified these notions in his concept of form *as* the final cause. The material cause of the atomists is incapable of explaining the *why* of becoming, he says, for it lacks that which the concept of becoming itself makes intelligible: the unity of the thing that becomes a whole. Those who see form as the only reality, however, cannot explain how this reality came to be, and so treat the form as eternal and everything else as illusion, and hence tell us nothing of the world. Thus for Aristotle genuine wholeness must be the product of becoming, but at the same time it cannot be the mere aggregation of parts. Instead, a true whole, that is, an individual exemplifying a natural species or class, emerges only where all parts are guided by a single purpose and strive to realize it.

> Natural things are exactly those things which do move
> continuously, in virtue of the principle inherent in
> themselves, towards a determined goal; and the final
> development which results from any one such principle
> is not identical for any two species, nor yet is it any
> random result; but in each there is always a tendency
> towards an identical result if nothing interferes.
> (*Physics*, II, viii)

Aristotle goes on to assert that if "natural things are exactly those things which do move continuously," then "unnatural"

things must be those which do not. The natural and the unnatural thus are distinguished by the criterion of regularity of
occurrence and, indeed, he asserts that this distinction must be
made *before* a scientific investigation of a thing can be undertaken.[26]

This method and metaphor are then applied to politics and
society. Men and women unite "because of natural instinct to
leave behind one of their own kind, and of the desire for self-
sufficiency." From this self-generated union come families,
clans, *gens, phratres,* and, eventually, city-states. The city-state
is thus the end of a natural, regular teleological evolution. It is
a species, a good, the fulfillment of man's nature as a political
animal. Not all peoples have reached this state of self-realiza-
tion, it is true. But Aristotle's theory is concerned with the
natural process of development, not with accidents or monstrosi-
ties. Not all acorns become oaks. In each particular case this
depends on local conditions of soil, climate, and the like. However, it is for this reason that in order to understand oaks or
anything else as a general class or species, science must focus
on their ideal development, that is, what they become "if
nothing interferes." Thus there are some things that simply
are not suited for scientific investigation (such as the "accidental" events of history), and even with proper scientific subjects (such as the *polis*), any occurrence that cannot be
associated with the unfolding of that thing's telic potential must
be treated as an "accident" and excluded from scientific study.

For Aristotle, then, these are the main components of the
organic metaphor:

1. Natural things, the proper subjects for science, are those
that change according to the law of their nature or telos, as
opposed to that which happens by chance, which is outside the
realm of science.

2. Even in the development of natural things, there can occur
accidental events; these also lie outside the scientific study of
that thing.

3. Change is natural, slow, regular, continuous, purposive,
directional, necessary, and self-generated. *Natura non facit
saltum;* nature does not make leaps.

4. Differences between examples of a natural class of things
can be explained in terms of their being in different phases of
the same evolutionary patterns. That is, the more primitive
examples have either started later or have been arrested in
their development by some impediment. Hence contemporary

primitive societies reveal what contemporary advanced societies were like at an earlier stage of growth.

At this point it may legitimately be asked, "So what?" Haven't the procedures of Aristotelian evolutionists like Comte and Spencer been "thoroughly discredited," as Howard Becker puts it, and hence may they not "be dismissed without further ado?" Could it not be said that even "by 1920 evolutionism in the social sciences was completely defunct?" (both quotations cited by Bock, 1956). Our answer to these questions is a resounding "No!" Indeed, we suggest that much of sociological theorizing continues to employ precisely the metaphor that supposedly was laid to rest many years ago. As evidence of this we will examine the work of the functionalist Talcott Parsons, the Chicago sociologist Robert Park, and retrospectively, the social Darwinist William Sumner.

In Parsons's view society is seen as a class or species, which must perform certain functions in order to maintain itself; these are system goal attainment, system pattern maintenance, system adaptation, and tension management. These functions are carried out by institutions, which are composed of roles, which are filled by individuals motivated by internalized cultural norms and values that help legitimize and hold the system together. Thus group action is regarded as an extrapolation of the social system, and individual action is treated as the expression of the individual's internalized role within the group. Action at each level is conceived as the outward expression of such elements as cultural demands, social norms, or institutional stresses of the next higher level. Interest is focused not on the social action itself, but only on selected aspects of interaction *insofar as they reflect the social system as a whole* (Parsons, 1951:29, 205). The social system – presupposed to have neat boundaries, integrated interdependency of parts, and telic goals – is not composed of individual people, but rather of social roles (Parsons and Shils, 1951:197). Variables such as "function" or "strain" are used to explain other variables such as "role performance" or "deviance."

This stress on functions does not exclude the possibility of explaining system change:

> If theory is *good theory* . . . there is no reason whatever to believe that it will not be *equally* applicable to the problems of change and to those of process within a stabilized system. (Parsons, 1951:535)

> At the most general theoretical levels, there is no difference
> between processes which serve to maintain a system and
> those which serve to change it. (Parsons, 1966a:21)

Yet in Parsons's major writings there is little to suggest that, as
the opposite of homeostatic stability, "change" could be anything
other than evolutionary biological growth.[27] Even in his explicit
treatment of change in *Societies: Evolutionary and Comparative
Perspectives*, Parsons stays well within the organic frame. Like
Greek and Christian scholars, eighteenth-century "moderns,"
and nineteenth-century champions of progress, Parsons suggests
that "human society" has generally passed through the primitive, intermediate, and modern stages. This is not merely a
logical taxonomy, any more than it was for Spencer or Comte.
On the contrary, the logical series is identified with "sociocultural evolution," which, "like organic evolution, has pro-
ceeded by variation and differentiation from simple to pro-
gressively more complex forms." Parsons's key explanatory
concept in this treatment is the "evolutionary universal . . .
[a] criterion derived from the famous principle of natural
selection."

This type of thinking also appears in "Full Citizenship for
the Negro American?" in which Parsons applies functional
evolutionism to a problem closer to home. The highest norm of
the American community, says Parsons, is full citizenship for
all members in the form of legal, political, and social inclusion.
"These three principal components of the citizenship complex
seem to constitute not only a rough temporal series, but also
a type of hierarchy." In applying this hierarchy to the history
of Negro *ex*clusion, Parsons first examines the origins of the
United States to discover there its natural direction of development. Although the first settlers were Anglo-Saxon, white, and
Protestant, there were enough sects, Catholics, and Jews present
to insure a pattern of toleration and eventual inclusion of
minorities. However, the realization of this central value of the
American creed was to be restrained by other values such as
federalism, with its permissive attitude toward local irregu-
larities, and private property, which tended to engender suspicion of government programs, particularly those seeking to
limit slavery. Moreover, equality for the Negro had to wait
until the system had absorbed other more easily assimilable
peoples: Slavs, Latins, and Jews from Europe. Beyond these
"always-present" factors of resistance," other events also slowed

down Negro progress. The Great Depression, World War II, the Cold War, and McCarthyism kept the Negro's case from the center of the public stage. Now that the civil rights movement has launched him on his deserved path, other events – black extremism, the Vietnam war – might again shove him off. Thus in a classical Aristotelian fashion, Parsons's model is one of gradual evolution toward the realization of goals that were found in the original nature of the entity under study.

In all such views, certain basic functions are seen as part of the "nature of society," that is, as part of its essential definition as a class. Hence these functions tend to be elevated to a status ontologically superior to that of the specific actions within specific societies which they are intended to explain. From a mechanistic viewpoint, this is a central weakness of the biological metaphor in that, just because of this dissociation of function and action, the functions tend not to be defined in terms of empirically observable conduct. The result is that while the concept of function or need can be invoked to explain certain behavior, the function cannot be known to have occurred independently of and antecedent to that same behavior. The occurrence of the dependent variable thus becomes the indicator for invoking the "explanatory" variable, thus providing no more than a redundant label for what was originally observed.

For example, Parsons attributes differences between societies to differences in their evolutionary levels or rates of growth, or to the intervention of "accidental obstacles" to this "natural development." But how is the *process* of evolution known except through the specific *events* for which it presumably accounts? Conversely, if intervening obstacles are dismissed as "accidental" (i.e., with no predictable pattern or regularity), how can they be accounted for in a scientific formulation? The explanatory variables are thus not amenable to observation *except* through the events they supposedly explain.

If we avoid accounting for differences between societies by rates of evolution or accidental obstacles, however, the unexplained differences would seem to violate Parsons's initial assumption of universal system needs. For, if the needs, goals or functions are universal, why are these not met through universal means, structures, and institutions? There are two principal ways functionalists have dealt with this problem: by positing various functional alternatives to the originally anticipated structures (Linton, 1964:253–287) or by referring to dysfunctions or deviance. If a given social practice serves the posited need or value, it is deemed functional; if it does not it is regarded as dysfunctional or deviant. Again, however, there is the problem of clarifying and operationalizing the concept of function in the first place so that it is observable independently of and antecedent to the structure to be explained. Without such clear operational definitions the concepts "functional," "alternative function," "dysfunctional," or "deviant" have no predictive power and instead become ex post facto classification devices, employed variously depending on which "higher" function has been posited. Moreover, to avoid arbitrariness in determining which higher function some social practice is supposed to serve (or inhibit), functionalists have posited numerous vague and conflicting hierarchies of needs or values of society as a whole.

This a priori reification of the concepts dysfunction and deviance can be understood, in Aristotelian terms, as a labeling of certain events as impediments that interfere with the natural functioning of the social system: "Deviance is a motivated tendency for an actor to behave in contravention of one of the more institutionalized patterns" (Parsons, 1951:250). Motivated, however, by what? (Koch, 1941; Bindra, 1959). If the source of the deviance were within the social system itself, the a priori assumption of system stability would be violated. Hence appeal is made to accidental external factors, for – if we understand deviance to be something *people* do – we are assured that the "personalities of the members are exogenous of the social system." The individuals composing the society or group thus become carriers or media for the expression of the operative endogenous functions, variables, or needs; stability remains a kind of biological homeostasis, a harmonious interfunctioning of the social parts.

Parsons and other functionalists, of course, have discussed the mechanisms by which a society moves from one species or stage to another. Wilbert Moore, for example, suggests that socialization is likely to produce more variation than uniformity. He also points to looseness of role specification, population growth, scarcities of desired goods, and conflicts of norms that, even in highly integrated systems, can be inherent sources of strain and transformation. Similarly, Merton has noted that "by focusing on dysfunctions as well as functions, this approach can assess not only the bases of social stability but the potential sources of change. . . . The stresses and strains in a social structure which accumulate as dysfunctional consequences of existing elements . . . will in due course lead to institutional breakdown and basic social change" (1957:40).

Still, how do we know what is dysfunctional and what is not? How can we identify an institutional breakdown or say that a new social system has emerged? How can we determine the most likely time, and the most probable rate, of social change? As in Aristotle's formulation, the answers to these questions can only be extrapolated from the nature of the beast itself – the social system – which was posited a priori in the first place. This is because all possible sources of change are either *inherent and imminent in the system itself or accidental events that lie outside it.* Thus, as Bock points out (1963:223), the functionalist/evolutionists are in the dilemma of being able to explain change only by violating their assumption of system homeostasis, and of being able to explain stability only by abusing their notion of the immanence of evolutionary growth.

In *Race and Culture* Robert E. Park also makes use of the organic metaphor. Park's famous "cycle of race relations" sees minority groups moving from contract to competition, accommodation, and assimilation. As Lyman has shown (1968; 1974) Park did not undertake any full-scale historical investigations of particular ethnic groups to see whether their histories fit this cycle. But indeed, according to the "comparative method" of his theory, it was not necessary that he should. Once the logical series was posited as a temporal one, any data on race relations could simply be slotted into the evolutionary scale. By knowing the stage of race relations at any given moment he could also know its future and its past. For, as with the acorn and the embryo, so the seed of assimilation is contained in conflicts of race. Thus Park wrote:

> It does not follow that because the tendencies to the
> assimilation and eventual amalgamation of races exists,
> they should not be resisted and, if possible, altogether
> inhibited. On the other hand, it is vain to underestimate
> the character and force of the tendencies that are drawing
> the races and peoples about the Pacific into the
> ever-narrowing circle of a common life. (1950:151)

Thus tendencies will draw the cycle on *even if* in practice these tendencies should be altogether inhibited! This is no paradox, of course, if we recall the doctrine of impediments, the accidental obstacles that may fall in the path of a thing's natural development. Indeed, Park and his students were quite aware of these obstacles. One "impediment" with which Park was particularly concerned was race prejudice: "People we know intimately we respect and esteem. In our casual contacts with aliens, however, it is the offensive rather than the pleasing traits that impress us. These impressions accumulate and reinforce natural prejudices" (1950:209, 230–243).

But while calling them "natural," Park dismisses these prejudices as though they were accidents in the Aristotelian sense. The fruit of such an analysis "is then presented as an analytic statement of what *must* happen, rather than a 'merely empirical' generalization of what *did* happen" (Bock, 1937: 237). Park thus never feels compelled to articulate the relationship between social organization, ethnic interaction, and prejudice as it is enacted in specific historical settings, thereby cutting off sociological analysis just where it should have begun (Lyman, 1968:18).

The organic metaphor thus has difficulties of both intension and extension – it tends to be circular in logic and unfalsifiable by experimental procedures. Despite this, however, it still retains enormous power and economy. It explains complex social processes in terms of biological ones that appear to be more familiar and more easily understood. Yet, as we have seen, the very acceptance and systematic elaboration of the metaphor has uncovered some of its internal contradictions and external limits. For example, in the organic metaphor we would expect the natural state or tendency of societies to be toward homeostasis; yet this would seem to challenge an equally natural tendency toward evolution. Conversely, as an external limit, we find that neither homeostatic nor evolutionary explanations give an adequate account of revolution.

William Graham Sumner provides a final example of how theorists may deal with such difficulties. In *Folkways* (1906:86) Sumner discusses revolutions from the standpoint of the evolutionary perspective. He assumes that revolutions are caused by the carryover from an earlier period of mores that have not properly evolved. Thus "In revolutions the mores are broken up." Yet Sumner seems aware of a contradiction, for he holds that "dogmas do not make mores"; revolutions, although they break down mores, cannot reconstruct a new set through their dogmas. Because of this reasoning he assumes that the old mores must inevitably reassert themselves, and with their reassertion the old ruling classes regain control and "set the society in its old grooves again." Revolution is made a chimera by counterrevolution; mores are created by evolution and only through evolution can they change. Revolutions are "explained" by being reduced to gradual change. What we see here is a theorist who has taken his metaphor to be literally true, an idolatry that, in this case, profanes the mystery of revolutionary change.

Mechanism

The first great crack in the organic metaphor came in the sixteenth and seventeenth centuries with the work of Galileo, Newton, Bacon, and Descartes. Life went out of nature. Physical imagery replaced that of the organism. Nature, and soon man and society, was seen as a machine. One of the first explicit transfers of mechanical thinking to the human realm is found in Hobbes' *Leviathan*:

> For seeing life is but a motion of limbs, the beginning
> whereof is in some principal part within; why may we not
> say, that all *automata* (engines that move by springs and
> wheels as doth a watch) have artificial life? For what is
> the *heart*, but a spring; and the *nerves*, but so many
> strings; and the *joints*, but so many wheels, giving motion
> to the whole body, such as was intended by the artificer.
> (1957:5)

This tradition was continued in philosophical radicalism, which Bentham defined "as nothing but an attempt to apply the principles of Newton to the affairs of politics and morals" (quoted by Matson, 1966:18). Such ideas were so widespread that they even found expression in the works of such dialectical thinkers as Marx and Freud. Invoking the model of physics, Marx claims to represent "the economic law of motion of modern society" as a natural law. In the preface to the second edition of *Capital* (Vol. 1) he quotes with approval the methodological assessment of a Russian reviewer:

> Marx seeks to demonstrate through precise scientific
> investigation the necessity of definite orders of social
> relations and to register as irreproachably as possible the
> facts that serve him as points of departure and
> confirmation . . . Marx considers the movement of
> society . . . as governed by laws that are not only
> independent of the will, consciousness, and intention
> of men but instead, and conversely, determine their will,
> consciousness, and intentions. (1946:16–17)

Equally startling is Freud's early "Project for a Scientific Psychology," the goal of which was "to furnish us with a psychology which shall be a natural science; ... to present psychical processes as quantitatively determined states of specifiable material particles and so to make them plain and void of contradiction" (1954:355). While neo-Marxists and neo-Freudians have revised these early metaphors, they persist with little change in the forms of behaviorist psychology and physicalistic sociology. As Karl Lashley puts it, "The essence of behaviorism is the belief that the study of man will reveal nothing except what is adequately describable in the concepts of mechanics and chemistry" (1923).

As we have seen, one of the epistemological ideals of this way of thinking is "objectivity," the ultimate expression of which would be machines measuring other machines. If this ideal cannot be achieved in full, it at least may be approximated by trying to *see* man as a subhuman entity and imagining oneself into the role of a recording device. The result of course is the highly controlled experiment with monkeys, pigeons, and rats. "Personally," says Tolman, "I am suspicious of ... verbal reports. I prefer to try to work out psychology with the aid of more gross forms of behavior. My motto for the present is: 'Rats, no men'" (1932). Tolman then goes on to make a surprisingly candid remark – given his commitment to objectivism – concerning the metaphoric style of his thought:

> [In planning and analyzing my rat experiments] I am openly ... casting concepts into a mould such that one can derive from one's own human, everyday experience. These hunches may then, later, be translated into objective terms. ... In my future work [I] intend to go ahead imagining how, *if I were a rat*, I would behave. ... And then eventually I shall try to state [the rules so derived] in some kind of objective and respectable sounding terms such as vectors, valences, barriers, and the like. (1938:24)

Tolman's formulation has been attacked, not only by nonmechanists, but also by other behaviorists who insist he has not gone far enough, in that he still implies a logical priority to consciousness and imagining, and "reduces" the rats upward to a humanlike status, when the whole point is to reduce humans, through the rat, to the model of machine. Thus, echoing Hobbes, Clark Hull states:

> One aid to the attainment of behavioral objectivity is to think in terms of the behavior of subhuman organisms,

such as chimpanzees, monkeys, dogs, cats, and albino rats. Unfortunately this form of prophylaxis against subjectivism all too often breaks down when the theorist begins thinking what he would do if he were a rat, a cat, or a chimpanzee. . . .

A device much employed by the author has proved itself to be a far more effective phrophylaxis. This is to regard, from time to time, the behaving organism as a *completely self-maintaining robot,* constructed of materials as unlike ourselves as may be. (1952:27, our italics)

Although his imagery normally is biological, Talcott Parsons also speaks of the "social system" in mechanical terms:

[There are] four fundamental generalizations for defining the equilibrium of a social system in terms of "four-dimensional space."

1. The Principles of Inertia: A given process of action will continue unchanged in rate and direction unless impeded or deflected by opposite motivational forces.
2. The Principle of Action and Reaction: If, in a system of action, there is a change in the direction of a process, it will be balanced by a complementary change which is equal in motivational force and opposite in direction.
3. The Principle of Effort . . .
4. The Principle of System-Integration . . . (1953:102)

In all these writings, through the medium of "operationism," abstract or ideal concepts are translated into discrete units of data. The subject and object are both collapsed into the operations of measurement. The recipe, in effect, defines the cake, regardless of who baked it and how it might taste (Lundberg, *et al.,* 1954:34). Thus Binet defines intelligence as what is measured by intelligence tests (1969). Chapin operationally defines social status in terms of a social status scale (1935). Rileys *et al.* see scales as providing "empirical representations of certain sociological concepts" (1954:7). Similar operational instruments are found in Bogardus's social distance scale, Thurstone's social attitude scale, Guttman's scalogram analysis, and the various ordinal measuring devices invented by Guttman and Lazarsfeld (Sjoberg, 1959:606; Douglas, 1971b; Gabaglio, 1888:1–36; Collins and Makowsky, 1972:219).

The home of the mechanical metaphor – the domain from which it is borrowed – is, of course, physics; and as the vocabulary of physics has changed so has that of physicalistic social

scientists. The simple levers and inclined planes of Galileo have
given way to the dynamo, electromagnetism, and the computer.
Thus, for example, in his effort to establish "A Basis for Social
Physics," Stewart incorporates electrical and molecular language:

> Our immediate quest is for uniformities in social behavior
> which can be expressed in mathematical forms more or less
> corresponding to the known patterns of physical science.
> Social physics so defined analyzes . . . sociological
> situations in terms of purely physical factors: time,
> distance, mass of material, and number of people, with
> recourse also to social factors which can be shown to
> operate in a similar way to two other physical agents,
> namely, temperature and electrical charge. . . . Social
> physics describes mass human aggregations of individuals
> as though they were composed of "social molecules" –
> without attempting to analyze the behavior of each
> molecule. (1952:110, 118)

Jacob Moreno carries the comparison one step further, or
lower, referring not to molecules but to "the social atom" as
"the smallest nucleus of an emotionally toned interpersonal
pattern in the social universe" (1946:229). Given the "lag"
between the source of such metaphors in physics and their use
in sociology, we await the discovery soon of social protons,
neutrons, and neutrinos.

A crucial test of the power of a metaphor is whether its
opponents wind up using it themselves. Thus, as we saw, the
functionalists who criticized the biological thinking of the evolutionists went on to establish a theory of social order that was
itself biological in conception. Similarly, many who have railed
against mechanism went on to develop their own mechanistic
theories. Thus, one can find social atomists accusing electricians
of mechanism, only to be accused of mechanism themselves by
social engineers. The revolt against atomism in psychology is a
good example of such a debate between submetaphors of the
same dominant root. Thus much of early Gestalt psychology
is clearly mechanistic. Kohler, for instance, insists that mental
facts are patterns or configurations that cannot properly be
reduced to atomistic elements (1947). Yet his conception of
the Gestalt pattern is itself couched in terms of electromagnetic
fields that are considered to be the physiological correlates of
these mental facts.

Kurt Lewin, who insists that he is doing away with metaphoric thinking, uses consolidated field physics as his metaphor of interaction. "We have tried," he says, "to avoid developing elaborate 'models'; instead we have tried to represent the dynamic relations between the psychological facts by mathematical constructs at a sufficient level of generality" (1951:21). Lewin then goes on to develop a (non-?) model of the "field of psychological activities" after the image of physical and geometrical space. Terms such as direction, vector, magnitude, distance, continuity and discontinuity, field, phase-space, tension, boundary fluidity, and force abound in his writings. All are transfers from an alien domain of discourse, but the borrowing has become so habitual that social mechanists tend to forget the interest on their debt.[28]

There is yet another mechanical metaphor, one more recent and subtle than those so far discussed. This is the description of human thought and conduct in terms of the operations of a computer. Here we must be careful to distinguish mathematical models from computer models. Mathematics traditionally has been the language of physics and, as such, the use of mathematical description often has been confused with physicalism or mechanism per se. While many materialists do employ a mathematical (or pseudo-mathematical) vocabulary, mathematics is itself a metaphoric system, independent of the machines, organisms, behavior, or whatever it may be used to describe.[29] As a system of purely formal relations, mathematics tends to be the choice metaphor for those wishing to describe the purely formal relations of any other realm of discourse, including that of machines. Yet it is important to note that mathematics and computers are not interchangeable realms. Indeed, in the very differences between the two lie the particular usefulness of computer modeling. As Hoggatt and Balderston (1963) have explained, computers make possible a degree of complexity in simulations that cannot be achieved through mathematics alone. And, of course, the greater the complexity of the model then the greater the possible degree of isomorphism between the computer iterations and the domain that the model is for. The logic involved, roughly, is to create a computer program that is structurally parallel to the known formal relations of that which is being modeled. The computer can then elaborate and extrapolate submetaphors that may be implicit in the initial set of structural relations. This can lead to new insights into the nature of that which is being modeled or, conversely, into the nature of the computer program. Thus, for example, in one model of a business firm long delivery delays appearing in the computer output made the analysts realize they had failed to account for the loss of customers due to such delays (Cohen and Cyert, 1965, Chapter 8). If isomorphism is achieved for areas of the business firm that are easily knowable, confidence is then increased that the model will be a good predictor or analog of areas that are less easily known – for example, marketing futures, savings on alternative production arrangements, and the like.

It should be clear that our purpose in undressing these metaphors is not to deplore metaphoric thinking, or even to criticize these particular metaphors as inadequate. However, once it is understood that they *are* metaphors, their relative adequacy in light of other possible metaphors may be more clearly seen.[30] Mechanism is a good place from which to see the tautological nature of much biologistic thinking. Conversely, the biological metaphor is more able to deal with immanent factors, intentionality, and transmogrification of a system than mechanism. Similarly, features peculiar to both these metaphors can be limned by light from the humanistic perspective. This is especially true when the same example is used to illustrate opposite points, thereby highlighting fundamental differences in the ways in which both conduct and knowledge are defined in each metaphor. For instance, Lazarsfeld and Barton speak of objective social science reporting:

> The reader who is unfamiliar with draft-horse judging
> will be aware that these are hardly instructions which
> anyone could follow and come to the same judgments; the
> rules work only where there is a common body of
> understanding as to what is meant by the various terms
> and what represents good and bad characteristics.
> *Nonetheless*, the adoption of this segmentation results
> in agreement within one or two points between experienced
> raters using the full hundred-point scale. (1951:167,
> our italics)

By reducing humans to horses, this illustrative metaphor underlines the assumptions that social actors have no view of their own conduct or that, if they do, it is sociologically irrelevant. Compare this with Charles Horton Cooley's comments on sympathetic understanding in "The Roots of Social Knowledge":

> There is, no doubt, a way of knowing people with whom
> we do not sympathize which is essentially external or
> animal in character. An example of this is the practical but

wholly behavioristic knowledge that men of much sexual experience sometimes have of women, or women of men – something that involves no true participation in thought and feeling. . . . Put rather coarsely, *a man sometimes understands a woman as he does a horse*; not by sharing her psychic processes, but by watching what she does. There is, in fact, a complete series in our knowledge of persons, from the purely external, like our knowledge of babies, of idiots, of the wildly insane, up through all grades to the completely internal or sympathetic, as when, in reading a meditative writer like Marcus Aurelius, we know his consciousness and nothing else. . . . There is no good reason to think that . . . statistical methods can anticipate that which, after all, chiefly distinguishes human life from physical processes, namely, originative mental synthesis. (1926:65, 77, our italics).

This assumption of originative mental synthesis is the unifying presupposition of the three metaphors we will treat below: the understanding of conduct as language, as drama, and as a game.

Language

One of the more recent developments in sociological thought is the view of social action as a kind of language. Indeed, this is the root metaphor underpinning at least three major schools: symbolic interactionism, ethnomethodology, and European structuralism. Practitioners of these schools differ in stressing either the iconic or the analogic side of their paradigm. Some understand language in a broad iconic sense to be any system of expression or communication by signs. Conventional, verbal language in this view is one such system of expression; but other "languages" also exist in the form of gestural communication, facial expressions, and moves in business or in war, art, ritual, and so on. Conventional language thus becomes one language among many, and language, in the broad sense, is seen as constitutive of (social) reality. Epistemologically, this view comes closer to what we discussed in Chapter 2 as symbolic realism.

A more limited, analogic use of the metaphor defines language in the narrow sense, as the grammatics, semantics, and pragmatics of speech. In this usage, other areas of behavior – gesture, ritual, and the like – are seen as being *like* language but not as languages themselves. Epistemologically, this view is more compatible with phenomenal and positivist notions of reality and truth in that language, as a symbol system, is distinguished from what is real or concrete.[31]

These two poles, however, are more analytic than descriptive, for many writers do not take a clear position with reference to them. For example, symbolic interactionists insist that "symbolic interaction is the fundamental datum in the approach of sociology to human conduct. It is the process from which all sociocultural patterns emerge, therefore it is the bench mark or – at least implicit – point of departure for all sociological analysis" (McKinney, 1970:236–237). But this, characteristically, is ambiguous, for it implies an ontological distinction between the fundamental data – which are symbolic – and emergent sociocultural patterns that are "real." Similarly, W. I. Thomas' dictum that "Situations that men define as real are real in their consequences" suggests a distinction between real consequences and unreal definitions. Erving Goffman's distinction between masks and selves is equally ambiguous but in an opposite sense: For Goffman the emergent selves seem to be less real than the symbolic masks.

In addressing such questions, ethnomethodologists, inspired by existential phenomenology, generally have opted for the broader, more radical use of the metaphor of language. Aaron Cicourel highlights this when he distinguishes ethnomethodological from linguistic approaches to language: "For the linguist the meaning of speech becomes fairly restricted; it is tied to the establishment of relationships and reference in speech through the use of formal types of reasoning that seeks to produce determinate outcomes. For the ethnomethodologist *talk and action are produced and understood as indexical displays of the everyday world*" (1974:99, our italics).[32]

The radical symbolic realism implicit here is stated directly by Harold Garfinkel, and in such a way as to include "objective" sociological theorizing itself:

> Let us be clear on this very important point. When we talk
> of "a world" or when we talk of "the world" we are
> talking *of a set of empirical constructs*. These are all of
> the sociologist's world. There is no reality beyond them.
> . . . This holds regardless of whether the empirical
> construct is a scientifically adequate one or not. The
> Judgment Day of the Seventh Day Adventist is as much
> an empirical construct and a specification of the world of

the Seventh Day Adventist as the psychologist's graph with its coordinates of blood sugar level and pancreatic secretion is for the physiologist an empirical portrait of his sympathectomized cats. Hence a construction like "a movement of the arm" or "a gesture of greeting," or "a symptom" is ontologically irreducible. The construction does not describe the world. It *is* the world. The construction is not an approximation to something beyond it; there is no question here of a "pie" that may be cut in many ways, but rather that the pie is found in the act of cutting.

The whole theoretical apparatus that has been elaborated here so far represents in effect a huge naming operation by which the object "a sociologically empirical world" is constituted in its meanings. Like any naming operation that deals with signals, it serves the function of providing the rules by which signals are transformed into perceptions. (1952:351, Garfinkel's italics)[33]

One way to limn the language metaphor is to compare it with other ways of thinking. For example, the very naming of a certain set of phenomena as "mental illness" presupposes an *organic* metaphor. In such a perspective, certain conduct is treated as symptoms of disease or malignancy. In contrast, Thomas Szasz defines the phenomena in the imagery of language. If mental illness were a disease entity, like an infection, says Szasz, "one could *catch* or *get* a mental illness, one might *have* or *harbor* it, one might *transmit* it to others, and finally one could *get rid* of it. . . . On the contrary, all evidence . . . supports the view that what people now call mental illnesses are, for the most part, *communications* expressing unacceptable ideas, often framed in an unusual idiom" (Szasz' italics).

A similar comparison can be made between linguistic and mechanical imagery. In the latter, corpuscles or waves of light strike the retina (the camera) and from there are transmitted to and decoded into certain stimuli by the brain (the telegraph, the computer) to which the body (the machine as a whole) responds. The metaphor of language, however, suggests several questions of "In what respect?" that might be put to the mechanical model of perception and behavior. Who determines what the camera will focus on and when it will take the picture? Who determines what, of that which is perceived, will be considered stimuli and what, of a wide range of possibilities, shall be the response? Is this a "ghost inside the machine?" What about self-reflection? Does the camera take pictures of itself? How does the camera come to be? Are people, like cameras or automatons, manufactured? Moreover, how do we know that the photographs are copies of some original when we have no access to that original except through the photograph? How do we distinguish between information or messages and mere sensa?

The answers to such questions are, of course, just the ones that can be elaborated from the linguistic metaphor. As Dewey, Bentley, and others have told us, we know what something is by its name. It is not a matter of the name *standing for* the thing as in Wittgenstein's early view. Instead, the "thing itself" is emergent in the process of its being named. For example, were I to observe X placing twelve yellow discs in front of Y, I could know that what I have observed is a "bribe," a "gift," or a "payment" only through some process of defining (the meaning of) the situation.[34] But to define the situation, that is, to give it a name, I must know the language. And constitutive of the language is not merely speech, but the entire body as well as anything the body may use as backdrop, setting, or prop. Goffman provides ample illustrations of such nonverbal communications:

> A girl having to pass through a knot of party guests to get to the bathroom employs a broad swimming motion to cut her way through, showing with these strokes that she has not been made bashful by her intent. A middle class, middle-aged man having forgotten a parcel on the counter of a repair store, returns twenty minutes later to retrieve it, breaks into a mock run as he enters the store, and shakes his head, silently broadcasting support of the bad opinion that others present might have of someone like himself who is so forgetful. (1971:135–136)

One test of the view of conduct as language may be made by examining one of its submetaphors: the assumption that behavior – being like, or as, a language – is learned. Hence, a foreigner would not know how to "speak" a given language of behavior; that is, he would not be able to understand the conduct of natives or to make his own conduct intelligible to them. This is seen easily enough in natural languages. For example, someone ignorant of French would not know what *chat* or *chien* meant, even though they might be familiar with cats and dogs. Similarly, an American familiar with "swishy gays" would be mistaken if he read this into males holding hands on the streets in New Delhi. A Westerner familiar with "anger" would not be able to read it in a Chinese's raising his eyebrows; nor would a Chinese read his version of anger in the increasing politeness of an Englishman.

To carry the illustration further, we may imagine a person who knew no *visual* language at all, as for example, a blind person who suddenly gained sight as an adult. The linguistic metaphor of perception would lead us to expect such a person to encounter "a bloomin', buzzin', confusion." And, indeed, in such cases this is exactly what appears to occur. But as he learns the language of visual perception, things begin to "speak" to the newly sighted. A certain array of sensa tells him that "it" is a "chair" and meant to be sat on; that the "cloudiness" says it may rain; that the "smiling" face says it is friendly.

In addition to symbolic interactionism and ethnomethodology, the other major school that takes language as its root metaphor is European Structuralism. This school has two principal antecedents: the social anthropology of Durkheim and Mauss, and the linguistic theories of Ferdinand de Saussure (Doroszewski, 1933). As is well known, Durkheim thought of "social facts" as "things"; yet in each attempt to define these facts more specifically, he found himself reintroducing the *phychical* – as for example, in his concept of "suicide," which depends on the *intention* of the actor. Faced with this paradox, but seeking to prevent sociology from collapsing back into psychology, Durkheim came to see the "facts" as representations not of *individual* intentionality but of a *collective* sense of moral bondedness. This *conscience collectif*, however, was conceived as ontologically autonomous of the conduct that it explained. Although a mainspring of history, it was not itself historical. The sociologist, too, was an absolute observer, standing outside of place and time; and what the analyst lacked in penetration into the inner life of individuals, he made up for in the certainty of his objectivity and logic.

Marcel Mauss, while not rejecting the teachings of his mentor, reveals Durkheim's limitations by going beyond them. The correlations and causal chains yielded through controlled comparison, says Mauss, do not by themselves give a full account. They leave a residue, so to speak, that causal analysis itself does not explain. This is evident enough in Durkheim's work, and such categories as "anomie" or "fatalism," refer to precisely these residues in his theories. Yet, because of the announced positivism of his method, the invocation of such concepts in Durkheim appears inconsistent, and adequate explanation is bought at the price of methodological contradiction.

In contrast, Mauss suggests that we read our way into the phenomenon, entering into it mentally, deciphering it much as we would a text. When we speak of *reading* a text, instead of *observing*, this reflects an implicit understanding that it is not the words as physical entities that is important but their meaning. Similarly, instead of merely observing conduct in its externals, Mauss would have us decipher it. For Mauss this text of behavior is constituted specifically of the exchanges that we enact through our institutions, the systems of reciprocity and equivalence that are expressed in the ways we work, make and use tools, fight wars, secure wives, or rear children (Mauss, 1967). The social fact is no longer an obdurate, concrete reality; instead it has become explicitly *symbolic*; it is a web, or language, of symbols with its own particular grammar and syntax, morphemes, and phonemes.[35]

This formulation resolved some of the difficulties in Durkheim's thought, but it let in others. For, once having grounded social reality in the symbolic, sociologists at the same instant inherited all the problems of symbology and, as the science of its privileged praxis, of linguistics as well. It is at just this moment, in the dialectic of ideas, that Saussure assumes preeminent importance.

As Saussure confronted it, nineteenth-century linguistics was "diachronic," largely a matter of tracing the origins of languages and the histories of words. The present world was "held constant," so to speak, and in light of this constancy it was thought that changes in language could be observed. Yet such study of the becoming of language, insisted Saussure, could never explain its *being*, the essential wholeness and inner logic that makes language comprehensible from one historical moment to the next. Thus Saussure made the seminal distinction between *la langue* and *la parole* – between the structures and forms of expression – as against their changing embodiments in particular acts of speech. *La langue* is constituted of the rules of the game of language, *la parole* of its particular moves; the former is synchronic and normative, the latter diachronic, historical.

Now it is not hard to see the parallel between Saussure's distinction and the distinction Durkheim makes between what is personal, idiosyncratic, and psychological as against the lawlike relationships of social *facts*, relationships that operate independently of the intentions of societies' members. But here the parallel ends. For unlike Saussure, Durkheim sought a concrete foundation for sociology. This led him to reify his concepts: On one hand, he grounds his social facts in a transcendental *conscience collectif*; on the other, just because of its occult nature, the *conscience collectif* can be envoked as an all purpose covering law to explain the meanings of statistics on individual acts.

In contrast, Saussure feels no need to decide this question: "When a science has no immediate recognizable concrete units, then it follows that such units are not really essential to it. In history, for instance, what is the basic unit? The individual, the period, the nation? No one is sure, but what difference does it make? Historical investigations may be pursued without a final decision on this point" (1965:149).

La langue is not granted a transcendental ontological status. But at the same time, neither is it made to refer to some reality outside of language. "The linguistic sign," he says, "unites not a thing and a name, but a concept and an acoustic image" (1965:98). Or, in the words of Jacques Lacan, "Only the relationship of one signifier to another signifier engenders the relationship of signifier to signified" (quoted by Wilden, 1968: 239).

The work of Claude Lévi-Strauss, the leading structural anthropologist, can be appreciated in light of this background. For, in conjoining the thought of Saussure with that of Durkheim and Mauss, Lévi-Strauss found in language the metaphor of structure that he needed to decode the workings of societies. Given two central assumptions – that spoken language is a sign *system* among many possible sign systems, and that sign systems have a hermetic, autoreferential character – the gate is thrown open for a fullblown hermeneutic of culture. Verbal sign systems – such as myths – become, in an obvious way, subjects for a linguistic type of analysis. But in a no less strict sense, so do *non-verbal* systems such as fashion, cooking, table manners, totemism, or kinship.[36] Thus, says Lévi-Strauss,

> marriage rules and systems of kinship are considered a
> kind of language, that is to say, a set of operations
> designed to ensure a certain type of communication
> between individuals and groups. That the "message" is
> here made up of the *women of the group* who *circulate*
> between the clans, dynasties or families (and not as in

language itself by the *words of the group* circulating
between individuals) does not affect the basic identity
of the phenomenon in both cases. (1963:69)

We said earlier that a metaphor informs the new domain of
application as well as the old domain from which it is borrowed. This is no less true in the present instance; for we have
here not only the metaphor of social relations as language, but
also a view of language as a social relation. This may be made
clearer by comparing the view of language of Husserl and
Heidegger as against that of Richards and Ogden. According
to Richards and Ogden, language is divided into three elements:
the symbolic act (of speech, writing, etc.), the meaning content
of that act, and the objective referent that the act and meaning
represent. Such a distinction invites a separation on the epistemological and ontological levels of the scientific and poetic uses
of language. In the first use the objective referent must be described according to certain "scientific" canons. In the second –
poetic – use of language, the referent becomes emotions or
states of feeling. Hence there is a schism between symbol and
reality, between feeling and rationality, between art and emotion as against science and knowledge.

With the downgrading of formalist epistemology, however,
and with the emergence of the philosophic trends discussed in
Chapter 2, such distinctions between cognition and emotion
come to seem less important, if not spurious. Instead, both
feeling *and* thinking, and indeed all acts of consciousness, are
seen as modes of being in the world. The question of what the
symbol refers to is bracketed; instead the problematics of
symbolization and of the constitution of objects intersubjec-
tively in consciousness are brought to the fore.[37]

This type of thinking has its parallels in Saussure's disconnection of the referential and his stress on the reflexive
nature of language. Yet it also casts a strong line to language-
based American sociologies discussed above. For, in light of
Saussurean and phenomenological bracketing, we can see more
deeply into the meaning of the radical empiricism of William
James, a philosophic godfather of symbolic interactionism.
From our new vantage point, the question with reference to
James becomes not "What is the objective world and what is
objective knowledge?" but, instead, "What are the varieties
of objective worlds and of objective ways of knowing?" The
implication and hope of such a perspective is for a theory of
social *realities* – their specifications and properties, their meth-

ods of construction, and their rules for testing and validation. One here is tempted to add also "their consequences for action"; yet this would falsify our point, for the realities or worlds that the sociologist studies are *constituted* of action, in the sense that action can be understood only as expressions of the particular language of that particular world. When the taken-for-granted fact world is thus brought into question, it becomes possible to go beyond Marxist, Weberian, social Durkheimian, or pragmatist theory. Schutz, for example, by differentiating various worlds of knowledge, is able to describe their properties with greater refinement than that provided by Marx's categories of ideology versus science, Weber's worlds of facts versus values, Durkheim's individual and collective representations, or the pragmatist stress on rational and instrumental action. Schutz advances the concept that such categories are drawn from lived experience, but that they can never encompass or exhaust such experience. Other forms of apprehension, such as the world of art, of play, of "being Burmese," or "making it on Wall Street," all have their own cognitive styles, with their own corresponding forms of self, sociality, and time. Each constitutes a world of meaning, a "language" unto itself.[38]

A central problematic here, of course, is that the sociological enterprise itself gets swept into this maelstrom of symbols. As a theory of languages, lived-models or worlds, sociology also must see itself as a kind of language and world, "objective" only in the sense that it has specified the conditions of the experience of "error." Yet the metaphor of language remains seductive because, while denying the possibility of absolute knowledge, or even knowledge with a statistically determinate probability, it at the same time presents a framework within which structure and consciousness, normative science and historical awareness, may be somehow reconciled.

Drama

Another root metaphor of human conduct, drawn like language from conduct itself, is the theater.[39] Like other root metaphors, the application of dramaturgical imagery to social life is often done unreflectingly, as a matter of habit. We speak of social roles, parts, and actors; we assume that "all the world's a stage" without thinking on the nature of "a stage" let alone the meaning of "a world." To gain a more explicit understanding of the limits and use of this metaphor we may ask, as before, in what respects are life and theater alike? Isomorphisms may be sought for numerous aspects of the theater: the author, audience, actors, performances, scripts, parts, and rehearsals; the distinction between real, nontheater selves and fictive characters or parts; and structural properties such as closure, completeness, and plot.

Before proceeding, a caveat is in order. In comparing respects of isomorphism of metaphors and their domains of application, we should remember that root metaphors are most useful when they claim selective isomorphism between domains, instead of an absolute correspondence. And indeed, the suggestiveness of the transfer generally is greater the less it is obvious. The statement, of a woman's hat, "It's a beehive," is a fairly transparent substitution, and hence not too instructive. But to say "The Taj Mahal!" (if that happens to be the *right* metaphor) tells us much more, just because of the indirection and surface strangeness of the juxtaposition. In a similar fashion, the criticisms and qualifications made below not only limit the dramaturgical metaphor; they also may refine it as a source and framework for insights and concepts.[40]

James Edie, in his commentary on Maurice Natanson's essay "Man as an Actor," provides a springboard for our discussion:

> What we in everyday life *lack* and what the actor in a
> stage-play *has* is an *author*. Whereas the existence of a
> play has a completeness, an inevitability, a wholeness . . .
> in its enactment, our own existence lacks these qualities
> altogether. We have no script according to which we can
> live our lives; we are both author and actor at once and it
> is precisely the freedom and openness, the unfinished
> character of our life-action and the unforeseeability of the
> consequences of our actions that distinguishes our
> experienced world of lived-time from that of aesthetic
> imagined time. (1967:225, Edie's italics)

Edie names two respects in which life is different from theater: the lack of an author and, flowing from this, the lack of structure, wholeness, and inevitability of experience. In treating these points, we ask again, in what respect? For example, it seems that in at least one respect our experience of the world is not as incomplete and fragmented as Edie makes it out to be. The very idea of "experience" or "having an experience" presupposes that certain phenomena have been defined as "events" and typified into a "set." A picnic, our trip to France, getting married, mother's operation, *become* experiences to the extent that they are organized in the imagination into beginnings, middles, and ends, or into some other principles of form, cogency, and closure. This can be taken as elemental to consciousness itself, in the sense that humans have "experience," while horses or fish only "live."[41]

Moreover, this same process of typification operates transsituationally, in such a way that we carry with us, so to speak, a stock shelf of predefinitions and structures that we draw on for various occasions. For example, when someone knocks on my door I know by the *cues* (not *clues* as in positive thought) that it is a "salesman" and, given this (as any door-to-door salesman knows) the exchange will proceed with a great deal of inevitability. People, of course, like actors, can "break role" and this is just where savoir faire, ad libbing, and "presence" become strategic. Yet all these respects are still within the terms of the root metaphor.

Now it may be objected that what we have described here is a retrospective, after-the-fact analysis, and that everyday life, as lived from moment to moment, does lack the logical, structural qualities that an aesthetically sensitive audience experiences *during the course* of the play. This point is valid, it seems to us, and it also introduces another refinement. For it is now apparent that the structure or inner logic of which Edie originally spoke can mean only the structure of the play *as perceived by the audience*. It is the onlooker (or the retrospective or prospective looker-on-himself) who perceives structure, and not the fictive actors engaged *within* the drama. But is it not precisely the *social theorist* who is the spectator of social life? Is it not he who can perceive the dramatic in what the actors take as mundane, or the mundane and (overly) predictable in what the actors take as (melo-) dramatic?

These observations give rise to others. We said before that the actor is not aware of the formal logic of his action while enacting it, but the sociologist is (or should be), and that this relationship parallels that between stage actors and their audience. This must be refined. For the "stage actor" is two persons: the professional actor and the character he is portraying. As the first, the actor clearly can and indeed must maintain an awareness of the logic of the play and his part in it. As Carnovsky puts it: "You see, a part is built up moment by moment. The actor . . . knows that in the third act he is going to have to justify what he does in the first act. The sense of form leads him into a development . . . so that [the action] . . . is unified" (Funke and Booth, 1961:282). At the same time, however, it is obvious that the actor, *as the character he is portraying*, does not have this formal, structural awareness. Carnovsky knows how fateful Lear's initial largesses will become, but *Lear* does not know and, indeed, it is on his ignorance, but the audience's foreknowledge, that the drama depends.

What this tells us, we think, is that people, like characters in dramas, don't always know what they are doing. Carnovsky, a great actor, is enabled to enact his intentions as an actor *through the role of Lear* because, in part, he possesses a *double* awareness: the naivete of the character locked in his role and the foreknowledge of the actor performing that role. But this simultaneous "nearness" and "farness" may also characterize people who are perceptive and competent in interaction in general. There are, of course, many poor actors. They cannot credibly represent that which they wish to seem. But again, is this not true also of life? Does not artistic integrity have its counterpart in the authenticity of the self?

Perhaps another nuance may be noted. There are many successful actors who patently do not have the type of consciousness described above. Yet here we would argue that such persons are not dramatic artists in the strict sense. They may simply happen to be cast so that they can "play themselves." They are one-role actors and hence not dramatic artists at all. Instead of having mastered their medium, they manage well only within their narrow range. Here again, there is a parallel in life. Most of us are poor actors, effective only in a narrow range of roles. Like the one-role actor who can do Shakespeare or Neil Simon, but not both, we can manage suburbia but not the slum, the businessman but not the lover. In contrast, the accomplished artist approaches each engagement with a certain reserve, an inner distance through which the role is seen as a mediation of the self. He recognizes the limits imposed by any mediation but, at the same time, is aware that the mediation can be made his instrument. The character he plays is "created" through his discipline, much as "character" for actors in the social world also is achieved through discipline and insight.

The question still remains as to the role of the author, "what we in everyday life *lack*," as Edie puts it, "and what a stage-play *has*." This seems to be a formidible obstacle, but Edie himself implies a way over it. "We [in everyday life] are both author and actor at once ... and it is precisely [this] that distinguish[es] our experienced world of lived-time from that of aesthetic imagined time." Again we ask, in what respect? To answer this, imagine a continuum of theater. At one end are marionettes, or mechanical dummies activated by a computer program. Further toward the middle of the continuum is the highly stylized ritual theater of, say, *Noh* plays, early Greek drama, or the court of Louis XIV. Still further along would be modern theater in which the actor's particular interpretation of his role becomes crucial. Then, well past the midpoint, we have the theater of, say, Genet, in which the author provides a scene, theme, and framework, but in which much of the action is improvised by the actors as they present it. Finally, at the far end of the continuum, we have "living theater" or "response theater" in which the play is entirely invented by the actors and audience as they go along. It seems to us that each point on this spectrum can properly be called theater. Yet between the two termini there is an exact reversal of the role of the author. At one end, the author is all, and the actors are absorbed into him; at the other end the actors and audience are all, and they absorb the author. Thus, insofar as our examples all are legitimate representatives of theater, that concept proves itself rich enough to contain the qualifications that Edie has made. One could go further, in fact, and speculate on the kinds of societies in which various ideas of the theater are likely to be found (Fergusson, 1949). Presumably, as social life varies, so will its characteristic form of drama. It would thus seem that what Edie deems an essential feature of "our experienced world of lived-time" – its lack of a script – is really a feature of our modern world but not necessarily of the worlds of others. Moreover, this lack of a script also is a feature of precisely the theater that is most characteristic of the modern age.

Edie's comment on life's lack of a script and author also can be dealt with on a deeper level. It may be accepted that we do not experience our lives as preordained.[42] *But neither did Macbeth.* Edie has misunderstood an essential aspect of the drama, an aspect that accounts for much of its metaphoric utility. The relevant isomorphism is not between our experience of freedom and the actor's experience that he is playing a part but between our consciousness and that of the character being portrayed. We and the actor may know that Macbeth cannot denounce his wife and save the king; but *Macbeth* doesn't! *He* experiences choice more fully than most of us and, indeed, were he not to, the moral drama would have no meaning. Yet it is this very ambiguity that makes the drama so useful a metaphor for social analysis. For it makes us hover, as it were, between freedom and determinism, between causality and consciousness, between the author and the audience, and between the actor and the character he presents. Each aspect or perspective can be simultaneously illuminated by the others. Conduct is conducted, intention is superintended, authority is authored, depth uses surface for concealment.

If every simulation is a dissimulation, then the dramatic simulation of a fiction on the stage falsifies its own fictional character and becomes, in some higher sense, real (see Griffith, 1967). Thus the real freedom that Macbeth experiences within the assumptions of his fiction becomes a representation of the fiction that our realities can make of our freedom. The determined, scripted nature of Macbeth's stage play becomes an intaglio of our worlds. Isomorphism is not identity. An exact opposite may be more instructive than an almost twin.

It remains for us now to illustrate the application of the dramaturgical metaphor to specific realms of social conduct. For this we may look at the writings of Erving Goffman and Lyman and Scott. Each of these writers stresses those aspects of the theater that are most isomorphic with the domains they study. Thus, in *The Presentation of Self in Everyday Life*, Goffman exploits the dialectic between the actor and his mask, between the actor and other actors who provide an intimate participating audience, and between the actors as a team and the broader public audience. Conduct is seen as aimed at creating and maintaining an image of the self before other members of the troupe. Yet to stage a larger social performance, team members must work together, maintaining separation between front and back stage, cueing each other, and so on. In elaborating these submetaphors, Goffman applies them to a wide range of social settings.

In another work, *Relations in Public*, the team aspect is diminished, and social theater becomes a one-man performance before an impersonal and psychically distanced audience. The performance of a restaurant staff before the diners, for example, may be thought of as a team performance with the audience on stage, as in theater in the round. But there is still a *back*stage – the kitchen, the boiler room – to which the actors can repair. In contrast, behavior in some other settings – in the street, on the beach – is often a one-man show. The team is not there for support and there may be no back stage for retreats. The elaboration of such concepts yields a framework and vocabulary by which a vast range of behaviors can be defined, cross-sorted, and organized.

One area of social life particularly lends itself to dramaturgical analysis: those situations in which persons have a sense
of being "on." Thus, not surprisingly, much of Goffman's
analyses are devoted to initiation ceremonies, rites of passage,
role conflict, stress situations such as those of sudden crisis, as
well as those aspects of mundane situations that sometimes call
for dissimulation or deceit – when, as Goffman puts it, "normal
appearances" must be sustained in abnormal conditions:

> Circumstances can cause the individual to feel that a
> whole flow of his complex activity is put on even though
> it is the same activity that was once "genuine."
> Dramaturgically, that is what lying is about. . . . To
> continue to cohabit with one's spouse while secretly
> having an affair, or to begin planning for the divorce
> before one's spouse knows that joint consideration of the
> possibility of separation is slated to be given, is to
> transform humdrum household activity into an ironic and
> perhaps nasty show. Ordinarily, then, what makes
> performances false is not the creation of a new, false
> routine but the continuation of an old, valid one under
> altered circumstances. (1971:272–273)[43]

A similar mode of perception informs the writings of Lyman
and Scott, particularly in their essays "On Coolness in Everyday Life" and "Stage Fright and the Problem of Identity." In
these essays they examine situations at the edge of conventional
frameworks. Through such extreme instances the authors try to
reveal the dramaturgical properties of conventional behavior.
Opportunities for the display of "coolness" are shown to occur
when dangers and stakes are high. The authors then elaborate
the respects of such circumstances, noting heightening of risks
due to prop failure, interruptions, intrusions from offstage, and
so on. The actor, but not necessarily the audience, must be
aware of the criticalness of such performances. In rituals of
passage, on the other hand, the audience shares the awareness
that "each actor is negotiating the identity of a character. The
audience is in a state of hyperconsciousness, which alerts it to
scrutinize each gesture for its apparent and subtle charactero-
logical meaning. Detecting some element of puzzlement or
incongruity, the audience is triggered into an even more enhanced stage of watchfulness" (1970:164).

Thus stage fright, or the display of coolness, may be expected
at all those points in the life cycle that are "first times," the
opening nights when poise is expected in the face of the as-yet-
unexperienced event. Examples include the nuptial bedding of

virgins, first days in school or in the new job, or the first witnessing of death. In all such situations at least one actor does
not know the rules or moves of the encounter, and must carry
off a performance before those who do. Immigrants, parvenus,
and newcomers of all sorts typically are in this situation. Negroes, homosexuals, and spies who "pass" may become masters
of it.[44]

These examples should show how a root metaphor can be
elaborated into an analytic framework capable of embracing
a vast range of data. This is not to say that the metaphor itself
constitutes a model or a theory. It does not. But it *does* provide
the basis for model building through systematic elaboration,
specification, and formalization.

Games

In its folk usage, the concept that "life is a game" goes back
centuries, if not millennia. In recent times the two areas in which
the game metaphor has been elaborated most are mathematics
and theory of language. Of the first, seminal work was done by
von Neumann and Morgenstern (1944) in their development
of a mathematical theory of games that could be applied to
economic and, presumably, other forms of behavior. In the
second area – theory or philosophy of language – the major
figure is Ludwig Wittgenstein, whose approach we will consider
shortly.

Mathematical theories of games tend to focus on calculating
the optimal move or choice among alternative means for achieving a given end. Formulas are developed for weighing risks,
costs, and potential benefits; options are arrayed; and then the
"rationally best choice" is determined. This type of thinking
has attracted not only mathematicians but also social scientists
whose theories assume that rational calculation, on the motivational or behavioral levels, is the prime mover of social conduct.
Thus, for example, economic theorists have employed the game
metaphor to model economic competition, while war planners
have used it to explain previous battles and generate scenarios
for possible future conflicts.

As with other models we have examined, mathematical game
theory has problems of internal clarity and consistency, and
of external isomorphism with its domains of application. At the
core of these difficulties is the concept of rationality (B. Wilson,
1970). If rationality is taken to mean maximization of profit,
we discover that the model is isomorphic with a relatively small

part of economic conduct (i.e., it doesn't cover subsidized status industries, "nonrational" choices of fun, politics, safety, tradition, etc.). On the other hand, if we take rationality to mean the calculation of efficiency of *means*, regardless of whether the end is profit, then we are left with a tautology, for virtually any outcome can be considered the "end," and the events antecedent to it reconstructed to show that no other set of actions could have led up to that unique denouement.

When applying the game model to aggregated data, the question of economic rationality becomes a heuristic assumption as to how the individual *must* act if he is to stay in business. Yet if the rationality that is presupposed in the model is never connected to the praxis of economic behavior, it becomes a redundant description of the statistics that it supposedly explains. For instead of speaking about how people behave, we are talking of the "behavior" of prices, demand, the market, and so on. This is of course a perfectly legitimate level of analysis. What is not legitimate is to invoke, at this level, explanatory concepts – such as rationality or motivation – that refer to individual intentionality. The metaphors are mixed and the theory becomes either circular or inconsistent.

Besides rationality, mathematical game theory assumes a number of other conditions that rarely are experienced in the realms for which the model is constructed. The postulates of a priori knowledge of possible outcomes, the unchangeability and singleness of values placed on them, and the alternation of moves of the participants (which overlooks the advantages of speed or surprise) are all "respects" not characteristic of most domains of social action. For example, von Neumann and Morgenstern imagine a zero-sum game in which each participant seeks the same end, in which the gain of one results in a commensurate loss for the other. In economic activity this "end" is money. Yet it is easy to see that:

1. Economic life generally cannot be characterized in zero-sum terms – that is, there often are mutual advantages among participants.

2. The "end" – money – has a variable meaning; that is, $100,000 may help push ITT toward "excess profit" and federal intervention; the same amount may be a windfall to the corner butcher. This also vitiates the zero-sum assumption, which requires transferability and commensurability of utils.

3. In the military application these difficulties are even greater. Military utils, such as ground gained or men lost, will

vary enormously in terms of such considerations as relative strength of forces, ideology, territoriality, and so on, respects of military conflict with which the mathematical game model is nonisomorphic.

One way around some of these difficulties is suggested by Olaf Helmer (1964). In his formulation players can be involved in a game that has many different prizes, some of which may require teamwork to win. Thus, the victory of one does not necessarily result in the loss to others. Utils need be neither commensurate nor transferable. Moreover, to the extent that each player can gain *something* from the play, the problem of rule enforcement is reduced. Finally, "instead of dealing with just one fixed competitive situation with well-determined outcome possibilities," Helmer's model appears "capable of handling a continual recurrence, a flux, of situations calling upon the participants to make decisions in the light of their preferences, capabilities, and attitudes" (1964:302).

The other major use of the game metaphor, inspired by Wittgenstein, focuses not on the theoretical rationality of action but on the assumption of its *rule boundedness* in practice. In this view social reality is seen as *constructed* in interaction. The "stakes" of the game are those things that only the players can extend or withhold: confirmation of a proffered identity, legitimacy of a proposed course of action, submission to the will of others, and so on. Terms used to denote this process are strategic interaction, impression management, the negotiation of identities, tactics, devices, maneuvers, and stratagems. The hypothetical elaborations built into the closed logic of the mathematical game model give way to the praxis and uncertainty of the game play itself, and the rationalistic presuppositions implied in mathematical thinking are replaced by a focus on the actual conduct of persons in situations in which the realization of their intentions depends on their taking into account the intentions and conduct of others.

How people put their lives together becomes the question. Thus Nels Anderson tells us "How the Hobo Meets His Problem," and how one goes about "Getting by in Hobohemia" (1923:IV, Ch. 4). Other studies of life-styles and occupational groupings, growing out of early Chicago research but increasingly inspired by European philosophy, tell us how the phenomenologically problematic is managed. In *Behavior in Public Places* (1963) Goffman speaks of "games of expression"; Joan Emerson's article "Behavior in *Private* Places" (1970), recounts the tactics by which gynecological examinations remain defined as such. In *Men Who Manage* (1959) Melville Dalton describes "Staff Counter Tactics," while Julius Roth's *Timetables* reports the strategies used by patients to "move along faster through the hospital" (1963:48–54). In *Making the Grade* Becker, Geer, and Hughes "observe students as they go about the task of finding out what the rules are and where they stand with respect to them" (1968:80). In *The Presentation of Self in Everyday Life* (1959) Goffman tells of "common techniques that persons employ to sustain . . . impressions" (1959: 15). In his essay "On Cooling the Mark Out" (1952) Goffman lists six strategies and four alternative ploys. Glaser and Strauss's work outlines "the tactics of various interactants as they attempt to manage changes of awareness context" (1964, 1968). An essay by Weinstein is titled "Toward a Theory of Interpersonal Tactics" (1966). Another by Goffman is called "Strategic Interaction" (1969).[45]

As with the mathematical version of the game metaphor, the interactionist approach also makes assumptions – not always consistent ones – relating to the three interrelated questions of consciousness, goal directedness, and rule boundedness. As we saw, some analysts have insisted that their assumption of consciousness or rationality is heuristic only, applying to the model but not necessarily to its domain of application. Conversely, it has been argued by Lyman and Scott that "consciousness is not in fact a problem of the model, but a potential condition of the empirical situation" (1970).[46]

Similar ambiguities appear in relation to the problems of rule boundedness and rationality in general. As Kenneth Boulding and others have noted (1963:150ff; Schelling, 1958, 1963), all conduct can be understood in terms of the actor's having some image of the state of the world, or to put it in more radical terms, every actor has a "world." It follows from this that the difference between rational and irrational behavior is that the latter is unresponsive to additional information and is inconsistent in its ordering of behavioral options. In this view the "world" of *homo economicus*, though consistent, is irrational in its rigidity. Yet this does not make it any less a world nor does it limit the applicability of the game model. For the rationality of the actor's world need not be a problem for the sociologist. It is, instead, a problem for the actor: To the extent that his world is irrational he comes to know this through his inability to realize his intentions. The social analyst, for his part, focuses

not on the objective rationality of these worlds but on the interactional origins and manifestations of various worlds from
the perspective and by the methods of the world that constitutes
social science.[47]

As seductive as such reasoning may be, it still leaves a
number of key questions unanswered. For example, if the
sociologist is interested in the behavioral expressions of various
worlds, will he not perforce be interested in the actor's ability
to realize his intentions? Moreover, if this ability depends on the
"rationality" of the actor's world, does not that world's rationality become a problem with which the sociologist must deal?
Furthermore, if all conduct is to be interpreted in terms of the
game model, how are we to distinguish game situations specifically from everyday life? Conversely, if we suppose that
the game model is an appropriate analytic tool for such "game
situations" but not for "everyday life," how then are we to
distinguish the perspective and interpretations of the actor in
the game situation from those of the sociologist using the game
model for analysis?

These ambiguities seem to be contained within the game metaphor itself. Perhaps because sociologists inherited the metaphor
from both mathematics and ordinary language philosophy, the
relationship between the *rules* of a game and its *moves* has not
been fully worked out in the root metaphor. Until this occurs it
is likely that the contradictions discussed above will continue to
reappear in the metaphor's particular applications.

In this section we have treated three relatively new metaphors
for conduct: language, drama, and games. At this point it may
be useful to see whether aspects of one do not amend limitations in the others. We will first compare games and ritual
drama, and then consider whether these can be interpreted as
submetaphors of language. One source of help in this may be
found in Lévi-Strauss' comments on the differences between
ritual drama and games. Games, he notes, disjoin people. At the
beginning of play all are ostensive equals under the rules, which
provide a preordained structure. But the vagaries of talent and
chance separate people into winners and losers. In ritual it is
exactly the opposite. It is the divisions – between the sacred and
the profane, between the initiated and the outsiders, between
the audience and the actors – which is established at the outset.
The structure thus lies not in the rules but in the events, not in
the pre-conditions but in the unfolding, by which all participants
are brought, as it were, to the winning side in a kind of communion.

What Lévi-Strauss shows, we believe, is the oppositeness-sameness of the root metaphors of drama and games. Moreover, his analysis reveals both of them to be symbolic expressions having definite structural properties, thus linking them both to the metaphor of language. An example in this connection is provided by K. E. Read, who reports that natives of New Guinea, who have learned to play football, will play numerous matches over several days, stopping only when both sides have reached the same score (1959:429). This can be seen as the turning of a game into a ritual or, put conversely, the performance of ritual through a game. The possibility of seeing game as ritual, and the reverse, thus allows the sociologist alternately to stress either conflict or harmony, rules or events, and calculation or conformity in his interpretation of conduct.

It is just such a tension that is at the heart of Simmel's formal sociology and Mead's and Cooley's theories of socialization (Mead, 1956). Simmel, for example, speaks of sociability as the "play form" of sociation. The ritual etiquette of the *salon* (or the saloon) are the training ground, and metaphor, for life. What gives Simmel's thesis bite, however, is that in its *formal* properties such ritualized play is akin to serious, but seemingly labyrinthine, activities such as economic bargaining, politics, or war (1950). Likewise, Mead's and Cooley's concepts of taking the role of others, and seeing ourselves as they do, is fundamental both to games as well as to play and, indeed, their thesis is that adult roles are learned in the ritual play of children.

The fusion of dramatistic and linguistic game images is of course extensive in current sociological writings. For example, Marvin Scott, in *The Racing Game*, says that "the jockey must at least *appear* to be riding energetically and cleanly. To bring off these appearances the jockey has developed certain *communication strategies – dramatic accentuation* and *concealment* or a combination of both" (1968, our italics). The imagery here is that of appearance and concealment as strategies in a communication game, the language of which is dramatic enactments. In *Passing On*, Sudnow describes the dramatic communication game engaged in by morgue attendants: "His chief and daily problem was going about the hospital without, wherever he went, appearing to others to be working. His problem generally was how to enter into any form or ordinary discourse without his affiliation with dead bodies intruding as a prominent way others attended to him. . . . He attempted to convey a sense of not being at work by developing clear styles" (1967:544ff). Labeling theory in general – insofar as it views conduct simultaneously as a process of reality definition through language, as a game of control or evasion, and as an enactment of desired identities – is a *situs* where these three metaphors may one day be fused.

Just as a discipline creates its own subject matter, an epistemology may create, or at least delimit, the discipline or domain of its relevance. In this sense, a poetic for sociology bears a privileged relation to the root metaphors discussed above. For what language, drama, and games all have in common is exactly what they share with art: They all are *autotelic, symbolic* activities. Enacting dramatic rituals, playing social games, entering into systems of language, all – like art – summon up their own realities and their own rules for understanding.

Social conduct is thus like art in this special sense – we cannot understand it except in terms of criteria that arise out of its own nature. Consider, for example, the following statements about a lemon tree:

1. Lemons are good for you.
2. Lemon trees grow well here.
3. That tree cost six dollars.
4. That species was introduced from Spain.
5. This tree has an elegant shape.

Each of the statements expresses a different interest or point of view. The first is medical, the second horticultural, the third economic, and the fourth historical. Only the fifth statement is aesthetical, and only from such a point of view does the tree *exist* as an aesthetic object – that is, as an object of aesthetic perception. Moreover, unlike the other four statements, the *interest* of the aesthetical perspective stops with the perceptual-contemplative act itself. The activity of aesthetic appreciation does not depend on the curative, botanical, economic, historical or any other antecedents or consequent features of the tree, but only on the fitness itself to perception. The tree, from this point of view, is its own end. Its meaning is to be.

Now the proposition that conduct is like art certainly is open to question. Indeed, on the face of it, such a concept seems to fly against massive organistic and mechanistic traditions that explain behavior as purposive or as caused. Even our severest critics, however, admit that at least *some* activities are *supposed* to be done only for their own sake, that on some occasions we are expected to enjoy ourselves simply "for the fun of it." We are not supposed to do business at a party, or to be so intent on winning that we are willing to cheat at tennis to do so. We may go to concerts to appear cultured, but we pretend that we go because we love music. Regardless of whether all our behavior is governed by the rule of disinterested interest, few deny that at least in some areas of life this rule exists.

If this is accepted the question then arises as to the relation between such autotelic areas of conduct – chiefly ritual drama and games – and social conduct in general, including the more purposive activities of survival and welfare. As we saw earlier, in terms of some formal properties, play activities seem to be mimetic of economic, political, and other realms of life. Yet by what reasoning can we account for such an isomorphism between autotelic and purposive social conduct?

To understand the underlying basis for such a similarity we may take a hint from Kant. Kant developed a strict formal theory of aesthetics and then asked what the relation was of aesthetic judgment to scientific or pure reason. Kant notes that in dealing with specific realms of data scientists speak in terms of causes and effects. Yet the very possibility of prescribing scientific laws itself presupposes some form or fitness of nature in its manifoldness and variety. Nature, taken as a whole, must have a fitness to perception, a certain self-contained, autotelic cogency, such that it is susceptible to decoding through the rule-bound inquiry that is science. In any case, says Kant, this is what we *must* assume if any rational inquiry is to be possible. This concept of an immanent and unfolding order in nature – yet an order not directed toward anything outside itself – represents "the unique manner in which we must proceed in reflecting upon objects of nature if we are to get a thoroughly coherent experience" (quoted by Friedrich, 1949:273). Biological or mechanical images of nature presuppose an aesthetical view of nature in the first place. Logically prior to the possibility of explaining nature in telic or causal terms, nature first must present itself in our perception as a coherent and *auto*telic object. There is thus a fusion, in aesthetic judgment, between the ultimate properties of nature and the ultimate prerequisites of thought.

Carrying Kant's reasoning a step further, such a relationship seems no less necessary between social conduct and the human studies. Rule boundedness and autotelic cogency must be imputed to nature for nature to be understandable in terms of the rule-bounded speculation that is science. Similarly, it seems equally required that behavior be construed as if it were rule

governed in order that it may be decoded by systematic socio-
logic thought.

These sets of relationships suggested by Kant may be taken
as emblematic of the relationship between autotelic social activities such as games and drama, social life in general, and our
manner of comprehending both. The first – games and drama –
must be understood in terms of their inner structures of rules
and events. But the understanding of social life, in general, as
we have seen, likewise requires us to assume that persons act
in accordance with rules. Unless seen from this perspective the
subject matter – *social* conduct – disappears. Hume puts this
neatly:

> In societies for play [i.e., sports clubs], there are laws
> required for the conduct of the game; and these laws are
> different in each game. The foundation, I own, of such
> societies is frivolous; and the laws are, in a great measure,
> though not altogether, capricious and arbitrary. . . . The
> comparison with social life in general . . . therefore, is
> very imperfect. We may only learn from it the necessity of
> rules, wherever men have any intercourse with each
> other. . . . It is impossible for men so much as to murder
> each other without statutes, and maxims. (1951:210)

Thus even causal or functional explanations must presuppose
a rule-bounded cogency in the objects of its analysis. (Indeed,
a major criticism of such explanations is that these presuppositions have remained inexplicit and unexamined.) These rules
emerge through typification. Social life is enacted – or at least
understood – through typifications, and social order lies in the
transsituational or rulelike quality these typifications come to
assume. In the game of baseball, certain actions *are* fouls,
strikes, or home runs because the rules of the game define them
as such, and to make of them something else would be to cease
to play baseball. Similarly, that a certain action *is* a murder,
and not an accident or euthanasia depends on (usually implicit)
rules that govern this area of conduct. To seek to explain social
actions without reference to their rulebounded character is to
cease to treat them as social.

Yet if rules must be presupposed in giving accounts of
conduct, how can sociology account for these rules? (see Blum,
1970; McHugh, 1970). The perplexity here is that unlike
things (or horses), both social actors as well as social scientists
construct their respective worlds in a rule-bounded fashion.
Unlike objects of nature, social actors themselves create rules

by which they understand and govern their conduct. In the natural sciences there is one level of consciousness to be accounted for – that of the scientist. But in sociology there are at least three levels: that of the actor in process of enacting conduct, that of the actor as he retrospectively or prospectively surveys his or other persons' actions, and that of the social scientist. Unlike the physicist with single vision, the sociologist may need a triple vision to save himself from "one-eyed intelligence."

There is thus a crucial lack of isomorphism between nature as Kant conceived it, and conduct as we understand it here. In treating this difference yet another metaphor may be useful – that of the difference between a puzzle and a game. Natural scientists, Kuhn tells us, solve *puzzles*. Puzzles, like games, are rule bounded; but *un*like game partners, the pieces of a puzzle don't talk back. A puzzle, then, is dehumanized, and it was precisely through such dehumanization of nature that Newton and others assimilated nature to a puzzle, and a mechanical one at that. Gods, people, spirits, and other *agents* were eliminated from the model, leaving instead bodies, forces, and factors.[48]

Whatever advantages the puzzle metaphor has for the natural sciences, it seems much less useful for understanding social *interaction*. It is precisely here, of course, that the game metaphor of conduct can be brought to bear. This metaphor affords the rule-bounded cogency of the puzzle model but, in addition, it leaves a place for consciousness, intentionality, and reciprocity of perspectives – the very constituents of action that is human. The ambiguous aspects of the game model discussed earlier are precisely the ones that separate a game from a puzzle, and human action from nonhuman events.

Perhaps one resolution of this problematic lies in the distinction between levels of consciousness just mentioned. Level one may be called "mundane" or "naive" consciousness, in which the actors have no explicit sense of following rules or engaging in strategies. Indeed, it is a major contribution of ethnomethodology to have discovered that actors, in the process of enactment, do not, and in fact can not, simply "follow the rules." Instead, rules must be interpreted as covering a given situation. But in this very interpretation the rules themselves are transformed.[49] Like meanings, rules are recreated in their invocations. Garfinkel, for example, shows how the application of "Some Rules of Correct Decisions That Jurors Respect" is subject to negotiation and redefinition (1967:104–115; see M. Douglas, 1973). In this case, the exercise of transsituational normative standards within a *specific* situation *can be seen as* a strategy by which actors try to make their definitions of the situation prevail. The degree of actual bargaining – and the degree of awareness on the part of the actors that bargaining is going on – may vary tremendously, from disinterested love to total war. Moreover, such bargaining and the awareness of it need not be symmetrical. Some actors generally will be more powerful or manipulative than others.

Yet even in a situation of complete harmony over the relevant rules of both procedure and purpose, the *potential* for conflict will remain. This is so if only because no set of rules can ever exhaust any given situation; some of the content inevitably escapes the form. And indeed, after a certain point the more the rules are elaborated the less they are intelligible. Legal documents and government regulations, for example, are notoriously precise *and* hard to understand. The ever-present indexicality of lived experience makes the governance of conduct by rules ever elusive.

In addition to these dimensions of awareness in the process of action, a second level is the actors' observational understanding of others and their prospective and retrospective comprehension of their own behavior. Such awareness tends to be rule bound and strategic in a much more explicit and regular fashion. "Why do you work hard?" "In order to get ahead." "Why is she so dressed up?" "In order to outclass Mrs. Jones." This type of understanding – what Lyman and Scott have called "Accounts" (1970:111–144) – requires an imputation of consciousness and intentionality to the actors. To *not* make such an imputation is to treat the actors as non- or subhuman, for example, as "crazy," "just a baby," or "media or carriers for the posited causes or functions." Accounts of fully human behavior are thus "in order to" or "because of" statements (Schutz, 1971).

The degree of *Verstehen* that such an account represents, however, will vary from actor to actor. Not everyone is highly reflective. But, again, to be human means to be capable of at least some reflection – that is, of some memory, imagination, and ordering of events. One variety of understanding in everyday life is that in which the actor imputes to himself or others *calculating* motives and *strategic* consciousness, as if they were in a "game situation." (The frequency of such an imputation is likely to vary with the degree to which the actor sees conflict as present in his world.)

A third level of consciousness is that of the sociologist who may employ the game model. For him the utility of the game model does not depend on the state of consciousness of the actors – whether naive or reflective or whatever. That the actors *be* conscious is important, of course, for without consciousness there can be no game, not even in potential. But no given *quality* of consciousness is required for the game model to be useful. One of the heuristic values of this model lies in its being open or neutral on this point; because of this openness the model is able to account for, or at least accommodate, different levels and modes of consciousness and their interactional consequences. In this sense, the rationality of the actor's world is not a prerequisite for using the game metaphor; it is, instead, an empirical datum that the metaphor can treat. It is a topic, rather than a resource, for explanation.

What distinguishes a game situation from everyday life is that in the latter conflict and strategic calculation is only potential, whereas in the game situation it has become manifest to at least one of the actors. Thus, as applied to everyday life, the game framework is an analytic model used by the researcher but unshared by the actors. In game situations, however, the actors *and* the sociologist share the game model. Yet there is one proviso: For the researcher the game model remains a model – now more descriptive than heuristic, but still more "as if" than literal. For (at least one of) the actors, however, the game perspective will be both a model *and* a behavioral norm, a guide not only to understanding but also to action. (This, by the way, does not mean that game strategists are scoundrels. The game model can serve moral persons in immoral situations just as well as the reverse.)

Such an analysis titillates more than it satisfies, but it may suggest possibilities for joining game and dramatic metaphors within a larger paradigm taken from language – that of symbolic communication.

5
Irony

When irony has first been mastered it undertakes a movement directly
opposed to that wherein it proclaimed its life as unmastered. Irony
now limits, renders finite, defines, and thereby yields truth, actuality,
and content; it chastens and punishes and thereby imparts stability,
character, and consistency. Irony is a disciplinarian feared only by
those who do not know it, but cherished by those who do. He who
does not understand irony and has no ear for its whisperings lacks
eo ipso what might be called the absolute beginning of the personal
life.
Kierkegaard (1965:339)

We said earlier that all knowledge is perspectival and hence
metaphoric. In this chapter we ask, What sort of a metaphor is
irony, and what special value has it for sociological thought?
Irony is a metaphor of opposites, a seeing of something from the
viewpoint of its antithesis. Put slightly differently, to render
something ironic is to take it from its conventional context and
place it in an opposite one. Through such a negation we become
more aware of what that thing is. In sociology this heightening
of awareness – which is the special value of irony – operates
on two principal levels: the lay and the professional. Insofar
as sociology is a "moral science" it must contribute to the
critical self-awareness of its lay audience. To the extent that
it is a science in a more formal sense, irony can serve a similar
critical and self-reflective function for professionals. In the
first instance, the "conventional context" that is reversed is a
widespread, complacently held belief. In the second case, the
"conventional context" is a theoretical one, a taken-for-granted
paradigm of normal science. In the first the audience is the
larger community and its ideologues, in the second it is the
community of scholars. In both these realms – the ethical and
the intellectual – irony may serve as an instrument of paradigm
innovation.

These two domains often are not separated in practice; the
line between "popular" and "serious" sociology, between intellectual power and public effect, is not always clearly drawn.
The two concerns are not mutually exclusive of course, nor will

we strictly separate them here. The greatest sociology simultaneously informs our theoretical *and* our ethical judgment. Weber, for example, helps us understand the hidden implications of Protestants' moral commitments while at the same time providing a general account of the relation between ideology and economics and the preconditions for peculiarly modern forms of thought.

In contrast to Weber's writings, some social theories are neither reflexive ethically nor innovative theoretically. Others, such as functional theory, tend to be highly ironic ethically but highly conventional theoretically. Ethnomethodology, on the other hand, ironizes functionalism as *theory*, just as functionalism ironizes popular beliefs. Yet ethnomethodology has yet to elaborate its own theoretical paradigm and, in the realm of values, its radical neutrality allows it to ironize dogma in general but not the specific contents of beliefs. One also could interpret neopositivist historicism in these terms. Bock's work, for example, ironically rebukes the functional evolutionists: "You thought you were studying social change," he seems to be saying, "but by placing your assertions in the context of a causal model of explanation, I have shown that you are not. In fact, because of your logical and theoretical assumptions, you *cannot* study social change." The contradiction between neopositivism's assertion of value neutrality and its indirect support of technicist social control also make it susceptible to ironization from, say, a Marxist perspective.

While such debates may be endless in practice, their main features have a limited number of logically possible combinations. This is shown in Figure 5.

Irony is a way of moving from conventional paradigms to

	Elaborating conventional paradigms	Inventing original paradigms
Of professional theory		
Of popular belief		

Figure 5

original ones, either on the level of professional theory or on the level of popular belief. In examining specific works we are likely to find few pure types. Some writings, while useful in unmasking popular pretensions, do not have the conceptual rigor and richness to be capable of elaboration into formal models. The reverse is also true: Some formulations can ironize professional conventions while having little impact on lay beliefs. On either the popular or the scholarly level, however, irony operates not merely as an ornament of style but as a logic of discovery.

The overwhelming bulk of effort in science and in ethics, of course, goes into extending the inherited insights rather than in finding new ones. In juridical work, for example, most decisions involve the application of existing precedents rather than the establishment of new ones. This more conventional work is a matter of elaborating the precedents case by case so they more completely cover their domains. Indeed, the nature of the law – and of science, art, or ethics – requires a division whereby most labor goes into elaboration, with sudden, seminal bursts of innovation. Thus changes in basic popular understandings, as in basic scientific theories, are relatively infrequent. Most scientists devote their careers to generalizing and detailing existing paradigms, rather than attempting formulations that might shatter the old frame of vision. In these senses, because it is an essentially negative movement, irony can never be the whole of social ethics or social theory. But it can be a method of innovation in each.

In this chapter we develop the idea of dialectical or dramatic irony as a principle of discovery in both formal and popular sociology. The "logic" of dramatic irony consists of three elements. First there is a juxtaposing of opposites, of thesis and antithesis, the association of which was unexpected. Then the peripety, or reversal from one term to its opposite, must be as inevitable as their initial association was unforeseen. Finally there is dramatic resolution, a synthesis of thesis and antithesis on a higher level. For example, theory, as dramatic closure and unity, shows us how and why Puritan ascetics become bourgeoise men of affairs, how capitalism becomes socialism, how socialists become oligarchs. The unanticipated juxtaposition makes the theory a discovery; the inevitability of the outcome is the dramatic equivalent of its logical cogency or empirical proof.

These concepts will be defined and then formulated into several "laws" of ironic effectiveness. The operation of these laws will be illustrated by examples from a wide range of sociological writings, with discussions in greater depth of Goffman and Sorokin. The chapter concludes with sections on "Irony as a Humanism" and "Irony as a Logic of Discovery," treating the relation of irony to values and to formal theory, respectively.

OF IRONY

There are four major modes of ironic expression: rhetorical irony, irony of manner, the irony of events, and dramatic or dialectical irony.[1] Each of these modes has a long history in literature and criticism, and each has a specific point of connection with the sociological enterprise. Rhetorical irony is, briefly, the stating of a meaning that is ambiguous, with the implication that the audience, the speaker, and the object are free to interpret the meaning in a sense opposite to the one conventionally assumed. The most frequent use of this mode is as an instrument of putting down one's enemies (or uplifting one's friends). The sweetest use of rhetorical irony is in pretending to take one's opponent's arguments seriously, and then showing their absurdity by defending them beyond credible limits. This was Hume's tactic against the argument of design in nature as a proof of God (Price, 1965), and it recurs today in debates between social scientists. Sheldon Wolin (1960), for example, extends the logic of Selznick to show that this professed democrat has the same theory of organization as the autocratic Lenin.

The irony of manner and the irony of events – the latter sometimes called cosmic irony – refer not to discourse but to action, the first on the level of face-to-face interaction, the second on the level of historical events. In irony of manner an ambiguous act is performed, the intentions and meaning of which are referred back to the audience, the actor, and the actor's mode of expression, the implication being that the message is the opposite of its medium. Classic examples of irony of manner are the behavioral ploys used by Socrates, St. Francis, and Jews at the Caliph's court. Contemporary instances would include sight gags or put-ons by hipsters, anarchistic artists, and symbolic revolutionaries. In a similar fashion, clients and subjects often ironize experts and sociologists, as when "Agnes" convinced Harold Garfinkel that he had always been a girl (1967).

In cosmic irony, or the irony of events, the source of the ambiguity is superhuman – "history," "fate," or "the gods," – as when events make a mishmash of sociological predictions, or when "the public will" subverts the well-laid plans of social engineers. Such impersonality led Hegel to call this "the objective irony of history" (1896:I:400). Here the ambiguity lies in the superhuman status of the agent – there is an air of magic because expected links of causation become mystified and blurred.

Our principal interest, however, is with dramatic or dialectical irony, what Kenneth Burke calls a "master trope . . . in the discovery and description of 'the truth' " (1969a:503). Dramatic irony differs from the other ironic modes on several counts. First, the events or situations through which dramatic irony is enacted are strictly bounded. The action must be created within two hours on the stage, or within fifty pages of an essay. This boundedness is less clear with the other modes, and hence they lend themselves less to the logical development of action within a pregiven frame.

Another difference lies in the relationship between the ironist and the audience. All irony depends on audience participation – it requires that the audience simultaneously perceive a multiplicity of perspectives. In ironies of speech or manner, however, it is the ironist himself who provides the point of audience involvement. The ironist is aware that the true meaning of his speech or gesture is the opposite of what his ignorant victim takes it to be, and the audience is allowed to enter into his perspective. With dramatic irony, however, the ringmaster disappears, and the audience is required to detect for itself contradictions that are inherent in the characters and their situations. In rhetorical irony the characters say the opposite of what they mean; the irony of manner lies in their seeming other than they are. But dramatic irony lies in the *structure* of contradictions and is revealed through the ripening of events. *Macbeth*, for example, would not be dramatic if its hero were half mad to begin with; it is the developing conflict between Macbeth's evil deeds and his moral abhorrence of them, as well as the reversal between his initial expectation and the outcome, that creates dramatic tension and resolution.

Moreover, in dramatic irony the higher knowledge of the audience takes the form of *fore*knowledge, an awareness of the foregivenness of how the action *must* take place. Indeed, it is precisely this knowledge of fore-given-ness that is the basis of sympathetic understanding, forgiveness, the logic of the drama, and dramatic resolution. Such foreknowledge may be conveyed by various devices. Primary among these is the protocol of the theater itself. Handbills and programs are distributed and, with a popular play, even the action may be known in advance. The audience also is aware of the unreality of the action, while the fictive characters are not – when murders are committed on stage, a character may call the police, but theatergoers will not. Other devices to induce foreknowledge are contained within the play proper. Shakespeare was fond of oracles and plays within the play. Other writers make one player more aware than others, as for example the adulteress in a comic love triangle. Many writers cut from one scene to another, with the audience but not the characters being aware of the immanent convergence of subplots. In a novelistic drama such as *Crime and Punishment*, we are kept in suspense not by our ignorance, but rather by the pregnancy of the opening lines, the early knowledge of the crime, and our awareness that the police inspector *also* knows who committed the crime. Limned by such foreknowledge, all action becomes infused with deeper meanings, with possibilities opposite to the intentions of the actors. And *we* are more aware of this than are the actors themselves.

Another aspect of dramatic irony is its more fully dialectical character. That is, not only is A opposed to B, as in other ironic modes; in addition, characteristically, A becomes B by avoiding B. Thus Moliere's Miser loses his money by seeking to preserve it; Oedipus becomes the killer of his father because he sought to save him. Not only is the *antithesis* stronger because of this hidden interdependence and reversal of opposites; there also is an explicit *synthesis* in the dramatic resolution or denouement: The Miser's larcenous servant marries his daughter, thus restoring his fortune but at the same time subverting his greed; Oedipus turns his light to darkness, his life-giving wife-mother takes her life.

All of the ironic modes discussed have at least two features in common: the opposition of incongruent images, characteristics, frameworks, or events; and a transcendent perspective in which these opposites unite. In rhetorical irony and irony of manner, opposition is stressed and the transcendent perspective is achieved through a compact of superior knowledge between the ironist and the audience. In cosmic irony the characters and events are allowed to speak with their own voices, and the transcendent perspective is achieved through dialectical reversal and synthesis. It is in dramatic irony, however, that all these features are conjoined within a single form. Because dramatic irony is the *representation and formalization* of antagonistic ambiguity, it subsumes the other modes within it. That is, ironies of speech, manner, or the cosmos all can be represented in a play, just as they all can be represented in a sociological theory. Indeed, it is difficult to imagine a form of dramatic irony that does not embody these other modes. What all ironies have in common is that they are a structure of ambiguities and contradictions. Yet because the very essence of the dramatic is to formally represent such structures, we may say that dramatic irony logically subsumes and completes the other modes. Having come this far in exploring the essence of irony, we find ourselves on the doorstep of sociological theory.

IRONY IN SOCIOLOGICAL THEORY

The features noted above suggest that irony is particularly suited for illuminating certain aspects of sociological theory. Yet recognition of this by sociologists themselves is infrequent and usually only implicit. Irony thus has remained a latent dimension of theory, one that we now wish to make manifest.

One discussion of irony as a way of sociological knowledge is Robert Merton's paper on "Manifest and Latent Functions" (1957:19–84). Merton criticizes some of the questionable postulates of functionalism and then suggests two major ways in which this theoretical perspective may be saved. He first calls for a clearer distinction between objective consequences and subjective dispositions – a suggestion that has been hailed by researchers who focus on problems of verification and of gathering statistical data.

Yet much less attention has been given to Merton's second recommendation – where he asserts that the prime instrument of sociological knowledge is an eye for paradox, contradiction, and reversals that are latent beneath the more obvious, manifest content of action:

> The distinction between manifest and latent functions serves further to direct the attention of the sociologist to precisely those realms . . . where he can most fruitfully apply his special skills. . . . It is precisely the latent functions of a practice or belief which are *not* common knowledge, for these are unintended and generally unrecognized social and psychological consequences. As a result, findings concerning latent functions represent a greater increment

in knowledge than findings concerning manifest functions. They represent, also, greater departures from "common-sense" knowledge about social life.

In short, it is suggested that the *distinctive* intellectual contributions of the sociologist are to be found primarily in the study of unintended consequences (among which are latent functions) of social practices, as well as in the study of anticipated consequences (among which are manifest functions). (1957:65–68, Merton's italics)

Other theorists, such as Moore and Tumin (1949), Louis Schneider (1949, 1962), Manfred Stanley (1972), David Matza (1969), and Richard Brown (1973), also have recognized the importance of dialectical irony in creating social theory. Matza, for example, suggests that:

Once the distinction between good and evil is made problematic, a similar insight may develop with respect to the relations between phenomena and their purported causes. . . . Accordingly, a stress on irony may be taken as a self-conscious reversal of the earlier correctional view that bad things were caused by bad conditions. Given the ironic tendency of naturalism, bad things could result from highly treasured and revered aspects of social life, and good things could be born of what was conventionally deemed evil. (1969:67–69)

Yet such statements hardly exhaust the salient types and levels of dialectical irony in social theory, nor do they focus on its peculiarly *logical* and dramatic character. Merton, for example, calls for studies that will show the specific relationships between latent and manifest functions, while Schneider urges researchers to trace the "transmutation mechanisms" that link the sides of dialectical equations. While agreeing with these suggestions, we would take them further, by carrying the implications of irony back to the presuppositions of sociological knowledge itself. In most treatments irony is considered a good source of hunches, or a way of dressing up an otherwise dull report. In this view, however, irony remains in the realm of art or beauty, strictly separated from science and truth. Irony is thus reduced to an inspiration or ornament of knowledge, while knowledge itself is seen as deriving from operational definitions, experimental tests, and multivariate analysis.

We are not claiming that operationalization and verification are "wrong," or even that they cannot be criteria of truth.

Instead, we recommend that they *are* such criteria, but not for the reasons often supposed. That is empirical specification has a truth value, but principally in terms of such *aesthetic* criteria of truth as those outlined in the previous chapter. For example, imagine a play in which both the motivations of the characters, as well as the practical possibilities of their actions, simply were not made credible. Because of this lack of truth value, the play would fail *aesthetically*. To be made credible, however, does not require correspondence to some reality independent of the drama but to reality as defined by the rules of that particular dramatic form. For example, a play about the gods may be made credible – that is, it will be a realistic representation – to an atheist as long as he accepts the conventions of religious drama and as long as the play conforms to those rules.

Within the terms of the symbolic universe of social science, something similar applies. A social theory will be inadequate if it fails to explain, on the motivational level, how X indeed came to cause Y. "The king died; then the queen died," is a correlation. But "The king died, then the queen died *of grief*," is a story with a plot, because it provides a motivational account of the correlation that identifies what is salient in it. Theories of conduct must have plots in this fashion (Forester, 1956; Mac-Iver, 1937:476–477; Furfey, 1953:72–73).

In addition to motivational plausibility, however, the theory also must show the practical feasibility of the actions. According to the rules of religious drama, a divine intervention is possible. According to the rules of court drama, the damsel may be saved by a knight but not by a serf. Like these other dramatic forms, science also has its rules for defining practical possibilities. These chiefly are the frequency of similar events having occurred in similar circumstances in the past. Operationalization and verification are, of course, ways of learning about such rates of occurrence and, within the assumptions of the modern scientific view, such rates of past occurrence may give us a very strong sense of inevitability about the future. What is important to remember is that our sense of inevitability – though it seems to be about the future – is, in fact, a creature of the past. And even then it is not the past in simple but the past as mediated by particular assumptions and procedures (operationalization, etc.).

Commonly, then, there are two ways to "make credible" a sociological theory – to provide the actors with plausible motives, and to demonstrate high rates of similar actions in similar situations. For example, we could reconstruct the motivational dynamics of actors in "ward politics" so that it appears credible, or even inevitable, that "bad" political machines produce "good" neighborhood welfare (Merton, 1957). Or, conversely, we could compare communities having machines and those not having them. If all those having machines also had good welfare, if those without machines had poor welfare, and if the two factors covaried sequentially in time, then we also would find it credible, or even inevitable, that "bad" machines cause "good" welfare. Adequate theory, like adequate plays, must supply credibility from both these sources.[2]

In these senses inevitability, or confident foreknowledge, is as much a criterion for science as it is a criterion for dramatic art. Moreover, in a cognitive aesthetic theory of truth, both these domains have common properties, in that both supply rules of boundary, cogency, and transformation that create the possibility of scientific and artistic meaning. To return to our earlier point, the spelling out of "transformation mechanisms" between latent and manifest functions is important because only in so doing – both motivationally and causally – can we provide the inevitability without which theories are dramatically, and hence intellectually, inadequate.

To be inevitable, however, does not guarantee that a play or prediction will be significant or interesting; inevitability may as likely signal boredom and trivia. To make a theory work, then, the inevitability has to be about the unexpected; there must be an *inevitable interdependency of incongruous opposites*. Such incongruity as perceived by the sociologist can refer to contradictions in the events themselves, in the expectations of the actors or the general public, in the official values of the society, or in the theories of the sociologist's professional colleagues. Indeed, to the extent that sociology becomes a hermetic science,[3] its discoveries will be chiefly ironizations of sociological, rather than popular, knowledge.[4]

A dramatic play and a sociological theory are both representations of experience, both are typifications of worlds. To be human – that is, to be a symbol maker – *means* to apprehend and communicate experience through typifications; yet as *students* of human conduct, both dramatists and sociologists must create typifications of these typifications. The question thus arises: How do the typifications of sociologists differ from those of the persons whom they study? The answer cannot lie in their degree of abstraction, for second-order generations are found in mundane reasoning as well as in social theory. Instead, we suggest that one essence of *sociological* typifications, or more precisely, what makes a typification valuable for sociology as a moral science, is that it ironizes the conventionally accepted typifications of everyday life.

Weber, for example, is interesting to professional scholars for what he has to say about the modern world and how it emerged from the varieties of world history. But on an ethical level, his work informs us because we expected that Christianity should lay a basis for public altruism rather than private avarice. What interest would his *Protestant Ethic and the Spirit of Capitalism* have on this level if the early Protestants had *not* turned piety into profit, or if they merely had been hypocrites rather than victims of historic irony? Similarly, how powerful would be Weber's insight into charisma and bureaucracy (1968) if the prophets really were bureaucratic types to begin with, or were using their charisma merely to capture administrative fiefs?

In contrast, it must be admitted, one finds many propositions such as "group equilibrium is a function of the extent to which group members ... conform with each other's expectations" (see Gouldner, 1959:423, for critique), or that "the more frequently persons interact with one another, the stronger their sentiments of friendship for one another are apt to be" (Homans, 1945:133). Yet by the same token, every such banality can be made to yield a genuine insight if seen from an ironical perspective as, for example, was done by Robert and Helen Lynd:

> In the second Middletown study the Lynds have given a classic analysis of the mind of middle-class America in their series of "of course statements" – that is, statements that represent a consensus so strong that the answer to any question concerning them will habitually be prefaced with the words "of course." "Is our economy one of free enterprise?" "Of course!" "Are all important decisions arrived at through the democratic process?" "Of course!" "Is monogamy the natural form of marriage?" "Of course!" (Berger, 1963:47)

Malcolm Muggeridge said that sociology departments, like topless waitresses and frozen lasagna, have become part of the American landscape. We would suffer this comparison only to the extent that social science is itself composed of "of course statements"; that is, only when sociology fails to be dramatic, only when it does not reveal unexpected relationships that have an ironic necessity, does it become banal. The value of a sociological contribution, then, can be enhanced in two possible ways: either by stressing the ironic incongruity, which heightens the instability of the opposites, the inevitability of the unexpected outcome, and the predictive power of the thesis; or by stressing the unawareness of the victims, which heightens the originality of the theoretical or ethical insight.

That sociological concepts must distance themselves from mundane ones has been noted by numerous writers. Alfred Schutz, for example, speaks of "the world as taken for granted . . . the way of life considered to be the natural, the good, the right one by members of the 'in-group' " (1971:I, 13). Similar notions are Sumner's concept of "folkways and mores" (1906), Durkheim's "collective thought," Park and Burgess's "consensus" (1924:163), Weber's "traditional behavior," Lynd's "of course statements," and Scheler's "relative natural aspect of the world." If such member conceptions constitute what Max Weber called an "enchanted garden," the job of the sociologist becomes that of pointing out the real toads that dwell in it.[5] Or, conversely, for those to whom everyday life is all too real, the sociologist may reenchant this world with the magic of elegant theory. The point in each case is that the sociologist must "estrange" taken-for-granted reality so that it appears in a new and previously unsuspected light; he must be the man who shouts "Theater!" in the middle of a crowded fire.

On the basis of these two concepts – inevitability and incongruity – we now formulate general "laws of irony," of dramatic tension and resolution, which may be taken as criteria of the potential fruitfulness of paradigm innovations in sociological theory. Tentatively, these laws may be stated as follows:

The greater the degree of incongruity,

> between latent and manifest content, or
> between intention and outcome, or
> between the innocence of the victim and the
> awareness of the observer, and

The greater the degree of inevitability,

> of the merging of logically opposed concepts, or
> of the reversal of events,

Then the greater the insight value of a sociological statement.

Or, put briefly, when the highest degree of incongruity is combined with the greatest degree of inevitability, there results a statement of the greatest theoretical value. The first part of this formula, in conventional terms, refers to the extent to which a statement is "original" or "significant"; the second part refers to the extent to which it is "valid" or presents us with a "proof."

Our purpose in what follows is merely to show that irony has been a central, though largely unrecognized, feature of much sociological thought – a latent criteria of truth that the dominant positivist epistemology has kept from becoming manifest. Our examples do not aim at exhausting the concept of irony, only at exhuming it. We thus limit ourselves to identifying three major types of dramatic irony in theories:

1. Unmasking.
   (A is not (merely) A, but (also) B.)
2. Functional interdependency of contraries.
   (A opposes, but at the same time depends on, B.)
3. Dialectical resolution of opposites.
   (A, in opposing B, becomes (like) B.)

Unmasking
We use the term "unmasking" in a theatrical rather than a moralistic sense. The skilled dramatist does not tell the audience that his characters are good when they appear bad, or the reverse. Instead, he lets such contradictions reveal themselves through the unfolding action. For the ironist human actions are such that to relate is to expose them. No moralistic name calling is required; indeed, the moral absolutism of the reformer is as inelegant as the "nothing but" reductivism of positivist defenders of the status quo. Unlike the hypocrite who hides evil in a cloak of virtue, or the reformer who strips away this cloak, the ironist is sufficiently distanced to enter into *either* of these roles, often simultaneously. That is, he is just as pleased to find goodness hiding within evil as he is to unmask evil posing as good.

Such a mode of perception, paradoxical or perverse as it may seem, remains in dialectical tension with mundane understanding. In this sense the "intellectual aha" that a nonspecialist may get reading good sociology can legitimately be followed by the question, "Now, why didn't I think of that?" This is because the subject matter of sociology is directly accessible to anyone with a disciplined imagination, in a way that that of chemistry or marine biology is not. It is partly for this reason that sociology has been called "the science of the obvious." Yet such a statement can be taken in two ways: It is a sling when seen to refer to sociologists' banalities about what actors know is complex. If we reverse this, however, and see sociology as ironic insight into what actors take as banal, then the jibe floats back to its sender. This point applies as much to the relations of sociologists with each other as it does to their relations with laymen. In popular sociology it is the common sense of the public that is ironized. In "serious" sociology, what is ironized is theory conventionally accepted by professionals. Banality is relative.[6]

Wherever sociological analysis is interesting, its basic concepts have this ironic edge. Unexpected similarities are revealed, as are unnoticed differences; opposites are seen to require each other or even to converge; sincerity is seen as bad faith, therapy as manipulation, law as opposed to order, evil as containing hidden good. Thus, for example, the study of personality, which begins by excluding social and cultural factors, leads one to the discovery of culture as that which makes personality determinate and real; apart from culture, personality is indeterminate, amorphous, potential (Diesing, 1971:213). A similar irony of unsuspected ambivalence is noted by V. W. Turner when he shows how the same Ndembu rituals that symbolize the unity and closeness of certain social relations also dramatize separation and conflicts (1964:21–27). Murphey's analysis of Taureg veiling practices (1964), and Radcliffe-Brown's of joking relationships (1952:109–110), respectively show the fur on the cobra, the fangs on the mouse.

The mutual implication of apparently exclusive concepts also is shown in Redfield's discussion of peasant and urban cultures (1953, 1960). Peasant culture, the "little tradition," differs from folk culture in that it is interdependent with the city, the carrier of the "great tradition." The two cultures – peasant and urban – are opposite and can be mutually destructive, yet one cannot survive without the other. Redfield's insight into the mutual implication of two terms often thought of as discrete may be expanded to the national and international scale. Here the peasant tradition is carried by Third World nations, who need the capital, technology, and ideas of the industrial nations, while these centers need the labor and materials of the peasant areas to survive. In this formulation, not only is internationalism implied in nationalism; also implied is the dependence of "master" nations on their "slaves" (see Hegel, 1942:203–204, 247–248).

Pointing out hidden relationships between opposites, or oppositions within apparent unities, will constitute a "discovery" only to the degree of incongruity that is noted in the terms and that is established between the new formulation and prior expectations. Thus, for example, "We are brothers under the skin" (McWilliams, 1951) is not a substantial contribution to knowledge when said of one's cousin or friend. But when analysts of leadership in small groups describe similarities between *The American Soldier* and "Cohesion and Disintegration in the Wehrmacht in World War II," we do find it news that GI's and Nazis bear a family resemblance. The American soldier, it turns out, was motivated not by democratic ideals so much as by fellowship with his comrades. Similarly, German troops were largely unconcerned with national propaganda; their will to fight, like that of the Americans, depended mainly on the character of face-to-face relationships within the combat unit (Stouffer, 1949; Shils and Janowitz, 1948; Little, 1964).

In like manner, the concept "bureaucracy" allows us to note similarities between the Catholic Church and General Motors, between altruistic service organizations and money-grubbing corporations, between Soviet socialism and Western capitalism, between ancient Egypt and the Austro-Hungarian state. The idea of "voluntary association" places a private London men's club in the same frame as a hobo camp – the members of both are exclusively male, leisured, discrete, snobbish, and subject to ostracism by their peers. In a similar fashion, Roland Barthes (1971) uses the concept "rationality" to show a similarity of consciousness between such unlikely compeers as Loyola, de Sade, and Fourier. Similarly, the idea of the "marginal man" allows us to see unexpected commonalities between immigrant German scientists and crazy poets, between pioneers and skid-row bums:

> The man whose restless disposition made him a pioneer
> on the frontier tends to become a "homeless man" – a hobo
> or vagrant – in the modern city. From the point of view of
> their biological predispositions, the pioneer and the hobo
> are perhaps the same temperamental type; from the point
> of view of their socially acquired traits, they are something
> quite different. (Park, in Anderson, 1923:8)

The sociologist's key unmasking device, then, is what Weber called the "general ideal type" (Rogers, 1969). Self-aware Protestants, for example, knew they shared something of a "Protestant ethic," or at least they were likely to become aware of it when they encountered slothful Catholics or gentry. Their "ethic" was a shared precept. Hard work, orderliness, thrift, and the like, were values that "everyone knew." Weber's great insight, then, was not in typifying the Protestant ethic as such. Instead, it lay in his seeing its unforeseen historical consequences, and its relationship to other, apparently unrelated, systems of belief. By transmuting the "Protestant ethic" into the broader typification, "inner-worldly asceticism," Weber was able to expose unsuspected relationships between Protestantism and ancient Judaism, Indian Jainism, and so on (Weber, 1963; G. Roth, 1971).

In this same tradition of unearthing unexpected similarities through ironic typifications, David Matza refines Edwin Lemert's concept of professionalism to include both physicians and whores:

> By prostitution, Lemert means the coincidence of three
> features: an exchange of sexual favor for material return;
> more or less indiscriminate indulgence with many persons;
> and a dissociation of deeper feelings from the physical
> act. If one omits the reference to the sexual act – the special
> province of prostitution – the elements of Lemert's
> conception suggest a similarity not limited to feminine
> activity. The rendering of a service for fee, the absence
> of discrimination in the choice of clientele (universalism),
> and a dissociation of deeper feelings from the service
> rendered (affective neutrality) are among the key elements
> of what is mainly a masculine activity – profession. There
> should be nothing surprising about this similarity:
> Prostitution is among the oldest of professions, and
> professionals always fear prostituting themselves. (1969:
> 83–84)

In addition to showing unsuspected similarities, ironic typifications can be equally effective in unmasking hidden differences and this, indeed, is its more frequent usage. Thus Veblen (1957) noted that people of wealth, or those wishing to appear wealthy, consume expensive goods not (merely) because such items are of better quality or value, but rather *because* they are expensive. That is, the more "frivolous" the expenditure, the more adequately it serves to symbolize that its consumer can "afford" it. As an expression of status, waste is efficient.

Fred Davis (1960) and Glaser and Strauss (1964, 1968), have made similar insights in their respective studies of uncertainty and information control in the practice of medicine. What appears as humane care to the individual may often be a cloak for administrative efficiency; what poses as honest uncertainty may instead be manipulation aimed at avoiding "scenes" that may be caused by bad news. R. D. Laing, in his reinterpretation of a case reported by Kraepelin, unmasks both the doctor *and* the patient. Laing first quotes Kraepelin's report to a lecture room of students on a patient showing signs of catatonic excitement:

> The patient I will show you today has almost to be carried into the room, as he walks in a straddling fashion on the outside of his feet. On coming in, he throws off his slippers, sings a hymn loudly, and then cried twice (in English), "my father, my real father! ". . . . The patient sits with his eyes shut, and pays no attention to his surroundings. He does not look up even when he is spoken to, but he answers beginning in a low voice, and gradually screaming louder and louder. When asked where he is, he says, "You want to know that too? I tell you who is being measured and is measured and shall be measured. I know all that, and could tell you, but I do not want to." When asked his name, he screams, "What is your name? What does he shut? He shuts his eyes. What does he hear? He does not understand; he understands not. How? Who? Where? When? What does he mean? When I tell him to look he does not look properly. . . . ," and so on. At the end he scolds in quite inarticulate sounds. . . . Although he undoubtedly understood all the questions, *he has not given us a single piece of useful information. His talk was . . . only a series of disconnected sentences having no relation whatever to the general situation* (Laing's italics).

Laing then presents his own interpretation of Kraepelin's material, in which patient is seen as ironinzing the doctor:

> Now there is no question that this patient is showing the "signs" of catatonic excitement. The construction we put on this behavior will, however, depend on the relationship we establish with the patient. . . . What does this patient seem to be doing? Surely he is carrying on a dialogue between his own parodied version of Kraepelin, and his own defiant rebelling self. "You want to know that too? I tell you who is being measured and is measured and shall be measured. I know all that, and I could tell you, but I do not want to." This seems to be plain enough talk. Presumably he deeply resents this form of interrogation which is being carried out before a lecture-room of students. He probably does not see what it has to do with the things that must be deeply

distressing him. But these things would not be "useful information" to Kraepelin except as further "signs" of a "disease." (1959:29–30)

It is significant that these examples are from the practice of medicine. The objectivity and professional distance of the doctor – or of the expert in general – puts him in a prime position to ironize the subjective pretensions of his clients.[7] Yet clients, and especially clients who have not voluntarily chosen their role, may also ironize the professional. This double irony is all the more powerful given the expert's assumption that he is in control of the exchange. We don't laugh when an old woman slips on the banana peel; the comic interest – and the potential ironic insight – is in proportion to the stuffiness of the victim, the social height from which he falls.

Another widely used form of unmasking is to show good cloaked as evil, and evil dressed as good. Thus Daniel Bell points out that organized crime fills a demand for numerous services, "humanizes" procedures that otherwise would be mediated by an impersonal bureaucracy, and provides an avenue of status mobility for disadvantaged groups (1960). In a similar fashion Bensman and Gerver discuss "Crime and Punishment in a Factory: The Function of Deviance in Maintaining the Social System" (1963). Likewise, Bayley (1966) notes that "The Effects of Corruption in a Developing Nation" aren't all bad:

Governments have no monopoly on correct solutions. . . . Corruption may serve as a means for impelling better choices, even in terms of government's expressed goals. . . . Contrary to common expectations, it . . . may result in increased allocations of resources away from consumption and into investment [and thus provide] a supplemental allocative mechanism compatible with the goals of economic development. . . . Nepotism in government hiring . . . can be looked upon as a substitute for a public works system. . . . Corruption [also] provides a means of giving . . . potentially disaffected groups . . . a stake in the system. Corruption may make the new system human in traditional terms, . . . reducing the harshness of an elite-conceived plan for . . . development . . . Among politicians [it] may act as a solvent for uncompromisable issues of ideology and/or interest, . . . [and it] may lessen potentially crippling strain [between politicians and the bureaucrats]. (1966)

In a similar vein, while conventional opinion holds that political bossism or social conflict in general is "evil," Merton, Coser, Bayley, Wildavsky, and other functionalists have asserted the virtues of such vices. Similarly, Lyman has argued that "the violent conflicts that erupted in Chinatown were also occasions and instrumentalities of order" (1961:340–377). Conflict, rather than an obstacle, is seen as the means by which society gets its business done. "Conflict . . . is always a transaction," says Coser (1956:37); says Blau, "Opposition is a regenerative force that introjects new vitality into a social structure and becomes the basis of social reorganization. It serves as a catalyst or starting mechanism of social change" (1964:301).

Having discovered a hidden order in chaos, the ironist also will seek chaos in what appears to be order. Thus certain theorists consider talk of "order" or "higher social purposes" as a rhetoric used to suppress the interests of less powerful groups. In terms of these two approaches, then, the debate between rational functionalists and conflict theorists can be seen as a battle as to who will out-ironize whom. The heavenly city of the functionalists has been challenged with studies of racial and ethnic particularism, discrimination of certain status groups in the labor market, the application of fundamentally irrelevant employment and promotion criteria, and other "irrational behaviors" (Collins, 1970; Brown, 1974, for summaries). At the same time, many functionalists have sought to explain such nonrational, nonuniversalistic behavior by interpreting it as aberrant, dysfunctional, an imperfection in an otherwise rational system, a vestige carried over from a less-advanced stage, an accidental obstacle to the natural course of development, or as an *apparent* exception that in reality has a hidden or latent function of systems maintenance (Parsons, 1951; Merton, 1957; Goode, 1973). Since the logic of each school of thought is open to criticisms based on the assumptions of the other, and since the disagreement is not concerning the "evidence" but its theoretical interpretation, it is hard to see how such debates could be resolved in terms of the correspondence theory of truth that sociologists traditionally have employed. On the other hand, such debates may be appreciated as dialectical drama. Both theories are ironic, and both take order and conflict as their data. But which is "appearance" and which is "essence"? In terms of our ironic criteria, the superior theory will be that which incorporates the broadest range of incongruous, contradictory, and apparently incommensurate data into a synthesis which has the most precisely cogent inevitability.

*Functional interdependency and dialectical resolution
of opposites*

Each level of sociological irony flows into and is contained by a dialectically "higher" level. Thus the irony of unmasking "leads to" the ironies of functional interdependency and resolution of opposites. These types of irony are at the core of what Merton has called the unanticipated latent consequences of purposive social action. Indeed, in addition to its conservative ideological appeal, it is just such irony which accounts, we believe, for the staying power and interest of functionalist social theory.

The unsuspected interdependency of opposites has long been noted by general theorists as well as by students of specialized areas of research. At least since Plato, social evolutionists have been aware that one state of affairs often gives rise to its apparent opposite. Other writers have sought to explain how human vices could somehow yield historical good. The eighteenth century, so rich in literary irony, had equal ironic insight into the history of human affairs. Vico noted that Providence so acts that ". . . out of the passions of men each bent on his private advantage, for the sake of which they would live like wild beasts in the wilderness, it has made the civil orders by which they may live in human society" (1948:56). Pointing to the "cunning of reason" and the "unsocial sociability" of men, Kant describes specific mechanisms by which war may result in universal peace (1949:116–131). Turgot, Hegel, Mandeville, Smith and many other eighteenth century thinkers had similar formulations.

In the nineteenth century sociologists were concerned with the great transformations from a feudal-traditional order to a democratic-capitalist one. Opposites such as community-society, authority-power, status-class, sacred-secular and, most embracingly, *Gemeinschaft* and *Gesellschaft*, are terms that today apply more to the Third World than to Euorpe or North America; yet the work of the nineteenth-century masters remains "classic" because of its style of thought and its insight into the ironic interplay of dialectical opposites.

In our time this type of thinking has been couched mainly in the vocabulary of latent and manifest functions or in terms of the dialectic between that which is free and that which is socially determined. MacIver, for example, points out that in addition to the overt effects of institutions which people may choose, "there are further effects . . . which lie outside the direct purposes of men [but which] may, though unintended, be of profound service to society" (1915). Other scholars have noted unsuspected functional interdependencies in such diverse areas as racial intermarriage (R. Adams, 1937; K. Davis, 1941; Merton, 1941); sociocultural change (Eisenstadt, 1963; Sorokin, 1957; Gluckman, 1968); stratification (K. Davis, 1942; Davis and Moore, 1945); affective frustration (Thorner, 1943); witchcraft and religion (Kluckhohn, 1944; Goode, 1951); personality dynamics (Freud, 1930; Mowrer and Kluckhohn, 1944); formal organizations (Selznick, 1949; Adams and Preiss, 1960; Blau, 1964; Gouldner, 1954); arms races, propaganda, and other national security issues (Parsons, 1954; A. K. Davis, 1947; Jahoda and Cook, 1952); programs aimed at curing social ills (Weaver, 1956; Simpson and Yinger, 1956:391); and virtually all other areas to which functionalists point as examples of the successful application of their approach. A limited selection from this literature should illustrate the ironic nature of the rest and, indeed, suggest that dialectical irony accounts for its theoretical teeth and claws.

Kingsley Davis's essay on prostitution, which he interprets as a pillar of female chastity, may be taken as a classic example of this type of thought. Davis first notes that "what the male has lost in frequency of intercourse with prostitutes he has gained in frequency with nonprostitutes." He then ironizes this by suggesting that:

> If we reverse the proposition that increased sex freedom among women of all classes reduces the role of prostitution, we find ourselves admitting that increased prostitution may reduce the sexual irregularities of respectable women.
> This, in fact, has been the ancient justification for tolerated prostitution – that it "protected" the family and kept the wives and daughters of the respectable citizenry pure. . . . Such a view strikes us as paradoxical, because in popular discourse an evil such as prostitution cannot cause a good such as feminine virtue, or vice versa. Yet, as our analysis has implied throughout, there is a close connection between prostitution and the structure of the family. (1961:283–284)

The interdependency of these opposites is at once practical and moral. Increased availability of prostitutes decreases pressure on men to seduce respectable virgins. However, were citizens aware of this latent function they would logically have to encourage it. Yet, in so doing, they would no longer be able to consider themselves upright citizens. The resultant attitude toward prostitution of "repressive tolerance" can be seen as a resolution of this contradiction. Moreover, by pushing Davis's argument to its logical "synthesis," we can see that the commonsense attitude that he ironizes in fact contains a hidden, self-protective wisdom. Ironic reflection thus can turn the analyst on his head even as he up ends the actors. Indeed, just such perspectives of incongruity are the hallmark of ironic insight.[8]

If encouraging a "moral" vice demoralizes those who encourage it, the same ambivalent contradictions may appear when one tries to suppress a vice that is not so good. For example, students of other forms of deviance, such as Matza, have noted that efforts to prohibit unconventional activities may force their practitioners to become even more unconventional. "The logic of ban creates the strong possibility that the subject will become even more deviant in order to deviate," [that is, in order to practice his deviation] (1968:148). Similarly, says Albert Cohen, "The rebuke which brings the incipient deviant back into line may further alienate the deviant who is somewhat further advanced" (1959:468). The reverse of this, when a deviant group bans nonmembers from its activities, may be equally ironic. Thus Becker (1963), Lofland (1966), Festinger (*et al.*, 1956), Schwartz (1968), Weber (1963), and others have pointed to the dialectic of exclusion, hostility, and recruitment in the transformation of cults into movements. Says Theodore Schwartz:

> Cult and opposition are part of a single system,
> indispensible to each other. . . . Secrecy is used to recruit
> as well as to exclude; skepticism, at a certain point, may
> be required of the entering cultist to renew and attest to
> dissonance on which the drama of conversion depends;
> the cultists not only recruit to add confirmation through
> numbers of believers, but they also exclude and elicit
> opposition to add . . . to their own drive and maintenance,
> or through exclusion, to recruit others to the larger
> interdependent system of which cult and opposition are
> both a part. (1968:27, 30)

The functional intedependency of opposites thus reveals the same drama as a "devil's dilemma" or an "impossible choice" as in high comedy or tragedy. If we choose duty, we must sacrifice love. If we avenge our father, we must murder our mother. If we halt prostitution, we subvert respectable women's virtue. If we maintain the purity of our cult we are likely to turn it into a mass movement. If we attempt to preserve the charisma of our leader, we may create an uncharismatic bureaucracy. Again referring back to our initial "laws of irony," such statements constitute "theoretical insights" in the exact degree of the oppositeness of the terms of the dilemma, the degree of confident unawareness of the actors, and the degree of inevitability to the observer of a reversed synthesis or denouement.

Most susceptible to ironization, then, will be the core myths of any group or culture, the "of course" statements that in America center around beliefs in fair play, free enterprise, democracy, and so on. In this sense, what constitutes "sociological knowledge" is irrevocably related to the general state of self-awareness of the culture in which sociologists write. By "culture," however, we mean both the popular understandings of laymen, as well as the taken-for-granted assumptions of professionals. In each case – whether popular or serious sociology – what constitutes an insight is relative to the sophistication of the audience. The higher their reflexive self-awareness, the higher the level to which sociological insight can and must ascend. Failing to do this, sociology becomes the science of the obvious in the negative sense, distinguishable only in its jargon from "what everyone knows."

In America, then, it is not surprising that the most striking formulations – especially in more popular sociology – concern just the values that Americans hold most dear. As Kingsley Davis uses prostitution to ironize monogamy as "the natural form of marriage," so Daniel Bell uses crime to ironize the values of ambition and success:

> Crime, in many ways, is a Coney Island mirror,
> caricaturing the morals and manners of a society. The
> jungle quality of the American business community,
> particularly at the turn of the century, was reflected in the
> mode of "business" practiced by the coarse gangster
> elements, most of them from new immigrant families, who
> were "getting ahead" just as Horatio Alger had urged.
> (1960:128)

Similar ironies have been the focus of theoretical writings on stratification, capitalism, and their relation to democracy. The thesis of Kingsley Davis and Wilbert Moore (1945), for example, despite ideological and empirical criticism, remains an important model of status and class. In their view the functioning of a democratic (or any other) society *depends on* status inequalities; without them the system would cease to exist. A more radical expression of this view is put forward by Michael

Lewis (1974), according to whom the very access to interclass mobility of most Americans creates status insecurities that seek outlet against some scapegoat, in this case the Negro, who is thereby forbidden to compete in the game of status achievement. Thus, paradoxically, openness among whites calls forth closedness against blacks; the racial caste system in America is a product of open-class mobility.[9]

A similar devil's dilemma was noted by Philip Selznick in his study *TVA and the Grass Roots* (1949). The federal agency, committed to building local democracy as well as power stations, but also needing to build its own constituency, encountered certain "inherent dilemmas": "Emphasis on existing institutions as democratic instruments may wed the agency to the status quo . . . and may shape and inhibit policy in unanticipated ways. . . . An attempt to carry forward a policy of nondiscrimination (as against Negroes) will not proceed very far when the instrument for carrying out this policy has traditions of its own of a contrary bent."

Other studies of the labor movement – such as Lipset, Trow, and Coleman's *Union Democracy* (1956) and its critique by Paul Jacobs (1958, 1963); Lyman's study of Chinese immigrants in relationship to the unions (1970:21–23, 115–116); and Hill and Ross's essays on racism as an instrument of labor organizing (1973, 1967) – all suggest that to realize competitive bargaining and democracy for white laborers seemed to have required, or to have led to, undemocratic treatment of workers of color.

Other scholars viewed democracy not so much as a good that produces evils, but instead looked at evils that result in the democratic good. Conflict functionalists such as Coser and Blau were mentioned earlier. Also in this vein is Tocqueville's study *The Old Regime and the French Revolution* (1955). It was not the Revolution that had destroyed traditional institutions of local self-government, Tocqueville discovered; instead, and contrary to conservative opinion, it was the French king himself.[10] Feudalism, which we had thought was the enemy of democracy, turns out to have been its protector.[11]

Tocqueville thus provides a transformation mechanism by which the destruction of feudal institutions may result in undemocratic centralism, or the reverse. Tocqueville's studies of the archives of French provincial towns, and his comparative analysis of these with the institutional development of England, Germany, and elsewhere, provide a powerful sense of inevitability to the dialectical relationship of apparent opposites. In contrast, Engels (1939) notes a relationship between ancient slavery and modern freedom, but without providing the same detailed linkage:

> It was slavery that first made possible the division between agriculture and industry on a considerable scale, and along with this, the flower of the ancient world, Hellenism. Without slavery, no Greek state, no Greek art and science; without slavery, no Roman Empire. But without Hellenism and the Roman Empire as a basis, also no modern Europe.
>
> We should never forget that our whole economic, political and intellectual development has as its presupposition a state of things in which slavery was as necessary as it was universally recognized. In this sense we are entitled to say: Without the slavery of antiquity, no modern socialism.

Bad yields good: Feudalism gives rise to democracy; slavery underpins socialism. Yet in the latter formulation we sense that a number of indispensable links have been omitted. Imagine an "inevitability scale" with "possible and plausible" at one end, "sufficient condition" at the other, and "necessary but not sufficient" somewhere in the middle. In terms of such a scale, taken from our "laws of irony," Tocqueville's formulation would score higher on "inevitability" because of its tighter logic and more thorough historical research. On this basis it would represent a "better" and "more interesting" theoretical formulation. However, in terms of our other law of irony, concerning the distance between dialectical opposites, Engel's pair is richer in contradiction; socialism and slavery seem highly opposed, while feudalism and American democracy share the notion of decentralized control. In terms of the degree of complacent unawareness of the actors, however, both formulations come out the same: Neither Hellenes and Romans nor feudal lords and early modern kings were aware of the potential consequences of their actions for either democracy *or* socialism. Similarly, there is not much difference in the degree in which our conventional views of these historical periods have been altered. Most people know Athens practiced slavery, just as most of us see the Magna Carta as a document of democracy. If our laws of irony are useful, they should illuminate in this way just those aspects that make one theoretical formulation more insightful than others.

GOFFMAN AND SOROKIN: TWO STYLES IN IRONIC SOCIAL THOUGHT

It might be said that the examples in the preceding section are superficial and unrepresentative. In response to such objections we explore the theories of two figures of unquestionable stature who, at the same time, appear to be far removed from each other: Erving Goffman and Pitirim Sorokin. While Goffman shows how consciousness reveals itself in passing encounters, Sorokin treats the unfolding of consciousness in historical civilizational systems. The first generally is considered a cynic, the second is a professed altruist. Yet despite such differences in moral and theoretical stance, the two share much that can be traced back to the dialectical sociology of Simmel. Like Simmel, both are "formal" sociologists in that they focus primarily on the descriptive analysis of the salient *types* or forms of face-to-face or systemic interaction, rather than concentrating on extrinsic analyses of causal relationships between such types. Both look to *style* as a principal expressive attribute of selves or systems. Both take as a basic category of analysis the actors' awareness of the consequences of conduct. Both make central use of the principle of peripety, or limit and reversal, in explaining the maintenance or transformation of governing definitions of reality. Both focus on the "tragedy of culture" – the evanescence of structure, its coming together and fading away, its fragility for persons and societies. Both stress the dialectic between self or spirit and their objectifications, mutually dependent and mutually subversive. Both employ dialectical irony as a basic mode of analysis.

Erving Goffman as dialectical ironist

At the turn of the century Emile Durkheim argued that a collective sense of moral bondedness, enacted through ritual and ceremony, is what holds society together. Durkheim tested this thesis at just those points where social order breaks down: Where the *conscience collectif* is weak we would expect to find deviation and disorder; where it is normal we should find low rates of social pathology; for example, rates of suicide are likely to be higher among groups that have the weakest sense of social filiation – unmarried men more than married, Protestants more than Jews, and nouveau riche or nouveau poor more than those with stable incomes and friendships.

Goffman took up Durkheim's insight that the normal can be understood through the abnormal, and he grounded Durkheim's

concept of *conscience collectif* in the interaction rituals of everyday life. Embarrassment, disability, scandals, mental illness,
faux pas, and awkward situations – these are Goffman's subjects. And, in illuminating them, he shows how psychiatrists
may be manipulated by their patients, how criminality provides
a model for understanding respectability, how work has the
game features of play, how the sancity of the self is revealed
through its profanation.

The social world for Goffman is play, in both the game
theoretical and dramaturgical senses. The "objective facts" of
the social world are seen as (material for) rituals of self-
presentation. These self-presentations are not "false" however,
for any counterstatement of the "objective facts" of the situation are seen as simply another representation.

> We now come to the basic dialectic. In their capacity as
> performers, individuals will be concerned with maintaining
> the impression that they are living up to the many
> standards by which they and their products are judged. . . .
> But, *qua* performers, individuals are concerned not with
> the moral issue of realizing these standards, but with
> the amoral issue of engineering a convincing impression
> that these standards are being realized. (1959:251)

This idea of the world as enactment has a number of descriptive and analytical advantages that lay largely in the
suitability of such imagery for ironic exposition. The social
world also has been pictured as an unfolding story, a tapestry,
or a canvas, and "dramatic tension" certainly occurs in these
"nondramatic" genres. Yet it is only in the theater that the
observer actually sees real people without free will (actors
playing roles) who are at the same time embodied fictions
acting (as though) of their own volition. Moreover, it is only
in the theater that the observer watches persons who *cannot*
know, by virtue of the rules of traditional play acting, that they
are being watched. The characters in a novel, of course, similarly cannot know that they are being read, but such characters
are only literary; unlike actors, they are not at the same time
real persons.

Modern theater, of course, has exploited the possibilities for
manipulating the aesthetic distance between the actor and the
audience, ironically alternating between reality and appearance
until the two are illuminated, confounded, or made to yield
some higher truth.[12] Bertolt Brecht's idea of the "alienation
effect" (1964) also makes use of this distance in that the source

of audience interest in the play lies in the tension between the play and life, not just in the dramatic tension internal to the play itself. This effect, as States puts it, is "a means of capitalizing on the actor's physical *existence* as a member of the audience's society at the same time that he is, *in essence*, a member of a fictitious society" (1971:176). Through ironic distance, then, the playwright or sociologist can not only "unmask" his actors, but also reveal unsuspected levels of the meaning and methods of their self-presentations.[13] "People 'lie psychologically'," says Pirandello (1952:xiv), "even as they 'lie socially'."

Rather than juxtaposing "real selves" and "false masks," however, Goffman draws no ontological distinctions between the two.[14] Instead he suspends the issue of the normative status of levels or types of reality, and examines *how* masks and selves dialectically come to be. For example, even in dealing with a bizarre social phenomenon, Goffman brackets the conventional idea that it is sick or crazy and instead seeks to understand it as emergent from *some* definition of the situation:

> As has been repeatedly shown in the study of nonliterate
> societies, the awesomeness, distastefulness, and barbarity
> of a foreign culture can decrease to the degree that the
> student becomes familiar with the point of view to life
> taken by his subjects. Similarly, the student of mental
> hospitals can discover that the craziness or "sick behavior"
> claimed for the mental patient is by and large a product
> of the claimant's social distance from the situation that the
> patient is in, and is not primarily a product of mental
> illness. (1961:130)

People are not, originally and in some factlike way, "mothers," "surgeons," or "crazy." Instead, they are cast into these roles by themselves and by others. Moreover, the actor always retains the possibility of a certain distance from the role. He may have the role thrust on him, and come to naively assume that he *is* the part. But he may also employ tactics of role avoidance or, once in a role, he may manipulatively exploit its possibilities. Thus conduct is not seen as simply "out there," a fact independent of any consciousness. Instead, even in the most extreme and coercive situations, conduct is understandable only as a project, in-order-to or because-of something in the actor's hierarchy of relevance. Eye contact, body gesture, even an old overcoat can be an instrument of engagement or evasion. "Since an overcoat *can* conceal clear evidence of migration, and since a personal front involving clothing accompanies our participation in every organization, we must appreciate that *any* figure cut by *any* person *may* conceal evidence of spiritual leave-taking" (1961:188, Goffman's italics; see Gogol, 1964).

This type of thinking is profoundly ironic, for it suggests that it is not the stimulus that determines the response, but that it is only through the "response" that the "stimulus" can be known. It is less the deviance that causes repression than the reverse; it is the cure that defines the disease. Thus agencies organized to help the blind teach sighted persons how to act like, or to become, blind men (R. Scott, 1969); ghetto schools, by holding special classes to help underachievers, encourage behavior that justifies the label; prisons, officially in the business of rehabilitation, instead serve as colleges of criminality; socially disruptive persons are taught how to act mentally ill by those wishing to give them care:

> I am suggesting that the patient's nature is redefined so that, in effect if not by intention, the patient becomes the kind of object upon which a psychiatric service can be performed. To be made a patient is to be remade into a serviceable object, the double irony being that so little service is available once this is done. (1961:379)

Moreover, once such casting takes place, a process that Goffman calls "looping" may occur – any attempt by the patient to affirm his sanity is reinterpreted as another manifestation of his disease. In this predicament the only way a "sick" person can achieve selfhood and autonomy is by utterly rejecting, and then outwitting, his would-be curers.

The dramatic model thus affords Goffman an ironic dialectical vehicle of description and analysis. Layer by layer of strategies and meanings emerge, each illuminated by the others. The actor is not (merely) what he seems: He is at once self and persona, autonomous as well as unfree. Others seek to cast him in roles, but these roles can be rejected, manipulated, subverted, or, "juggled." Those seeking to change his fate often seal it. Moreover, unlike the cosmic irony of Sorokin, the dialectical engine in Goffman's writings is the all too humanness of persons: the psychological and social lies we tell to ourselves and to each other. What Matza says about casting speaks for Goffman as well:

> In Darwin's natural selection evolution occurs without Author. Human selection restores active authority to a

central place, but an irony is maintained. Being merely
human, he who casts another as deviant may intend
something quite different or, if conscious of his activity,
may view it as quite inconsequential, as *following* the
formation of character rather than contributing to it.
In the human realm, the irony of selection is that it is done
with good intentions; not with no intentions whatsoever.
Self-deception, bad faith, the limitations of perspective and
short-sightedness replace the fully blind forces of nature.
Motive restored, consequence becomes more devious.
(Matza, 1969:157)

This use of irony to unfold layers of consciousness and expression may be restated in terms of a formal model as, for
example, Muecke has done in his treatment of irony in literature. To illustrate this we may begin with a fairly simple
passage, one that Goffman himself might quote. In *Northanger
Abbey*, Mr. Tilney has been introduced to Catherine Morland:

After chatting for some time on such matters as naturally
arose from the objects around them, he suddenly addressed
her with – "I have hitherto been very remiss, madam, in
the proper attentions of a partner here; I have not yet
asked you how long you have been in Bath; whether you
were ever here before; whether you have been at the
Upper Rooms, the theatre, and the concert; and how you
like the place altogether. I have been very negligent – but
are you now at leisure to satisfy me in these particulars?
If you are I will begin directly."

"You need not give yourself that trouble, sir."

"No trouble I assure you, madam." Then forming his
features into a set smile, and affectedly softening his voice,
he added with a simpering air, "Have you been long in
Bath, madam?"

"About a week, sir," replied Catherine, trying not to
laugh.

"Really!" with affected astonishment.

"Why should you be surprised, sir?"

"Why, indeed!" said he, in his natural tone – "but some
emotion must appear to be raised by your reply, and
surprise is more easily assumed, and not less reasonable
than any other. – Now let us go on. Were you never here
before, madam?"

"Never, sir."

"Indeed! Have you yet honored the Upper Rooms?"

"Yes, sir, I was there last Monday."
"Have you been to the theatre?"
"Yes, sir, I was at the play on Tuesday."
"To the concert?"
"Yes, sir, on Wednesday."
"And are you altogether pleased with Bath?"
"Yes – I like it very well."
"Now I must give one smirk, and then we may be rational again."
Catherine turned away her head, not knowing whether she might venture to laugh. (J. Austen, 1818:25–26)

This little scene, which could have been taken from life as well as from literature, can be interpreted as presenting several stages or dimensions. We can see, for example, levels in the art of conversation, which have their analogue in the development of art in general and, parallel to this, several levels in development of sociation which have their analogue in the art of sociological interpretation. In formal terms, following Muecke, these may be divided as follows.

Stage 1. Natural, spontaneous conversation. The equivalent in art would be the stage, perhaps in folk art, at which a dance or ballad is composed with complete spontaneity and un-self-consciousness. The counterpart in sociology would be an account of interaction by a participant who was not being self-consciously theoretical, as, for example, the autobiography W. I. Thomas commissioned a peasant to write.

Stage 2. "Making conversation," saying the right things on acceptable topics. The equivalent in art is the work consciously but not self-consciously composed within an acceptable tradition – "hack work" by competent professionals. The equivalent in sociology might be statistical studies of the dating behavior of coeds, which makes no methodological or theoretical innovations (cf. Cooper, 1971:10–13).

Stage 3. Being aware of the artificiality of pretending to converse naturally. An artist stymied by his consciousness of the artificiality of art is in a similar position, as is the sociologist aware that his descriptive analyses can never capture the nature of his subject matter as lived experience.

Stage 4. One way out of this impasse is available to highly spirited persons, or to persons of normal passions in extreme situations: to sweep away conventions and express one's feelings directly. The prototype of this in art is the *Sturm und Drang* genius. The counterpart in sociology is the bold specu-

lator who presents radically original hypotheses despite a lack
of data or the hostility of conventional opinion.

Stage 5. But the artist is in an unfree condition as long as he is
possessed by creative fervor, as is the case in Stage 4. To recover his freedom he must impose upon his inspiration the
self-limitation of irony. Thus Thomas Mann writes that "In matters of style I really no longer admit anything but parody"
(1947:179). Similarly, in the conversation quoted above, Henry
Tilney parodies artificial conversation – he uses artificiality to
destroy artificiality, and so he becomes free on a higher level.
Likewise, in sociological interpretation, Goffman suspends notions of real selves versus false masks, and instead uses each
to unmask the other, thereby liberating the analyst and enabling
him to understand the situation on many levels at once. Such a
perspective unites both subjectivity and objectivity, allows us
to fill the demands of both causal and interpretive knowledge,
and does what Schlegel required of "every good poem," that it
"must be at the same time wholly conscious and wholly in-
stinctive" (1957:113), a movement, as Mann put it quoting
Merezhkovsky, "from unconscious creation to creative consciousness" (1960:88–89).

In presenting this model we have focused on the conversation
as conducted by Mr. Tilney. But it is easy to imagine that
Catherine Morland, or someone else, could turn the irony back,
perhaps by assuming an air of indignation at Mr. Tilney's
flippancy or, conversely, by responding to his questions with
elaborate seriousness. The first tactic tends to be used by persons of moral authority – executives to staff and fathers to children, for example. It turns the tables on the ironist's mocking
the conventional. The second tactic is more often employed
by people commissioned to carry out commands: bureaucrats,
children, and underlings of all sorts. This tactic ironizes one's
own conventionality. In both cases, as soon as more than one
participant becomes self-aware in the setting, the gamelike
qualities of the social drama become explicit. Such "dramatic
tension" can, of course, be seen in virtually any situation of
conflict or choice. For example, family versus career: Although
the psychologist sees it as an "inner conflict" within the actor,
the sociologist understands it as a conflict of the actor's kins-
men against his work group. Passion versus propriety: Will
the count bed Hildegard, or will he wed her first? – a "personal"
choice that also can be seen as a social drama between competing classes. In this manner interaction can be construed as

games of information and control between teams, groups and organizations, as well as among individuals:

> Since we all participate on teams we must all carry within ourselves something of the sweet guilt of conspirators. And since each team is engaged in maintaining the stability of some definitions of the situation, concealing or playing down certain facts in order to do this, we can expect the performer to live out his conspiratorial career in some furtiveness. (Goffman, 1959:105)

While Howard Becker makes bigots the butt of his implicit irony and Thorstein Veblen mocks academics and the leisured class, the favorite subjects of Erving Goffman are the professional and his clients. In decoding Goffman's discussions of mental patients and their doctors in mental asylums, for example, we note five logical levels in terms of our model.

Stage 1. The "sick" person's behavior and other laymen's response to it. Goffman describes these naturalistically, but his analysis then goes on to ironize what he has observed:

> Ordinarily the pathology which first draws attention to the patient's condition is conduct that is "inappropriate in the situation." But . . . diagnostic decisions can become ethnocentric, the server judging from his own culture's point of view individuals' conduct that can really be judged only from the perspective of the group from which they derive. Further, since inappropriate behavior is typically behavior that someone does not like and finds extremely troublesome, decisions concerning it tend to be political. . . . (1961:363–364)

While using dramaturgical imagery to ironize people's pretensions to honesty and directness, however, Goffman at the same time ironizes the drama itself: In a basic sense there is no difference between the face and the mask. The face *is* the mask, in that the face is used as an instrument to convey impressions of ourselves to others. But even here the dialectic is reintroduced, for to speak of "impressions of ourselves" implies that there *is* a "self" that the impressions are impressions *of*. By exploiting such ambiguities between formal appearances and ineffable essence, Goffman ultimately debunks the pretensions of sacred ritual itself. He disenchants the status of everyone, including himself, by suggesting that underneath it all "our . . . everything is not very much."

The wife of the patient may be quite unaware of her "conspiratorial" relation with the psychiatrist (or with the dentist, priest, etc.). Yet in this role she initiates possible degradation ceremonies for her husband. Instead of gratitude at her benevolence, the patient may feel abandoned and betrayed (1961: 136–141).

Stage 2. Making a professional diagnosis. The expert translates the spontaneous "natural" behavior of laymen into the vocabulary of a codified tradition. The irony here, as noted earlier, is that the professional sees himself as merely responding to the patient's conduct. As Goffman shows, however, the "response" casts the patient into a role which the doctor then interprets as the "stimulus" of his own action.

Stage 3. Awareness of the artificiality of "therapy." The therapist is perceived as not being able to deliver the therapy that he has prescribed, yet the patient by now is also shown to be socially incompetent or, at least, incapable of doing very much about his situation.

Stage 4. The underlife of the mental asylum is revealed for what it "really is." The dehumanization of enforced institutionalization is described, as are countertactics employed by patients to preserve some sense of self.

Stage 5. Transcendence of each pair of opposites is mastered. There also is a convergence of the moral meaning with the theoretical insight. At this moment in the context and sequence of his argument Goffman emerges as a subtle, conservative Durkheimian. Beyond unmasking personal and institutional falsity, Goffman reveals the *functional necessity* of formalisms in everyday life. The analyst describes the dialectical relation of role casting and role evasion – the need for social order (the good intention) and the psychic exploitation (the bad result) involved in actually implementing social control. Mental illness is not a crime but a punishment, the social "justice" of which is itself poetic. The failure to live up to the rules of social encounters requires retaliation by one's fellows in order that those rules remain alive; as the self is derived from others, so by others it is taken away.

Pitirim Sorokin and the dialectics of social and cultural change

Unlike Goffman, Sorokin self-consciously is in that biogenetic tradition that seeks to explain the origins to total sociocultural systems:

> ... this means that any sociocultural system, as soon as it emerges as a system, bears in itself its future destiny. To

use Aristotle's example, an acorn as soon as it emerges
bears in itself its destiny, namely the unfolding destiny of
an oak and of nothing else. So with the initial system of
any plant or animal organism. The same is still truer of a
sociocultural system. (1957:640)

The above, of course, is fully vulnerable to the mechanists'
criticisms discussed in Chapter 4. Yet Sorokin appears to
have the virtues of his faults, for his most brilliant ideas are
just those which help him overcome the limits of the biological
metaphor. Three of these ideas are:

1. The restriction of the principle of immanence to logicomeaningful systems.

2. The empirical specification of transformation mechanisms
by which historical dialectics take place.

3. The use of dialectical modes other than immanentalism.

Aristotle defined a class or species as "things which do move
continuously, in virtue of the principle inherent in themselves,
towards a determined goal; . . . in each there is always a tendency towards an identical result if nothing interferes (*Physics*,
II, viii). So far this could be Sorokin. But, unlike some other
modern theorists, Sorokin does not then "explain" change in
terms of some generalized inner "tendency." Instead, he insists
that immanentalism applies only to logicomeaningful systems,
whose very integratedness and adaptability make them highly
resistant to external influence. Yet, "The *Dynamics* clearly states
that only a few total cultures of a few societies and periods reach
the highest possible integration. . . . Even in such *Hochkulteren*
these supersystems unify only their significant part, and not
their total culture. In other words, these supersystems are neither
coextensive nor equivalent with the total human culture" (1964:
407).

Other cultural expressions that do not display this unity are
explicable in terms other than the immanentalist principle. At
the same time, however, Sorokin takes pains to specify the
nature of logicomeaningful entities or cultural supersystems in
terms *independent* of their tendency toward self-transformation.
Insofar as he is successful in this, Sorokin avoids the Aristotelian tautology that a thing is the cause of itself.

A second major contribution of Sorokin's theory is his
specification of a number of devices by which systems appear
and reappear. One such explanation is logical. Sorokin does
not view social change as "ever-linear, ever-new, or strictly
circular." Systems come and go, but they do so neither in a

steady progressive development nor in an ever repeating cycle. Instead, says Sorokin, there are a limited number of basic civilizational cognitive systems. As one of these reaches the point of entropy its replacement must take the form of at least one of the others, though *which* once it will be is not strictly determined by the one that went before. Thus change is neither progressive nor cyclical, but fluctuating. The limited number of possible systems, and the limitations within each system, results in a dialectical playing off of each against the others.

Beyond this general formulation, however, Sorokin notes a number of specific empirical mechanisms of dialectical change. One example of this is Sorokin's treatment of "the tragic and immanent destiny of the Ascetic Ideational culture system to turn into the Active Ideational." As more people follow an Ascetic Ideational way and an organization arises, organizational necessities tend to become an end in themselves, and the ascetic purity of the original movement becomes contaminated. Success in the world is bought at the price of disfigurement of the spirit:

> When we read about the activities of St. Paul, the great
> organizer of Christianity, we notice at once how he had to
> busy himself with worldly matters and how the empirical
> world caught him more and more in its web . . . most of the
> matters in which his flock involved him, from riots and
> politics to property and wealth, were of this world.
> (1941:I, 35–36)

A slightly different mechanism comes from the fact that saints often become objects of veneration and, as such, they draw crowds, stimulate markets and trade, and create prosperity, thereby endangering asceticism again, even if the ascetic leaders themselves remain pure (1941:III, 223–224). A third mechanism is suggested by the view that large numbers of followers cannot in any case attain or long remain at the Ascetic Ideational level (1941:I, 135). Success of a church brings an increase of adherents, but this very increase means that the beliefs adhered to will be significantly changed. "The tragedy of vulgarization and decisive disfiguring of any complex and great and sublime system of cultural values when it infiltrates and roots itself among the large masses is that . . . such success is invariably bought at the cost of . . . simplification and distortion" (1941:IV, 82, 84, 259, n. 83).

Finally, it should be noted that Sorokin does not restrict himself to immanentalism, but makes use of a number of dialectical procedures. As pointed out by Gurvitch (1962), the dialectical method involves five different operational procedures: complementarity, mutual implication, ambiguity, polarization, and reciprocity of perspectives. At least four of these dialectical procedures have been used by Sorokin: in his construction of his "Integral system of philosophy, sociology, and personality structure" (1963); in his concept of inorganic, organic, and superorganic levels of reality (1954); and in his discussions of the social, cultural, and personal aspects of superorganic reality (1957, 1963). Concerning his theory of ideational-sensate-idealistic supersystems, Sorokin himself states that

> without a use of dialectical procedures of complimentary, mutual dialectical implication, dialectical polarization, and dialectical reciprocity of perspective, it is hardly possible to define and study adequately social or cultural systems as *Ganzheiten* (quite different from congeries); their meaningful causal unity, their triple interdependence of parts upon the whole, upon each other, and of the whole upon the parts, and other basic characteristics. (1964:404)

These efforts by Sorokin do not entirely save him from critics who attack his theory as tautological, empirically weak, and lacking in predictive power. Insofar as such criticisms are valid, however, they can be seen in the same light that we have used to illuminate Sorokin's virtues. This may be represented formally as follows:

Tautological logic and definitions	$=$	Lack of dramatic tension
Empirical weakness	$=$	Lack of a sense of inevitability
Lack of predictive power	$=$	Lack of foreknowledge on the part of the observer

The "scientific" weaknesses of Sorokin's theory are thus dramaturgical or aesthetic ones as well.[15]

IRONISM AS A HUMANISM

The "homeless mind" of modern man wanders in a wilderness not of nature but of conflicting social forces (Berger *et al.*, 1973). "We live as the ancients did," says Weber, "only . . . in a different sense. . . . As Hellenic man at times sacrificed to Aphrodite and at other times to Apollo, and, above all, as everybody sacrificed to the gods of his city, so do we still nowadays, only the bearing of man has been disenchanted and denuded of its mystical and genuine plasticity. Fate, and certainly not 'science,' holds sway over these gods and their struggles" (1946: 148).

The gods are not only the competing ideologies of the market-place or of political groups. They are also, and above all, the various compartments into which modern life has been divided – the worlds of work, of family, of ideas, and so on endlessly, each with its own rituals and deities, each seemingly unrelated to the totems and rites of the others. Everyday life thus becomes a kind of manic sacrificing, propitiating now to one god, now to its rivals. The choice of a career, the possibility of creating one's own persona, appeared in the nineteenth century and even then entailed both the evaluation of various professions and political regimes as alternative life forms, as well as a dissatis-faction with any ultimate option. When Balzac and Stendhal were writing, few people imagined that society could be re-structured. Yet today in advanced industrial nations most per-sons can envision alternative futures. The relativization of *race*, *milieu*, *moment* through heightened communication and social and geographic mobility has had its counterpart in a *psychic* mobility, the capacity to imagine oneself into different identities and situations. The view that "Anything is possible," held in the nineteenth century by social philosophers and marginal men, today seems an almost universal article of faith. As Herbert Fingarette says, "It is the special fate of modern man that he has a 'choice' of spiritual visions. The paradox is that although each requires complete commitment for complete validity, we can today generate a context in which we see that no one of them is the sole vision" (1963:236).

Such a relativization of values has implications for sociology even more than for other aspects of contemporary culture. Sociology, with one foot in the basements of metaphysics and the other on the escalator to power, stands astride these contradic-tions. Sociology is the "new science" in its application of Cartesian rationality and Baconian empiricism to social data, as well as in Vico's anti-Cartesian sense of being the study of the world that we have created and to which we belong. Yet sociology is the new science in yet another and more important way, in its peculiarly modern response to the relativization and "absurdity" of modern life.

This peculiar sensibility – much of which is ironic – makes

the sociologist, like the artist, an outsider. In his professional
perspective he is irrevocably separated from unreflective men.[16]
He avoids both the underdistance of those who live within their
social myths, as well as the overdistance of the positivist who
assumes the thingness of what he sees. In contrast to both, what
is "ironic" from the sociological perspective is that people act,
or can be treated, as objects when in fact they are, or can be,
human. To *be* ironical the sociologist must apprehend situations
in terms of the dialectic between his own knowledge and the
unawareness of others. His irony requires that his "victim"
interpret ambiguous action differently from those "in the know."
But it also requires that these differing levels of awareness be
joined in a structured synthesis.[17]

The ironic stance thus has the dispassion or overview in which
opposites converge. But it is objective in the further sense that,
in the very possession of this greater knowledge of the dialectical
outcome of the situation, the ironicist *objectifies* the persons
under study, he makes of them objects. This process of objectifying also contains its opposite; to see the irony of a person acting
as an object is, at the same instant, to assume that he is capable
of acting as subject. In this fashion *irony humanizes as it objectifies*. For, if only humans can be ironical, it is equally true
that only humans can be ironized. To see people as merely
animals is to commit the reductive fallacy; but to see animals
or things in ironic situations is to commit the pathetic fallacy.
If we laugh at our dog for not getting a joke it is because we have
mistakenly imputed to it the capacity for a human kind of
understanding. Conversely, to see persons as victims of irony –
to see them "object-ively" – is to turn them into animals or
things. Bergson's theory of humor makes a similar point: "The
attitudes, gestures and movements of the human body are
laughable in exact proportions as that body reminds us of a mere
machine. . . . We laugh every time a person gives us the impression of being a thing" (1956:79–97).

This very vulnerability to irony also implies the capacity to
avoid being a victim. Unlike the behaviorist who treats persons
as mere objects, in the ironic mode the subject nature of persons
is brought to awareness dialectically, when juxtaposed with its
contrary, the perception of persons behaving *as though* they were
things. The ironic stance transcends the object-subject dualism
by seeing each half of this pair, when posited alone, as susceptible to ironization by the other. Through such a dialectic between subjectivity and objectivity the ironist can achieve a per-

spective of both these perspectives, incorporating even while transcending them (Burke, 1969a:512). None of the participating subperspectives are treated as either precisely right or precisely wrong. Each is a voice, or position, which, in interacting with the others, contributes to the development of the whole.

The sense of superior knowledge, or *fore*knowledge, the outsiderness or distance, the timelessness of a perspective that hovers over earthly transformations, all suggest God, or Satan, as the master ironist, the "Aristophanes of Heaven" as Heine called him. Classical literature abounds in images of gods laughing at men. Scholastics also spoke of God as the dreamer of the dream we live, or as the spectator of the *theatrum mundi*. For from God's ultimate perspective all human actions take on a penultimate character, and hence they are subject to irony to the extent that humans take them as absolute (Bonhoffer, 1967). To God's archetypal ironist, man plays the archetypal victim. Enmeshed in the contingent, unfree but believing ourselves masters, or free but acting as slaves, humanity plays out its comedy for the heavens.

Given God as the archetypal ironist, it is natural that many human ironists have seen themselves as partaking in the divine. "Supreme Irony reigns in the conduct of God as he creates men and the life of men. In earthly art Irony has this meaning – conduct similar to God's" (Solger; cf. Sedgewick, 1948:17). This notion of the artist as god was voiced by eighteenth-century Britons such as Scaliger, Sidney, and Shaftesbury; the view of God as artist was held by such nineteenth-century Germans as Goethe, Schelling, and Schlegel. In his study of Unamuno, José Mora draws a parallel between the writer and God who, in dreaming forth the world, creates a "kind of cosmic novel." More recently, a divinely ironic perspective, or what Peter Berger calls "Christian faith," has been seen to have a direct bearing on sociological inquiry:

> The Christian faith, when it is true to itself and really is
> "in the world but not of it," provides distance from society
> and thus creates opportunities for perception. Thus the
> Christian faith relates to the enterprise of the social sciences
> not only because of its radical challenge to social delusions
> and alibis. In a more benign way, as it were, it relates to
> the "sociological imagination" (Mills) by way of the
> cosmic perspective on the social carnival. (1969:132)

To the extent that the ironist takes his activity as godlike, however, he becomes himself a proper subject of irony. Just

when he thinks he has cornered the market on reason and freedom the ironist exhausts his credit. For the confidence and
mastery he feels at this moment is an exact replica of the pre-
sumptive confidence and mastery he is laughing at in his victim.
By savoring his superior knowledge, by relaxing in Nature's
throne, as Verlaine put it, *"de splendeur, d'ironie, et de
sérénité,"* the ironist assumes a complacent unawareness that
vitiates his own position.[18]

Moreover, the ironist not only may be subjected to irony from
a higher level than his own; he also may be ironized by what he
finds out. The sphinx may indeed have no secret; but, as Oedipus
discovered, she also may hold secrets better left untold. The
ironist may find himself caught in an endless regress of ironies;
the "infinite heights" may turn out to be the bottomless depths.

None of us is utterly safe from ironization. The absolute
defense against irony would itself be ironizable in its absoluteness. Circumspection, a sense of relatively, tentativeness in
making judgments, can be carried only so far; beyond a certain
point the lack of confidence in the future, a desire to avoid being
surprised, itself becomes a pose. This point is made in Kafka's
story *The Burrow* (1971) in which a molelike creature, when
emerging above ground for air, must constantly guard that no
enemies are sniffing around his hole. Yet he is faced with a
dilemma: Are there really no enemies about? Or is their non-
appearance due only to the fact that he is out there watching for
them?

Any desire to obtain absolute knowledge is potentially ironizable by the fact that all knowledge is mediated. Indeed, what
is called methodology in the social sciences can be understood
ironically as an effort to bypass some mediations (the subjective ones) only to replace them with others (objective ones).
And, if this is true of knowledge in general, it is particularly
true of knowledge of conduct. As MacIver puts it,

> Social facts are all in the last resort *intelligible* facts. When
> we know why a government falls or how a price is deter-
> mined . . . our knowledge is different in one vital respect
> from the knowledge of why a meteor falls or how the moon
> keeps its distance from the earth. . . . Facts of the second
> kind we know only from the outside; facts of the first kind
> we know, in some degree at least, from the inside. . . . It is
> because . . . there is always an inside story, or in other
> words a meaning, in human affairs that we never attain
> more than partial or relative truth. Here is the paradox of

knowledge. The only things we know as immutable truths are the things we do not understand. The only things we understand are mutable and never fully known. (1938:124) MacIver's notion also is expressed in such dictums as "The more we know, the less we understand," or "The higher the validity the lower the significance." In the same spirit is the definition of experts as "persons who know more and more about less and less, until finally they come to know everything about nothing." In this sense, what Jack Burnham says about art history can apply to all the human studies:

> The most impeccable scholarship, utilizing newly verified documents, voluminous footnotes, and convincing empirical generalizations about the development of the art impulse, only succeeds in further indoctrinating us into the art mystique. There is a perverse condition here . . . the more we learn circumstantially about the art historical phenomenon, the more we are convinced that art is essentially unknowable and spiritual in substance. (1971:2)

The ability to ironize others, then, may bring with it awareness that one's own pretentions to knowledge may themselves be ironized. And such an awareness may give rise to a peculiar serious unseriousness, a kind of sympathetic play. Beyond the offensive ironization of others, and the defensive circumspection to avoid being ironized oneself, there emerges an attitude of innocence, gaiety, and compassion, an attitude as close to joy, grace or enlightenment as social thinkers are likely to get. Nietzsche meant something like this when he spoke of "the gay wisdom," as do Mannheim (1956:240) and Berger (1963) when they refer to the "ecstasy" of sociological awareness. Similarly, Jankelevitch writes that "Irony is the somewhat melancholy gaiety which discovery of a plurality inspires in us" (1950:29) or, as Anatole France puts it, "The irony I invoke is not cruel. It mocks neither love nor beauty. It is mild and benevolent. Its laughter calms anger, and it is this irony that teaches us to make fun of the fools and villains whom otherwise we might have been weak enough to hate" (1935:IX:450).

This, we believe, recaptures some of the original meaning of *humanitas*. When Marsilio Ficino defined man as a "rational soul participating in the intellect of God, but operating in a body," he saw humans as at once subject and object, at once free as well as finite. And Pico della Mirandola's essay "On the Dignity of Man" does not say that man *is* the center of the world, but only that God *placed* man in the center of the universe so that he might be conscious of where he stands, and so free to decide "where to turn." As Panofsky tells us,

It is from this ambivalent conception of *humanitas* that humanism was born. It is not so much a movement as an attitude which can be defined as the conviction of the dignity of man, based on both the insistence on human values (rationality and freedom) and the acceptance of human limitations (fallibility and frailty); from this, two postulates result – responsibility and tolerance. (1955:2)

Irony, then, at a more complete moment, expresses not merely a proud humility which says "There but for the grace of God . . ." On a deeper level it also expresses a kinship with the victim, a bondedness in which the ironist realizes his freedom only through his "victim," and in which the victim regains his subjectivity only through being ironized. By defiling that which has been taken as sacred, the ironist at the same time purifies the sacred of its religiosity, and thereby joins himself and that which is cleansed in a new communion. When people's pretensions are ironized, their humanity again becomes accessible to compassion and to love. The ironist does not objectify persons in order to remain in the emperium. Instead he cleanses himself and his subject of finitude, and in this baptism rejuvenates and fortifies their joint humanity.[19]

IRONY AS A LOGIC OF DISCOVERY

By unmasking popular dogmas irony can create greater moral awareness and tolerance. In this sense ironism is a humanism. But in relation to *sociological* rather than *social* paradigms, irony may function as a mode of theoretical discovery.

As we have seen, the question of paradigm innovation or theoretical discovery often is relegated to "art" – more a matter for the muses than for logic. Indeed, logic of method in sociology generally refers only to procedures of empirical verification of problems that already have been defined. "The design of experiments . . . is often such that the problem, the puzzle, is, so to say, ready made. It is provided; only the solution is contingent" (Merton, 1959:xii). Yet perhaps more fundamental to science than problem solving is problem *formulation.* Discovering new problems is the first step to creating new paradigms. Solving *existing* problems is part of the elaboration of paradigms already accepted. Thus what Darwin says about biological theory would seem equally to apply to the human studies: "You would be surprised at the number of years it took me to see clearly what some of the problems were which had to be solved. . . . Looking back, I think it was more difficult to see what the problems were than to solve them."

Yet the logic of discovery involved in problem and paradigm invention often is overlooked in discussions of sociology's methods. And where it is treated the recommendations tend to be naive. Consider, for example, Ralf Dahrendorf's statement of what he means by a problem:

> What I mean is that at the outset of every scientific
> investigation there has to be a fact or set of facts that is
> puzzling the investigator: . . . workers in the automobile
> industry go on strike; . . . Socialist parties in
> predominantly Catholic countries of Europe seem unable
> to get more than 30 per cent of the popular vote;
> Hungarian people revolt against the Communist regime.
> There is no need to enumerate more of such facts; what
> matters is that every one of them invites the question
> "Why?" and it is this question, after all, which has always
> inspired that noble human activity in which we are
> engaged – science. (1958:123)

Yet this fails to distinguish the curiosity of the scientist or artist from that of ordinary newspaper readers, aphasics who can not understand their worlds, or fools or children incessantly asking "Why?" If the asking of this question were enough to turn a situation into a *scientifically relevant* problem then, as Merton says, "problems for sociological investigation could be multiplied at will by turning to any compendium of social data – say the many volumes of the U.S. Census – and routinely affixing the question "Why?" to each set of facts reported there (1959:xi).

Our contention, of course, is that much of the potential fruitfulness of situations as new *sociological* problems lies in their ironic incongruity. As we noted earlier, the starting point of irony is what Kenneth Burke calls "perspective by incongruity, . . . a method for gauging situations" by seeing them in terms of their opposites (1964:94). But is it true that all incongruous situations provoke insights, or only the ironic ones? In his study of incongruity and humor, Herbert Spencer quotes Bain's list of *non*-ironic incongruities; these may help us define *ironic* incongruity by negation:

A decrepit man under a heavy burden, five loaves and two
fishes among a multitude, and all unfitness and gross
disproportion; an instrument out of tune, a fly in ointment,
snow in May, Archimedes studying geometry in a siege,
and all discordant things; a wolf in sheep's clothing, a
breach of bargain and falsehood in general; the multitude
taking the law into their own hands, and everything of the
nature of disorder; a corpse at a feast, parental cruelty,
filial ingratitude, and whatever is unnatural; the entire
catalogue of the vanities given by Solomon are all
incongruities, but they cause feelings of pain, anger,
sadness, loathing, rather than mirth. (Quoted by Spencer,
1892:II, 463)

Thus there are different types of incongruity; not all of them
are funny or ironic, not all of them yield dialectical knowledge.
Compare the above, for example, with Mark Twain's assertions
that "The reports of my death have been greatly exaggerated,"
Will Rogers's quip that Abraham Lincoln built with his own
hands the log cabin he was born in, or Anatole France's remark
in *Thäis* that "It is a maxim of our father that there is in every
god an element of the divine." These incongruities are *ironic*
because they bring before our eyes *logical* contradictions,
rather than mere opposition or reversals of chance events. In
Mark Twain's statement there is an opposition of the logically
incompatible concepts of *degree* of accuracy of the reports and
the *finality and absoluteness* of death. The Rogers' statement in-
verts our assumption of generational, sequential time, whereas
France's remark suggests that divinity, which defines gods
as a class category, is something they do not entirely possess.[20]

Thus the maxim that "Brevity is the soul of wit" is a *logical*
proposition. The compactness of ironic incongruity is an expression of the principles of simplicity and parsimony. Occam's
razor is the cutting edge of wit. Exploding opposites and pithy
epitomizations have an immediacy and impact which disappear
if the contradiction has to be explained. Irony makes possible
a moment of insight; the juxtaposition of logically incongruous
frameworks forces upon us an awareness which is deeper than
the denotative surface of what is being told. For example,
compare: "Often individuals who go to excessive lengths to
justify their conduct, in so doing create the impression that they
really are guilty of having done something wrong" and "*Qui
s'excuse, s'accuse.*" The logic of the second expression is
superior to that of the first because it enriches and creates interconnections with a minimum of resources; in contrast, the

heaviness of the first expression drags down a potentially spritely idea.

The incongruities cited by Spencer, therefore, like the sets of facts listed by Dahrendorf, are not ironical nor insight provoking because they express no logical contradiction. An instrument out of tune, a fly in the ointment, a government falling, the Hungarian uprising, may provoke us to corrective action, in that they abuse our habits and conventions. But they teach us little new about how we think and see our worlds. They are not opposites that clash logically or challenge our assumptions about the *nature* of order. And, hence, they do not prod us toward deeper understanding of our paradigmatic presuppositions. Admittedly, irony is often thought of as a game or play, while science or logic tend to be characterized as serious enterprises. Yet the notion of a game also implies boundaries and rules – features of all logical activities. Playing a game, even the game of irony, involves an implicit commitment to some structural and postulation system, some rules of logic.

Irony is thus a method of discovery in that it functions to illuminate relationships between various contents and new and unexpected frames. These relationships, of course, are revealed negatively, as irony affirms rules of consistency through opposition and contradiction. By working out the negative implications of a term – whether in conduct or in theory – one can see whether the sign system implied by that term is really consistent.

Structuralists provide many examples of this. Using Greimas's model, for instance, we could understand a given tribe's marriage rule as the sign S. Opposed to this would be those practices that violated the rule, such as incest, or perversion, that is, —S. The strict negative of the rules, then, would be all conduct not included under them, such as sexual activity of children, S. The fourth term, the contrary of that which is prohibited, would not take us back to the original S, but would result in —S as, for example, the practice of male adultery, which though prohibited by the marriage rules may not be abnormal. Similarly, one may understand the concept love as S; its contrary, —S, is hate; its strict negative, S, would be indifference, while the anti, anti S, —S, would be all other feelings. All these, it should be noted, are implied in the original concept love. In this sense, love is a relational term, defined in a dialectically stuctural manner by its contraries. Greimas's model of the meanings and transformational functions of every semantic unit thus shows, in a real sense, how logical structure is *con*structed dialectically.

Fredric Jameson (1975:13–24) applies this schema to a

number of concept clusters in his analysis of Max Weber's thought as dramatic narrative. For example, Weber's four basic types of social action can be seen as an expression of latent dialectical structure in Figure 6. The initial sign (S) "rationality," in the sense of conduct rationally directed toward profit, has its contrary (−S) in behavior rationally directed toward ethical ends. The strict negative (S) of the initial sign is emotional behavior, while the contrary of the strict negative (−S) is traditional behavior.

In these examples the internal logic of the sign systems has shown itself to be consistent through negation. Our efforts to ironize them instead revealed their implicit logical strengths. While the materials with which Weber or Greimas work clearly are different from those of the dramatist, physicist, or musician, an ironizing style of thought even where "unsuccessful" still can elucidate underlying logical or structural principles which lend all symbol systems order and rational interrelation.

We have said that irony can bring humility by making us aware of the limits of our knowledge. Yet just because of its power to reveal inconsistencies between paradigm and experience, or within our paradigms, irony is a privileged means of paradigm innovation. When theories or paradigms stand before us confidently cogent and ontologically secure, we can elaborate their contents with the methods they provide. But a chief function of irony is to lift these contents out of their conventional frame and, by placing them in an opposite context, to mystify conventional methods. This paradox and ambiguity, created by an ironic formulation, are the first steps to a reformulation of conventional thought. Our apprehension – in the senses both of "anxious dread" and of "awareness at hand" – is akin to what we experience when a mystery confronts us, when, as Natanson puts it, "our inquiry strikes itself, that is, when the inquirer

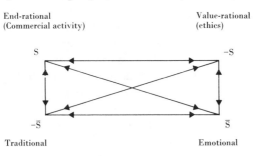

End-rational
(Commercial activity)

Value-rational
(ethics)

S   −S

−S̄   S̄

Traditional   Emotional

Figure 6

meets his own image in the course of his inquiry . . . Its pecu-
liarity – a methodological uncanniness – consists in the fact that
inquirer and inquiry at one and the same time intersect and
astonish each other" (1970:144; see Marcel, 1969:8). The self-
irony of dialectical knowledge is just such a mystery, a confrontation of objectivity and humanity, created by a distanced
yet vulnerably involved ironist. At such a moment the dispassion
we had previously assumed is revealed to have passions of its
own.

T. S. Eliot said that "There are lines, in a play by one of the
supreme poetic dramatists, in which we hear a more impersonal
voice still than that of either the characters or the authors"
(quoted by Wheelock, 1963:29). Such unspoken lines slip away
when we attempt to find them in the surface of the text. Like a witti-
cism when explained, we lose the mysteries emergent from irony
when we reduce them to discrete problems and familiar theories.
Familiar problems by definition are soluable with existing
methodology. We find them complete before our eyes. We lay
siege and grasp their solutions. But in the open, multi-visioned
world of moderns – who are aware of the disjunction between individual freedom and social form – the social world
is experienced more as a mystery than as a problem. Unlike a
problem – a fortress to be penetrated and conquered – the
mystery of social life is something that we, as persons and as
social scientists, are directly involved in ourselves. It is a sphere
where the distinction between what is in us and what stands outside and before us loses its validity. The mysteries revealed by
irony can, of course, be reduced to problems and, though their
nature be corrupted, they will be made amenable to unreflective
techniques. On the other hand, we can go beyond the battle of
opposites and listen to that still more impersonal voice which
irony reveals. In seeking to plumb the depths out of which social
reality and knowledge emerge, we may receive of irony that
"mastered moment" when the sociologist, rather than abandoning himself to alienated objectivism, preserves his stance as
scholar who is present in the world. As such he can respect the
evanescent quality of his subject matter while pursuing the
dialectic between the institutional and the noninstitutional, between objectified knowledge and what is precognitively known.

As an instrument of such a confrontation, irony starts with an
ambiguity. But this ambiguity, rather than being resolved, is
first developed into a full contradiction. Through such a development – by pushing a proposition to its limits and then past

its limits – we discover the boundaries of its proper domain. This moment is crucial if the irony is to be mastered, for it is then that the mind shifts gears, as it were, and circles back upon itself in a larger orbit. What was an unsolvable contradiction in the first circle becomes its own solution from the perspective of the second. The mental processes which were stymied by a mystery become available for scrutiny, and in terms of this larger, self-reflective framework, our initial perplexity becomes a commentary on the mystery itself. Indeed, as we develop the initial obscurity of our subject matter – the apparent impossibility of correlations, the apparent senselessness of certain acts – it is seen to have been part and parcel of our earlier point of view. By reversing and then expanding our perspective, the method *and* the content come to be seen in one frame; indeed, our methods themselves are seen to have provided the preconditions of our confusion. In this manner the naive self-confidence of propositions can be unmasked as hiding latent antitheses; and the mysteries of such contradictions can be seen in a wider circle to contain their own solutions.

By such processes thought attempts to liberate itself, to become aware of its own bad faith, its own interests and "social lies." Such a liberation is a potential contribution of irony. But, unlike elaborations of existing paradigms, this paradigm reversal and transcendence must be done, as it were, by its own bootstraps. To climb out of its hermetic bottle, thought must use the subject-object distinction, the separation between form and content, as rungs in a ladder, each form itself becoming the content of the form constituted by the next higher rung, each subjectivity transmogrified into an object of higher self-reflective awareness. And the outcome of this is no proof either of correspondence or of some closed and perfect symmetry. The proof, if there is one, lies instead in the shock, or failure, of recognition, the ego chill in the moment when the mind confronts itself.

6
Coda

The problem is to recognize which interest groups are exerting
preponderant influence and for what purposes. ... Our theme,
therefore, is the need to subject the gothic mysteries of science and
technology to ordinary ... political judgment.
H. L. Nieburg (1970)

CONCLUDING ARGUMENT

Our discussions of point of view, metaphor, and irony lead
us back to the initial question of the relationship between logic
and feeling, between science and art. As we have noted, many
thinkers insist on a strict separation of these two realms:

I certainly have no objection to the aesthetic, to
imagination, and so forth. I've written novels, I write
poetry when I can't sleep at night – and sometimes I think
of chucking sociology and scholarship to devote myself
fully to these alternate pursuits of reality. Thus I'm
perfectly willing to concede epistemological status to
aesthetic modes of apprehension. *But one must keep these
modes distinct from the modes of philosophical reason and
the scientific inquiry.* If one doesn't, one ends up in the
night in which all cognitive cats are grey, in which lucidity
is lost. (Berger, private correspondence, 1972, italics in
original)

Coming from a sociologist who also is a novelist and a philosopher, Peter Berger's remarks provide a neat counterpoint to the
argument we hope to summarize here: that aesthetic judgment is
presupposed by logical, and sociological, inquiry.

Of help in this project is Marie Swabey's discussion of logical
or postulational systems. Swabey distinguishes postulates *from*
which we reason and the principles in accordance *with* which
we reason:

(1) the first, are free assumptions of a point of view, optimal conveniences, differing from one scheme of thought to another, and (2) the second, [are] a group of comprehensive regulations necessary to all systems, the basic logic of sanity and rationality. These latter are the principles of consistency and inference. As such they are not factual (psychical or physical) laws but cannons of validity, constituting the comprehensive framework of both thought and things, principles whose certification is discursive in that they are reaffirmed in their very denial (1961:17).

This distinction is useful in describing various paradigms or symbol systems, their internal structures, and their external relations. In the elaboration of all such paradigms or "rules of projection" – whether they be Boolean algebra or Swift's *Tale of the Tub* – adherence is required not only to the internal rules of the postulational system chosen but also to the principles of formal expression in general.

Having noted these features common to both science and art, several further comments become possible. It is clear that art and science are different in that they assume different postulational systems *from* which to reason – they are different kinds of games. Moreover, since both are systems for structuring appearance, both must presuppose principles of structural cohesion and order, that is, the principles in accordance *with* which we reason. Such principles are implicit in the relationship between the rules of any game and its moves, a relationship that must be maintained regardless of what kind of game is being played or what are the strategies of the players. Without such a relationship the term "game" would have no meaning; similarly, without principles with which we construct relationships between form and content, theory and evidence, neither art nor science would "make sense."

The dichotomy posited by both positivism and romanticism thus must be rejected on *logical* grounds. These grounds are provided not only by innovations in the philosophy of science but also by criticisms of conventional theories of art. First, the view that aesthetic values are entirely immediate and self-evident – that is, are not justified by canons of reason – provides no means for differentiating which values are aesthetic to begin with. There is of course an element of the incommunicable in every perception, including scientific ones. But if we maintain that all axiological criteria are undefinable, we have posited a private language that no one can understand but ourselves and this, as Wittgenstein showed, contradicts itself.

A second view of aesthetics, rather than spiritualizing judgments of value into self-evident intuitions, instead reduces them to behavior. A. J. Ayer puts this succinctly:

> Our conclusions about the nature of ethics apply to aesthetics also. Aesthetic terms are used in exactly the same way as ethical terms . . . words such as "beautiful," "hideous" are employed, as ethical words are employed, simply to express certain feelings and evoke certain responses. . . . As in ethics there is . . . no sense in attributing objective validity to aesthetic judgments, and no possibility of arguing about questions of fact. . . . Aesthetic criticism purposes not to give knowledge but to communicate emotions. (1946:170–171)

This type of thinking, which reduces all value statements to statements of behavior, all normative statements to ones of fact, also contains a contradiction, as critics of logical positivism have noted. For the very assertions of facticity, causality, and procedures of verification are themselves criteria of value and validity. Scientific inquiry, like artistic inquiry, rests not on self-given facts but on rules of structural coherence (Swabey, 1961:227–247; 1954:250; 1955:143). These rules are themselves values, and they are not located in facts or direct intuitions, nor are they mere behavioral indicators of emotion. Instead, values – such as truth, beauty, or what have you – are the principles by which facts and intuitions are organized and apprehended.

As a privileged vocabulary or metalanguage for speaking of symbol systems in general, however, aesthetics calls for some treatment beyond that appropriate to the rules of intraparadigm discourse. Gödel's proof may aid us on this point (1962).[1] In his critique of Russell and Whitehead's *Principia Mathematica*, Gödel shows how any structure or class concept must justify itself in terms of some higher structure. Hence, any new structure, structural anomaly, or conflict between structures, implies a metastructure that will emerge in the epistemic justification of the terms being examined. There is thus, in the dialectical process of structure creation, an ever-near possibility of the "peaking out" or ratiocination, an encounter with the mysteries that lie outside our current frames of discourse. On one side we face the Spinozan requirement of having to know all implicit structures in order to understand the contents of any one structure "in itself." On the other side, the attempt to specify these implicit structures itself yields further structures on yet higher levels.

In confronting these difficulties, the temptation becomes almost irresistible to halt and declare "whereof one cannot speak, thereof one must be silent." In just this spirit many writers have invoked "intuition" as the means by which one apprehends what appear to be ultimate, ineffable unities or systems (Sorokin, 1954:364ff). This is expressed in such mystical symbols as God, the Tao, Nirvana, or Absolute Mind, or in Husserl's essences, Plato's forms, or Chomsky's and Lévi-Strauss's deeper structures of the mind.

Yet, if we cannot fully name such implicit higher or deeper structures, how then can we know them? Or put more radically, how can we know that there *are* such things? Might not these structures, as with Kant's transcendental ego and things in themselves, prove to be redundant categories, epiphenomena of that which we *can* know and describe? Is our positing of higher, more ultimate structures a chimerical dream of unmediated knowledge, emerging from the nature of language itself and having no referent beyond that language? Many thinkers have, in fact, denied the existence of metaphysical structures altogether, and instead have insisted that ultimate reality lies in phenomenal facts. Thus Otto Neurath, one of the founders of logical positivism, tells us that "The conclusion of the *Tractatus*, 'whereof one cannot speak, thereof one must be silent,' is at least grammatically misleading. It sounds as if there were a 'something' of which we could not speak. We should rather say 'if one really wishes to avoid the metaphysical attitude entirely, then one will 'be silent,' but not 'about something' " (in Ayer, 1966:284).

Yet to answer Neurath, our being silent, if it is not about something, is also not about nothing. Instead, the posture of being silent, but not about something, is itself a postulational position, a choice "about" a number of key issues. Indeed, it was precisely an attempt to be silent that made the logical positivists so un-self-conscious of their own axiological presuppositions, the postulates from which they reasoned. Their unwillingness to acknowledge that their inquiries were based on certain normative game rules forced them to choose between either a barbaric physicalism or a kind of antiempirical intuitionism, an idealism of language (Passmore, 1966:390).

The difficulties the Vienna Circle had in dismissing "supraphysical" notions are instructive. They suggest that there is a certain necessity of speculation about the not-something whereof we are silent. The point, we think, is not whether there is or is not such a "something." Rather it is that the assumption of and quest for such higher structures is indispensable to any rational inquiry, scientific, ethical, or otherwise. Put in terms of Gödel's proof, only by assuming a higher order outside our paradigms are we provided the possibility of ordering the materials that occur *within* them. Moreover, the more general our causal explanations become, and the deeper goes our understanding, then the more ultimate will be that ultimate which our inquiry, of necessity, must presuppose. The paradox of necessary but unknowable ultimates is thus dissolved. Higher-order structures are not essences or forms that we must know in themselves; instead, the very positing of them provides the implicit principles for the discovery and organization of what we already can apprehend.

This line of argument suggests the need and possibility of a framework that integrates yet transcends the opposition between the dominant paradigms of sociological discourse. We spoke of such a transcendental framework at the end of Chapter 4, where we drew on Kant's *Critique of Judgment*; our discussion here is an extension of those points. It will be remembered that for Kant aesthetic judgment is the domain of the principles with which we reason, the home of such prerequisites to rationality as "fitness to perception" or "autotelic cogency." These principles, says Kant, must be (thought of as) part of nature in order for science to be possible. We can now take this thinking a step further. In Chapter 5 we stressed the ethical side of sociology, its use not only as a way of formally representing the world, but also – through irony – as a way of overcoming "social lies" and institutional bad faith. At this point Kant's formulation is helpful again. For another question now puts itself before us: What is the relationship between the more mimetic and analytic side of sociology, stressed in our discussion of metaphor, and the more ethical side stressed in our treatment of irony?

Kant asks a very similar question when he considers the relationship between pure and practical reason, between science and ethics. Kant first asserts that both science and ethics "have their own proper jurisdictions over their content, and since there is no higher (*a priori*) jurisdiction over their content the division of philosophy into theoretical and practical parts is justified" (1949:268). Kant then introduces the possibility that in our "higher thinking faculties there is yet a link" between these two jurisdictions: "This link is the *power of* [*aesthetic*] *judgment,* and by analogy we may reasonably surmise that it also contains, if not a special law-giving authority, at least its own principle for discovering laws, even if this principle is merely subjective a priori" (1949:268).

In developing this idea, Kant asserts that the possibility of prescribing scientific laws requires us to posit some form or fitness of nature. This transcendental concept of an imminent and unfolding order in nature

is abundantly evident from the maxims of judgment upon which we rely a priori in investigating nature, e.g., the law of parsimony, and which only deal with the possibility of experience, and consequently the possibility of the knowledge of nature. This concept only represents the unique manner in which we must proceed in reflecting upon objects of nature if we are to get a thoroughly coherent experience. (1949:273, 275)

The ultimate framework of science thus must be an aesthetic one, for aesthetic judgment is the domain of order and cogency, of fitness and form. Yet given that aesthetic judgment underlies the possibility of knowledge of nature, how does this relate to the possibility of practical or moral reason? Kant notes that aesthetic judgment supplies a priori principles of cohesion for scientific inquiry, that is, the principles in accordance with which scientists reason. In so doing, however, the mind itself has created the possibility or ultimate framework for its own inquiry. Such a "determinability through the intellectual faculty" of the higher structural order (or what Kant calls the "supersensible substratum"), is an exercise and demonstration of our volitional consciousness, and hence of the possibility of moral law. "Thus judgment makes possible the transition from the realm of the concept of nature to that of the concept of freedom" (1949:282).

If we follow Kant's formulation, then, there is a sense in which aesthetics is the master science. Durkheim said that "Logic is the morality of thought; morality is the logic of action." It also has been said that "The beauty of formulas is logic; the logic of beauty is form." The rightness of both these statements hinges on the necessity of aesthetic judgment, by which each of these domains is governed. Art, science, and conduct each reason *from* different postulates, but they all reason in accordance with such principles as concinnity, parsimony, and so on. All modes of structuring appearance – whether through theoretical inquiry or rational action – are sensical only if (we assume) they cohere in this fashion.

Awareness of the necessarily symbolic nature of knowledge also brings the possibility of a deeper, more reflective appreciation of the aesthetic properties of symbol systems per se. Indeed, with the suspension of correspondence theories of truth, aesthetic principles such as cogency, consistency, and economy become principal criteria for determining what constitutes an accurate report, a valid explanation, or a meaningful statement. As a semiotic, or master-science of symbols, aesthetics is the domain of just these criteria. Thus, rather than being banished from the kingdom of philosophic and scientific inquiry, as Berger would have it, aesthetics is a prince and prime contender for the throne.

ON THEORY AND PRACTICE

There is yet another implication of what we have said so far, one that returns us to the question first asked in our preface – that of the relationship between theoria and praxis (Lobkowicz, 1967). In one sense our aesthetic model could hardly seem more removed from the world of action. Our metacriteria would appear to have taken us away from conduct, through sociology, and into a rarefied emperium. We must now come down from Mt. Olympus to the stones and furrows of enactments.

But perhaps this distance is not so great after all. For in our aesthetic terms no opposition is posited between purely cognitive knowledge and purely mindless action. Instead, in a cognitive aesthetic even the most formal paradigmatic knowledge is always embedded in, and is an active making of, a world. Just as paradigms reach for higher epistemic structures, so they also are grounded in the life-worlds of their makers. Similarly, in symbolic realism action must be the enactment of projects, the expression of an intentional consciousness, or it is not action at all, but only mere "events." Thus, instead of independent opposites, theoria and praxis become two moments in the same dialectic.

Even given this, however, we still can never formally know all that we experience, nor can we enact all that we know. One expression of this ambiguity of knowledge and action – a mutual dependency and a mutual tension – lies in the contradiction between logical validity and pragmatic meaning. Formal logic tells us why we cannot say "waste is efficient" without contradicting ourselves. Yet in practice in some situations we *can* meaningfully make such a statement. Sociology, standing between philosophy and social action, has the task of explicating this paradox. Yet if sociology assumes for its *own* metastructure the scientific realist or logical positivist view, it perforce must consider the above statement nonmeaningful – "illogical," "confused," "crazy" – noise to be screened out by objective measures. Scientific realism sees science as *the* reality; other paradigms are viewed as inferior – they are ideology, expressions of emotion, or primitive pre-science.[2]

In contrast, for the symbolic realist both science or logic as well as practical action are "worlds" – albeit worlds with varying degrees of cogency, perspicuity, and so on. Yet neither has ontological priority. Instead of attempting to reduce all worlds to the world of science, the symbolic realist seeks to illuminate each in light of the others, and to examine the purposes each most effectively serves. In symbolic realism "reality" is seen as emergent from *all* symbol systems, only one of which is science. Thus science may be seen as "irrational" (or perhaps "un-oneiric") if one adopts the viewpoint of mythology, while from the viewpoint of science it is easy to see mythic reality as "mere myth." Similarly, cubist art is "unrealistic" from the perspective of the Renaissance, just as the linear, progressive history of moderns is unrealistic from the viewpoint of the all-at-once moral symbolism of medievals.

To relate this more directly to contemporary praxis, consider how theoretical and political considerations interact to define what constitutes a social problem, or a legitimate or feasible solution. From the symbolic realist's viewpoint, no set of behaviors is inherently a social problem (or anything else). Social problems are constructed. They are "symbolic public realities" that emerge from a process of inventing and imposing definitions. But what is the role of lay knowledge in this process? Of the paradigms used in professional research? What part is played by organized constituencies and public agencies, or by the ruling class? May not a problem be defined as such by a group seeking its mission, a group whose "cure" will be the paradigm that defines the "disease"?

In the history of conflicts, issues come to be "owned" by groups that establish themselves as the legitimate guardians of those domains of life. The Church, for example, once controlled the paradigms of economic morality; now this is left to personal conscience, market regulatory commissions, and the corporate elite. What roles do various forms of knowledge play in this process? How do groups "disown" a problem the way, say, the auto and alcohol industries have disowned drunk driving? What are the political implications of various epistemologies which, as the justifications for truth claims, help legitimize policy recommendations? As frameworks of realness and meaning, how do different paradigms contribute to (or detract from) the objectivity or propriety of requests for public credence and action? How is it that some metaphors are elaborated into paradigms while others, equally fruitful in formal terms, are not? How is it that some paradigms come to be accepted as real while others, though no less cogent or articulate, are labeled fiction or utopia? How are various paradigms, once established as legitimate, used as rhetorics or justifying actions which may have been decided on very different bases?

Such questions return us to our original concern with relationships between epistemology, social theory and methods, and applied social change. But insofar as sociology assumes scientific realism, it can do little to answer these questions. For in scientific realism present values and social structure are taken as given, out there and factlike, and with such a view social theory cannot inform social action beyond advising on the costs and benefits of alternatives within the status quo.[3] With scientific realism as their epistemology, the social and policy sciences render themselves incapable of reflecting on their own political and ethical position. And with this forfeiture they inevitably drift into the mindlessness that they so circumspectly seek to avoid. The value-freedom by which sociology and policy analysis ironize popular beliefs is itself ironized by their becoming the unwitting (if not witless and willing) instruments of technocractic domination.

More sensitive social scientists have been aware of this, but they generally have lacked the epistemic framework that would enable them to incorporate the political use of social theory as itself an element in a larger, more dialectical, approach to societal analysis. In contrast, by adopting an aesthetic perspective, a groundwork is laid for analysis that could criticize both itself as well as existing institutions and that could help bridge the gap between questions of technical efficiency and formal proofs, and questions of values and human needs.

Formerly, contending paradigms could be judged from the perspective of a primary one – science, or divine will, was seen as the measure of all things. But today with our almost direct intromission of ideas into practice, of practical innovations summoning up their own formal theories, paradigms tend to be tested in the process of their realization (Foss, 1971:247). Rather than "feedback from reality" today we have "feed-*forward into* reality," since today paradigms can be massively enacted even as they are being invented. Theoretical knowledge is the modern basis for design, and design errors – say in a canal lock on the Great Lakes – can kill a species, in this case the disappearance of lampreys. Applied to humans instead of fish, this is what Camus meant when he referred to Stalin's murders as "crimes of logic," design errors in the practical paradigm for a new society. The deaths "resulted from" the paradigm. But today our problems are global and, at the extreme, ecocide can be the result of paradigm errors.

In such a situation the old relationship between theoria and praxis is radically rearranged. The thinker is now the thinker-apparatchik or the thinker-pioneer. Our poetic for sociology sees formal thought as a game, but it also recognizes that the toy soldiers have real guns.

One example of this political dimension of formal thought is cybernetic systems theory, which can be seen as an effort to name, and hence to evoke, an entire social order. According to cybernetic theorists, society is (or is like) a great computer, with its input and output, its feedback loops, and its programs; this machine – society – is guided by a servomechanism – the technoadministrative elite. To see this imagery as a *metaphor*, however, is to reject it as a literal description, to unmask it as a legitimating ideology, and to begin criticizing it as a rhetoric of persuasion. By doing a close literary textual analysis, for example, it becomes clear that in the imagery of social cybernetics there is an atrophy of the very vocabularies of citizenship, moral responsibility, and political community. Instead, the machinery of governance, initially conceived as serving human values, tends to generate its own self-maintaining ends. Objectivity and reason are defined in terms of efficiency for systems maintenance, while feelings and morality are relegated to the private realm. The polity – the arena for the institutional enactment of moral choices – dissolves upward into the state, or downward into the individual whose intentionality is now wholly privatized and whose actions, uprooted from an institutional context, are bereft of social consequence and hence of moral meaning (see Burke, 1973b).

To see paradigms for discourse through a poetic, then, is to recognize that they provide the frameworks for structuring appearance, for creating that which becomes accessible to us as reality. Accordingly, the sociologist is no longer in the grandstand watching ideas and behaviors pass in review. Instead, as part of the parade, he can either clear or clutter up the way. To understand that formal thought has this power – power to name the right and true – is to understand that intellection is a highly political act.

In this state of affairs, the very potency of formal thought has transvalued the legitimacy and purposes of its instrumental applications. Formerly, rationality was seen as an instrument to serve values whose justification lay beyond the domain of instrumental reason itself. Yet when all forms of thought – scientific as well as ethical – are justified in terms of their rationally calculated utility, then rather than serving human purposes, the dehumanizing, objectifying properties of positivist thought become ends in themselves. At the same time, however, if we deny that some ideas are of practical utility, we will have consigned ourselves to contemplative passivity in the face of genuine social crises.

In its ultimate form, this conflict between technicism and humanism is expressed as a choice between survival or dignity (Stanley, 1977). Given such apocalyptic global potentials as Malthusian food scarcities, nth country nuclear wars, and atmospheric pollution, many thinkers have advocated (or warned against) technology as a means of salvation. Yet, carried to its ultimate application, technology means the instrumental use of not only tools, but also of reason, and of persons themselves. Thus survival in postindustrial society may require that the status "human" be demoted to that of a "factor of production," a thing possessing no *intrinsic* worth, dignity, or moral agency. This would be the end of humanism.

We thus are confronted with a two-sided problem: Those wishing to defend humanism against technicism tend to be wedded to a romantic vocabulary that is inadequate for articulating their cause. Likewise, those wishing to apply knowledge to social purposes often are unfamiliar with the moral philosophical problems associated with the instrumental use of reason. And this problem is itself but another version of the conflict between positivism and romanticism with which we began this essay – the conflict between rational, scientific, or empirical modes of thinking versus intuitive, metaphysical, evaluative ways of feeling; between increasing demands for elite technical knowledge to manage the complex institutions of advanced industrial society, and increasing needs for non-alienating modes of work and governance.

A chief claimant to the systematic knowledge that might resolve these dilemmas is the community of social scientists and social systems engineers. Both inside and outside this community it is expected that its research can and should be translated into social problem-solving technologies (i.e., public "policies"). Yet this trend has been accompanied by criticism of the instrumental use of reason – that is, the emergent dissident literature of alienation and authenticity. The irony, however, is that both these camps justify their positions on "humanistic" grounds. One side says that if knowledge cannot be used to solve human problems it is worthless. The other side sees these same problems as manifestations of a consciousness already dehumanized by the technological attitude itself. It goes without saying that intensification of this polarization would be catastrophic for a truly humane culture. Of central importance, then, is an analysis of the conceptual and *preconceptual* foundations of humanism and of the epistemic and political economic relationships between knowledge for its own sake and knowledge for use.

To address these questions effectively, sociology must pursue existential, as well as propositional truths. Philosophers often distinguish these two kinds of truth: the Aristotelian concept of "speaking the truth," or the truth of propositions, as contrasted to truth as an authentic response to reality, a "being in truth" (Kecskemeti, 1952:15, 31).[4] The first refers to hypotheses advanced within some disciplinary framework; it is a truth of discourse. The second is mainly an act, a feature of existence; it involves "witnessing," not in the sense of being an uninvolved observer but in the sense of bearing witness, of being a representative *of* truth rather than merely re-presenting it. This distinction between propositional and existential truth – truths of theoria and truths of praxis – is paralleled by two aspects of sociological theories. Such theories not only are "about" their various domains; they also reflect and create the context and consciousness from which they emerge. Beyond its scientific import, sociological theory is also a collective cry of anguish, a witness to the various truths, and lies, of our times.

In this sense social theories can be on the side either of piety or of profanation, in favor of order or of renovation. They can sanctify the conventional by formalizing it into occult language or they can demystify the sacrosanct by formally exposing its contradictions. Just as psychoanalytic theory can expose the private dream, socioanalytic theories can expose public illusions. What is solipsism or neurosis for the individual, however, on the level of society is not the sacred as such, but rather the "sacred cows," the human extensions that have been reified into idols. In and through this social theory can be a kind of loyal, though not always legal, opposition. In opening the sacred to scrutiny, sociology at once profanes and purifies it. Sociology's truth is truth in the original Greek sense; "the unconcealing of what is concealed" (Heidegger, *passim*).[5] Such a revealing is less a destruction than a revelation of what is held to be sacred, an uncovering of that society's ultimate concerns. The view that sociological demystification is necessarily a fall from grace thus expresses the very mentality that dialectical sociology criticizes from within. "The secular is the sacred integrated, rather than degraded or displaced" (Hartman, 1970:156). The self-consciousness of social theory as constituting existential truth thus serves as a means of transcending the relativism and pessimism that has come with sociology's "disenchantment" of the modern world. For this unmasking mode of thought can be turned on sociology itself, thereby creating new frames of reference from which to judge the adequacy of social theory as an expression of, and witness to, contemporary history and society (Wolff, 1970:41).

Most often, however, such a self-consciousness has brought with it relativism and doubt. Part of this unease seems due to the dissonance between the mobile, synergistic character of modern experience, and the static, positivistic epistemology by which we measure whether such experience counts as knowledge. Karl Mannheim, in a letter to Kurt Wolff, states this well:

The inconsistencies in our whole outlook . . . are due to the fact that we have two approaches which move on different planes. . . .

To use a simple analogy, what happens is that in our empirical investigation we become aware of the fact that we are observing the world from a moving staircase, from a dynamic platform and, therefore, the image of the world changes with the changing frames of reference which various cultures create. On the other hand, epistemology still only knows of a static platform where one doesn't become aware of the possibility of various perspectives and, from this angle, it tries to deny the existence and the right of such dynamic thinking. . . .

I want to break the old epistemology radically but have
not succeeded yet fully. . . . Nothing is more obvious than
that we . . . think on the basis of changing frames of
reference, the elaboration of which is one of the most
exciting tasks of the near future (quoted by Wolff,
1970:36).[6]

This essay is a contribution to the task outlined by Mannheim.
In this sense our project – a poetic for sociology – is an attempt to provide an epistemic self-consciousness for sociological
thought, but one that would be reflexive rather than absolutist or
solipsistic. Given such a framework, we no longer are forced to
choose between two sociologies: one positivist, which tells us
everything about society and nothing about our selves; the other
romantic, which expresses insight into moral agency but lacks
empirical rigor. We can begin instead to cast such sterile
dichotomies aside – scientific sociology can be seen as interpretive, while insight or interpretation can be made a disciplined,
rule-bound procedure. On such a basis the possibility is opened
for creating a form of discourse that is self-reflective of both
its postulational admissibility as well as its existential fitness.
Such discourse would constitute a theoretical praxis that is also
praxiological theory; it would not demand of us that we abandon our profession in order to profess our lives; its methodological self-consciousness could also constitute a *method of*
self-consciousness for sociologists, and for peoples, in their
struggles for emancipation.

Notes

Chapter 1. *Poetics and sociology: an invitation*

1 Merleau-Ponty also warns that "we must be fully aware of the *obscurantist* consequences of our failure to use [science and ontology] to illuminate each other.... We would have to hide from the scientist the 'idealization' of brute fact which is nevertheless the essence of his work. He would have to ignore the deciphering of meanings which is his reason for being, the construction of intelligible models of reality without which there would be no more sociology today than there would formerly have been Galilean physics" (1964: 98–99).

2 The term *language game* is borrowed from Wittgenstein, who uses it in his critique of his earlier logical atomism. In Wittgenstein's later view, language is not a matter of words being a static reflection of things. Instead, language is an *activity* bound by *rules* and taking place within a *social context*. In particular cases language does name or describe, but there are many other uses of language as well: giving orders, framing conjectures, telling jokes, praying and, by extension, doing sociology or some other discipline. The forms of words – such as verbs or nouns – appear on the surface to be the same; yet in terms of its depth grammar each word has a different function depending on the language game within which it is used. As Wittgenstein says, "Here the term 'language *game*' is meant to bring into prominence the fact that the *speaking* of language is part of an activity, or of a form of life.... It is interesting to compare the multiplicity of the tools in language and of the ways they are used, the multiplicity of kinds of word and sentence, with what logicians have said about the structure of language" (1953, para. 23, Wittgenstein's italics). See Chapter 4 of the present essay for more on the game metaphor.

3 Jack Douglas also has spoken of paradigm imperialism: "As in any science, we have our *paradigm-imperialists*: in *The Structure of Social Action* Talcott Parsons tried to show that there was an implicit paradigm for all social action in the works of Durkheim, Weber, Marshall, and Pareto; Kingsley Davis and others argue that structural-functionalism *is* sociology – the whole truth and the only truth; Otis Dudley Duncan and others argue that *only*

the ecological model will allow us to achieve the true goals of sociology" (1971:45, Douglas' italics, in Tiryakian).

To counteract such partisanship, Maurice Stein (1963:177) seeks to encourage "a plurality of languages": "We need the vivid description prose of the community sociologist. How valuable would *Middletown* have been had the Lynds been confined to structural functional jargon? Yet we also need Mills' passionate indignation, Riesman's subtle discursive essays, Erving Goffman's keen eye for the underside of everyday life and certainly the lucid propositions of Robert Merton. When a given language or mode of presenting theories is taken as the *only* correct mode, the presenter runs the risk of cutting himself off from fruitful alternatives."

4 For example, survey methods have been used by both experimenters and historians in order to get at larger ranges of data. The neologism "statistical-experimental" thus lumps together a number of research strategies. A researcher can be experimental in qualitative fashion, e.g., in carrying out field experiments or observing "natural" experiments such as disasters in a community or region. Quantitative research can analyze aggregate data such as census data or survey data without being experimental. Both quantitative and qualitative research can analyze the relationship between variables as well as describe characteristics of actors and their behavioral context. To insist that quantitative research is nomothetic would equate it with inductive research, which is clearly not the case. There is a good deal of quantitative research that uses a deductive approach. (See Braithwaite's discussion of induction and deduction [1953], and Josiah Royce on "The Mechanical, the Historical, and the Statistical" [1914].) A similar merging of distinctions is found in Thomas Wilson's conception of "normative paradigm" (1969) which lumps together functionalist and positivist approaches, while his "interpretive paradigm" conflues symbolic interactionism with ethnomethodology. Our classifications are thus not meant as absolute, exhaustive, or mutually exclusive; they are presented as signposts to help the reader locate his own position as he wanders in the swamps. For our larger argument, the main point here is not the shapes of divisions within our discipline, but that they exist.

5 What is said has little to do with either range or scale of problem. The interpretive approach can be applied to a huge subject – say the rationalization of society under Protestant capitalism – or to a tiny one – say a street-corner gang (Weber, 1958; Whyte, 1969). Similarly, the statistical-experimental approach can be applied to a large range of data – such as suicide in modern Europe – or to a relatively narrow range – such as leadership in small groups (Durkheim, 1951; Homans, 1945).

6 For other discussions of theories of the middle range see Zetterberg (1954), Hankins (1956), Nehnevajsa (1956), and Rossi (1956); all cited by Merton (1957:10, n. 4). Bensman and Vidich (1960:577) point out that "other studies addressed to issues in the relationship between theory and research are represented in the work of Mills, Blumer, Becker, Abel, A. K. Davis, Becker and Boskoff, Znaniecki, Borgatta and Meyer; Coser and Rosenberg; and Goode and Hatt, to mention only a few. All these authors have criticized the hiatus between low-level theory dealing with factually exact minutiae and the world-sweeping generalizations of theorists who appear to fail to appreciate the time-consuming task of systematically gathering and interpreting data."

7 Another example of the indifference of functional logic to the range or scale of the data is provided by three essays in medical sociology by Parsons and Fox, Edward Suchman, and Donald Ball, respectively. The Parsons and Fox essay stakes out the high ground by functionally interrelating "Illness, Therapy, and the Modern Urban American Family." Although the explanation presented is largely a redundant description of

data that is presumed, few would argue that this limitation disbars the essay from membership in the functionalist camp. The second essay, explicity indebted to Parsons, relates "Social Patterns of Illness and Medical Care," finding that "cosmopolitan" groups are "more likely to hold a 'scientific' health orientation while 'parochial' groups adhered to [a] 'popular' health orientation." Although this contention is supported by impressive statistical-demographic data, the formulation of the problem in the first place, and the interpretation of the resultant statistical correlations, presupposes that "people seeking medical care and the practitioners of medical care" are "two components of an interacting social system." This qualifies the article as structural-functionalist and, with key variables such as "ethnic traditionalness" and "attitudes toward health care," it brands the piece as functionalism of the middle range. The third paper, by Donald Ball, is "An Abortion Clinic Ethnography." Because it focuses on directly observed interactions and situated strategies of image maintenance and people processing, it might be thought that this is not really a functionalist essay. The underlined terms in the quotation below, however, make it clear that Ball has adopted the basic functionalist assumptions of telos and system. "In the case of the abortion clinic the rhetoric *operates to subvert* the conventional world's view of abortion, and *to generate* a picture of legitimate activity. Fundamentally, the question thus becomes: What techniques *are utilized* via this rhetoric *to neutralize* the context of deviance in which the clinic operates, *so as to enhance* the parallels with conventional medical and social situations and *thus derive* a kind of 'rightness' or legitimization? How, in other words, are the setting and action qua impressions *manipulated to maximize* the clinic's image over and above successful performance of its task and [*to*] *contradict* the stereotypic stigma of deviance? Specifically, how does the clinic (1) *minimize the possibilities of trouble* with frightened or recalcitrant patrons; (2) *generate the patron satisfaction necessary for referral system maintenance*; (3) *present an image which will provide the most favorable self image or identity for the actors involved*, whether patron or staff?" (our italics).

This indifference to sacle is also found in other theoretical approaches. In phenomenological sociology, for example, the writings of Berger and Luckman on the construction of reality, legitimization, and institutionalization take on highly general questions, as do the works of Burkart Holzner, Georges Gurvitch, and Jürgen Habermas. The midrange of phenomenological sociology is thinner, but Scott and Lyman's work on student politics, Jack Douglas' on deviance, David Sudnow's on death in hospitals, and Aaron Cicourel's on juvenile justice demonstrate that first rate phenomenological studies of specific institutions or problem areas are possible. At the micro-level, there are numerous contributions from Garfinkel, Cicourel, Sacks, Pollner, Zimmerman, Wieder, and others. In their *programmatic* statements, ethnomethodologists eschew the aprioristic tendencies of functionalism; yet their *empirical* writings are much akin to those of aprioristic symbolic interactionists whom they attack. See the Bibliography for references.

8 See Birnbaum (1969b) for a rather full bibliography on the crisis going on *within* Marxist sociology.

9 The term "behavioral sciences" is used advisedly. Bernard Berelson, a leading behaviorist, gives credit for the substitution of this label for "social science" to the Ford Foundation. The Foundation, eager to support studies that would result in "objective behavioral knowledge," encouraged the adoption of a Watsonian approach. As Seligman notes: "Support for the new concept was lent by politicians who established the National Science Foundation in 1946; they eschewed the use of the term 'social science' because it suggested 'politics, socialism, or some form of social philosophy'." See Ben B. Seligman (1968:76–79).

10 For a discussion of the social indicators movement, the Year 2000 studies, and similar activities, see Manfred Stanley (1973).

11 Related to this third argument are discussions of the "public interest" and also of the relationship between pluralism of private values and the value-freedom of public discourse. On the former see Joseph Tussman (1960) and Michael Walker Walzer (1970). On the latter see Kingsley Davis, "American Society: Its Group Structure."

12 See Amitai Etzioni (1968, Chapter 9). Also see Norman Birnbaum: "Knowledge has become a factor of production, in the form of the technological derivatives of scientific inquiry and in the indispensable contribution of other forms of knowledge. Indeed, the ... fusion of administrative, political and productive processes in neocapitalism ... has made it difficult to specify where precisely production stops and the administration begins, and has rendered virtually impossible a distinction between 'political' and 'economic' decisions" (Birnbaum, 1969a:234–235).

13 This discussion transcends the rather superficial debate between American and Soviet sociologists. Indeed, the neo-Marxism that we speak of here is in many respects opposed to Soviet Marxism, particularly insofar as the former has incorporated ideas from Nietzsche, Husserl, and Heidegger, and has expanded its critique to all industrial societies, not just capitalist society. Alvin Gouldner's criticisms of both American *and* Soviet sociology, for example, is along the lines of the Frankfort School. But despite this Gouldner winds up in a position exactly the opposite of what C. Wright Mills recommended. Instead of moving from biography to history, thereby turning personal troubles into social issues, Gouldner's concept of reflexiveness would have us turn our social situations into personal reflections on the problem of "being a sociologist and being a person." Like C. Wright Mills' recommendations, those of Robert Merton also were inverted. Instead of middle-range theories, what advanced under Merton's banner was theoretical embroidery of the same old statistical research.

14 We wish to stress that our use of the term "humanist" is restricted to thought or activity – in this case sociology – which is based on the assumption of people's capacity for meaning creation and moral agency. While the term "existential" captures much of this, it excludes other sociologies that also stress meaning creation, for example, symbolic interactionism. The word "human" or "humane" is currently associated with the psychology of Maslow, the phenomenology of the Duquesne University philosophers, and a number of neo-Marxists. Despite these ambiguities, as well as the general "mushiness" of its popular use, we find "humanist" to be the least inadequate term to distinguish the theories discussed from functionalism and positivism.

15 Again there are nuances that should not be overlooked. Parsons, for example, opposes some policies but favors contemporary culture. Redfield, in contrast, is a Rousseauian who opposes modern society *and* culture.

16 Here too, of course, there are ambiguous cases, mainly depending on whether the term *phenomenologist* refers to the early Husserl or to the late Husserl as interpreted by Heidegger and Sartre. For example, some phenomenologically inspired ethnomethodologists can be seen as extreme positivists seeking to take the closest possible look at their data. For them Husserl's dictum "Back to the things themselves!" is taken literally. Other phenomenological sociologists, such as Lyman and Scott, stress the existential side, thereby relinquishing any claim or hope of ultimates, either in theory or in data.

17 This dilemma also can be stated in terms of the functionalist versus positivist versus phenomenological approaches to historical sociology. A major critique of functionalism-evolutionism from a neopositivist viewpoint was

made by Teggart, Hogden, and Bock. They pointed out that, aside from specific empirical problems, the functionalist approach had logical difficulties that rendered its theses incapable of being tested empirically. Put simply, the neopositivists insisted that the causes of social change cannot be contained in the thing that is changing itself; or, in formal terms, the functionalist explanation is tautological because the dependent and independent variables are both known by the same indicator. These neopositivists then offered an alternative approach of their own (and tried to demonstrate it in Teggert's *Rome and China* and Hodgen's *Early Anthropology*). This explanation, again simply put, is that change occurs when a critical event takes place *outside* the thing to be explained. Such an event may come from another society (e.g., trade with China changed the Roman Empire). Within a single, hermetic society (e.g., Japan in the eighteenth century), the event will be found in one institutional area that causes change in another. Thus, while asserting a commitment to positivist methods of observation and verification, the above view rejects the functionalist assumptions of rationality in social order, systemic interdependence of institutions within a society, and "functions" that explain institutional or social systemic "evolution."

The Teggartian view can look to certain streams in modern philosophy for support, particularly logicians' analysis of the Aristotelian tautology and Ryle's demonstration that to be a cause a thing must be an event (not a process or a law). Other modern philosophic developments, however – namely those related to phenomenology – have led to criticism of the Teggart-Bock formulation. The focus of such criticism is on the questions What is an event? What is our unit of study and how can we know it?

In the positivist approach concepts of alternative possible "causes" are operationalized, and indicators are developed by which an "event" is measured and defined. In contrast, phenomenologists see this procedure as a violation of the integrity of the subject matter; instead one must suspend judgment as to the existence or nonexistence of phenomena (in this case an historical event) as a precondition to the intuitive apprehension of its essence. The interest is not in whether the event was a cause, or even if it actually – in some naturalistic sense – took place; instead, the interest is on the constitution of the historical phenomena in consciousness.

One implication of such methodological radicalism is that history becomes eternally present – it can never be more than what we think it is. As the study of "the past," history is logically impossible. But even if one accepts this and still insists on doing history – even if the concept of historical causation is accepted as a rhetoric for describing the contents of consciousness in the present – there still remain problems in defining "What is an event?" For if phenomenology does not tell us what an event is, it does indicate what an even *is not*: A historical event must refer to that which can be apprehended interpersonally in *somebody's* everyday life. Hence events cannot be reified forces or generalizations such as "increased trade throughout the third century" or "the tide of expectations unleashed by the French Revolution."

This basic commitment to using data that emerge from everyday life has been accompanied – not surprisingly – by a tendency to ask and study questions relating to settings small enough for one to "get at" the data as it is constructed in consciousness through interaction. Yet, while this responds in part to the question originally put to Teggart, phenomenological social-historical research has raised new dilemmas of its own: How do we move from a history of consciousness to a history of action? How do we move from a *micro* cnception of "event" to an explanation of macrosocietal questions? And, most radically: How is history possible?

Chapter 2. *Cognitive aesthetics, symbolic realism, and perspectival knowledge*

1 "Questions Concerning Certain Faculties Claimed for Man"; "Some Consequences of Four Incapacities"; and "Grounds for Validity of the Laws of Logic: Further Consequences of Four Incapacities," reprinted in the *Collected Papers of Charles Sanders Peirce*, edited by Charles Hartshorne and Paul Weiss, Vol. V. Compare these essays with Heidegger's insistence that Descartes never accounted for the *sum* that was presupposed by the *cogito* (Heidegger, 1962:24).

It also is interesting to compare Peirce's phenomenology, or what he called "phaneroscopy," with that of Husserl. Peirce wrote: "It will be plain from what has been said that phaneroscopy has nothing to do with the question of how far the phanerons it studies correspond to any realities. It religiously abstains from all speculation as to any relations between its categories and physiological facts, cerebral or other. It does not undertake, but sedulously avoids, hypothetical explanations of any sort. It simply scrutinizes the direct appearances, and endeavors to combine minute accuracy with the broadest possible generalization. The student's great effort is not to be influenced by any tradition, any authority, any reasons for supposing that such and such ought to be the facts, or any fancies of any kind, and to confine himself to honest, singleminded observation of the appearances. The reader, upon his side, must repeat the author's observation for himself, and decide from his own observation whether the author's account of the appearances is correct or not" (quoted by Herbert Hensel, 1967:40–41).

Other echoes of Peirce's criticism of the "foundation metaphor" can be found in W. V. O. Quine, "Two Dogmas of Empiricism" (1964); Wilfred Sellars, "Empiricism and the Philosophy of Mind" (1963); and Paul Feyerabend, "Explanation, Reduction, and Empiricism" (1962).

2 Berkeley and Hume were virtually ignored by British positivist philosophers in the eighteenth and nineteenth centuries. The actual line of development in the eighteenth century was from Locke to Stewart and Hartley to Mill and the Scottish associationists. For example, Laplace's universal determinism – a locus classicus of naive positivist thought – is exactly the opposite of Berkeley's antimaterialism and Hume's skepticism. Similarly, John Stuart Mill had read neither Berkeley nor Hume. Their main influence was on Kant, and hence on German idealism and its relativistic successors. Only in the twentieth century are Berekely and Hume revived in their homeland and honored retrospectively for their usefulness in creating a sophisticated pragmatic version of positivism to replace the older naive form.

3 For example, Willard Quine, a student of Carnap, argues that "entification" – the process by which objects are formed in consciousness – begins "at arm's length... under conspicuously intersubjective circumstances" (1960: 1). Similarly, Karl Popper distinguishes his position from that of "naive empiricists," allowing that ... "The empirical basis of objective science has thus nothing 'absolute' about it. Science does not rest upon rock-bottom. The bold structure of its theories arise, as it were, above a swamp. It is like a building erected on piles. The piles are driven down from above into the swamp, but not down to any natural or 'given' base; and when we cease our attempts to drive our piles into a deeper layer, it is not because we have reached firm ground. We simply stop when we are satisfied that they are firm enough to carry the structure, at least for the time being" (1959: 11).

However, such statements do not constitute agreement with the conceptual catholicism implicit in a *strong* symbolic realist approach. For the neopositivist, science – although now admittedly a symbol system – is still thought of as the most privileged one. Sellars, for example, says that it is reasonable to accept the conceptual structure of science as standing behind the manifest images of the phenomenal world, thereby replacing Kant's *Dinge an sich* (1968:Ch. 7). Also see articles by Zelditch and by Verba in Vallier (1971), and Randall Collins's review of their volume in *Contemporary Society*, 1973. Also see Kuhn: "Karl Popper and I both insist that scientists may properly aim to invent theories that *explain* observed phenomena and that do so in terms of *real* objects.... On the other hand, Sir Karl and I are united in opposition to a number of classical positivism's most characteristic theses. We both emphasize, for example, the intimate and inevitable intanglement of scientific observation with scientific theory; we are correspondingly skeptical of efforts to produce any neutral language of observation" (1970:2, Kuhn's italics).

Also see Popper: "the theory of scientific objectivity...can only be clarified through such social categories as, for example – competition (both of individual scientists and of different schools); tradition (namely, the critical tradition); social institutions (such as, for example, publications in different competing journals and through different competing publishers; discussions in congresses); power of the state (namely, political tolerance of free discussion)" (in Adorno, 1969:113).

4 This insistence on experience as the context of inquiry may be fruitfully compared to Kierkegaard's idea that concrete individual existence can never be *Aufgehoben*. Peirce's statement that "the idea of the other, of *not*, becomes a very pivot of thought" could be taken from Sartre's *Critique of Dialectical Reason*. See Bernstein (1971:182).

5 For criticisms of Goodman's accounts (1960, 1968), see Harris (1973:323–327), Savile (1971:3–27), and Rudner and Scheffler (1972).

6 See Edwyn Bevan: "I remember once at Oxford, at the Ashmolean, looking through, not very carefully, a series of water-colors by Turner of Oxford, and when I went out again from the Museum into the Oxford streets, it all looked different; there were new lights on trees and houses; it all looked like a painted picture by Turner" (1938:278).

Also see Victorino Tejera's discussion of why "a description is often a judgment with little problematic about it.... Descriptions are, after all, judgments, even if settled judgments; and the mistaken belief grows that there is such a thing as purely descriptive discourse" (1965).

7 In his essay "On Realism in Art" Roman Jakobson provides some useful examples: "The perception of those of a more conservative persuasion continues to be determined by the old canons; they will accordingly interpret any deformation of these canons by a new movement as a rejection of the principle of verisimilitude, as a deviation from realism. They will therefore uphold the old canons as the only realistic ones. Thus, in discussing meaning *A* of the term 'realism' (i.e., the artistic intent to render life as it is), we see that the definition leaves room for ambiguity:

A_1: The tendency to deform given artistic norms conceived as an approximation of reality;

A_2: The conservative tendency to remain within the limits of a given artistic tradition, conceived as faithfulness to reality.

"Meaning *B* presupposes that my subjective evaluation will pronounce a given artistic fact faithful to reality; thus, factoring in the results obtained, we find:

B_1: I rebel against a given artistic code and view its deformation as a more accurate rendition or reality;

B_2: I am conservative and view the deformation of the artistic code, to which I subscribe, as a distortion of reality.

"The concrete content of A_1, A_2, B_1, and B_2 is extremely relative. Thus a contemporary critic might detect realism in Delacroix, but not in Delaroche; in El Greco and Andrej Rublev, but not in Guido Reni; in a Scythian idol, but not in the Laocoön. A directly opposite judgment, however, would have been characteristic of a pupil of the Academy in the previous century. Whoever senses faithfulness to life in Racine does not find it in Shakespeare, and vice versa.

"In the second half of the nineteenth century, a group of painters struggled in Russia on behalf of realism (the first phase of C, i.e., a special case of A_1). One of them, Repin, painted a picture, "Ivan the Terrible Kills His Son." Repin's supporters greeted it as realistic (C, a special case of B_1). Repin's teacher at the Academy, however, was appalled by the lack of realism in the painting, and he carefully itemized all the instances of Repin's distortion of verisimilitude by comparison with the academic canon which was for him the only guarantee of verismilitude (i.e., from the standpoint of B_2). But the Academy tradition soon faded, and the canons of the "realist" Itinerants (*peredvizhniki*) were adopted and became social fact. Then new tendencies arose in painting, a new *Sturm und Drang* began; translated into the language of manifestos, a new truth was being sought.

"To the artist of today, therefore, Repin's painting seems unnatural and untrue to life (i.e., from the standpoint of B_2). In turn, Repin failed to see anything in Degas and Cezanne except grimace and distortion (i.e., from the standpoint of B_2). These examples bring the extreme relativity of the concept of 'realism' into sharp relief" (1971:41–42).

Also see Capon (1965) and Ortega y Gasset in *Velázquez* (1959:34, 135). Ortega conceives of art as derealization, and is convinced that realism is "the negation of art." His defense of Velázquez is that the latter's alleged realism is but a variety of the irrealism of all great art. Similarly, in *Idea del Teatro* he talks of transmigrations into unreal worlds of fun and joke, and stresses that a really great novel does not refer to anything outside itself.

8 See L. Wertenbaker's comments on Picasso's *Les Demoiselles d'Avignon*: "[It] achieved a basic breakthrough in art, effectively ending the long reign of the Renaissance ... a revolutionary call for wholly fresh perceptions. The viewer is made to abandon his preconceived ideas of form, to forget natural appearance altogether, to look at the fragments that make up his nudes as pure forms in themselves ... its distortions of face and figure and placement force the viewer to look everywhere at once" (1957:53, 55).

9 It is worth noting that when philosophers of science speak of the verification of scientific laws they invariably choose as their examples laws about which there is virtually no doubt. What they describe, then, is not the logic or process of discovery – as we are attempting here – but the practical demonstrating of what is already known. This is often stated fairly baldly: "The philosopher of science is not much interested in the thought processes which lead to discovery" (Reichenbach, 1949:289); or "The gist of the scientific method is ... verification and proof, not discovery" (Mehlberg, 1955:127). When evidence of the process of discovery intrudes on such accounts, it generally is speedily consigned to "psychology."

10 As Cassirer puts it: "Just as scientific theory is not to be judged by referring back to the experience which it reconstructs but to its own standards of theoretical completeness, so art is not to be judged in terms of its 'imitation' of perception.... There is no privileged status for science over art or any other symbolic formation which constitutes some kind of interpretation of experience" (1955:II, xiv–xv).

11 Merleau-Ponty distinguishes awareness of the preobjective elements of experience and the reflective determination of the meanings and structure of a situation: "To return to the things themselves is to return to that world which precedes knowledge, of which knowledge always speaks, and in relation to which every scientific schematization is an abstract and derivative

sign-language, as is geography in relation to the countryside in which we
have learnt beforehand what a forest, a prarie or a river is" (1964:ix).

See also Victorino Tejera: "Thus nonobjective, as in pragmatism, means
preobjective, not subjective. And if indeed the prerational, nonthetic, preobjective domain is like William James's world of pure experience or
Dewey's indeterminate qualitative situation, then *judgments* about what
'requirednesses' ought to be acted upon will be reached in a manner similar
to that in which Dewey has said judgments are reached in clarifying or
making determinate a given situation" (1965:158).

Also Polanyi: "In relying for its own interest on the antecedent interest
of its subject matter, science must accept to an important extent the pre-
scientific conception of these subject matters. The existence of animals was
not discovered by zoologists, nor that of plants by botanists, and the
scientific values of zoology and botany is but an extension of man's pre-
scientific interest in animals and plants. Psychologists must know from
ordinary experience what human intelligence is, before they can devise tests
for measuring it scientifically, and should they measure instead something
that ordinary experience does not recognize as intelligence, they would
be constructing a new subject matter which could no longer claim the
intrinsic interest attached to that which they originally chose to study"
(1958:139).

12 See A. J. Greimas: "Signification is thus nothing but such transposition
from one level of language to another, from one language to a different
language, and meaning is nothing but the possibility of such *transcoding*"
(1970:13).

But the facility with which one mode of expression can be transcoded
into another reflects not only the skill of the interpreter; it also may
indicate the extent to which a culture has achieved what Sorokin called
a "logicomeaningful unity" of its symbolic forms (1957). For example, the
lines of a baroque snuff box, held at arms length, can be made to almost
exactly overlay the lines of a baroque church. Panofsky offers a negative
example to make a similar point: "Just as it was impossible for the Middle
Ages to elaborate the modern system of perspective, which is based on the
realization of a fixed distance between the eye and the object and thus
enables the artist to build up comprehensive and consistent images of visible
things; so was it impossible for them to evolve the modern idea of history,
based on the realization of an intellectual distance between the present and
the past which enables the scholar to build up comprehensive and consistent
concepts of bygone periods" (1955:51).

The "golden ages" we sometimes speak of – Periclean Athens or Weimar
in the days of Goethe – all seem to be characterized, and perhaps created
in part, by the mutual resonances and enrichments which each form of
expression gave to the others. Whether this is achievable in fragmented
mass cultures – or whether it is any longer an appropriate goal – is a question we moderns must ask of ourselves.

Chapter 3. *Point of view*

1 The relevant passage in Leibniz's letter is as follows: "He who finds pleasure
in the contemplation of a beautiful picture and would suffer pain if he saw
it spoiled, even though it belongs to another man, loves it so to speak with
a distinterested love; but this is not the case with he who thinks merely
of making money by selling or getting applause by showing it, without
caring whether it is spoiled or not when it no longer belongs to him"
(quoted by Osborne, 1968:179).

2 On the aesthetic attitude or point of view see Jerome Stolnitz, "On the
Origins of 'Aesthetic Distinterestedness,'" *The Journal of Aesthetics and*

Art Criticism (JAAC), XX/2 (Winter 1961, 131–143); "Some Stages in the History of an Idea," *The Journal of the History of Ideas,* XXII/2 (April–June 1961, 189); "A Third Note on Eighteenth-Century Distinterestedness,'" *JAAC,* XXII/1 (Fall 1963, 69f); Marcia Allentuck, "A Note on Eighteenth-Century 'Disinterestedness'," *JAAC,* XXI/1 (Fall 1962, 89); Gilbert-Kuhn, *A History of Esthetics,* revised ed. (Bloomington: Indiana University Press, 1954, 322); D. W. Gotshalk, "Aesthetic Attitude" in *Dictionary of World Literature,* J. T. Shipley, ed. (Paterson, N.J.: Littlefield & Adams, 1960, 7); Hunter Mead, *An Introduction to Aesthetics* (New York: Ronald Press, 1952, 17).

Some scholars have questioned the utility of discussions of aesthetic perception. Rather than focusing on the subjective contents of perception, they say, it is more fruitful to examine the grounds for aesthetic *judgments,* that is, to analyze the language and reasons used to describe or defend aesthetic evaluations concerning form, presentness, etc. Such a position, it seems to us, is based on a very ungenerous account of theories of aethetic perception, reducing them to a kind of subjectivist sensationalism, to which cognition can then be opposed. In contrast, for us the particular value of aesthetic perception lies in its transcending such dichotomies as cognitive versus emotive, or objective versus subjective. As H. D. Aiken says, "Any interest, as it approaches maturity, tends to become aesthetic.... It is certainly true that the aesthetic response is not a limited or partial version of some other sort of human concern.... But whatever limitations its own integral character imposes upon aesthetic experience, its domain is sufficiently commodious to include... the full range of what, all too obscurely, we lump together under the rubric of cognitive meaning" (1961: 273).

Arriving at a similar position from the opposite direction, Professor Haezrahi tells us that "reason plays the same part in shaping our aesthetic perceptions, as the artist does in creating a work of art. It carves a portion out of the stream of our sense-impressions, in a way similar to that in which the artist demarcates the boundaries of his subject. Again it introduces an order and coherence into its sensual material, akin to the pattern imposed by the artist on his material when he fashions it into a work of art. Thanks to this integrating, harmonizing, shaping activity shared alike by reason in the aesthetic experience, and by the artist in his work, natural things when they become objects of aesthetic perception seem to resemble works of art, and works of art to resemble living organisms....

"This unity in spite of the variety and multitude of sense-impressions it contains, is yet easily surveyed by the mind because of its orderly well-knit structure. This structure, the pattern and articulation of the complex unity, are so very apparent and clear, so very transparent to the mind, that the whole complex acquires a quality of lucidity, of necessity, of harmony. This air of being a coherent and harmonious cosmos, of an almost organic body is due to the thorough way in which the various sense-impressions have been pervaded, dominated and welded together by an exercise of reason" (1956:32, 27–28). See also Beardsley (1970), Cohen (1965), Ziff (1962), and Paul Taylor (1961:109).

3 It could be argued that the disconnection of the mundane world, and the existential shock of recognition that may come after one has entered a contemplative mode, requires that the places and spaces for such reflection be physically as well as psychically set apart from ordinary reality. Thus we have monasteries, as well as the monastic character of universities. "If we examine the settings for artistic behavior, says Morse Peckham, "we find the same phenomenon. The Japanese niche with its flower arrangement and its single painting, the picture frame which by bounding the perceptual field makes it easier to ignore what lies outside of it, the quiet museum of

art, in which everyone talks in hushed tones, if at all, in which the guard
upbraids the noisy, the darkened concert hall and theater, the defined space
before or around a great building – all these stages for the perceiver's role
are marked by psychic insulation" (1965:82).

4 Perhaps the quickest way to understand the nature of such a suspension of
conventional reality, suggests Natanson, "is to compare it with the act of
trying to take a fresh look at something or someone you already have quite
fixed ideas about. Looking at the face of someone you know intimately and
have seen daily over a period of years may mean not really seeing that
individual at all.... A sudden change in the appearance of a friend may
cause us to look closely, to 'take a second look'.... Or, on occasion, we
suddenly *see* the Other because of the glance of a third person.... A
situation may in fact call for a strategy of review in an almost literal sense
of that word.... In some professions, a 'distancing' of the self from its involvement with Others is essential to the success of the relationship"
(1970:9).

For an example of such a moment see Virginia Woolf: "So that is
marriage, Lily thought, a man and a woman looking at a girl throwing a
ball. That is what Mrs. Ramsay tried to tell me the other night, she thought.
For Mrs. Ramsay was wearing a green shawl, and they were standing close
together watching Prue and Jasper throwing catches. And suddenly the
meaning which, for no reason at all, as perhaps they are stepping out of
the Tube or ringing a doorbell, descends on people, making them symbolical,
making them representative, came upon them, and made them in the dusk
standing, looking, the symbols of marriage, husband and wife. Then, after
an instant, the symbolical outline which transcended the real figures sank
down again, and they became, as they met them, Mr. and Mrs. Ramsay
watching the children throwing catches" (1955:110–111).

5 See Bernard J. Boelen: "Insofar as 'di-*stance*' is an actual 'standing' in the
presence of the structural 'unity' of existence, there is ontological 'nearness.'
Insofar as '*di*-stance' is the ex-sistential 'standing-*apart*' of the unitary structure of ex-sistence, there is ontological '*remoteness.*' Everything becomes at
the same time infinitely remote and infinitely close – The space which opens
up in the aesthetic phenomenon is the very 'open-ness' of the comprehensive
universality of primordial wonder.... The revelation of original space makes
us aware of the fact that we are not spatialized on the bases of our *body*
alone, but rather on the bases of our 'Being-in-the-world.' We are not
'spatialized' in the passive sense of an 'established fact,' but rather 'specializ-
ing' in the active sense of 'opening up the world.' Bullough in his discussion of 'aesthetic distance' was right when he spoke of 'the *action* of
distance' " (1968:185–186, Boelen's italics).

For Husserl's treatment of the concept of distancing see "Method of
Clarification. The 'Nearness' and 'Remoteness' of Given Data" in *Ideas:
General Introduction to Phenomenology* (Vol. I, Secs. 67–71, 1931:75).

Hans Georg Gadamer speaks of the importance of a simulataneous nearness and farness with reference to historical hermeneutics: "A placement
between strangeness and familiarity exists between the historically intended,
distanced objectivity of the heritage and our belongingness to a tradition.
In this "between" is the true place of hermeneutics. ... Its temporal distance not only allows certain prejudgments peculiar to the nature of the
subject to die out but also causes those which lead to a true understanding
to come forward" (1965:279, 282, Gadamer's italics).

6 One of the earliest modern thinkers to develop these notions into a general
theory of art was the Russian Formalist Victor Shklovsky. Rather than
speaking of subjectivity and objectivity, Shklovsky opposes habituated and
original perception, unreflective, mechanical action as against experience
that is actually lived. In these terms art, or aesthetic perception, allows

us to see things freshly by distancing or defamiliarizing them. "Habituation devours work, clothes, furniture, one's wife, and the fear of war." Yet by making strange the familiar (*ostranenie*) aesthetic perception enables us to "recover the sensation of life; art exists to make one feel things, to make the stone *stony*" (1965:12).

7 For discussions of the practical and technical problems as well as many of the advantages and disadvantages of participant observation see especially the following: Florence R. Kluckhohn, "The Participant Observer Technique in Small Communities," *American Journal of Sociology*, XLVI (November 1940, 331–43); William F. Whyte, *Street Corner Society* (Chicago: University of Chicago Press, 1943, Preface, pp. v–x) and also his "Observational Field-Work Methods" in Marie Jahoda, Morton Deutsch, and Stuart W. Cook (eds.), *Research Methods in the Social Sciences* (New York: Dryden Press, 1951, II, 393–514); Marie Jahoda et al., "Data Collection: Observational Methods," ibid. (Vol. I, Chap. v); Benjamin D. Paul, "Interview Techniques and Field Relations" in A. L. Kroeber et al. (eds.), *Anthropology Today: An Encyclopedic Inventory* (Chicago: University of Chicago Press, 1953, 430–51); and Edward C. Devereux, "Functions, Advantages and Limitations of Semi-controlled Observations" (Ithaca, N.Y.: Staff Files, "Cornell Studies in Social Growth," Department of Child Development and Family Relationships, Cornell University, 1953). Also George McCall and J. L. Simmons, eds., *Issues in Participant Observation* (Reading, Mass.: Addison-Wesley, 1969); John Johnson, *Doing Field Research* (New York: Free Press, 1975); and Jack D. Douglas, *Investigative Field Research* (forthcoming, 1977).

8 David Riesman notes that "for decades, the pictures of primitive character brought back by anthropologists, no matter how well intended, were used by the denizens of Western industrialized civilization, either to preen themselves on their progress or to damn their cities, machines, or customs by reference to a constructed preliterate Eden—all, of course, under the guidance of such supposedly scientific terms as 'folk society,' 'Gemeinschaft,' 'sacred society,' and other such phrases" (1952:333).

9 On a more mundane level, graduate students are warned to take notes on everything "new" that they encounter during field research, the assumption being that discovery lies in the perspective of the outsider; once one becomes a member, experience becomes routinized and insight cease. Indeed, unlike the sociologist or the foreigner, or the person who simply is "out of it," to be a member means that one takes as *un*problematic the background rules which "everyone" knows. See Blanche Geer, "First Days in the Field" (1964).

10 Simmel makes a point about social forms similar to that which these investigators have been reaching empirically: "Even from their most punctilious observance [of rules of courtesy], we must not infer any positive existence of the esteem and devotion they emphasize; but their slightest violation is an unmistakable indication that these feelings do *not* exist. Greeting somebody in the street proves no esteem whatever, but failure to do so conclusively proves the opposite." See Georg Simmel, "The Negative Character of Collective Behavior" in Simmel (1950:400–401).

11 See Harold Garfinkel: "The members of the society uses background expectancies as a scheme of interpretation. With their use actual appearances are for him recognizable and intelligible as the appearances-of-familiar-events. Demonstrably he is responsive to this background, while at the same time he is at a loss to tell us of what the expectancies consist.... For these background expectancies to come into view one must either *be a* stranger to the 'life as usual' character of everyday scenes, or *become estranged* from them" (1967:35–37, our italics).

12 Deviants may be "cases" of course, as well as people. See Merton (1959: xxxii): "Because such inconsistencies set the stage for instituting new

problems, many... authors... search actively for 'deviant cases' – cases that depart from a prevailing pattern.... Appropriately investigated, the exception can improve the rule." See also Sjoberg (1959:359), and Lazarsfeld and Rosenberg (1959:167–174).

13 The use of "distancing" in literature was part of the same "discovery of society" that expressed itself in the realistic novel, the emergence of the social sciences as intellectual disciples, and that seems to be reconverging in a theater *and* a sociology of the absurd (Lyman and Scott, 1970, 1976). Thus each of the techniques for distancing mentioned in our text with reference to sociology have their cognates in art.

As Boris Tomashevsky notes, "Swift uses these methods of defamiliarization extensively in *Gulliver's Travels* in order to present a satirical picture of the European social-political order, Gulliver, arriving in the land of the Houyhnhnms (horses endowed with reason), tells his master (a horse) about the customs of the ruling class in human society. Compelled to tell everything with the utmost accuracy, he removes the shell of euphemistic phrases and fictitious traditions which justify such things as war, class strife, parliamentary intrigue, and so on. Stripped of their verbal justification and thereby defamiliarized, these topics emerge in all their horror. Thus criticism of the political system – nonliterary material – is artistically motivated and fully involved in the narrative" (1956:86).

As a giant in Lilliput, Gulliver also was located physically and socially for an optimal distance. Such a distanced point of view is achieved in this case by what Burke calls a "perspective by incongruity" (1964:94). This can be conveyed through numerous literary devices: the mountain and the plain, as in *The Magic Mountain* by Thomas Mann or *The Tartar Steppe* by Buzzati; the man and the animal, as in Anatole France's *Penquin Island*; animal fables from the *Pancatantra* to *Metamorphosis*; the earth and the cosmos as in Voltaire's *Micromegas*; or in other disjunctions of size, geography, social relatedness, or psychic set (Todorov, 1969:46–50).

Other devices include the repetition of a familiar phrase or motif until its conventional, referential meaning becomes absurd and we see it as an ontic unity in its own right. Kierkegaard developed a panoply of techniques for shaking people into awareness. These went under such names as ambiguity, incognito, the maieutic attitude, conscious duplicity, existential reduplication, immediate pathos, causing to take notice, accepting the other's illusions (and pretentions) as real money, teleological suspension of the ethical, and repetition (as contrasted with recollection). The last two terms come from Kierkegaard's *Repetition* and are its themes. The others are limned in *The Point of View*. See Benjamin Nelson's Preface in Kierkegaard (1962). In describing his point of view as an author, Kierkegaard uses images of the spy, the outsider, the subversive, and the underground man.

The sociologist, like the artist or underground man, makes himself known by indirection. Like a synthesis hovering over two contraries – the conventional expectation and the distanced view of it – his presence in the world is an emergent from the contradictions, that he reveals. To understand the true believer he may "reverse the proposition and look at the matter from the point of view of the Untrue Believer" (Murphey, 1971:143). The viewpoint of Swift is neither Gulliver's nor the Houyhnhnms'; instead Swift's message, as with the moral meaning of sociological writing, lies precisely in that which is unstated but which is immanent in the juxtaposition of the high and the low, the natives and the stranger. Sociological distance thus has several dimensions – a distance *from* previous concepts, and *from* previous value judgments, *toward* a theoretically and morally questioning stance.

14 For important treatments of point of view as a mimetic technique see Jacques Souvage, *An Introduction to the Study of the Novel* (Ghent: Wetenschappelijke Uitgeverij, 1965); Leon Surmelian, *Techniques of Fiction Writing* (New York: Doubleday, 1968); Robie Macauley and George

Lanning, *Technique in Fiction* (New York: Harper & Row, 1964); Shiv Kumar and Keith McKean, *Critical Approaches to Fiction* (New York: McGraw-Hill, 1968); Wayne Booth, *The Rhetoric of Fiction* (Chicago: University of Chicago Press, 1961). In *The Craft of Fiction* Percy Lubbock notes that "The whole intricate question of method, in the craft of fiction, I take to be governed by the question of the point of view – the question of the relation in which the narrator stands to the story" (1957:251).

15 A typology closely parallel to that of Pouillon is found in Gold, 1969. Though using nonaesthetic language, Gold in effect distinguishes four levels of authorial voice: complete observer, observer-as-participant, participant-as-observer, and complete participant.

16 Lewis uses other novelistic techniques as well: selection of a single day as the unit of study, which, he recognizes, "has been a common device of the novelist" (p. 4). Another technique "is to select for intensive study a problem or a special event or crisis to which the family reacts" (p. 4). A third technique, which Lewis uses but does not specifically note, is "cultural connotation," the use of rich associative language to create a paradigmatic thickness to objects so that they become symbolic embodiments of larger meanings. Lewis also tries to balance dialogue and summary, showing and telling. We have chosen the point-of-view technique for more detailed examination because of its epistemological implications. For Lewis' claims to the objectivity of his work see Lewis (1970). Many of our comments on Lewis were first suggested by Michel Benamou.

17 Gustave Flaubert, in a letter to Mademoiselle Leroyer de Chantepie dated March 18, 1857: "The illusion of truth in *Madame Bovary*... comes from the very objectivity of the work. It is one of my principles that one must not write oneself into one's work. The artist must be... invisible yet all-powerful; we must sense him everywhere but never see him" (quoted by Allott, 1959:271).

18 For other examples of the use of members' speech to create near-distance see Ned Polsky (1967, Chapter 2). Polsky expounds the pool hustler's argot: speed, heart, short-con, dumping, lemoning, the fish, and so on. Goffman treats the gambler's concepts of "hotness" (in Archibald, 1966:154) and "action" (Goffman, 1967:181–194), and the con man's notion of "cooling the mark" (Goffman, 1952). Hunter examines such concepts as "real thinkers" and "good old boy" to clarify the ideology of the power elite in Atlanta (Hunter, 1953).

Thomas and Znaniecki take the logically ultimate step in this direction by including in their study, *The Polish Peasant in Europe and America*, an autobiography written by an immigrated Polish peasant. Much of the richness of this classic, of course, is due to Thomas' having balanced such near-distanced material with far-distanced analytic treatments. Moreover, Thomas could play outsider to Znaniecki's insider concerning Polish culture, while these roles could be reversed with reference to America. In this connection, Robert Merton's paper, "Insiders and Outsiders: A Chapter in the Sociology of Knowledge," can be reinterpreted as an essay on point of view (Merton, 1972:9–47).

19 For a similar debate see Radcliffe-Brown versus Murdock concerning Australian marriage rules; Lawrence and Murdock (1949), Radcliffe-Brown, *American Anthropologist* (1951: 53:37–55), Elkin (1953), and Leach (1951:31–34). On who governs the American city see Dahl (1961), Hunter (1953), and Banfield and Wilson (1963).

20 Our discussion focuses mainly on techniques for gaining multiple points of view in testing hypotheses, looking, so to speak, from the theoretical level "down" onto the data. But our comments apply equally well if one were looking "up" from the data to various theories. Bensman and Vidich provide an example of this: "How is it possible to comprehend and interpret

the relationships between local and external action in a way that is true to the basic facts and elements observed? We turned our attention to various unsystematic and unsystematized theories developed in the past to handle similar data and problems: those of Redfield, Weber, Tönnies, Veblen, Merton, Lynd, Warner, Mills, Sapir, and Tumin. In each case we applied their perspectives to our data. In effect, we asked: 'What in their theories would permit us to comprehend our data?'

In the case of each theory which our initial finding made salient, we had a directive for data which could be elicited by further field research. Thus, for example, Veblen's study of the country town makes the point that the political conservatism of rural life rests in the rural village because economically it dominates the surrounding agricultural area. We did not find this to correspond with our observations and could only account for the difference by noting that Veblen wrote in a day when rural banks were strong and apparently autonomous agencies. While many things in Veblen's study of the country town rang true, it did not provide us with a basis for further investigation of our particular problem. On the other hand, Sapir's analysis of spurious culture, which emphasizes the role of cultural imports, directed us to view all phases of the cultural life of the community as a successive series of imports made at different times since 1890. In short, existing theory gave our field work a focus, and we could conduct it along the lines thereby suggested.

"Theories were helpful in opening our eyes to specific facts about our problem. For example, Sapir called our attention to the agencies of cultural penetration; Mills and Selznick, to the agencies of institutional penetration and organizational co-optation. In some instances a theorist's minor point became a central point to us, while his central point seemed irrelevant. In no case did we view any theory as offering us a solution to our problem, nor did we use any one theory exclusively to direct our observations. Research, for us, did not demonstrate, document, or annotate theory, but rather it exhausted the theories that came to our attention. Sapir's theory of the genuine culture was exhausted when nothing was found in the cultural life of the community that was indigenous to it – when everything cultural could be traced to an external source. In our procedure a theory was exhausted if and when it either yielded little follow-up data or if the data suggested by the theory were not forthcoming."

Bensman and Vidich are also sensitive to the role point of view played for the *subjects* of their study: "Farmers as a class, for example, were the only group directly protected and aided by federal legislation, but not all farmers responded similarly to the benefits it brought them. A farmer's reaction to federal legislation had an important effect on his local class position. Small businessmen had lost their monopoly of the local market to the large urban chains, and they responded to the loss in a psychologically and economically defensive manner. The connections of the professional class to the outside world were almost exclusively cultural, but these enhanced their prestige in the local community, etc. In examining the problem of penetration, we could not look at the town as a unified whole but had to examine how each class was related to the outside world.

"As a result of these observations it was necessary to recast our problem as a consideration of class. Class had to be considered, however, in terms not only of the specific problem of mass society but also of the general theories of class. In posing our problem as a class problem, again a whole range of new theories was evoked, including those of Warner, Lynd, Kaufman, Hollingshead, Weber, and Marx. However, again, theories of class were not considered *sui generis* but rather as pragmatic devices which would bring us to a solution to the original problem; that is, the alternative data which would be selected by different theories were considered initially only in terms necessary to solve the problem of the relationship of the local structure to the mass society, using as many dimensions as theory would allow. The new focus meant making an examination of all relevant class data....

"Theories of class led to another refocusing of the problem, this time in the area of politics. It became apparent that members of different classes played different roles in local political life. Accordingly, we considered the political theories of Weber, Centers, Marx, V. O. Key, Mosca, Neumann, Michels, and Mills.

"Each successive application of theory, derived in each instance from stimulation given by the immediately preceding investigation, caused us to take into account new orders of data which in turn forced us to select different types of theory" (1960:577–584).

21 *Tristam Shandy*, like Sartre's *Nausée*, Beauvoir's *Mandarins*, and Moravia's *Conjugal Love*, also are novels of a man trying to write a novel, simultaneous presentations of what the novel is about and the author's self-reflections on the process of writing it.

Chapter 4. *Metaphor*

1 But Aristotle also implies that metaphor might be used as a means of discovery: "Words express ideas, and therefore those words are most agreeable that enable us to get hold of new ideas. Now strange words simply puzzle us; ordinary words convey only what we know already; it is from metaphor that we can best get hold of something fresh" (*Rhetoric*, 1410b).

2 There are some who would oppose such an extension of meaning. For example, W. B. Stanford (1936:103): "If the term *metaphor* be let apply to every trope of language, to every result of association of ideas and analogical reasoning, to architecture, music, painting, religion, and to all the synthetic processes of art, science, and philosophy, then indeed metaphor will be warred against by metaphor...and how can its meaning stand."

3 Nathan Edelman, in his study "The Mixed Metaphor in Descartes," notes two central images by which the philosopher describes himself: as traveler and as architect. Although speaking to the same point – a straight road for the traveler, a solid foundation for the architect – the two figures are engaged in contrary activities. As Edelman puts it, "The one – always pressing forward – drives on, pulls ahead, explores without end. The other – in order to build upward – digs in, and stays on the spot, upon a rock that is immovable.... Thus it seems to have been with Descartes. He could reach out for utmost certitude, but withal could not outgrow a native uncertainty.... Are certitude and incertitude polar opposites or twin states of the human mind?" (1974:120).

4 For a neurological view of the role of imagery in cognition see Jason W. Brown (1972). "Regarding this iconic:analogic breakdown," Brown notes that it may "be an index of the extremes of the semantic field of the core item. In a sense metaphor is like a 'word association.' In speech or poetry the expositional function of language may be metaphorized. Word associations employ language in its referential aspects, so in a sense one gets only the resonance of the metaphor (see C. Jung, studies in word association). There are many workers in neurology and psychology (Luria in Moskow, Pribram in Palo Alto) who conceptualize cognitive action in terms of spatial, simultaneous systems and temporal, successive systems. Perception has basically this spatial, all-at-once character; meaning-experiences are sudden and powerful and the mental content is close to thought and the image life. Language on the other hand is a serial system mainly, in which meaning is stretched out over time. Could this iconic:analogic dichotomy be translated into a simultaneity:successivity dichotomy? If so, you're on

solid ground" (private correspondence, October 27, 1972). Also see Shaffer (1974:7–13) for a neurophysiological view.

5 Kandinsky, in *Reminiscences* (1913), also describes the creative imagination in terms similar to Eliot's: "Not only the stars, moon, woods, flowers of which the poets sing, but also a cigarette butt lying in the ash-tray, a patient white trouser button looking up from a puddle in the street, a submissive bit of bark that an ant drags through the high grass in its strong jaws to uncertain but important destinations, a page of a calendar which the conscious hand reaches to tear forcibly from the warm companionship of the remaining block of pages – everything shows me its face, its innermost being, its secret soul, which is more often silent than heard. Thus every still and every moving point (=line) became equally alive and revealed its soul to me."

Compare this to the advice given by the painter Kuo Hsi (1020–1090) in his *Lin Ch'uan Kao Chih* (Essay on Landscape Painting), one of the most famous works of Chinese aesthetics: "If you wish to record these wonders of creation, you must first be filled with enthusiasm for their beauty, then you must give yourself over to a detailed confrontation with them and sate yourself with them completely. So you must wander about in them and sate your eye with them; after you have arranged the impressions in your breast you will paint all this with complete ease and fluency, without your eye being aware of the painting-silk and your hand of the brush and ink, and everything will be your own individual image of them."

The reader also may be reminded of the Japanese *haiku* or of Chinese nature poetry. Where Western aesthetics has tended to be analogic and naturalistic, that of the Chinese is basically iconic and spiritual. Note such terms as "spirit resonance," "bone structure," and "life rhythm" as applied to paintings. See Munro, Siren, Sze, and Rowley.

6 What we have here in embryo is a linguistic theory of perception that adumbrates Whorf, Mead, Merleau-Ponty, and others. Edward Sturtevant's discussion of the origin of language is explicitly Nietzschean: "Voluntary communication can scarcely have been called upon except to deceive; language must have been invented for the purpose of lying" (1947:48).

7 This interplay of meanings may also be called "poetic tension." This tension can vibrate on two dimensions: the *in*tension of iconic implication, and the *ex*tension of the analogic relation. The properties of these dimensions may be suggested by these clusterings of terms:

Iconic	*Analogic*
diaphor	epiphor
plurisignation	simile
economy	range
condensation	reference
synoptic	comparative
sameness	likeness
quality	relation

Diaphor and epiphor are treated by Wheelwright (1962:70ff); plurisignation and simile are discussed in Wheelwright (1968:105ff). Similar distinctions are made by Sosensky, though he restricts the term "metaphor" to the iconic type only and then asserts that science, being analogic, is nonmetaphorical. The term "icon" for a kind of mental construct can be traced back to Charles Peirce (II, 247): "An *Icon* is a sign which refers to the Object that it denotes merely by virtue of characters of its own and which it possesses, just the same, whether any such Object actually exists or not." For other dyadic theories of metaphor, or language and thought in general, see Roman Jakobson (1956:55–82); Frazer (1951:12–14); Veach

(1969) ; and Ricoeur (1972). Frazer, much like Sosensky, distinguishes analogical from what he calls "fetishistic" thinking. Also see Jameson (1972:122–123).

8 Our argument also was suggested by Vico, who argued that the transparent certitude of mathematical reasoning derives solely from the fact that we ourselves create the "world of forms and numbers" with which mathematics deals, its elements being fictions that we have freely devised.

9 In Figure 7 are visual metaphors for what was said in the text.

10 A similar conclusion is reached by Braithwaite (1953:50–87, esp. p. 76) but through a different type of analysis.

11 The isomorphism of mice and men also was a question for medieval theologians. Their debate was whether a mouse that nibbles the consecrated wafer has partaken of the body of Christ. While they spoke of spirit and ritual rather than of consciousness and conduct, the logic of their debate is ironically similar to the contemporary "scientific" one.

12 Robert K. Merton (1969:xxvii) also speaks of the importance of finding "strategic materials for specific inquiry into a general problem," though he does so without acknowledging that what is involved here is the discovery of a pungent metaphor: "The history of sociology has its own complement of cases in which long-dormant problems were brought to life and developed by investigating them in situations that strategically exhibited the nature of the problem. Inquiry into the modes of interdependence between disparate social institutions was greatly advanced by Weber's decision to study the general problem in the particular instance of the connections between ascetic Protestantism and modern capitalism. The problem of the social bases of moral indignation, integral to an understanding of mechanisms of social control, required the finding of situations in which people react strongly to violations of social norms even though they are not directly injured by them. George Mead and Durkheim clarified the problem by proposing the study of systems of punishment, not with respect to the traditional question of their effects in curbing crime, but with respect to their other functions for the community. William F. Ogburn and Dorothy S. Thomas seized upon the occurrence of simultaneous multiple discoveries and inventions as a peculiarly strategic point of departure for clarifying the role of cultural factors in innovation. Robert Park focused on the behavior of immigrants as providing strategic materials for investigating the problem of the marginal man, who is oriented toward the competing values of different groups in which he fails to find full acceptance, a problem integral to current work on reference groups. In instances of this sort, a decisive turn was taken by the location of strategic materials for specific inquiry into a general problem."

The question as to what, exactly, constitutes the "strategicness" of such materials is, of course, one which our discussion of metaphor hopes to answer.

13 Paul Armer presents a similar example with reference to the flight of birds and of planes, and their "resolution" in aerodynamic theory (1963:398). Also see K. Gunderson (1964:60–71) and Anderson and Moore (1966).

14 Rashevsky's analogy of rumors and diseases is actually itself a metaphor on the biological theory of the lynx-rabbit cycle as propounded, for example, by A. J. Lotka (1925). For other theories analogous to this cycle see Richardson's theory of international competition in *Generalized Foreign Politics*, and George Homans's and Leon Festinger's models of interpersonal communication, as mathematically formulated by Herbert Simon (Festinger and Thibaut, 1951 and Simon, 1952:202–211). Also see Shibutani (1966).

15 One could argue that the use of metaphor here is not merely illustrative, because Simmel presents a model for a certain form of feeling. The distinction between illustrative metaphor and metaphor as model depends on

POETIC METAPHOR
(Inner life and
visualizable phenomena)

"Joyous undulation"   "Reason is a charioteer"

Form of joy   d — b   Visualizable waves   Form of reason   d — b   Visualizable charioteer

Feeling-of-waves   Presential reality of reason

SCIENTIFIC METAPHOR
(Formal — i.e., mathematical — theory
and visualizable phenomena)

The universe is a machine

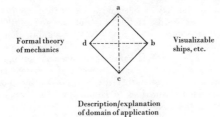

Formal theory of mechanics   d — b   Visualizable ships, etc.

Description/explanation
of domain of application

SOCIOLOGICAL METAPHOR

(a) "Scientific" imagery   (b) "Artistic" imagery

Society is a machine,
organism, etc.   Conduct is enactment,
language, etc.

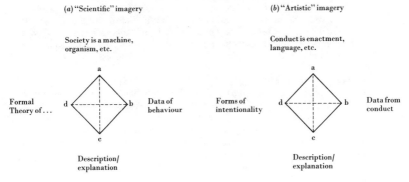

Formal Theory of ...   d — b   Data of behaviour   Forms of intentionality   d — b   Data from conduct

Description/
explanation   Description/
explanation

Figure 7

the degree to which the metaphor is elaborated, and the cutoff point between types is necessarily a matter of judgment.

16 On the relationship between models and theories, we agree with Simon and Newell in W. D. White (1956:66): "In contemporary usage the term 'model' is, I think, simply a synonym for 'theory.' However, the persons who arranged this meeting did *not* presumably intend that 'model' should mean simply 'theory.' I suspect ... that by 'model' they meant 'mathematical theory,' and they intended to exhibit in this arena another installment of the prolonged guerrilla warfare between mathematics and language. With respect to these hostilities ... I stand with J. Willard Gibbs: 'Mathematics *is* a language.' "

Also see Black (1962:238); Churchman *et al.* (p. 157); and Willner (1967:23): "Successful models are representative in that they not only are constructed to represent isomorphically certain abstracted factors of a set of empirical phenomena or 'domain of application,' but they also correspond to a formal system or validated theory for that set of phenomena."

17 For a similar definition – although of "form" rather than of "system" – see Merleau-Ponty: "We shall say that there is form whenever the properties of a system modify themselves for every change effected upon a single one of its parts, and on the contrary, conserve themselves when they all change by maintaining the same relationship between themselves" (1967:50).

18 A remark in Hegel's essay, "Dramatic Motivation and Language," may be helpful in this point. Hegel is speaking of the relation of the Greek gods to the natural order they were supposed to symbolize. Olympian theology, he says, was not a case of an allegorical separation of nature as against its human personification in the god, to be regarded as a theology in which the god *rules* nature; in other words, Helios was not the god of the sun but, instead, the sun *as* God (*States*, 1971:xix). Now, assuming that a similar "divinity" might exist in the world of social relations, we might think of the factors noted by Klapp not as causes of a person's getting a certain label but as the process by which certain elements of a system get labeled as causes. We might also remember that this process has no more obligation to those factors than the sun had to Helios, and that other ages will have their own names for these mysteries.

19 For a view of analytic induction as a method of defining essences rather than as controlled comparison in the statistical sense, see Znaniecki (1968: 249–331) and Robinson (1951, *passim*).

20 In Popper's view there is no "logical method of having new ideas, or a logical reconstruction of this process." His position, he says, "may be expressed as saying that every discovery contains an 'irrational element,' or a 'creative intuition,' in Bergson's sense. In a similar way Einstein speaks of '... the search for universal laws from which a picture of the world can be obtained by pure deduction. There is no logical path,' he says, 'leading to these laws. They can only be reached by intuition, based on something like an intellectual love (*Einfuhlung*) of the objects of experience" (1959:32).

Popper's concept of "insight" is similar to that of Gestalt psychologists. See, for example, Lewin (1951:252ff). Also see Samuel Johnson's literary criticism for another perspective on the same question: "The thing to be communicated was not emotion in all the flux and flurry of its original presence in the human soul. It is never a stream of consciousness. It is emotion selected and generalized into the simple universals that move men everywhere. To generalize an emotion was not, as the romantics tended to believe, to evaporate it but rather to make it available." (Hagstrum, 1952:47).

21 It should be clear that what we have said above is not limited to a simple four-point metaphor, which may be thought of as an icon for the larger

system of implications with which it is gravid. Nor must analogs be verbal representations – they could be expressed mathematically, diagrammically, physically (e.g., the protein model made of the sticks and balls of a child's erector set), etc.

22 See Paul Klee: "Even a glimpse through a microscope reveals to us images which we should deem fantastic and overimaginative if we were to see them somewhere accidentally, and lacked the sense [i.e., paradigm] to understand them" (quoted by Read, 1955:107).

23 R. D. Laing also uses this metaphor to illustrate the difference between existential and positivistic approaches in psychology (1965:20).

24 A list of "organistic" writers that we gleaned from Teggert, Bock, and Nisbet includes the following names: Aristotle, Ecclesiastes the Preacher, Euripides, Plato, Seneca, Thucydides, Vergil, Aquinas, Augustine, Roger Bacon, Francis Bacon, Jean Bodin, the Marquis de Concordet, Denis Diderot, Fontenelle, Pascal, Rousseau, Tocqueville, Voltaire, Hegel, Herder, Robert Bellah, Gordon Childe, Auguste Comte, Emile Durkheim, Engels, Sir James Frazier, Freud, Hobhouse, George Homans, Marion Levy, Robert Lowie, Robert MacIver, Sir Henry Maine, Malinowski, Marx, George Herbert Mead, Robert Merton, Lewis Morgan, Pareto, Parsons, W. W. Rostow, Saint-Simon, Selznick, Smelser, Sorokin, Spengler, Spencer, William Graham Sumner, Toynbee, Trotsky, Edward Burnett Tylor, Westermark, and Leslie White. To this list we add Cassierer, Husserl, Kant, Hobsbawm, Robert Park, A. Lane-Fox Pitt-Rivers, Tönnies, Adam Wildavsky, and Florian Znaniecki, as well as other writers mentioned in this connection in our text. See Teggert (1941); Bock (1956); Nisbet (1969).

25 The obvious candidate exception to this claim is *The Republic*. Here Plato has Socrates assert that *arete* is not the right of the stronger, but the effective harmony of the whole. To demonstrate this Plato shifts from the micro- to the macrosocietal level of analysis. "That which is writ large," says Socrates, "is easier to read than that which is writ small." We can know individual *arete* by examining the *arete* of the body social as a whole. And, like any organism – a statue is the illustrative metaphor used – the excellence of the body social lies in maintaining the harmonious inter-functioning of its parts which, of course, must remain subordinate to the whole. Hence it follows that individual virtue lies in each person's performing his particular function or role within the body social.

26 Aristotle says: "That a science of the accidental is not even possible will be evident if we try to see what the accidental really is. We say everything is either is always and of necessity ... or is for the most part, or is *neither* for the most part, *nor* always and of necessity, but merely as it chances.... The accidental, then, is what occurs, but not always, nor for the most part. Now we have said what the accidental is, and it is obvious why there is no science of such a thing; for all science is of that which is always or for the most part, but the accidental is in neither of these two classes." (*Metaphysics*, XI, viii).

27 In this Parsons goes far beyond his predecessors. Where Maine posited an evolution from status to contract, Tönnies from community to society, Durkheim from mechanical to organic solidarity, Redfield from folk to urban, and Becker from sacred to secular society, the "permutations and combinations" of Parsons's "pattern variables" yield no less than thirty-two distinct possible species.

28 It should be noted that, contrary to much opinion, the replacement of classical mechanics by quantum mechanics does not wipe the books clean. As Polanyi points out: "The behavior of human beings whose particles were ruled by the equations of quantum mechanics would be completely pre-determined by these, except for a certain range of random variations which would be strictly unaccountable. Since human judgment is anything

but a strictly unaccountable random choice, a quantum mechanical automaton is no better a representation of intelligent behavior than a mechanical automaton would be; and it offers no possibility either for the presence of human consciousness" (1958:390, n.1).

29 That this distinction often has not been made is well known to critics of mechanistic social science. For examples of the error see Zipf (1949), Parsons (1937:78–81), Dodd, and Rashevsky. For critiques see Sorokin (1956) and Peter Park (1969). In his *Philosophy of Physical Science* (1939), Eddington quotes a poem by W. J. M. Rankine (*Songs and Fables*, 1874), which seems apposite here:

"Let x denote beauty, y manners well-bred,
z fortune (this last is essential),
Let L stand for love – one philosopher said –
Then L is a function of x, y and z,
Of the kind that is known as potential.

"Now integrate L with respect to dt
(t standing for time and persuasion),
Then, between proper limits, 'tis easy to see
The definite integral Marriage must be
(A very concise demonstration.)"

30 For an example of the self-consciousness that we advocate see George Kubler: "The biological model was not the most appropriate one for a history of the things. Perhaps a system of metaphors drawn from physical science would have clothed the situation of art more adequately than the prevailing biological metaphors: especially if we are dealing in art with the transmission of some kind of energy; with impulses, generating centers, and relay-points; with increments and losses in transit; with resistances and transformers in the circuit. In short, the language of electrodynamics might have suited us better than the language of botany; and Michael Faraday might have been a better mentor than Linnaeus for the study of material culture" (1962:9).

31 See A. D. Ritchie: "As far as thought is concerned, and at all levels of thought, it is symbolic process. It is mental not because the symbols are immaterial, but because they are symbolic" (1936). Suzanne Langer, in taking issue with Ritchie, makes a distinction similar to the one we advance here: "As a matter of fact, it is not the essential act of thought that is symbolization, but an act *essential to thought*, and prior to it. Symbolization is the essential act of mind; and mind takes in more than what is commonly called thought" (1942:41).

32 On the meaning of "indexical" see Garfinkel (1967) and Cicourel (1974:74–98).

33 What Garfinkel says of the irreducibility of verbal constructions is equally true of nonverbal ones. For example, in *Being and Nothingness* (1956: 346–347), Sartre writes: "These frowns, this redness, this stammering, this slight trembling of the hands, these downcast looks which seem at once timid and threatening – these do not *express* anger; they *are* anger. But this point must be clearly understood. In itself a clenched fist is nothing and means nothing. But also we never perceive a *clenched fist*. We perceive a man who in a certain situation clenched his fist. This meaningful act considered in connection with the past and with possibles and understood in terms of the synthetic totality 'body in situation' *is* the anger" (Sartre's italics).

34 Goffman offers the example of a man driving through a red light. "What is he doing? What has he done?" Goffman lists no less than twenty-four plausible definitions of the situation. Summarizing, he says: "So our man

has passed through a red light. But at his hearing when the judge asks him what he was doing running a red light, he will provide an argument as to what was really happening. Obviously, what makes driving through a red light a discernible, isolable event is that a rule stipulated in regard to the light was broken. The objective 'fact,' then, must be as variable as is the individual's possible relation to the rule" (1971:102–103, note).

If conduct is a language, then social theory becomes, in Charles Peirce's words, "pure rhetoric," the (aesthetic) theory of the language of behavior. In these terms Goffman may be criticized for confining himself to lexography; he writes dictionaries of behavior when our more pressing need is for books of grammar and syntax.

35 To see reality as symbolic, however, is not to throw empirical verification out the window. On the contrary, it is to suggest that "empirical verification" be understood as referring back to an intersubjective *social* world in which the investigator inexorably plays a part. We must accept Durkheim's dictum to treat social facts as things, *as well as* Weber's response that social facts are *not* things. The way over this contradiction is to recognize that all the things in our worlds are socially mediated, all are given up to us through intersubjective symbolic action, all are apprehended in (however primitive) a social-historical consciousness. The absolute separation between theory and reality, between values and objectivity, between meanings and facts turns out to be unnecessary and misleading. As Sartre says, "social facts are things to the extent that *all things*, directly or indirectly, are social facts" (1956:246). Also see Merleau-Ponty, "From Mauss to Claude Lévi-Strauss," in *Signs*, pp. 114–125, and J. Monnerot, *Les faits sociaux ne sont pas les choses* (Paris: 1946).

36 The references here, of course, are to Roland Barthes's *Système de la mode* (Paris: Seuil, 1967), and to Lévi-Strauss's *Le Cru et le cuit* (Paris: Plon, 1964); *L'Origine des manières de table* (Paris: Plon, 1968); *Le Totemisme aujourd'hui* (Paris: Presses universitaires de France, 1962); and *Les Structures élémentaires de la parenté* (Paris: Presses universitaires de France, 1949). The quotations from Saussure and Lévi-Strauss were translated by Fred Jameson. A full English translation of Lévi-Strauss' essay "Language and the Analysis of Social Laws," from which this is taken, appears in *Structural Anthropology*, translated by Jacobson and Schoepf (New York: Basic Books, 1963).

37 It may be argued that the structuralists do not disconnect the symbol from a nonsymbolic empirical referent in quite as strict a manner as our discussion here might suggest. For, if the symbol itself is referential only to other symbols, there also appears the idea that the structure of these referential relationships, in some larger sense, corresponds to a thing-in-itself. In Lévi-Strauss this *Ding an sich* appears to be "nature" or "the deeper structures of the mind." In Barthes there is a feeling for social and ideological materials, in Althusser a sense of history. See Jameson (1972:109).

38 John Staude (1972:267–268) says that "It is a postulate of humanistic sociology...that the modes of human being include many intentional 'worlds'; i.e., the world of being-alone (privacy), the world of being-close-to-another (intimacy), the world of being-isolated or cut-off from others (alienation)...and the world of being-a-part of a collectivity (solidarity). The world of the alien or the outsider (the stranger) is different from the world of the insider. Furthermore, we can move from one world to another. Note: These situations are not simply feelings (I feel isolated). They are modes of human being (I am isolated). They are not merely subjective states, they are *existential* states."

39 Besides the works cited in this section, important sociological studies from the dramaturgical perspective include Berryman (1962), Burns (1972),

Evrienoff (1970), Ichleiser (1970), Louch (1966), Messinger et al. (1962), and Stanford Lyman and Marvin Scott (1976).

40 See Cicourel (1970:28), for a similar criticism made from an ethnomethodological perspective.

41 See Wilhelm Dilthey [(1958:VIII, 194) and as quoted by R. Palmer (1969: 107)]: "That which in the stream of time forms a unity in the present because it has a unitary meaning is the smallest entity which we can designate as an experience. Going further, one may call each encompassing unity of parts of life bound together through a common meaning for the course of life an 'experience' – even when the several parts are separated from each other by interrupting events."

An extraordinarily similar idea is expressed by John Dewey: "We have *an* experience when the material experienced runs its course to fulfillment. . . . A situation, whether that of eating a meal, playing a game of chess, carrying on a conversation, writing a book, or taking part in a political campaign, is so rounded out that its close is a consummation and not a cessation. Such an experience is a whole and carries with it its own individualizing quality and self-sufficiency. It is *an* experience" (1958:35).

42 This obviously is a heuristic assumption, for the consciousness of many groups and times does appear to have the scripted, authored aspect that Edie denies. In fact, what Edie described as "lived-time" refers to a form of secular, individualized consciousness that is virtually unique to the modern West.

43 This quotation suggests several avenues worth exploring that lie beyond our present focus. But it may be noted that the dramaturgical model need not be restricted to those areas of life that involve deception. On the contrary, such special situations parallel what is a special aspect of drama: the portrayal of deception within the normal appearances created by the play as a whole. In comedies such as *Two Gentlemen of Verona* or *The Miser*, good is achieved by a real character impersonating a false one. In tragedies such as *Othello* or *Richard III*, an evil usurper presents *himself* as though he were good. In other plays, like other life situations, the action is conducted wholly in terms of normal appearances, with only the *audience* being aware of consequences unbeknown to the actors. As we have seen, in such plays the higher knowledge of the audience is paralleled in life by that of the social observer. See Anne Righter (1962).

Also note that Goffman's notion of deception on the level of personal relations has great affinity with Marx's thoughts on ideology and false consciousness on the macrosocial level. In Marx's formulation, intellectuals in the hire of the ruling class refine and systematize the ideas of their patrons. These ideas become the ruling ideas of the society because the ruling class controls channels of communication. The ideology thus becomes fixed in art, religion, and public discourse. It takes on an autonomous, objectified character that might not change *even if* the material base and class structure of the society changes. Thus ideas and forms of expression may continue to prevail despite their disalignment with "reality" and their inappropriateness to authentic relationships and felt social needs. See Marx's discussion of the "Mystery of the Fetishistic Character of Commodities" in *Capital*, as well as *The German Ideology*. See Blumer (1958).

44 In another essay, "Toward a Sociology of the Absurd" (1970), Lyman and Scott claim as their precursor Machiavelli who, they argue, posited life as a "theater of the absurd" and then set about defining the rules of effective performance. Whereas Machiavelli wrote for aristocrats, today everyman must be his own Prince, for everyman today must enact what he wishes to seem. In this light, what Castiglioni and others did for the courtier, Goffman and his students are doing for today's middle class. The parallel cries

out for a treatment in terms of the historical sociology of ideas. See also Merleau-Ponty, "A Note On Machiavelli" in *Signs* (1964).

45 It is striking that most of these studies do not explicitly acknowledge the game metaphor from which their insight and imagery are drawn. The metaphor thus may be called a root one because it is widespread, but latent. Such a lack of explicitness has contributed to what John Lofland calls "analytic interruptus," the failure to elaborate the initial sensitizing metaphor into a full-blown formal theory. See Lofland, "Interactionist Imagery and Analytic Interruptus," mimeo, Sonoma: California State University (January 1969).

46 Note that Saussure also struggled with this problem. At first, like Wittgenstein, he compared language to a game of chess, in order to illustrate the idea of a rule-bounded system. Later however, Saussure noted that whereas the rules of chess are constant, those of language evolve in the process of their enactment. "In order for the chess game to resemble the game of language at every point, one would have to suppose an unconscious or unintelligent player."

See *Cours de linguistique generale* (p. 43), as well as Jameson (1972: 20–22) and Alfred Schutz, "The Problem of Rationality in the Social World" in Schutz (1964, esp. pp. 72–76). Also see Aaron Cicourel's criticism of the *dramaturgical* metaphor: "[This] metaphor...is defective in explaining how actors are capable of imitation and *innovation* with little or no prior rehearsal, just as a child is capable of producing grammatically correct utterances that he has never heard and is capable of understanding utterances that have never been heard before" (1970:28).

47 Alfred Schutz makes some interesting remarks on precisely this point: "We have to distinguish between rational constructs of models of human actions on the one hand, and constructs of models of rational human actions on the other. Science may construct rational models of irrational behavior, as a glance in any textbook of psychiatry shows. On the other hand, common-sense thinking frequently constructs irrational models of highly rational behavior, for example, in explaining economic, political, military and even scientific decisions by referring them to sentiments or ideologies presupposed to govern the behavior of the participants. The rationality of the construction of the model is one thing and in this sense all properly constructed models of the sciences – not merely of the social sciences – are rational; the construction of models of rational behavior is quite another thing. It would be a serious misunderstanding to believe that it is the purpose of model constructs in the social sciences or a criterion for their scientific character that irrational behavior patterns be interpreted as if they were rational" (1970:279–280).

48 Early modern thinkers rejected Aristotle's organic, anthropomorphic view of nature in favor of a mechanistic view. It is curious that mechanism should today be rejected in favor of a human-centered view, which we here are saying is based on the model of art. This series of changes brings us full circle, in a sense, in that Aristotle's theory of nature originally was developed on the metaphor of art. Aristotle's dictum that art imitates nature has been interpreted mechanistically by moderns to mean that art is a copy of some objective natural reality. But in speaking of nature, Aristotle was referring to its immanent, autotelic, self-coming-to-be. Art "imitated" nature in the sense that nature – being governed by its own aesthetic logic – had already imitated art. For an exposition of this view see Victorino Tejera (1965:45–49). See also Omar K. Moore and Alan R. Anderson (1965). An animistic view of nature lies behind Wald's discussion of confidence levels in the behavioral sciences (1950). Also see O. K. Moore (1957:69–74).

49 Durkheim logically deduced the same point that Garfinkel discovered empirically. In his treatment of the normative backgrounds of activity, Durkheim insists that the validity and understanding of the stated terms of a contract depend on unstated and essentially unstatable terms that the contracting parties take for granted but that bind and cover their transactions.

Chapter 5. *Irony*

1 For treatments of the nature and varieties of irony see Knox, *The Word Irony and Its Context*; D. C. Muecke, *The Compass of Irony*, and Kierkegaard, *The Concept of Irony*. These seminal works can lead the reader to others. The four major modes of ironic expressions that we defined obviously are not the only possible typology. The rationale for our division is twofold: It has some justification in the history of the concept, and it most naturally leads up to dramatic or dialectical irony, which is the type that most illuminates sociological theory.

2 A contrary example is provided by Margaret Hodgen's *Change and History*, a study in the neopositivist tradition of Teggart and Bock. This work shows high correlations between technological innovations and other types of events but is dubious about plausible motives for actors. Unlike Merton's thesis concerning ward politics, Hodgen's formulation is nonironic. It overturns neither conventional theory nor lay assumptions. This difference also makes clear how "popular" irony operates in the realm of values. No amount of unexpected juxtaposition and peripety is ironic unless one believes that good government *should* produce good welfare.

3 When we speak of sociology as a hermetic science, we are merely distinguishing sociology from society. What Northrop Frye says about physics and art criticism is apposite: "Physics is an organized body of knowledge about nature, yet the student says that he is learning physics, not that he is learning nature. Art, like nature, is the subject of systematic study, and has to be distinguished from the study itself, which is criticism. It is therefore impossible to 'learn literature'; one learns about it in a certain way, but what one learns, transitively, is the criticism of literature" (quoted by F. Jameson, "History and the Techniques of Literary Criticism," San Diego: Dept. of Literature, University of California, mimeo., p.1).

4 See Merton (1959:xv, fn.5): "This is not the place to consider...the relations between the socially plausible...and the true.... It may be enough to suggest that the independence between the two confronts the sociologist with some uncomfortable alternatives. Should his systematic inquiry only confirm what had been widely assumed...he will of course be charged with 'laboring the obvious'....Should investigation find that widely held social beliefs are untrue...he is a heretic, questioning value-laden verities. If he ventures to examine socially implausible ideas that turn out to be untrue, he is a fool....And finally, if he should turn up some implausible truths, he must be prepared to find himself regarded as a charlatan."

5 Actually Weber used "enchanted garden" to refer to premodern non-rationalist modes of thought. The image originally appears in the works of Schiller.

6 Harold Garfinkel argues that sociology has been an irony of common sense language with scientific language. He proposes a further ironization of the latter. This, of course, is not inconsistent with our argument here. See Richard Hill and Kathleen Crittenden (1968:13–15). Also see Harvey Sacks (1963:1–16). The intellectual career of Herbert Blumer is instructive in this connection. For examples of major essays ironizing sacred cows of the *profession*, see Blumer (1931, 1954, and 1956).

7 Laing's discussion of Kraepelin also can be interpreted in terms of different levels or points of view. Note, for example, how the construction of the events is transformed depending on whether the observer assumes a stance of superiority to the subject, as does Kraepelin, or of equality, as is the case with Laing.

Also apposite are examples from other professions, such as career counseling or police work. On the former, Burton Clark (1960) discovered that career counseling also serves as a cooling-out process for people who aren't making it in college; unbeknown to the clientele, career counseling is the organization's way of getting rid of those who fail. Regarding police work, Jerome Skolnick notes that law and order often are conflicting goals: "When law is used as the instrument of social order, ɪt necessarily poses a dilemma. The phrase 'law and order' is misleading because it draws attention away from the substantial incompatibilities existing between the two ideas. Order under law suggests procedures different from achievement of 'social control' through threat of coercion and summary judgment.... In short, 'law and order' are frequently found to be in opposition, because law implies rational restraint upon the rules and procedures utilized to achieve order. Order under law, therefore, subordinates the ideal of conformity to the ideal of legality" (1966:9).

8 Davis' use of the term "cause" (in the fourth to last line) presumes a greater inevitability than he has made credible. The existence of prostitution may make it easier for virtuous women to stay that way, but "cause" implies a stronger necessity than this.

9 While Lewis makes a strong case for inevitability on the motivational level, he misses it entirely on the level of practical necessity. For example, the historical sequence of slavery and open-class mobility tended to be just the reverse of what he assumes; other societies have equal or greater mobility, but less racism, and so forth.

10 What is ironic and original in relation to popular opinion of course may be conventional wisdom among professionals. In the present example, Tocqueville's findings are treated by scholars as merely one instance illustrating a general theory of organizations. See Collins and Makowsky (1972:61).

11 One also could argue that rather than "protecting" democracy, feudalism kept it from being fully realized. Such a view *could* be an ironic insight to the extent that feudalism is presumed to have been a liberating force. For an example see R. Brown (1972:1–13).

12 Pirandello contrasts himself to positivistic social scientists: "while the sociologist describes social life as it presents itself to external observation, the humorist, being a man of exceptional intuition, shows – nay, reveals – that appearances are one thing and the consciousness of the people concerned, in its inner essence, another" (1952:xiv).

See also Wylie Sypher: "Those in the thrall of carnival come out, for a moment, from behind the facade of their 'serious' selves, the facade required by their vocation. When they emerge from this facade, they gain a new perspective upon their official selves and thus, when they again retire behind their usual *personae*, they are more conscious of the duplicity of their existence" (1956:221).

13 A favorite unmasking technique of Goffman is to place jarring opposites within a single frame. For example: "The fact – at least in our society – is that a very limited set of ritual enactments are available for contrite offenders. Whether one runs over another's sentence, time, dog, or body, one is more or less reduced to saying some variant of 'I'm sorry.'... A single ritual idiom of remedial moves must be called on whether a toe has been accidently stepped on or a destroyer accidently sunk (1971:117–118). Elsewhere Goffman says, "Taking the hat off ... marked an occasion when a

gentleman was...oriented to the presence of some sacred object, such as a lady, a casket, or the flag" (1971:92n.).

14 Goffman quotes Santayana to show (or shield?) his own position: "Masks are arrested expressions and admirable echoes of feeling, at once faithful, discreet, and superlative. Living things in contact with the air must acquire a cuticle, and it is not urged against cuticles that they are not hearts; yet some philosophers seem to be angry with images for not being things, and with words for not being feelings. Words and images are like shells, no less integral parts of nature than are the substances they cover, but better addressed to the eye and more open to observation. I would not say that substance exists for the sake of appearance, or faces for the sake of masks, or the passions for the sake of poetry and virtue. Nothing arises in nature for the sake of anything else; all these phases and products are involved equally in the round of existence" (1922:131–132, quoted on flypage of Goffman, 1971).

It also should be said, in Goffman's defense, that Alvin Gouldner's critique on this issue stays wholly within a moralistic and naturalistic framework and thus quite misses the nature and value of Goffman's ironic stance (Gouldner, 1970:378–390). Also see Simmel, *Fragmente* (Ch. VI), "Zur Philosophie des Schauspielers."

15 Ways in which Goffman's and Sorokin's works might complement each other also are worth exploring. For example, Goffman has been criticized for lacking a macropolitical context for his microsocietal analyses. Yet just such a context might be supplied by Sorokin's concept of civilization. Similar interpretations could be made on the questions of values and of historical change. See Alan Dawe's "The Underworld-view of Erving Goffman" for relevant criticisms and Stanford Lyman's "Civilization: Contents, Discontents, Malcontents" for a possible solution.

16 What Thomas Mann's Tonio Kröger says about the "curse" of literature could apply equally to the social sciences: "It begins by your feeling yourself set apart, in a curious sort of opposition to the nice, regular people; there is a gulf of ironic sensibility, of knowledge, scepticism, disagreement, between you and others" (1958:153–154).

17 At stake here is not only the maintenance of a critical reflective consciousness but also the problem of intersubjectivity at a basic political level. As Sartre puts it: "*If* a concrete dialectic (*dialectique située*) is to be possible, a social conflict...must be *in principle* understandable to the third parties who depend upon it without participating in it, or to the witnesses who watch it from outside without being in the least involved in it.... This third party, by its mediation, realizes the transcendent and objective unity of the positive reciprocities.

"This formal characteristic does not preclude degrees in the reciprocal understanding of adversaries. Circumstances decide this, and one may be 'handled like a child,' 'manipulated,' etc.... If one of the adversaries ceases to understand, he is the *object of the Other*" (1960:753–754, Sartre's italics).

18 Muecke notes this resemblance of the ironist and his victim by pointing out that "a portrait of someone smiling, but not smiling at anything represented in or implied by the portrait, may be interpreted either as a portrait of someone smiling ironically or as an ironical portrait of someone smiling with foolish self-satisfaction. Evelyn Waugh evidently felt the truth of this since he speaks of 'the sly, complacent smile of la Gioconda'" (1969:229). See also K. Burke (1973a), "The Virtues and Limitations of Debunking."

19 See Thackery's *Mr. Brown's Letters to His Nephew*: "A literary man of the humoristic turn is pretty sure to be of a philanthropic nature, to have a great sensibility, to be easily moved to pain or pleasure, keenly to appreciate the varieties of temper of people round about him, and sympathize

in their laughter, love, amusement, tears. Such a man is philanthropic, man-loving by nature, as another is irascible, or red-haired, or six feet high."

Also see Carlyle's attempt to describe the humor of Jean-Paul Richter: "Fundamentally it is genuine humour, the humour of Cervantes and Sterne, and produce not of Contempt but Love, not of superficial distortion of natural forms, but of deep and playful sympathy with all forms. It springs not less from the heart than from the head; its result is not laughter, but something far kindlier and better; as it were, the balm which is generous spirit pours over the wounds of life, and which none but a generous spirit can give forth. Such humour is compatible with tenderest and sublimest feelings, or rather it is incompatible with the want of them."

Both the above passages are quoted by Harry Levin, who himself writes: "As the focus of humor is shifted from actor to spectator, from the individual whose oddities are noted to the writer who is taking note, a more sympathetic relation seems to develop between the two. Ridicule gives way to empathy; the characterization becomes the author's mouthpiece, not his victim; and the author himself becomes a role-player, a practical joker, a collector of hobby-horses" (1972:13).

20 Obviously those who interpret rhetorical irony or wit from a biological or phenomenal perspective will overlook this logical dimension. Freud, for example (1960), suggests that wit, while employing certain intellectual techniques, is "essentially a weapon *against logic*, stemming from the irrational unconscious, and being in fact a device to gain pleasure by eluding reason through substituting the infantile for the adult state of mind." We agree with Freud that wit and irony are a victory over repression, but the victory is that of intellection rather than of unreason. See Swabey (1961: 69–102) and Mary Douglas (1968). Also see Anton Ehrenzweig (1953) for an extension of the Freudian analysis of wit to aesthetic pleasure.

Chapter 6. *Coda*

1 Even within a given domain of discourse innovations require a kind of conflict and pyramiding by which the structure of *new* paradigms hover over or are immanent in the old. And, with the acquisition of synoptic or overviewing vision of different frames of discourse, this emergent effect is clearer still. See Lovejoy (1926), Bergmann (1944), Arnheim (1971), and Adelman (1966). Gendron (1970:151) also implies this when he tells us that "there are serious difficulties in making sense of the concept of (scientific) rationality when applied to *inter-* or *extra-*framework discourse" (our italics). Yet an aesthetic concept of rationality may be just what is needed to provide such extraframework sense.

John Platt speaks of "hierarchial jumps" or "hierarchical restructuring" as "the interactions jumping *across* the system level between old subsystems and the new supersystem that is process of formation." Platt also considers the relationship between the subrational and superrational: "There is a curious connection between things we regard as subrational and as superrational. Thus, in *The Ides of March*, Thornton Wilder has Caesar say that four things keep him from being sure there are no Gods. They are: love, mystical experiences connected with his epileptic seizures, creative acts such as poetry, and his sense of destiny. Today, most of us would likewise regard love or great music as uplifting experiences – and yet, viewed cynically, these would seem to be no more than sexual or rhythmic excitations of the lower nervous system. These are all nonrational responses of some part of the brain.... Why then the sense of enlargement, of Godhood, in intelligent and active men? – for I believe that we, as well as Wilder and his Caesar, are not deceived in this leap of insight.

"The answer is, I think, that these nonrational experiences differ from simple lower operations, like shivering or good digestion, because they refer to and help us integrate with ... a larger system than isolated man. Love, whether purely sexual or more sublimated, means biological continuity and an enlargement to include and respond to another person or a family or all mankind. Poetry or great music are creative acts that build up larger architectonic patterns for both the composer and the audience. Such acts of hierarchical growth are never rationally deducible from the smaller system-structures that precede them, as Arthur Koestler and Michael Polanyi have emphasized. Similarly, mystical experiences or a sense of destiny, as suggested for Caesar, can represent insights and identification with a larger ongoing universe in which the individual becomes a creative part" (1970:52). On emergent properties in sociology see Nagel (1952:7–32), Parsons (1949:33ff), Coleman (1964:241), and Edel (1956: 167–195).

2 In sociology's attempt to relate theory and practice – to reconcile the logical meaning of contradiction with the social contradiction of logic – the concept of alienation may be strategic (Seeman, 1959). One meaning of alienation is that the logic of one's world fails to be confirmed by the facts of one's experience. We refer not to disconfirmation of the contents of one's world, but of one's world as such. The scientist, for example, is not alienated from the world of science if his hypothesis is falsified by an experiment. But he may be alienated if his moral existence comes to falsify science as a whole. Imagine, for instance, the Quaker physicist who realizes his theories, no matter what he does with them, lead to bigger and better bombs.

In the above instance a "sane" personal paradigm is disconfirmed by the "war madness" of a paradigm that is widely shared. But alienation also may result from the opposite: when "sane" others label one's personal world as "mad." In what neurologists call aphasic and schozophrenic paralogic, for example, deductions are reached through the fusion of two items that are equated with the same predicate, as in $A = B$, $C = B$, ergo $A = C$. But in paralogic this becomes:

Indians are swift.
Stags are swift.
Ergo: Indians are (swift as) stags.

The "logic" here is impeccable if one understands it in terms of schizophrenics' world. Yet for all practical purposes people who call Indians stags are called crazy (Ergo: stags are crazy?)

Earlier (Ch. 4:163) we discussed Kenneth Boulding's distinction between rational and irrational behavior. Rational behavior, says Boulding, is responsive to new information and consistent in its ordering of behavioral options. Irrational behavior is not. But as symbolic realists we must ask "Unresponsive, etc., from what point of view?" For is it not possible that much behavior that is labeled "irrational" may possess a responsiveness, consistency, and order that simply is not manifest in the structurings of its appearances from an alien point of view? Could it be that what Scheff, Szasz, and Laing tell us about the labeling of people's worlds as "mentally ill" is true of worlds and paradigms in general? Which paradigms get accepted as legitimate and which are rejected as "primitive," "crazy," or "irrational?" Our aesthetic criteria for determining the fitness of paradigms do not necessarily determine their acceptance in practice, for this is also a question of power.

3 Habermas has argued for a dialectical sociology that would be motivated by an emancipatory interest, and the intent of which would be the liberation of individuals from alien structures and definitions that arise out of systems of domination. In contrast, he says, the interest of positivism is technical: "Empirical analytic sciences disclose reality insofar as it appears

within the behavioral system of instrumental action. In accordance with their immanent meaning, nomological statements about this subject domain are thus designed for a specific context in which they can be applied – that is, *they grasp reality with regard to technical control that, under specified conditions, is possible everywhere and at all times*" (1971:195).

4 Kurt Wolff also notes this difference between existential and propositional truth as related to sociological theory (1970:45–46). Wolff reminds us that this distinction corresponds to that between mathematical time and "inner" time or *durée*. On this latter distinction see Schutz (1945:538–542), Sorokin (1943), and Stravinsky (1956:31–34). Also see Simmel's essay on "The Nature of Philosophy": "Is there anyone nowadays, who still asks whether Plato's theory of ideas or the pantheism of the Stoics is 'correct,' whether Nicholas of Cusa's concept of God as the 'coincidence of contra- dictions' or Fichte's world-creating self 'corresponds to the facts,' or whether Schelling's doctrine of the identity of nature and mind or Schopenhauer's metaphysics of will is 'true'? All these views have been frequently and conclusively 'refuted.' Yet in each case, the human type which set down its reactions to existence in these 'errors' has survived all refutations and, in its own way, has lent those doctrines an immortal significance. *In any case, the criterion of truth of these doctrines is not to be obtained from the point to which the factual assertion refers but from the point from which it comes.* This, as is evident, is the attitude which gives rise to the complaint against philosophy … that it anthropomorphizes the world" (1959:299–300; our italics).

5 For Heidegger's discussions of art as "the-putting-itself-into-work of truth" (*Das Sich-ins-Werk-Setzen*), see Heidegger, "Der Ursprung des Kunstwerks" in Holzwege (1957, 25–28, 40–42, 45, 50), *Ienfuhrung in die Metaphysik* (1958, 77–78, 156), *Sein und Zeit* (1960, 212ff), *Vom Wesen der Wahrheit* (1954), "Die Frage nach der Technik" in *Vortrage und Aufsatze* (1954, 43) ; and elsewhere.

6 To quote Mannheim in our Coda is not to agree with all his formulations. For critical examinations of Mannheim's works see Alexander von Schelting (1934:94–100 and 117–67 and 1936:664–74), Hans Speier (1937:155– 166), Maurice Mandelbaum (1938: 67–82), Arthur Child (1941a:204– 207, 1941b:410–411, and 1947:18–34), Robert K. Merton (1941:125–147), Virgil G. Hinshaw (1943:XL:57–72), and Jacques J. Maquet (1951:esp. Chapters 3 and 5).

Bibliography

In mounds of books
  where verses lie buried,
you may find by chance
  iron-filed lines of poems;
handle them with the care
  that respects
ancient
  but terrible weapons
Mayakovsky (1960:226)

Abel, Theodore. "The Operation Called *Verstehen*," *American Journal of Sociology*, 14, 3 (November 1948), 211–218. In Herbert Feigl and May Brodbeck, eds. *Readings in the Philosophy of Science*. New York: Appleton-Century-Crofts, 1953.

Abrams, Meyer Howard. *The Mirror and the Lamp*. New York: Oxford, 1953.

Adams, Richard, and Preiss, J., eds. *Human Organization Research*. Homewood, Ill.: Dorsey, 1960.

Adams, Romanzo. *Interracial Marriage in Hawaii*. New York: Macmillan, 1937.

Adelman, Frederick. *The Quest for the Absolute*. The Hague: Nijhoff, 1966.

Adorno, Theodor W., et al. *The Authoritarian Personality*. New York: Harper & Row, 1950.

"Einleitungsvortrag zum 16. Deutschen Soziologentag." In *Spatkapitalismus oder Industriegesellschaft?* Stuttgart: 1969.

Der Positivismusstreit in der deutschen Soziologie. Berlin: Neuwied, 1969.

Aiken, Henry David. "Some Notes Concerning the Aesthetic and the Cognitive." In Morris Philipson, ed. *Aesthetics Today*. Cleveland: World, 1961.

Alleman, Beda. "Metaphor and Antimetaphor." In Stanley R. Hopper and David L. Miller, eds. *Interpretation: The Poetry of Meaning*. New York: Harcourt, Brace & World, 1967.

Allentuck, Marcia. "Expression, 'Aesthetic Silence,' and Information Theory." In Jan Aler, ed. *International Congress on Aesthetics, 5th Amsterdam, 1964*. The Hague: Mouton, 1968.

Allott, Miriam. *Novelists on the Novel*. London: Routledge, 1959.

Almond, Gabriel, and Verba, S. *The Civic Culture*. Princeton, N.J.: Princeton, 1963.

Althusser, Louis. *For Marx*. Ben Brewster, trans. New York: Pantheon, 1969.

American Sociological Review, "A Review Symposium on Harold Garfinkel," 33, 1 (February 1968), 122–130.

Anderson, Alan Ross. *Minds and Machines*. Englewood Cliffs, N.J.: Prentice-Hall, 1964.

Anderson, Alan Ross, and Moore, Omar K. "Models and Explanations in the Behavioral Sciences." In Gordon V. Di Renzo, ed. *Concepts, Theory, and Explanation in the Behavioral Sciences*. New York: Random House, 1966.

The editions listed in the Bibliography are those used by the author in his research and do not necessarily reflect the dates of first publication.

Anderson, Nels. *The Hobo.* Chicago: University of Chicago Press, 1923.

Archibald, Katherine, ed. *Strategic Interaction and Conflict.* Berkeley: Institute of International Studies, 1966.

Arendt, Hannah. *On Revolution.* New York: Viking, 1966.

Crises of the Republic. New York: Harcourt, Brace, Jovanovich, 1972.

Aries, Philippe. *Centuries of Childhood. A Social History of Family Life.* New York: Knopf, 1970.

Aristotle. *Works.* W. D. Ross, ed. London: Oxford, 1967.

Armer, Paul. "Attitudes Toward Intelligent Machines." In E. A. Feigenbaum and J. Feldman, eds. *Computers and Thought.* New York: McGraw-Hill, 1963.

Arnheim, Rudolf. *Visual Thinking.* Berkeley: University of California Press, 1971.

Ashby, W. R. *An Introduction to Cybernetics.* New York: Wiley, 1956.

Athey, K. R., Coleman, J. E., Reitman, A. P., and Tang, J. "Two Experiments Showing the Effect of the Interviewer's Racial Background on Responses to Questionnaires Concerning Racial Issues," *Journal of Applied Psychology,* 44 (1960), 244–246.

Austin, Jane. *Northanger Abbey.* London: Murray, 1818.

Ayer, Alfred Jules. *Language, Truth and Logic.* New York: Dover, 1946.

ed. *Logical Positivism.* New York: Free Press, 1966.

Bacon, Francis. "*De augmentis scientiarum.*" In Ellis and Heath Spedding, eds. *The Works of Francis Bacon.* New York: 1864. Vol. 1, pp. 415–838.

Ball, Donald W. "An Abortion Clinic Ethnography," *Social Problems,* 14 (Winter 1967), 293–301.

Banfi, Antonio. "L'Humanisme et la Culture Contemporaine," *Comprendre,* No. 5 (1956).

Banfield, Edward C. *Big City Politics.* New York: Random House, 1965.

Banfield, Edward C., and Wilson, James Q. *City Politics.* Cambridge, Mass.: Harvard, 1963.

Bann, S., and Bowlt, J. E., eds. *Russian Formalism.* New York: Barnes and Noble, 1973.

Barthes, Roland. *Systeme de la mode.* Paris: Seuil, 1967.

Sade, Fourier, Loyola. Paris: Seuil, 1971.

Bartlett, Maurice S. *Essays on Probability and Statistics.* New York: Wiley, 1962.

Bateson, Gregory. "Experiments in Thinking About Observed Ethnological Material," *Philosophy of Science,* 8, 1 (1941), 53–68.

Bauer, Raymond A. *Social Indicators.* Cambridge, Mass.: M.I.T., 1966.

Bayley, David H. "The Effects of Corruption in a Developing Nation." *Western Political Quarterly,* 19 (1966), 719–32.

Beardsley, Monroe C. "The Aesthetic Point of View." In Howard E. Kiefer and Milton K. Munitz, eds. *Perspectives in Education, Religion and the Arts.* Albany: State University of New York, 1970.

Beattie, John. "Understanding and Explanation in Social Anthropology." In R. Manners and D. Kaplan, eds. *Theory in Anthropology.* Chicago: Aldine, 1968.

Beauvoir, Simone de. *The Mandarins.* L. M. Friedman, trans. Cleveland: World, 1956.

Becker, Howard S. "Interpretive Sociology and Constructive Sociology." In Georges Gurvitch and Wilbert E. Moore, eds. *Twentieth Century Sociology.* New York: Philosophical Library, 1945.

Outsiders, Studies in the Sociology of Deviance. New York: Free Press, 1963.

Becker, Howard S. and Geer, Blanche. "Participant Observation and Interviewing: A Comparison." In Jerome G. Manis and Bernard N. Meltzer, eds. *Symbolic Interaction, a Reader in Social Psychology.* Boston: Allyn and Bacon, 1967.

Becker, Howard S.; Geer, Blanche; and Hughes, Everett. *Making the Grade: The Academic Side of College Life.* New York: Wiley, 1968.

Bell, Daniel. *End of Ideology.* New York: Free Press, 1960.

"Notes on the Post Industrial Society." *The Public Interest,* No. 6 (Winter 1967), 24–35, 102–118.

ed. *Toward the Year 2000.* Boston: Houghton Mifflin, 1968.

The Coming of Post-Industrial Society. New York: Basic Books, 1973.

Bellah, Robert N. "Christianity and Symbolic Realism." *Journal for the Scientific Study of Religion*, 9, 2 (Summer 1970), 89–96, 112–115.

Benney, M.; Riesman, D.; and Star, S. "Age and Sex in the Interview." *American Journal of Sociology*, 62 (1956), 143–152.

Bensman, Joseph, and Gerver, Israel. "Crime and Punishment in the Factory: The Function of Deviance in Maintaining the Social System." *American Sociological Review*, 28, 4 (August 1963), 588–598.

Bensman, Joseph, and Vidich, Arthur. "Social Theory in Field Research" *American Journal of Sociology*, 65, 6 (May 1960), 577–584.

Bentham, Jeremy. "The Rationale of Reward" (1825). In *The Works of Jeremy Bentham*. New York: Russell & Russell, 1962.

Bentley, Arthur F. *Inquiry into Inquiries, Essays in Social Theory*. Boston: The Beacon Press, 1954.

Berger, M., Abel, T., and Page, C. H., eds. *Freedom and Control in Modern Society*. New York: Van Nostrand, 1954. See H. Alpert, "Robert M. MacIver's Contributions to Sociological Theory," Ch. XIII.

Berger, Peter L. *The Precarious Vision: An Essay on Social Perception and Christian Faith*. Garden City, N.Y.: Doubleday, 1961.

Invitation to Sociology. Garden City, N.Y.: Doubleday, 1963.

"Christian Faith and the Social Comedy." In M. Conrad Hyers, ed., *Holy Laughter; Essays on Religion in the Comic Perspective*. New York: Seabury, 1969.

Berger, Peter, Berger, Brigette, and Kellner, Hansigfried. *The Homeless Mind: Modernization and Consciousness*. New York: Random House, 1973.

Berger, Peter and Luckmann, Thomas. *The Social Construction of Reality*. Garden City, N.Y.: Doubleday, 1966.

Berggren, Douglas. "The Use and Abuse of Metaphor." *Review of Metaphysics*, 16, 2 (December 1962), 237–258; and 16, 3 (March 1963) 450–472.

Bergmann, Gustav. "Holism, Historicism and Emergence," *Philosophy of Science*, 11, 4 (October 1944), 209–221.

Bergson, Henri Louis. *Le rire: essai sur la signification du comique*. Paris: Presses universitaires de France, 1965. In Wylie Sypher, trans. and ed. *Comedy*. Garden City, N.Y.: Doubleday, 1956.

Bergstraesser, Arnold. "Wilhelm Dilthey and Max Weber: An Empirical Approach to Historical Synthesis." *Ethics*, 57 (January 1947), 109.

Bernstein, Richard. *Praxis and Action*. Philadelphia: University of Pennsylvania Press, 1971.

Berryman, Gerald D. *Behind Many Masks; Impression Management in a Himalyan Village*. Human Organization, monograph no. 4. 1962.

Bevan, Edwyn Robert. *Symbolism and Belief*. London: Allen and Unwin, 1938.

Bierstedt, Robert. "A Critique of Empiricism in Sociology." *American Sociological Review*, 14 (October 1949), 584–592.

Bindra, Dalbir, W. *Motivation: A Systematic Reinterpretation*. New York: Ronald, 1959.

Binet, Alfred. *The Experimental Psychology of Alfred Binet*. Robert H. Pollack and M. W. Breuner, eds. New York: Springer, 1969.

Birdswhistell, Ray L. *Kinesis and Context: Essays on Body Motion Communication*. Philadelphia: University of Pennsylvania Press, 1970.

Birnbaum, Norman. "The Crisis in Marxist Sociology," *Social Research*, 35, 2 (Summer 1968), 348–380.

The Crisis of Industrial Society. New York: Oxford, 1969b.

"On the Idea of Political Avant-Garde in Contemporary Politics: The Intellectuals and the Technical Intelligencia." *Praxis*, Nos. 1 and 2, (1969a).

Black, Max. *Models and Metaphors: Studies in Language and Philosophy*. Ithaca: Cornell, 1962.

"Metaphor." In Francis J. Coleman, ed. *Contemporary Studies in Aesthetics*. New York: McGraw-Hill, 1968.

Blau, Peter M. *Exchange and Power in Social Life.* New York: Wiley, 1964.

"The Comparative Study of Organizations." *Industrial and Labor Relations Review,* 18, 3 (April 1965), 323–338.

Blum, Alan F. "Theorizing." In Jack D. Douglas, ed. *Understanding Everyday Life.* Chicago: Aldine, 1970.

Blumer, Herbert. "Science Without Concepts," *American Journal of Sociology,* 36 (January 1931), 515–531.

"Public Opinion and Public Opinion Polling." *American Sociological Review,* 13 (October 1948), 542–554.

"What is Wrong with Social Theory." *American Sociological Review,* 19 (February 1954), 3–10.

"Sociological Analysis and the Variable." *American Sociological Review,* 21 (December 1956), 683–690.

"Race Prejudice as a Sense of Group Position." *Pacific Sociological Review,* 1 (Spring 1958), 3–6.

Symbolic Interactionism. Englewood Cliffs, N.J.: Prentice-Hall, 1969.

Bock, Kenneth. *The Acceptance of Histories: Toward a Perspective for Social Science.* Berkeley: University of California Press, 1956.

"Evolution, Function, and Change," *American Sociological Review,* 28 (April 1963), 229–237.

Boelen, Bernard J. *Existential Thinking.* Duquesne: Duquesne University Press, 1968.

Bogardus, Emory Stephan. *Fundamentals of Social Psychology.* New York: Appleton-Century, 1931.

Bonhoeffer, Dietrich. *Letters and Papers from Prison.* New York: Macmillan, 1967.

Booth, Wayne. *The Rhetoric of Fiction.* Chicago: University of Chicago Press, 1961.

Borges, Jorge Luis. "Partial Enchantments of the Quixote." in *Other Inquisitions, 1937–1952.* New York: Washington Square Press, 1966, pp. 45–48, quoting Josiah Royce, *The World and the Individual.* New York: Macmillan, 1899.

Boring, E. G. *The Physical Dimensions of Consciousness.* New York: Century, 1933.

Boulding, Kenneth E. *Conflict and Defense: A General Theory.* New York: Harper & Row, 1963.

The Image. Ann Arbor: The University of Michigan Press, 1966.

Braithwaite, Richard Bevan. *Scientific Explanation.* Cambridge, Mass.: Harvard, 1953.

"Models in the Empirical Sciences." In Ernest Nagel, Patrick Suppes, and Alfred Tarski, eds. *Logic, Methodology, and Philosophy of Science.* Stanford: Stanford, 1962.

Brant, C. S. "On Joking Relationships." *American Anthropologist,* 50, 1 (January–March 1948), 160–162.

Brecht, Bertolt. *Brecht on Theatre: the Development of an Aesthetic.* John Willett, ed. and trans. New York: Hill and Wang, 1964.

Briefs, Henry. *Three Views of Method in Economics.* Washington: Georgetown University Press, 1960.

Brodbeck, May. "Models, Meaning, and Theories." In Llewellyn Gross, ed., *Symposium on Sociological Theory.* New York: Harper & Row, 1959.

Brooks, Cleanth. "Metaphor, Paradox, and Stereotype." *British Journal of Aesthetics,* 5, 4 (October 1965), 315–318.

Brown, Jason W. *Aphasia, Apraxia and Agnosia; Clinical and Theoretical Aspects.* Springfield, Mass.: Charles C Thomas, 1972.

Brown, Richard H. "Industrial Capitalism in Early Tokugawa Japan: A Political Interpretation." *Journal of Asian History,* 6, 1 (1972), 1–13.

"Economic Development as an Anti-Poverty Strategy: Notes on the Political Economy of Race." *Urban Affairs Quarterly,* 9, 2 (1973), 165–210.

"L'Ironie dans la theorie sociologique," *Epistemologie Sociologique,* No. 15–16 (1973), 63–96.

Bruner, Jerome S. et al. *A Study of Thinking.* New York: Wiley, 1956.
    Beyond the Information Given; Studies in the Psychology of Knowing. New York: Norton, 1973.
Bruyn, Severyn. *The Human Perspective in Sociology.* Englewood Cliffs, N.J.: Prentice-Hall, 1966.
Buckley, Walter Frederick. *Sociology and Modern Systems Theory.* Englewood Cliffs, N.J.: Prentice-Hall, 1967.
    Modern Systems Research for the Behavioral Scientist. Chicago: Aldine, 1968.
Bullough, Edward. " 'Psychical Distance' as a Factor in Art and as an Aesthetic Principle." In Frank A. Tillman and Steven M. Cahn, eds. *Philosophy of Art and Aesthetics.* New York: Harper & Row, 1969
Burke, Kenneth. *Perspectives by Incongruity.* Bloomington: Indiana University Press, 1964.
    A Grammar of Motives. Berkeley: University of California Press, 1969a.
    A Rhetoric of Motives. Berkeley: University of California Press, 1969b.
    "The Virtues and Limitations of Debunking." In *The Philosophy of Literary Form.* Berkeley: University of California Press, 1973a.
    "The Rhetoric of Hitler's Battle." In *The Philosophy of Literary Form.* Berkeley: University of California Press, 1973b.
Burnham, Jack. *The Structure of Art.* New York: Braziller, 1971.
Burns, Elizabeth. *Theatricality, A Study of Convention in the Theatre and in Social Life.* London: Longmans, 1972.
Burns, Tom, and Stalker, George M. *The Management of Innovation.* London: Tavistock, 1961.
Burtt, E. A. *The Metaphysical Foundations of Modern Science.* Garden City, N.Y.: Doubleday, 1954.
Bush, Douglas. *Science and English Poetry.* New York: Oxford, 1950.
Buzzati, Dino. *The Tartar Steppe.* Stuart C. Hood, trans. New York: Farrar, Straus & Young, 1952.
Campbell, D. T. "Recommendations for APA Test Standards Regarding Construct Trait or Discrimination Validity." *American Psychologist,* 15 (1960), 546–553.
Campbell, D. T. and Fiske, D. W. "Convergent and Discriminant Validation by the Multitrait-Multimethod Matrix." *Psychological Bulletin,* 56 (1959), 81--105.
Campbell, N. R. *Physics, The Elements.* Cambridge: Cambridge, 1920.
Campbell, Norman. *What is Science?* London: Methuen, 1921.
Cantril, H. *Gauging Public Opinion.* Princeton, N.J.: Princeton, 1944.
Capon, Eric. "Theatre and Reality." *British Journal of Aesthetics,* 5, 3 (July 1965), 261–269.
Carnap, Rudolf. *Introduction to Semantics.* Cambridge, Mass.: Harvard, 1942.
    "Inductive Logic and Science." *Proceedings of the American Academy of Arts and Sciences,* 80 (1953).
Cassirer, Ernst. *Language and Myth.* New York: Harper & Row, 1946.
    The Philosophy of Symbolic Forms. New Haven: Yale, 1955.
Castaneda, Carlos. *The Teachings of Don Juan: A Yaqui Way of Knowledge.* Berkeley: University of California Press, 1968.
Chapin, Francis Stuart. *Contemporary American Institutions.* New York: Harper, 1935.
Child, Arthur. "The Problem of Imputation in the Sociology of Knowledge." *Ethics,* 51 (January 1941), 200–219.
    "The Theoretical Possibility of the Sociology of Knowledge." *Ethics,* 51 (July 1941), 392–418.
    "The Problem of Truth in the Sociology of Knowledge," *Ethics,* 58 (October 1947), 18–34.
Churchman, C. W. *Introduction to Operations Research.* New York: Wiley, 1957.
Cicourel, Aaron V. "Basic and Normative Rules in the Negotiation of Status and Role." In Hans Peter Dreitzel, ed. *Recent Sociology, No. 2.* New York: Mac-Millan, 1970.
    "Ethnomethodology." In Aaron V. Cicourel, *Cognitive Sociology: Language and Meaning in Social Interaction.* New York: Free Press, 1974.

The Social Organization of Juvenile Justice, New York: Wiley, 1968.

"Generative Semantics and the Structure of Social Interaction." In Aaron V. Cicourel. *Cognitive Sociology: Language and Meaning in Social Interaction.* New York: Free Press, 1974.

Cognitive Sociology: Language and Meaning in Social Interaction, New York: Free Press, 1974.

Clark, Burton. "The Cooling-Out Functions in Higher Education." *American Journal of Sociology*, 65 (May 1960), 569–576.

Clark, Kenneth. *Dark Ghetto.* New York: Harper, 1965.

Clifford, Derek. *Art and Understanding.* Greenwich, Conn.: New York Graphic Society, 1968.

Coleman, Francis J. *Contemporary Studies in Aesthetics.* New York: McGraw-Hill, 1968.

Cohen, Albert K. "The Study of Social Disorganization and Deviant Behavior." In Robert K. Merton, Leonard Broom, and Leonard S. Cottrell, eds. *Sociology Today.* New York: Basic Books, 1959.

Cohen, Kalman, and Cyert, Richard. "Computer Models in Dynamic Economics." *Quarterly Journal of Economics*, 75, 1 (February 1961), 112–127.

Cohen, Marshall. "Aesthetic Essence." In Max Black, ed. *Philosophy in America.* Ithaca: Cornell, 1965.

Coleman, James J. *Introduction to Mathematical Sociology.* New York: Free Press, 1964.

Coleridge, Samuel Taylor. *Biographia Literaria.* George Watson, ed. New York: Everyman's Library, 1956.

Collins, Randall. "Sociology Building." *Berkeley Journal of Sociology*, 14 (1969), 73–83.

"Book Review of *Comparative Methods in Sociology*, edited by Ivan Vallier." *Contemporary Sociology: A Journal of Reviews*, 2 (Summer 1973), 376–379.

Conflict Sociology, Toward an Explanatory Science. New York: Academic, 1975.

Collins, Randall, and Makowsky, Michael. *The Discovery of Society.* New York: Random House, 1972.

Cooley, Charles Horton. *Human Nature and the Social Order.* New York: Scribners, 1902.

Social Organization. New York: Scribners, 1909.

"The Roots of Social Knowledge." *American Journal of Sociology*, 12 (July 1926), 59–79.

Cooper, David. *The Death of the Family.* New York: Pantheon, 1971.

Coser, Lewis. *The Functions of Social Conflict.* Glencoe, Ill.: Free Press, 1956.

Cox, Harvey. *The Feast of the Fools: A Theological Essay on Festivity and Fantasy.* Cambridge, Mass.: Harvard, 1969.

Crane, Ronald S. *The Languages of Criticism and the Structure of Poetry.* Toronto: University of Toronto Press, 1953.

Cressey, Donald R. "Criminal Violation of Financial Trust." *American Sociological Review*, 15 (December 1950), 738–743.

Croce, Benedetto. *Aesthetic as Science of Expression and General Linguistic.* New York: Noonday, 1955.

Cyert, Richard M., and March, James G. *A Behavioral Theory of the Firm.* Englewood Cliffs, N.J.: Prentice-Hall, 1963.

Dahl, Robert Alan. *Who Governs? Democracy and Power in an American City.* New Haven: Yale, 1961.

Dahrendorf, Ralf. "Out of Utopia: Toward a Reorientation of Sociological Knowledge." *American Journal of Sociology*, 64 (1958), 115–127.

Dalton, Melville. *Men Who Manage.* New York: Wiley, 1959.

"Preconceptions and Methods in *Men Who Manage.*" In Phillip Hammond, ed. *Sociologists at Work.* New York: Basic Books, 1964.

Davis, A. K. "Some Sources of American Hostility to Russia." *American Journal of Sociology*, 53, 3 (November 1947), 174–183.

Davis, Fred. "Uncertainty in Medical Prognosis, Clinical and Functional." *American Journal of Sociology*, 66 (July 1960), 41–47.

Davis, Kingsley. "Intermarriage in Caste Societies," *American Anthropologist*, 43, 3 (July–September 1941), 376–395.

"A Conceptual Analysis of Stratification." *American Sociological Review*, 7, 3 (June 1942), 309–321.

Davis, Kingsley. "Some Principles of Stratification." *American Sociological Review*, 18 (August 1953), 394–397.

"The Myth of Functional Analysis as a Special Method in Sociology and Anthropology." *American Sociological Review*, 24 (December 1959), 757–772.

"Prostitution." In Robert K. Merton and Robert A. Nisbet, *Contemporary Social Problems*. New York: Harcourt, Brace & World, 1961a.

"American Society: Its Group Structure." *Contemporary Civilization*, No. 2 (1961b), 171–186.

Davis, Kingsley and Moore, Wilbert E. "Some Principles of Stratification," *American Sociological Review*, 10 (April 1945), 242–249.

Denzin, Norman. *The Research Act; A Theoretical Introduction to Sociological Methods*. Chicago: Aldine, 1970.

Descartes, René. *Oeuvres*. Paris: L. Cerf, 1897–1910. Haldane and Ross, trans. *Philosophical Works*. Cambridge: University Press, 1911–1912.

Dewey, John. *Essays in Experimental Logic*. New York: Dover, n.d.

The Quest for Certainty; A Study of the Relation of Knowledge and Action. New York: Putnam, 1929.

Logic: The Theory of Inquiry. New York: Holt, 1938.

Art as Experience. New York: Capricorn Books, 1958.

Dewey, John, and Bentley, Arthur F. *Knowing and the Known*. Boston: Beacon Press, 1949.

Diesing, Paul. *Patterns of Discovery in the Social Science*. Chicago: Aldine, 1971.

Dilthey, Wilhelm. *Gesammelte Schriften*. Stuttgart: B. G. Teubner, 1958.

Pattern and Meaning in History: Thoughts on History and Society. H. P. Rickman, ed. New York: Harper & Row, 1962.

Dodd, Stuart Carter. *Dimensions of Society: A Questionnaire Systematics for the Social Sciences*. New York: Macmillan, 1942.

Doroszewski, W. "Quelques remarques sur les rapports de la sociologie et de la linguistique: Durkheim et F. de Saussure." *Journal de psychologie normale et pathologique*, 30 (1933), 82–91.

Dostoyevsky, Fgodor M. *Crime and Punishment*. Constance Garnett, trans. New York: Modern Library, 1950.

Douglas, Jack D. *Understanding Everyday Life*. Chicago: Aldine, 1970.

Observations of Deviance. New York: Random House, 1970.

"The Theory of Objectivity in Sociology." Mimeographed. San Diego, Calif.: Department of Sociology, University of California at San Diego, 1971.

"The Rhetoric of Science and the Origins of Statistical Social Thought: The Case of Durkheim's *Suicide*." In Edward A. Tiryakian, ed. *The Phenomenon of Sociology*. New York: Appleton-Century-Crofts, 1971a.

Existential Sociology. New York: Cambridge, 1977.

Douglas, Mary. "The Social Control of Cognition: Some Factors in Joke Perception." *Man*, N.S. 3, 3 (September 1968), 361–367.

Rules and Meanings: The Anthropology of Everyday Life. Baltimore: Penguin, 1973.

Dreitzel, Hans Peter. *Recent Sociology, No. 2, Patterns of Communicative Behavior*. New York: Macmillan, 1970.

Dufrenne, Mikel. *Language and Philosophy*. Bloomington: Indiana University Press, 1963.

Duhem, Pierre. *La Theorie physique*. Paris: 1914.

Durkheim, Emile. *Suicide*. John A. Spaulding and George Simpson, trans. New York: Free Press, 1951.

The Elementary Forms of Religious Life. Joseph W. Swain, trans. New York: Free Press, 1965.

The Rules of Sociological Method. Sarah A. Solovay and John H. Mueller, trans. New York: Free Press, 1964.

Durkheim, Emile, and Mauss, Marcel. *Primitive Classification*, Rodney Needham, trans. Chicago: The University of Chicago Press, 1967.

Dyson, A. E. *The Crazy Fabric, Essays in Irony*. New York: St. Martin's Press, 1965.

Eddington, Arthur. *Philosophy of Physical Science*. New York: Macmillan, 1939.

Edel, Abraham. "The Concept of Levels in Social Theory." In Llewellyn Gross, ed. *Symposium on Sociological Theory*. New York: Harper & Row, 1956.

Edelman, Nathan. "The Mixed Metaphor in Descartes." In *The Eye of the Beholder*. Baltimore: Johns Hopkins University Press, 1974.

Edie, James. "Comments on Maurice Natanson's Paper 'Man As Actor.'" In Erwin W. Straus and Richard M. Griffith, eds. *Phenomenology of Will and Action: The Second Lexington Conference on Pure and Applied Phenomenology*. Pittsburgh: Duquesne University Press, 1967.

"William James and Phenomenology," *The Review of Metaphysics*, (June 1970), 23.

Eggan, Fred. "Social Anthropology and the Method of Controlled Comparison." *American Anthropologist*, 56, 5 (October 1954), 743–763.

Ehrenzweig, Anton. *The Psychoanalysis of Artistic Vision and Hearing: A Theory of Unconscious Perception*. London: Routledge, 1953.

Ehrmann, Jacques, ed. *Structuralism*. Garden City, N.Y.: Doubleday, 1970.

Eichenbaum, Boris M. "Thematics." In Lee T. Lemon and Marion J. Reis, eds. and trans., *Russian Formalist Criticism: Four Essays*. Lincoln: University of Nebraska Press, 1965.

"The Theory of the Formal Method." In Ladislav Matejka and Krystyna Pomorska, eds. *Readings in Russian Poetics: Formalist and Structuralist Views*. Cambridge, Mass.: M.I.T., 1971.

Eisenstadt, S. N. *The Political Systems of Empires*. New York: Free Press, 1963.

Eliot, Thomas S. *The Sacred Wood: Essays on Poetry and Criticism*. New York: Barnes & Noble, 1960.

Elkin, A. P. "Murngin Kinship Re-examined," *American Anthropologist*, 55, 3 (August 1953), 412–419.

Emerson, Joan. "Behavior in Private Places: Sustaining Definitions of Reality in Gynecological Examinations." In Hans Peter Dreitzel, ed., *Recent Sociology, No. 2, Patterns of Communicative Behavior*. New York: Macmillan, 1970.

Engels, Frederick. *Herr Engen Duhring's Revolution in Science (Anti-Duhring)*. New York: International Publishers, 1939.

Etzioni, Amitai. *A Comparative Analysis of Complex Organizations*. New York: Free Press, 1961.

The Active Society. New York: Free Press, 1968.

Evrienoff, Nicolas. *The Theatre in Life*. New York: Benjamin Blom, 1970.

Feibleman, James K. *The Institutions of Society*. London: Allen & Unwin, 1956.

Feigl, Herbert. "Logical Empiricism." In Dagobert H. Runes, ed., *Twentieth Century Philosophy*. New York: Philosophical Library, 1943.

Feigl, Herbert, and Brodbeck, May, eds. *Readings in the Philosophy of Science*. New York: Appleton-Century-Crofts, 1953.

Feigl, Herbert, Scriven, Michael, and Maxwell, Grover, eds. *Concepts, Theories and the Mind-Body Problem*. Minneapolis: The University of Minnesota Press, 1967.

Ferguson, Donald N. *Music as Metaphor; The Elements of Expression*. Minneapolis: The University of Minnesota Press, 1960.

Image and Structure in Chamber Music. Minneapolis: The University of Minnesota Press, 1964.

Ferguson, Thomas. "The Political Economy of Knowledge and The Changing Politics of Philosophy of Science." *Telos* 15 (Spring 1973), 125–137.

Fergusson, Francis. *The Idea of a Theatre: The Art of the Drama in Changing Perspective*. Garden City, N.Y.: Doubleday, 1949.

Festinger, Leon, Riecken, H., and Schacter, S. *When Prophesy Fails*. Minneapolis: The University of Minnesota Press, 1956.

Festinger, Leon, and Thibaut, John. "Interpersonal Communication in Small Groups." *Journal of Abnormal Psychology*, 46, 1 (January 1951), 92–99.

Feyerabend, Paul K. "An Attempt at a Realistic Interpretation of Experience." *Proceedings of the Aristotelian Society*, 58 (1957), 143.

"Explanation, Reduction and Empiricism." In *Minnesota Studies in the Philosophy of Science*. Vol. 3. Herbert Feigl and Grover Maxwell, eds. Minneapolis: The University of Minnesota Press, 1962.

"Against Method: Outline of an Anarchistic Theory of Knowledge." In Michael Radner and Stephen Winokur, eds. *Minnesota Studies in the Philosophy of Science*. Vol. 4. Minneapolis: University of Minnesota Press, 1962.

"Problems of Empiricism." In Robert Colodny, ed. *Beyond the Edge of Certainty*. Englewood Cliffs, N.J.: Prentice-Hall, 1965.

Fichte, Johann Gottlieb. *Science of Knowledge*. Peter Heath and John Lachs, eds. and trans. New York: Appleton-Century-Crofts, 1970.

Ficino, Marsilio. *Opera omnia*. Torino: Bettega de'Erasmo, 1962.

Fingarette, Herbert. *The Self in Transformation*. New York: Basic Books, 1963.

Forster, E. M. *Aspects of the Novel*. New York: Harcourt, Brace & World, 1956.

Foss, Laurence. "Art as Cognitive: Beyond Scientific Realism." *Philosophy of Science*, 38 (June 1971), 234–250.

Foster, George. "Interpersonal Relations in Peasant Societies." *Human Organization*, 19, 4 (Winter 1960–1961), 174–178.

France, Anatole. *Thais*. Ernest Triotan, trans. New York: Boni and Liveright, 1902. *Penguin Island*. A. W. Evans, trans. New York: Dodd, Mead, 1922.

"Le Jardin d'Epicure," *Oeuvres Completes*, vol. 9. Paris: Calmann-Levy, 1935.

Frankfort Institute for Social Research, *Aspects of Sociology*. Boston: Beacon Press, 1972.

Frazer, Sir James George. *The Golden Bough*. New York: Macmillan, 1951.

Freud, Sigmund. *Wit and Its Relation to the Unconscious*. New York: Moffat, Yard, 1916.

The Ego and the Id. London: Hogarth, 1930.

"Project for a Scientific Psychology." *Complete Works*. Vol. 1. London: Hogarth, 1954.

Freudenthal, Hans, ed. *The Concept and Role of the Model in Mathematics and the Natural and Social Sciences*. New York: Gordon and Breach, 1961.

Friedrichs, Robert W. *A Sociology of Sociology*. New York: Free Press, 1970.

Frisby, David. "The Popper-Adorno Controversy: The Methodological Dispute in German Sociology." *Philosophy of the Social Sciences*, 2 (1972), 105–119.

Fromm, Erich. *Marx's Concept of Man*. New York: Ungar, 1961.

Funke, Lewis, and Booth, John E. *Actors Talk About Acting: Fourteen Interviews with Stars of the Theatre*. New York: Random House, 1961.

Furfey, Paul Hanly. *The Scope and Method of Sociology; A Metasociological Treatise*. New York: Harper, 1953.

Gabaglio, Antonio. *Teoria Generale de la Statistica: Parte Storica*. Vol. 1. Milano: Hoepli, 1888.

Gadamer, Hans-Georg. "Asthetik und Hermeneutik." In Jan Aler, ed. *International Congress on Aesthetics, 5th Amsterdam*. The Hague: Mouton, 1968.

Wahrheit und Methode: Grundzuge einer philosophischen Hermeneutik. Tubingen: J. C. B. Mohr, 1965. Garrett Barden and John Cumming, trans. and eds. *Truth and Method*. Seabury Press, 1975.

Galileo, Galilei. *The Achievement of Galileo*. Henry Paolucci, ed. New York: Twayne, 1962.

Garfinkel, Harold. "The Perception of the Other: A Study in Social Order." Ph.D. dissertation, Harvard University, 1952.

Studies in Ethnomethodology. Englewood Cliffs, N.J.: Prentice-Hall, 1967.

Garner, W. R. "Contest Effects and the Validity of Loudness Scales." *Journal of Experimental Psychology*, 48, 3 (September 1954), 218–224.

Garner, W. R., Hake, H. W., and Erikensen, C. W. "Operationism and the Concept of Perception." *Psychological Review*, 63, 3 (May 1956), 149–159.

Geer, Blanche. "First Days in the Field." Phillip Hammond, ed. *Sociologists at Work*. New York: Basic Books, 1964.

Gendron, Bernard. "The Foundations of Scientific Realism: A Critical Review of W. Sellars' *Science and Metaphysics.*" *International Philosophical Quarterly*, 10, 1 (March 1970), 129–151.

Gibbs, J. Willard. *Collected Works*. New Haven: Yale, 1957.

Gide, André. *The Counterfeiters*, Dorothy Bussy, trans. New York: Knopf, 1955.

Girard, René. "Tiresias and the Critic." In Richard Macksey and Eugenio Donato, eds. *The Structuralist Controversy*. Baltimore: Johns Hopkins, 1972.

Glaser, Barney, and Strauss, Anselm. "Awareness Contexts and Social Interaction," *American Sociological Review*, 29, 5 (October 1964), 669–678.

The Discovery of Grounded Theory. Chicago: Aldine, 1967.

Time for Dying. Chicago: Aldine, 1968.

Gluckman, Max. "The Utility of the Equilibrium Model in the Study of Social Change." *American Anthropologist*, 70, 2 (April 1968), 219–237.

Gödel, Kurt. *On the Formally Undecidable Propositions of Principia Mathematica and Related Systems*. London: Oliver and Boyd, 1962.

Goffman, Erving. "On Cooling the Mark Out: Some Aspects of Adaptation to Failure." *Psychiatry*, 15, 4 (November 1952), 451–463.

The Presentation of Self in Everyday Life. Garden City, N.Y.: Doubleday, 1959.

Encounters. Indianapolis: Bobbs-Merrill, 1961.

Asylums: Essays on the Social Situation of Mental Patients and Other Inmates. Garden City: Doubleday, 1961.

Behavior in Public Places; Notes on the Social Organization of Gatherings. New York: Free Press, 1963.

Interaction Ritual: Essays on Face-to-Face Behavior. Garden City, N.Y.: Doubleday, 1967.

Strategic Interaction. Philadelphia: University of Pennsylvania Press, 1969.

Relations in Public: Microstudies of the Public Order. New York: Basic Books, 1971.

Goffman, W., and Newel, V. A. "Communications and Epidemic Processes." *Proceedings of the Royal Society*, A, 298 (1967), 316–334.

Gogol, Nokolai V. "The Overcoat." In Constance Garnett, trans. *Collected Tales and Plays*. New York: Pantheon, 1964.

Gold, Raymond. "Roles in Sociological Field Observation." In George McCall and J. L. Simmons, eds. *Issues in Participant Observation*. Reading, Mass.: Addison-Wesley, 1969.

Gombrich, Ernst Hans. *Meditations on a Hobby Horse, and Other Essays*. London: Phaidon Press, 1965.

Goode, William J. *Religion Among the Primitives*. Glencoe, Ill.: Free Press, 1951.

"The Protection of the Inept." *American Sociological Review*, 32, 1 (February 1967), 5–19.

Goodman, Nelson. *The Structure of Appearance*. Cambridge, Mass.: Harvard, 1951.

"The Way the World Is," *Review of Metaphysics*, 14, 1 (September 1960), 48–56.

The Language of Art. Indianapolis: Bobbs-Merrill, 1968.

Gotschalk, D. W. *The Structure of Awareness, Introduction to a Situational Theory of Truth and Knowledge* Urbana: The University of Illinois Press, 1969.

Gouldner, Alvin W. *Patterns of Industrial Bureaucracy*. Glencoe, Ill.: Free Press, 1954.

"Organizational Analysis." In Robert K. Merton, Leonard Broom, and Leonard S. Cottrell, eds., *Sociology Today*. New York: Basic Books, 1959.

"Anti-Minotaur: The Myth of a Value-Free Sociology." *Social Problems*, 9, 3 (Winter 1962), 199–213.

The Coming Crisis in Western Sociology. New York: Basic Books, 1970.

Greer, Scott A. *Last Man: Racial Access to Union Power*. Glencoe, Ill.: Free Press, 1959.

The Logic of Social Inquiry. Chicago: Aldine, 1969.

Greimas, A. J. *Du Sens*. Paris: Seuil, 1970.

Griffith, Richard M. "Simulation and Dissimulation." In Erwin W. Straus and Richard M. Griffith, eds. *Phenomenology of Will and Action, The Second Lexington Conference on Pure and Applied Phenomenology*. Pittsburgh: Duquesne University Press, 1967.

Gunderson, K. "The Imitation Game." In A. R. Anderson, ed. *Minds and Machines*. Englewood Cliffs, N.J.: Prentice-Hall, 1964.

Gurvitch, Georges. *Dialectique et Sociologie*. Paris: Flammarion, 1962.

    Traite de Sociologie. Paris: Presses universitaires de France, 1967.

    The Social Frameworks of Knowledge. Margaret Thompson and Kenneth Thompson, trans. Oxford: Blackwell, 1971.

Gusfield, Joseph. "The Literary Rhetoric of Science: Comedy and Pathos in Drinking Driver Research." Mimeographed. San Diego, Calif.: University of California at San Diego, 1974.

Habermas, Jürgen. *Theorie und Praxis: Socialphilosophische Studien*. Neuwied am Rhein: Luchterhand, 1967.

    Knowledge and Human Interests. Boston: Beacon Press, 1968.

    Technik und Wissenschaft als "Ideologie." Frankfurt am Main: Suhrkamp, 1969.

    "Toward a Theory of Communicative Competence." In Hans Peter Dreitzel, ed. *Recent Sociology No. 2*. New York: Macmillan, 1970.

Haezrahi, Pepita. *The Contemplative Activity*. New York: Abelard-Schuman, 1956.

Hage, Jerald, and Aiken, Michael. "Relationships of Centralization to Other Structural Properties." *Administrative Science Quarterly*, 12, 1 (June 1967), 72–92.

Hagstrum, Jean H. *Samuel Johnson's Literary Criticism*. Minneapolis: University of Minnesota Press, 1952.

Hahn, Robert A. "Understanding Beliefs: An Essay on the Methodology of the Statement and Analysis of Belief Systems." *Current Anthropology*, 14, 3 (June 1973), 207–229.

Hammond, Phillip E. *Sociologists at Work*. New York: Basic Books, 1964.

Hankins, Frank H. "A Forty Year Perspective." *Sociology and Social Research*, 40, 6 (July–August 1956), 391–398.

Hanson, Norwood R. *Patterns of Discovery: An Inquiry into the Conceptual Foundations of Science*. Cambridge: Cambridge, 1958.

    Observation and Explanation: A Guide to the Philosophy of Science. New York: Harper & Row, 1971.

Harré, Rom. "Architectonic Man." In Richard H. Brown and Stanford M. Lyman, eds., *Structure, Consciousness, and History*. Cambridge: Cambridge, forthcoming.

Hart, Ray L. *Unfinished Man and the Imagination*. New York: Herder and Herder, 1968.

Hartman, Geoffrey. "Structuralism: The Anglo-American Adventure." In Jacques Ehrman, ed. *Structuralism*. Garden City, N.Y.: Doubleday, 1970.

Hausman, Carl R. "Understanding and the Act of Creation." *Review of Metaphysics*, 20, 1 (September 1966), 89–112.

Hayner, Norman. "Hotel Life and Personality." In Ernest W. Burgess, ed., *Personality and the Social Group*. Chicago: The University of Chicago Press, 1929.

Hegel, G.W.F. *Lectures on The History of Philosophy*. London: 1896.

    Philosophy of Right (1921), T. M. Knox, trans. Oxford: Clarendon, 1942.

Heidegger, Martin. *Being and Time*. New York: Harper, 1962.

Heine, Heinrich. *Werke*. Berlin: Volksbushne Verlags-and Vertriebs, 1925.

Helmer, Olaf. "The Game-Theoretical Approach to Organization Theory." In John R. Gregg and F.T.C. Harris, eds., *Form and Strategy in Science*. Dordrecht: D. Reidel, 1964.

Helmer, Olaf, and Rescher, Nicholas. *On the Epistemology of the Inexact Sciences, P-1513*. Santa Monica, Calif.: Rand Corporation, 1958.

Hensel, Herbert. "Phenomenon and Model." In Erwin W. Strauss and Richard M. Griffith, eds., *Aisthetis and Aesthetics*. Pittsburgh: Duquesne University Press, 1970.

Herder, Johann Gottfried von. *Abhandlung uber den Ursprung der Sprache*. Leipzig: Brandstetter, 1901.

Hesse, M. "The Explanatory Function of Metaphor." In Y. Bar-Hillel, ed., *Logic, Methodology, and Philosophy of Science*.

Hesse, Mary B. *Models and Analogies in Science*. Notre Dame, Ind.: University of Notre Dame Press, 1970.

Hill, Herbert. *Caste and Class in American Labor*. Englewood Cliffs, N.J.: Prentice-Hall, 1973.

Hill, Richard, and Crittendon, Kathleen, eds. *Proceedings of the Purdue Symposium on Ethnomethodology*. Institute for the Study of Social Change Monograph Series No. 1. Lafayette, Ind.: Purdue University, 1968.

Hinshaw, Virgil G. The Epistemological Relevance of Mannheim's Sociology of Knowledge." *Journal of Philosophy*, 40, 4 (February 1943), 57–72.

Hobbes, Thomas. *Leviathan*. Oxford: Basil Blackwell, 1957.

Hodgen, Margaret T. *The Doctrine of Survivals*. London: Allerson, 1936.

Change and History. Viking Fund, Publications in Anthropology No. 18. New York: Wenner-Gren, 1952.

Early Anthropology in the Sixteenth and Seventeenth Centuries. Philadelphia: University of Pennsylvania Press, 1964.

Hodges, H. A. *The Philosophy of Wilhelm Dilthey*. London: Routledge, 1952.

Hofstadter, Albert. *Truth and Art*. New York: Columbia, 1965.

Hoggatt, A. C., and Balderston, F. E., eds. *Symposium on Simulation Models*. Cincinnati: Southwestern Publishing, 1963.

Holzner, Burkart. *Reality Construction in Society*. Cambridge, Mass.: Schenkman, 1968.

Homans, George. *The Human Group*. New York: Harcourt, Brace & World, 1945.

Hopkins, Terrance, and Wallerstein, Immanuel. "The Comparative Study of National Societies." *Social Science Information*, 6, 5 (October 1967), 25–58.

Horowitz, Irving. *The New Sociology*. New York: Oxford, 1964.

Hospers, John. *Meaning and Truth in the Arts*. Hamden, Conn.: Archon, 1964.

Hull, Clark L. *Behavior System: An Introduction to Behavior Theory Concerning the Individual Organism*. New Haven: Yale, 1952.

Hume, David. *Enquiries Concerning Human Understanding*. Oxford: Clarendon, 1951.

Humphreys, L. G. "Note on the Multitrait-Multimethod Matrix." *Psychological Bulletin*, 57 (1960), 86–88.

Hungerland, I. C. *Poetic Discourse*. University of California Publications in Philosophy, No. 33. Berkeley: University of California Press, 1958.

Hunter, Floyd. *Community Power Structure*. Chapel Hill: The University of North Carolina Press, 1953.

Hussain, Fakhir. *Le Jugement esthétique. Inventaire des Théories. Essai de Méthodologie*. Paris: Lettres Modernes, Minard, 1967.

Husserl, Edmund. *Ideas: General Introduction to Phenomenology*. W. R. Royce Gibson, trans. London: Allen and Unwin, 1931.

Hutten, Ernest H. "The Role of Models in Physics." *The British Journal for the Philosophy of Science*, 4, 16 (February 1954, 284–301.

Hyers, M. Conrad. "The Dialectic of the Sacred and the Comic." In M. Conrad Hyers, ed. *Holy Laughter: Essays on Religion in the Comic Perspective*. New York: Seabury, 1969.

Hyman, H. H., Cobb, W. J., Feldman, J. J., Hart, C. W., and Stember, C. H. *Interviewing in Social Research*. Chicago: The University of Chicago Press, 1954.

Hyman, Stanley Edgar. *The Tangled Bank: Darwin, Marx, Frazer, and Freud as Imaginative Writers.* New York: Atheneum, 1962.

Ichleiser, Gustav. *Appearances and Realities, Misunderstandings in Human Relations.* San Francisco: Jossey-Bass, 1970.

Jacobs, Paul. "Union Democracy and the Public Good." *Commentary,* 25, 1 (January 1958), 68–74.

The State of the Unions. New York: Atheneum, 1963.

Jahoda, Marie, and Cook, S. W. "Security Measures and Freedom of Thought: An Exploratory Study of the Impact of Loyalty and Security Programs." *Yale Law Journal,* 61, 3 (March 1952), 296–333.

Jakobson, Roman. "Two Aspects of Aphasic Disturbances." In Jakobson and Halle, *Fundamentals of Language.* The Hague: Mouton, 1956.

"On Realism in Art." In Ladislav Matejka and Krystyna Pomorska, eds. *Readings in Russian Poetics: Formalist and Structuralist Views.* Cambridge, Mass.: M.I.T., 1971.

James, William. *The Writings of William James,* John J. McDermott, ed. New York: Random House, 1967.

Jameson, Fredric. *The Prison House of Language.* Princeton, N.J.: Princeton, 1972.

"History and the Techniques of Literary Criticism." Mimeographed. San Diego, Calif.: University of California at San Diego, 1973.

"Max Weber's Pessimism: A Structural Analysis of Late Nineteenth Century Thought." In *German Criticism.* Vol. 1. New York: Free Press, 1975.

Jankelevitch, Vladimir. *L'Ironie, ou la Bonne Conscience.* Paris: Presses Universitaires de France, 1950.

Jaspers, Karl. *Truth and Symbol (from "Von der Wahrheit").* New York: Twayne, 1959.

Journées Internationales d'Etudes sur les Méthodes de Calcul dans les Sciences de l'Homme. *Calcul et Formalisation dans les Sciences de l'Homme.* Paris: Centre National de la Recherche Scientifique, 1968.

Kafka, Franz. *The Complete Stories.* New York: Schocken Books, 1971.

Kahn, Herman, and Weiner, Anthony J. *The Year 2000: A Framework for Speculation on the Next Thirty-three Years.* New York: Macmillan, 1967.

Kahn, R. L., and Cannell, C. F. *The Dynamics of Interviewing: Theory, Technique and Cases.* New York: Wiley, 1957.

Kant, Immanuel. *The Philosophy of Kant.* Carl J. Friedrich, ed. New York: Modern Library, 1949.

Kaplan, Abraham. *The Conduct of Inquiry.* San Francisco: Chandler, 1964.

Kardiner, Abram. *The Individual and His Society.* New York: Columbia, 1939.

Katz, D. "Do Interviewers Bias Poll Results?" *Public Opinion Quarterly,* 6, 2 (Summer 1942), 248–268.

Kerlinger, Frederick N. *Foundations of Behavioral Research.* New York: Holt, 1973.

Kierkegaard, Soren. *Repetition: An Essay in Experimental Psychology,* Walter Lowrie, trans. Princeton, N.J.: Princeton, 1946.

The Point of View for My Work as an Author. Benjamin Nelson, ed. New York: Harper & Row, 1962.

The Concept of Irony. Lee M. Capel, trans. New York: Harper & Row, 1965.

Kinsey, Alfred C. *Sexual Behavior in the Human Male.* Philadelphia: Saunders, 1948.

Sexual Behavior in the Human Female. Philadelphia: Saunders, 1953.

Kitto, H. D. *Form and Meaning in Drama.* New York: Barnes & Noble, 1957.

Poesis. Berkeley: University of California Press, 1966.

Klapp, Orrin E. "The Fool as a Social Type." *American Journal of Sociology,* 55, 2 (September 1959).

Kluckhohn, Clyde. *Navaho Witchcraft.* Cambridge, Mass.: Peabody Museum, 1944.

Knox, Norman. *The Word Irony and Its Context.* Durham, N.C.: Duke, 1961.

Koch, Sigmund. "The Logical Character of the Motivation Concept." *Psychological Review,* 48, 1 (January 1941), 15–38.

Koestler, Arthur. *The Act of Creation.* New York: Macmillan, 1964.

Koehler, Wolfgang. *Gestalt Psychology: An Introduction to New Concepts in Modern Psychology.* New York: New American Library, 1947.

Kolakowski, Lesek. *Toward a Marxist Humanism: Essays on the Left Today.* New York: Grove Press, 1968.

Krasnow, H. S., and Merikallio, R. A. "The Past, Present, and Future of General Simulation Languages," *Management Science,* II 2 (November, 1964), 236–267.

Kubler, George. *The Shape of Time: Remarks on the History of Things.* New Haven: Yale, 1962.

Kuhn, Thomas S. *The Structure of Scientific Revolutions.* Chicago: The University of Chicago Press, 1962.

"Logic of Discovery or Psychology of Research?" In Imre Lakatos and Alan Musgrave, eds. *Criticism and the Growth of Knowledge.* Cambridge: Cambridge, 1970.

Kumar, Shiv and Kieth McKean. *Critical Approaches to Fiction.* New York: McGraw-Hill, 1968.

La Capra, Dominick. *Emile Durkheim: Sociologist and Philosopher.* Ithaca: Cornell, 1973.

Laing, R. D. *The Divided Self.* London: Tavistock, 1959.

Landar, Herbert. *Language and Culture.* Oxford: Oxford, 1966.

Landheer, Barth. "Presuppositions in the Social Sciences," *American Journal of Sociology,* 37, 4 (January 1932), 539–546.

Lane, Michael, ed. *Introduction to Structuralism.* New York: Basic Books, 1970.

Langer, Susanne. *Philosophy in a New Key.* Cambridge, Mass.: Harvard, 1942.

Lashley, Karl S. "The Behavioristic Interpretation of Consciousness." *Psychological Review,* 30, 4 (July 1923), 237–272.

Lawerance, W. E. and Murdock, G. P. "Murngin Social Organization." *American Anthropologist,* 51, (1949), 58–65.

Lazarsfeld, Paul F., and Rosenberg, Morris. *The Language of Social Research.* New York: Free Press, 1955.

Leach, Edmund R. "The Structural Implications of Matrilateral Cross-cousin Marriage." *Journal of the Royal Anthropological Institute,* 81 (1951), 23–56.

ed. *The Structural Study of Myth and Totemism.* London: Tavistock, 1967.

Rethinking Anthropology. New York: Humanities Press, 1968.

Claude Lévi-Strauss. New York: Viking Press, 1970.

Lee, Dorothy. "Linguistic Reflections of Wintu Thought." *International Journal of American Linguistics,* 10, 4 (1939), 181–187. In *Freedom and Culture.* Englewood Cliffs, N.J.: Prentice-Hall, 1959.

Lemon, Lee T., and Reis, Marian J., eds. and trans. *Russian Formalist Criticism: Four Essays.* Lincoln: University of Nebraska Press, 1965.

Lenski, G. E., and Leggett, J. C. "Caste, Class, and Deference in the Research Interview." *American Journal of Sociology,* 65 (1960), 463–467.

Lerner, Daniel, ed. *Parts and Wholes.* New York: Free Press, 1963.

Levin, Harry. "Veins of Humor." In *Howard English Studies 3.* Cambridge Mass.: Harvard, 1972.

Lévi-Strauss, Claude. *Les Structures elementaires de la parente.* Paris: Presses universitaires de France, 1949.

Tristes tropiques. Paris: Plon, 1955.

"La Structure et la forme, reflexions sur un ouvrage de Vladimir Propp." *Cahiers de L'Institut de science économique appliquée* (Recherches et dialogues philosophiques et économiques, 7), no. 99. Paris, 1960.

Le Totémisme aujourd 'hui. Paris: Presses universitaires de France, 1962.

Structural Anthropology, Jacobson and Schoepf, trans. New York: Basic Books, 1963.

Le Cru et le cuit. Paris: Plon, 1964.

The Savage Mind. Chicago: The University of Chicago Press, 1967.

L'Origine des manières de Table. Paris: Plon, 1968.

Lewin, Kurt. *Field Theory in Social Science.* New York: Harper, 1951.

Lewis, Michael. "Social Inequality." In Jack Douglas, ed., *American Social Problems in an Age of Revolution*. forthcoming.

Lewis, Oscar. *Life in a Mexican Village: Tepoztlan Restudied*. Urbana: The University of Illinois Press, 1951.

Five Families, Mexican Case Studies in the Culture of Poverty. New York: Basic Books, 1959.

Anthropological Essays. New York: Random House, 1970.

Lewontin, R. C. "Models, Mathematics and Metaphors." In John R. Gregg and F.T.C. Harris, eds. *Form and Strategy in Science*. Dordrecht: D. Reidel, 1964: 274–296.

Liebow, Elliot. *Talley's Corner*. Boston: Little, Brown, 1967.

Linschoten, Hans. *On the Way Toward a Phenomenological Psychology: The Psychology of William James*. Amedeo Giorgi, trans. Pittsburgh: Duquesne University Press, 1968.

Lindesmith, Alfred. *Addiction and Opiates*. Chicago: Aldine, 1968.

Linton, Ralph. *The Study of Man*. New York: Appleton-Century-Crofts, 1964.

Lipset, Seymour, Trow, Martin, and Coleman, James. *Union Democracy*. Glencoe, Ill.: Free Press, 1956.

Little, Kenneth. "The Political Function of the Poro." *Africa*, 25, 4 (1965).

Little, Roger W. "Buddy Relations and Combat Performance." In M. Janowitz, ed. *The New Military*. New York: Russell Sage Foundation, 1964.

Llewellyn, Karl, and Hoebel, E. A. *The Cheyenne Way*. Norman: University of Oklahoma Press, 1941.

Lobkowicz, Nicholas. *Theory and Practice; History of a Concept from Aristotle to Marx*. Notre Dame, Ind.: University of Notre Dame Press, 1967.

Lofland, John, and Stark Rodney. "Becoming a World-Saver: A Theory of Conversion to a Deviant Perspective." *American Sociological Review*, 30, 6 (December 1965), 862–875.

Lofland, John. *Doomsday Cult: A Study of Conversion*. Englewood Cliffs, N.J.: Prentice-Hall, 1966.

"Interactionist Imagery and Analytic Interruptus." Mimeographed. Sonoma, Calif.: California State University at Sonoma, 1969.

Lotka, Alfred J. *Elements of Physical Biology*. Baltimore: Williams & Wilkins, 1925.

Louch, A. R. *Explanation and Human Action*. Berkeley: University of California Press, 1966.

Lovejoy, Arthur O. "The Meanings of 'Emergence' and Its Modes." *Proceedings of the Sixth International Congress of Philosophy*, 6 (1926), 20–33.

Lubbock, Percy. *The Craft of Fiction*. New York: Viking, 1957.

Lukács, Georg, *History and Class Consciousness: Studies in Marxist Dialectics*. Cambridge, Mass.: M.I.T., 1971.

Theory of the Novel. Cambridge, Mass.: M.I.T., 1971.

Lukes, Steven. *Emile Durkheim: His Life and Work*. London: Penguin, 1973.

Lundberg, George. "The Natural Science Trend in Sociology." *American Journal of Sociology*, 61, 3 (November 1955), 191–202.

Lundberg, George, Schrag, Clarence C., and Larsen, Otto. *Sociology*. New York: Harper, 1954.

Lyman, Stanford M. "The Structure of Chinese Society in Nineteenth Century America." Ph.D. dissertation, University of California at Berkeley, 1961.

"The Race Relations Cycle of Robert E. Park." *Pacific Sociological Review*, 11, 1 (Spring 1968), 16–22.

The Asian in the West. Reno: Desert Research Institute, 1970.

Lyman, Stanford M., and Scott, Marvin B. *A Sociology of the Absurd*. New York: Appleton-Century-Crofts, 1970.

The Drama in Social Reality. New York: Oxford, 1976.

Lynd, Robert S., and Lynd, Helen M. *Middletown: A Study in Contemporary American Culture*. New York: Harcourt, Brace, 1929.

Middletown in Transition: A Study in Cultural Conflict. New York: Harcourt, Brace, 1937.

Macauley, Robie, and Lanning, George. *Technique in Fiction.* New York: Harper & Row, 1964.

MacCormac, Earl R. "Metaphor Revisited." *Journal of Aesthetics and Art Criticism,* 30 2 (Winter 1971), 239–250.

Machiavelli, Niccolo. *The Prince.* New York: Washington Square Press, 1963.

MacIver, Robert M., *Society: An Introductory Analysis.* New York: Holt, 1937. *On Going to College.* New York: Oxford, 1938.

Macksey, Richard, and Donato, Eugenio. *The Structuralist Controversy: The Language of Criticism and the Sciences of Man.* Baltimore: Johns Hopkins, 1972.

Malinowski, Bronislaw. "The Psychology of Sex and the Foundations of Kinship in Primitive Societies." *Psyche,* 4 (1924), 98–129. *The Father in Primitive Psychology.* New York: Norton, 1927. *The Sexual Life of Savages.* London: Routledge, 1929.

Mandelbaum, Maurice. *The Problem of Historical Knowledge: An Answer to Relativism.* New York: Liveright, 1938.

Mandeville, Bernard. *The Fable of the Bees: or Private Vices, Public Benefits.* Douglas Garman, ed. London: Wishart, 1934.

Mann, Thomas. *The Magic Mountain.* H. T. Lowe Porter, trans. New York: Knopf, 1939. "Anna Karenina." In *Essays of Three Decades.* H. T. Lowe-Porter, trans. New York: Knopf, 1947. "Tonio Kröger." In H. T. Lowe-Porter, trans. *Death in Venice and Seven Other Stories.* New York: Vintage, 1959. "The Art of the Novel." In H. M. Block and H. Salinger, eds. *The Creative Vision.* New York: Grove Press, 1960.

Manning, Peter, "Existential Sociology." Mimeograph, Department of Sociology, Michigan State University: East Lansing, 1972. *Ideology and Utopia.* New York: Harcourt, Brace, 1966.

Manning, Peter, "Existential Sociology." In Jack D. Douglas, ed., *Existential Sociology.* New York: Appleton-Century-Crofts, 1975.

Maquet, Jacques J. *The Sociology of Knowledge: A Critical Analysis of the Systems of Karl Mannheim and Pitirim Sorokin.* Boston: Beacon Press, 1951. "Objectivity in Anthropology." *Current Anthropology,* 5, 1 (February 1964), 47–55.

Marcel, Gabriel. *Being and Having: An Existentialist Diary.* New York: Harper & Row, 1965. *The Philosophy of Existence.* Freeport, N.Y.: Books for Libraries Press, 1969. *Problematic Man.* Brian Thompson, trans. New York: Herder and Herder, 1967.

Marcuse, Herbert. *Studies in Soviet Marxism.* New York: Columbia, 1958. *Studies in Critical Philosophy.* Boston: Beacon Press, 1973.

Marle, René. *Introduction to Hermeneutics.* E. Froment and R. Albrecht, trans. New York: Herder and Herder, 1967.

Martindale, Don. *The Nature and Types of Sociological Theory.* Boston: Houghton, Mifflin, 1960.

Martineau, Harriet. *Society in America.* Garden City, N.Y.: Doubleday, 1962.

Marx, Karl. *A Contribution to the Critique of Political Economy in Karl Marx, Selected Works.* Moscow: Cooperative Publishing Society, 1935. *Capital.* New York: Everyman's Library, 1946. "Theses on Feuerbach." In Lewis Feuer, ed. *Marx and Engels: Basic Writings on Politics and Philosophy.* Garden City, N.Y.: Doubleday, 1959.

Maslow, A. H. *Meaning and Interpretation.* University of California Publications in Philosophy, No. 25. Berkeley: University of California Press, 1950.

Masterman, Margaret. "The Nature of a Paradigm." In Imre Lakatos and Alan Musgrave, eds. *Criticism and the Growth of Knowledge.* Cambridge: Cambridge, 1970.

Matejka, Ladislav, and Pomorska, Krystyna, eds. *Readings in Russian Poetics: Formalist and Structuralist Views.* Cambridge, Mass.: M.I.T., 1971.

Matson, Floyd. *The Broken Image: Man, Science, and Society.* Garden City, N.Y.: Doubleday, 1966.

Matza, David. *Becoming Deviant.* Englewood Cliffs, N.J.: Prentice-Hall, 1969.

Mauss, Marcel. *The Gift: Forms and Functions of Exchange in Archaic Societies.* New York: Norton, 1967.

Mayakovsky, Vladimir. "At the Top of My Voice." In Patricia Blake, ed. *The Bedbug and Selected Poetry.* New York: Meridian Books, 1960.

Mayenowa, Maria Renata. "Semiotics Today: Reflections on the Second International Conference on Semiotics." *Social Science Information,* 6, 2–3 (1967), 59–64.

McClosky, Mary A. "Metaphors," *Mind,* 73, 290 (April 1964), 215–233.

McHugh, Peter. "On the Failure of Positivism." In Jack D. Douglas, ed. *Understanding Everyday Life.* Chicago: Aldine, 1970.

McKeon, Richard. "Philosophy and Method." *Journal of Philosophy,* 48, 22 (October 1951), 653–682.

McKinney, John C. "Sociological Theory and the Process of Typification." In John C. McKinney and Edward A. Tiryakian, *Theoretical Sociology, Perspectives and Developments.* New York: Appleton-Century-Crofts, 1971.

McWilliams, Carey. *Brothers Under the Skin.* Boston: Little, Brown, 1951.

Mead, George Herbert. *Mind, Self, and Society.* Chicago: The University of Chicago Press, 1934.

Mead, George Herbert. "Play the Game, and the Generalized Other." In Anselm Strauss, ed. *The Social Psychology of George Herbert Mead.* Chicago: The University of Chicago Press, 1956.

Mehlberg, Henry. *The Reach of Science.* Toronto: University of Toronto Press, 1958.

Merleau-Ponty, Maurice. *The Primacy of Perception.* Evanston, Ill.: Northwestern University Press, 1964.

The Structure of Behavior. Alden L. Fisher, trans. Boston: Beacon Press, 1967.

Signs. Evanston, Ill.: Northwestern University Press, 1969.

Merton, Robert K. "Karl Mannheim and the Sociology of Knowledge." In *Social Theory and Social Structure.* New York: Free Press, 1957.

"Intermarriage and the Social Structure." *Psychiatry,* 4, 3 (August 1941), 361–374.

"The Role of the Intellectual in Public Bureaucracy." In *Social Theory and Social Structure.* New York: Free Press, 1957.

Social Theory and Social Structure. New York: Free Press, 1957.

"Insiders and Outsiders: A Chapter in the Sociology of Knowledge." *American Journal of Sociology,* 78, 1 (July 1972), 9–47.

Messinger, Sheldon L., Sampson, Harold, and Towne, Robert. "Life as Theatre: Some Notes on One Dramaturgic Approach to Social Reality." *Sociometry,* 25, 1 (March, 1962), 98–110.

Mill, John Stuart. *On Liberty.* London: Oxford, 1966.

Miller, Libuse Lukas. *Knowing, Doing and Surviving: Cognition in Evolution.* New York: Wiley, 1973.

Mills, C. Wright. *The Sociological Imagination.* New York: Oxford, 1959.

Sociology and Pragmatism. New York: Oxford, 1966.

Mischel, T. "Personal Constructs, Rules, and the Logic of Clinical Activity." *Psychological Review,* 71, 3 (May 1964), 180–192.

Moles, Abraham A. *Information Theory and Aesthetic Perception.* Joel Cohen, trans. Urbana: The University of Illinois Press, 1965.

Moliere. *The Miser.* Wallace Fowlie, trans. Great Neck, N.Y.: Barron's Educational Series, 1964.

Monnerot, Jules. *Les faits sociaux ne sont pasdes choses.* Paris: Gallimard, 1946.

Moore, Omar K. "Divination–A New Perspective." *American Anthropologist,* 59, 1 (February 1957), 69–74.

Moore, Omar K., and Anderson, Alan R. "Puzzles, Games and Social Interaction." In David Braybrooke, ed. *Philosophical Problems of the Social Sciences.* New York: Macmillan, 1965.

Moore, Wilbert E. "A Reconsideration of Theories of Social Change." *American Sociological Review,* 25, 6 (December 1960), 810–818.

"Predicting Discontinuities in Social Change." *American Sociological Review,* 29, 3 (June 1964), 331–338.

Moore, Wilbert E., and Tumin, Melvin M. "Some Social Functions of Ignorance." *American Sociological Review,* 14, 6 (December 1949), 787–795.

Mora, Jose Ferrater. *Unamuno, A Philosophy of Tragedy,* Philip Silver, trans. Berkeley: University of California Press, 1962.

Moravia, Alberto (pseud. for Alberto Pincherle). *Conjugal Love.* Angus Davidson, trans. New York: Farrar, Straus and Young, 1951.

Moreno, Jacob L. *Psychodrama.* New York: Beacon House, 1946.

Morpuego-Tagliabue, Guido. *L'Esthetique Contemporaine.* Milan: Marzorati, 1969.

Morris, Charles. *Six Theories of Mind.* Chicago: The University of Chicago Press, 1932.

Writings on the General Theory of Signs. The Hague: Mouton, 1971.

Mowrer, O. H., and Kluckhohn, C. "Dynamic Theory of Personality." In J. M. Hunt, ed. *Personality and Behavioral Disorders.* New York: Ronald, 1944.

Muecke, Douglas Colin. *The Compass of Irony.* London: Methuen, 1969.

Muller, Friedrich Max. *The Science of Language.* New York: Scribners, 1891.

Munro, Thomas. *Oriental Aesthetics.* Cleveland: Press of Western Reserve University, 1965.

Murphey, Robert F. "Social Distance and the Veil." *American Anthropologist,* 66, 6 (December 1964), 1257–1274.

Murphey, Robert F. *The Dialectics of Social Life.* New York: Basic Books, 1971.

Murray, John Middleton. *Countries of the Mind.* London, 1931.

Myrdal, Gunnar. *An American Dilemma.* New York: Harper, 1944.

Nadel, S. F. *The Theory of Social Structure.* New York: Free Press, 1964.

Nagel, Ernst. "Wholes, Sums, and Organic Unities." *Philosophical Studies,* 3 (1952), 17–32.

Nash, Harvey. "Freud and Metaphor." *Archives of General Psychiatry,* 7, 2 (July 1962), 17–32.

Natanson, Maurice. "Causation as a Structure of the *Lebenswelt.*" In *Literature, Philosophy and the Social Sciences.* The Hague: Nijhoff, 1962.

"Man as an Actor," in Erwin W. Strauss and Richard M. Griffiths, eds. *Phenomenology of Will and Action, The Second Lexington Conference on Pure and Applied Phenomenology.* Pittsburgh: Duquesne University Press, 1967.

The Journeying Self, A Study in Philosophy and Social Role. Reading, Mass.: Addison-Wesley, 1970.

Navasky, Victor. *Kennedy Justice.* New York: Atheneum, 1971.

Needham, Rodney. *Belief, Language and Experience.* Oxford: Blackwell, 1972.

Nehnevajsa, Jiri. "Reflections on Theories and Sociometric Systems." *International Journal of Sociometry,* 1 (1956), 8–15.

Nelson, Benjamin. *The Idea of Usury: from Tribal Brotherhood to Universal Otherhood.* Princeton, N.J.: Princeton, 1949.

Introductory comment to Norman O. Brown, "Apocalypse: The Place of Mystery in The Life of the Mind." *Harpers Magazine,* May 1961, 45–47.

" 'Probabilists,' 'Anti-Probabilists' and the Quest for Certitude in the sixteenth and seventeenth Centuries." In *Proceedings of the Xth International Congress for the History of Science.* Vol. 1. Paris: Herrmann, 1965.

"Histories, Symbolic Logics, Cultural Maps." *The Psychoanalytic Review,* 55, 3 (1968), 332–522.

"Is the Sociology of Religion Possible?" *Journal for the Scientific Study of Religion,* 9, 2 (Summer 1970), 107–111.

Newton, Isaac. *Sir Isaac Newton's Mathematical Principles of Natural Philosophy and his System of the World*. Berkeley: University of California Press, 1960.

Nieburg, Harold L. *In the Name of Science*. Chicago: Quadrangle, 1966.

Nietzsche, Friedrich. *Joyful Wisdom*. New York: Ungar, 1960.

"Uber Wahrheit und Luge im aussermoralischen Sinn" (On Truth and Lie in an Extra-Moral Sense). In *Werke in drei Banden*. Karl Schlechta, ed. Vol. 3. Munchen: 1960.

Nisbet, Robert A. "Sociology as an Art Form." *Pacific Sociological Review*, 5, 2 (Fall 1962), 67–74.

Social Change and History: Aspects of Western Theory of Development. New York: Oxford, 1969.

Odgen, C. K., and Richards, I. A. *The Meaning of Meaning; A Study of the Influence of Language Upon Thought and of the Science of Symbolism*. New York: Harcourt, Brace & World, 1946.

O'Neill, John. *Sociology as a Skin Trade*. New York: Harper & Row, 1972.

Osborne, Harold. *Aesthetics and Art Theory: An Historical Introduction*. New York: Dutton, 1968.

The Art of Appreciation. London: Oxford, 1970.

Palmer, Richard. *Hermeneutics; Interpretation Theory in Schleirmacher, Dilthey, Heidegger, and Gadamer*. Evanston, Ill.: Northwestern University Press, 1969.

Panofsky, Erwin. *Meaning in the Visual Arts*. Garden City, N.Y.: Doubleday, 1955.

Park, Peter. *Sociology Tomorrow*. New York: Pegasus, 1969.

Park, Robert. *Race and Culture*. Glencoe, Ill.: Free Press, 1950.

Human Communities. New York: Free Press, 1952.

Park, Robert E., and Burgess, E. W. *Introduction to the Science of Sociology*. Chicago: The University of Chicago Press, 1924.

Parsons, Talcott. *The Structure of Social Action*. Glencoe, Ill.: Free Press, 1949.

The Social System. Glencoe, Ill.: Free Press, 1951.

"Evolutionary Universals in Society," *American Sociological Review*, 29, 3 (June 1964), 339–357.

Essays in Sociological Theory. Glencoe, Ill.: Free Press, 1954.

Societies: Evolutionary and Comparative Perspectives. Englewood Cliffs, NJ.: Prentice-Hall, 1966.

"Full Citizenship for the American Negro? A Sociological Problem." In Talcott Parsons and Kenneth B. Clark, eds. *The Negro American*. Boston: Houghton Mifflin, 1966.

Parsons, Talcott, and Shils, Edward A., eds. *Toward a General Theory of Action*. Cambridge, Mass.: Harvard, 1951.

Parsons, Talcott, and Fox, Renee. "Illness, Therapy and the Modern American Family." *Journal of Social Issues*, 8, 4 (1952), 31–44.

Parsons, Talcott, Bales, R. F., and Shils, E. A. *Working Papers in the Theory of Action*. Glencoe, Ill.: Free Press, 1953.

Passmore, John. *A Hundred Years of Philosophy*. Baltimore: Penguin, 1966.

Peckman, Morse. *Man's Rage for Chaos: Biology, Behavior, and the Arts*. New York: Chilton, 1965.

Peirce, Charles S. *Collected Papers*. Charles Hartshorne and Paul Weiss, eds. Cambridge, Mass.: Harvard, 1960.

Pepper, Stephan. *World Hypotheses*. Berkeley: University of California Press, 1942.

Peters, R. S. *The Concept of Motivation*. London: Routledge, 1960.

Petrovic, Gajo. *Marx in the Mid-Twentieth*. Garden City, N.Y.: Doubleday, 1967.

Pirandello, Luigi. *Naked Masks: Five Plays*. New York: Dutton, 1952.

Pico della Mirandola, Giovanni. *Oration on the Dignity of Man*. A. Robert Caponigri, trans. Chicago: Henry Regnery, 1956.

Plato. *The Republic*. F. M. Conford, trans. New York: Oxford, 1964.

Platt, John. "Hierarchial Restructuring." *General Systems:* 15 (November 1970), 49–54.

Polanyi, Michael. *Personal Knowledge: Toward a Post-critical Philosophy*. Chicago: The University of Chicago Press, 1958.

Polsky, Ned. *Hustlers, Beats, and Others.* Chicago: Aldine, 1967.

Polya, George. *Mathematics and Plausible Reasoning.* Princeton, N.J.: Princeton, 1954.

Popper, Karl. *The Logic of Scientific Discovery.* New York: Basic Books, 1959.

Conjectures and Refutations; The Growth of Scientific Knowledge. London: Routledge, 1963.

Pouillon, Jean, *Temps et Roman.* Paris: Gallimard, 1946.

Pribram, Karl H. *Languages of the Brain.* Englewood Cliffs, N.J.: Prentice-Hall, 1971.

Price, John V. *The Ironic Hume.* Austin: University of Texas Press, 1965.

Psathas, George. *Phenomenological Sociology.* New York: Wiley, 1973.

Quine, Willard Van Orman. *Word and Object.* Cambridge, Mass.: M.I.T., 1960.

From a Logical Point of View. Cambridge, Mass.: Harvard, 1964.

Rabinowitch, Eugene. "Integral Science and Atomized Art." *Bulletin of the Atomic Scientist,* 15 (February 1959).

Radcliffe-Brown, Alfred R. *The Andaman Islanders.* Glencoe, Ill.: Free Press, 1948.

"Murngin Social Organization." *American Anthropologist,* 53, 1 (January 1951), 37–55.

"On Joking Relationships," and "A Further Note on Joking Relationships." In *Structure and Function in Primitive Society.* New York: Free Press, 1952.

Radnitzsky, G. "Ways of Looking at Science" *Scientia,* 104 (1969), 49–57.

Randall, John H. Jr., and Haines, George. "Controlling Assumptions in the Practice of American Historians." *Theory and Practice in Historical Study: A Report of the Committee on Historiography,* Bulletin 54. New York: Social Science Research Council, 1946.

Rao, Calyampudi, ed. *Contributions to Statistics.* New York: Pergamon Press, 1965.

Rapoport, Anatol. "Lewis Richardson's Mathematical Theory of War." *Journal of Conflict Resolution,* 1, 3 (September 1957), 249–299.

"Some Systems Approaches to Political Theory." In D. Easton, ed. *Varieties of Political Theory.* Englewood Cliffs, N.J.: Prentice-Hall, 1966.

N-Person Game Theory. Ann Arbor: The University of Michigan Press, 1970.

Rashevsky, Nicholas. *Mathematical Biology of Social Behavior.* Chicago: The University of Chicago Press, 1951.

Read, Herberd E. *Icon and Idea: The Function of Art in the Development of Human Consciousness.* Cambridge, Mass.: Harvard, 1955.

Read, K. E. "Leadership and Consensus in a New Guinea Society." *American Anthropologist,* 61, 3 (June 1959), 425–436.

Redfield, Robert. *Tepoztlan, A Mexican Village.* Chicago: The University of Chicago Press, 1930.

The Folk Culture of Yucatan. Chicago: The University of Chicago Press, 1941.

"The Art of Social Science." *American Journal of Sociology,* 54, 3 (November 1948), 181–190.

The Primitive World and its Transformations. Ithaca: Cornell, 1953.

The Little Community. Chicago: The University of Cihcago Press, 1955.

Reichenbach, Hans. *Einstein: Philosopher-Scientist.* Evanston, Ill.: Northwestern University Press, 1949.

Richards, I. A. *The Philosophy of Rhetoric.* New York: Oxford, 1936.

Richards, I. A., Ogden, C. K., and Wood, J. *The Foundations of Aesthetics.* London: Allen & Unwin, 1921.

Richardson, Lewis Fry. *Arms and Insecurity; A Mathematical Study of the Causes and Origins of War.* Pittsburgh: Boxwood Press, 1960.

Rickert, Heinrich. *Science and History; A Critique of Positivist Epistemology.* George Reisman, trans. Princeton, N.J.: Van Nostrand, 1962.

Ricoeur, Paul. *The Symbolism of Evil.* Boston: Beacon Press, 1967.

"La Metaphore et le probleme central de l'herméneutique." *Revue philosophique de Louvain,* 4th ser., 10, 5 (February 1972), 93–112.

Riesman, D. "Orbits of Tolerance, Interviewers and Elites." *Public Opinion Quarterly,* 20, 1 (Spring 1956), 49–73.

"Some Observations on the Study of American Character." *Psychiatry*, 15, 1 (August 1952), 158–161.

Riesman, D., and Ehrlich, J. "Age and Authority in the Interview." *Public Opinion Quarterly*, 25 (Spring 1961), 39–56.

Riezler, Kurt. *Man, Mutable and Immutable: The Fundamental Structure of Social Life*. Chicago: Henry Regnery, 1950.

Righter, Anne. *Shakespeare and the Idea of the Play*. New York: Barnes & Noble, 1962.

Riley, Matilda, Riley, John, and Toby Jackson. *Sociological Studies in Scale Analysis*. New Brunswick, N.J.: Rutgers University Press, 1954.

Ritchie, Arthur David. *The Natural History of Mind*. London: Longmans, 1936.

Robinson, D. and Rohde, S. "Two Experiments with an Anti-Semitism Poll." *Journal of Abnormal and Social Psychology*, 41, 2 (April 1946), 136–144.

Robinson, James M. "Theology as Translation." *Theology Today*, 20, 4 (January 1964), 518–527.

Robinson, W. S. "The Logical Structure of Analytic Induction." *American Sociological Review*, 16, 6 (December 1951), 812–818.

Also see Alfred R. Lindesmith. "Comment on W. S. Robinson's 'The Logical Structure of Analytic Induction'." *American Sociological Review*, 17, 4 (August 1952), 492–493; and W. S. Robinson, "Comments and Rejoinder," ibid., 494.

Rodin, Auguste. *Art*. Paul Gsell, comp. and Romilly Fedden, trans. London: Hodder and Stoughton, 1912.

Rogers, Rolf E. *Max Weber's Ideal Type Theory*. New York: Philosophical Library, 1969.

Ross, Arthur, and Hill, Herbert, eds. *Employment, Race, and Poverty*. New York: Harcourt, Brace & World, 1967.

Rossi, Peter H. "Methods of Social Research, 1944–1955." In Hans L. Zetterberg, ed. *Sociology in the United States of America: A Trend Report*. Paris: UNESCO, 1956.

Roth, Guenther. "Max Weber's Comparative Approach and Historical Typology." In Ivan Vallier, *Comparative Methods in Sociology*. Berkeley: University of California Press, 1971.

Roth, Julius. *Timetables: Structuring the Passage of Time in Hospital Treatment and Other Careers*. Indianapolis: Bobbs-Merrill, 1963.

Rousseau, Jean Jacques. *Oeuvres completes*. Bernard Gagnebin et Marcel Raymond, eds. Paris: Gallimard, 1959–1969.

Rowley, G. *Principles of Chinese Painting*. Princeton, N.J.: Princeton, 1959.

Royce, Josiah. "The Mechanical, the Historical, and the Statistical." *Science*, N.S., 39, 1006 (1914), 551–566.

Rudner, Richard. "On Semiotic Aesthetics." *Journal of Aesthetics and Art Criticism*, 10 (1951), 66–77.

Rudner, Richard and Scheffler, Israel, eds. *Logic and Art: Essays in Honor of Nelson Goodman*. Indianapolis: Bobbs-Merrill, 1972.

Rugg, Harold. *Imagination*. New York: Harper, 1963.

Ruitenbeek, H. M. *Creative Imagination*. Chicago: Quadrangle, 1965.

Ryder, Arthur W., ed. and trans. *The Panchatantra*. Chicago: The Chicago University Press, 1925.

Ryle, Gilbert. *Dilemmas*. Cambridge: Cambridge University Press, 1954.

Sacks, Harvey. "Sociological Description." *Berkeley Journal of Sociology*, 8 (1963), 1–16.

"The Search for Help: No One to Turn To." Unpublished Ph.D. dissertation, University of California at Berkeley, 1966.

Sacksteder, William. "Diversity in the Behavioral Sciences." *Philosophy of Science*, 30, 4 (October 1963), 375–395.

"Inference and Philosophic Typologies." *The Monist*, 48, 4 (October 1964), 567–601.

St. Simon, Claude Henri. *Selected Writings*. F. Markham, trans. Oxford: Blackwell, 1952.

Santayana, George. *Soliloquies in England and Later Soliloquies*. New York: Scribner, 1922.

Sartre, Jean-Paul. *Being and Nothingness*, Hazel E. Barnes, trans. New York: Philosophical Library, 1956.

Nausea. Lloyd Alexander, trans. Norfolk, Va.: New Directions, 1959.

Critique de la Raison dialectique. Paris: Gallimard, 1960.

Saussure, Ferdinand de. *Cours de linguistique generale*. Paris: Presses universitaires de France, 1965.

Saville, Anthony. "Nelson Goodman's 'Languages of Art': A Study." *British Journal of Aesthetics*, 11, 1 (Winter 1971), 3–27.

Schaffer, Robert D. "Cerebral Lateralization: The Dichotomy of Consciousness." *International Journal of Symbology*, 5, 2 (July 1974), 7–13.

Scheff, Thomas J. "Control Over Policy by Attendants in a Mental Hospital." *Journal of Health and Human Behavior*, 2 (1961), 93–105.

Becoming Mentally Ill. Chicago: Aldine, 1966.

Scheflen, Albert E. *Body Language and the Social Order, Communication as Behavioral Control*. Englewood Cliffs, N.J.: Prentice-Hall, 1972.

Schelling, Thomas C. "The Strategy of Conflict: Prospectus for a Reorientation Game Theory." *Journal of Conflict Resolution*, 2, 3 (September 1958), 203–264.

Strategy of Conflict. Cambridge, Mass.: Harvard, 1960.

Schlegel, Friedrich, von. *Literary Notebooks, 1797–1801*. Hans Eichner, ed. Toronto: University of Toronto Press, 1957.

Schmidt, Paul, trans. *Arthur Rimbaud: Complete Works*. New York: Harper & Row, 1975.

Schneider, David M. *The Relevance of Models for Social Anthropology*. A.S.A. Monograph 1. London: Tavistock, 1965.

Schneider, Louis. *The Freudian Psychology and Veblen's Social Theory*. New York: King's Crown Press, 1948.

"The Role of the Category of Ignorance in Sociological Theory: An Exploratory Statement." *American Sociological Review*, 27, 4 (August 1962), 492–508.

"Toward Assessment of Sorokin's View of Change." In G. K. Zollschan and W. Hirsch, eds. *Explorations in Social Change*. Boston: Houghton Mifflin, 1964.

The Sociological Way of Looking at the World. New York: McGraw-Hill, 1975.

Schon, D. *The Displacement of Concepts*. London: 1963.

Schrodinger, Edwin. "Science, Art, and Play." In *Scientific Theory and Man*. New York: Dover, 1935.

Schroyer, Trent. "A Reconceptualization of Critical Theory." In J. David Colfax and Jack D. Roach, eds. *Radical Sociology*. New York: Basic Books, 1971.

The Critique of Domination: The Origin and Development of Critical Theory. New York: Braziller, 1973.

Schutz, Alfred. "The Stranger." *American Journal of Sociology*, 49, 6 (May 1944), 499–507. In Arvid Brodersen, ed. *Collected Papers II: Studies in Social Theory*. The Hague: Nijoff, 1964.

"On Multiple Realities," *Philosophy and Phenomenological Research*, 5, 4 (June 1954), 533–576

On Phenomenology and Social Relations. Helmut R. Wagner, ed. Chicago: The University of Chicago Press, 1970.

Collected Papers. Maurice Natanson, ed. The Hague: Nijhoff, 1971.

Schwab, Joseph, "What Do Scientists Do?" *Behavioral Science*, 5, 1 (January 1960), 1–27.

Schwartz, Theodore. "Beyond Cybernetics: Constructs, Expectations and Goals in Human Adaptation." mimeographed. San Diego, Calif.: University of California at San Diego, 1968.

Scott, Marvin B. *The Racing Game*. Chicago: Aldine, 1968.

Scott, Marvin B., and Lyman, Stanford M. *The Revolt of the Students*. Columbus: Charles E. Merrill, 1970.

Scott, Robert A. *The Making of Blind Men; A Study of Adult Socialization*. New York: Russell Sage Foundation, 1969.

Sedgewick, Garnett G. *Of Irony, Especially in the Drama*. Toronto: University of Toronto Press, 1948.

Seeman, Melvin. "On the Meaning of Alienation." *American Sociological Review*, 24, 6 (December 1959), 783–791.

Segall, Marshall H., Campbell, Donald T., and Herskovits, Melville J. *The Influence of Culture on Visual Perception*. Indianapolis: Bobbs-Merrill, 1966.

Seligman, Ben. B. "The State of the Social Sciences." *Commentary*, 46, 4 (October 1968), 76–79.

Sellars, Wilfred. "The Language of Theories." In Herbert Feigl and Grover Maxwell, eds. *Current Issues in the Philosophy of Science*. New York: Holt, Rinehart & Winston, 1961.

Science Perception and Reality. New York: Humanities Press, 1963.

Science and Metaphysics. New York: Humanities Press, 1968.

Selznick, Philip. *TVA and the Grass Roots*. Berkeley: University of California Press, 1949.

Seward, Georgene, ed. *Clinical Studies in Culture Conflict*. New York: Ronald Press, 1958.

Shaftesbury, Anthony Ashley Cooper. *Second Characters or the Language of Forms*, Benjamin Rand, ed. New York: Greenwood Press, 1969.

Shibles, Warren A. *An Analysis of Metaphor*. The Hague: Mouton, 1971.

Shibutani, Tamotsu. "Reference Groups as Perspectives," *American Journal of Sociology*, 60, 6 (May 1955), 562–569.

Improvised News: A Sociological Study of Rumor. Indianapolis: Bobbs-Merrill, 1966.

Shils, Edward A. and Janowitz, Morris. "Cohesion and Disintegration in the Wehrmacht in World War II." *Public Opinion Quarterly*, 12, 2 (Summer 1948), 280–315.

Shklovsky, Victor. *O teorii prozy*. Moscow: 1929.

"Art as Technique." In Lee T. Lemon and Marian J. Reis, eds. and trans. *Russian Formalist Criticism: Four Essays*. Lincoln: University of Nebraska Press, 1965.

Shubik, Martin. *Strategy and Market Structure*. New York: Wiley, 1959.

Game Theory and Related Approaches to Behavior. New York: Wiley, 1964.

Simmel, Georg. *The Sociology of Georg Simmel*. Glencoe, Ill.: Free Press, 1950.

et al. "The Ruin." In Kurt H. Wolff, ed. *Essays on Sociology, Philosophy and Aesthetics*. New York: Harper & Row, 1965, pp. 259–266.

Fragmente and Aufsatze. Hildesheim: Olms, 1967.

"On the Concept and the Tragedy of Culture" in *The Conflict in Modern Culture*. New York: Teachers College Press, 1968.

Simon, Herbert A., "A Formal Theory of Interaction in Social Groups." *American Sociological Review*, 17, 2 (April 1952), 202–211.

Simon, Herbert A. and Newell, Allen. "Models: Their Uses and Limitations." In Leonard D. White, ed. *The State of the Social Sciences*. Chicago: The University of Chicago Press, 1956.

Simpson, George E., and Yinger, J. Milton. "The Sociology of Race and Ethnic Relations." In Robert K. Merton, Leonard Broom, and Leonard S. Cottrell, eds. *Sociology Today*. New York: Basic Books, 1969.

Racial and Cultural Minorities: An Analysis of Prejudice and Discrimination. New York: Harper & Row, 1972.

Siren, Oswald. *The Chinese on the Art of Painting*. New York: Schocken-Bailey, 1963.

Sjoberg, Gideon. "Comparative Urban Sociology." In Robert K. Merton, Leonard Broom, and Leonard S. Cottrell, eds. *Sociology Today*. New York: Basic Books, 1959.

"Operationalism and Social Research." In Llewellyn Gross, ed. *Symposium on Sociological Theory*. Evanston, Ill.: Row, Peterson, 1959.

Skinner, B. F., *Science and Human Behavior*. New York: Macmillan, 1953.

Skolnick, Jerome. *Justice Without Trial*. New York: Wiley, 1966.

Smith, Adam. *An Inquiry into the Nature and Causes of the Wealth of Nations*. New York: A. M. Kelley, 1966.

Sociological Review. "New Approaches in Sociology." N.S. 21, 1 (February 1973), 1–182.

Solger, Karl Wilhelm Ferdinand. *Vorlesungen uber Asthetik*. Darmstadt: Wissenschaftliche Buckgesellschaft, 1962.

Sophocles. *Oedipus the King, and Oedipus at Colonus*. Charles R. Walker, trans. Garden City, N.Y.: Doubleday, 1966.

Sorokin, Pitirim. *Social and Cultural Dynamics*. New York: Bedminster Press, 1941.

——— *Sociocultural Causality, Space, Time*. Durham, N.C.: Duke University Press, 1943.

——— *The Ways and Power of Love*. Boston: Beacon Press, 1954.

——— *Social and Cultural Dynamics*, abrg. ed. Boston: Extending Horizons Books, 1957.

——— *Society, Culture and Personality*. New York: Cooper Square Publishers, 1962.

——— "Reply to My Critics." In Philip Allen, ed., *Pitirim Sorokin in Review*. Durham, N.C.: Duke University Press, 1963.

——— "Comments on Schneider's Observations and Criticisms." In G. K. Zollschan and W. Hirsch, eds. *Explorations in Social Change*. Boston: Houghton Mifflin, 1964.

Sosensky, Irving. "The Problem of Quality in Relation to Some Issues in Social Change." In G. K. Zollschan and W. Hirsch, eds. *Explorations in Social Change*. Boston: Houghton Mifflin, 1964.

Southall, Aidan. "Community, Society, and the World in Emergent Africa." In Manfred Stanley, ed. *Social Development: Critical Perspectives*. New York: Basic Books, 1972.

Souvage, Jacques. *An Introduction to the Study of the Novel*. Ghent: Wetenschappelijke Uitgevrij, 1965.

Spector, Jack. *The Aesthetics of Freud*. New York: Praeger, 1972.

Speier, Hans. "Review of Mannheim's *Ideology and Utopia*." *American Journal of Sociology*, 43, 1 (July 1937), 155–166.

Spencer, Herbert. *Essays: Scientific, Political, and Speculative*. New York: Appleton, 1892.

Stanford, W. Bedell. *Greek Metaphor*. Oxford: Blackwell, 1936.

Stanley, Manfred. "Technicism, Liberalism, and Development: A Study in Irony as Social Theory." In M. Stanley, ed. *Social Development*. New York: Basic Books, 1972.

——— "Prometheus and the Policy Sciences: Alienation as the Decline of Personal Agency." In Frank Johnson, ed. *Alienation: Concept, Term and Meanings*. New York: Seminar Press, 1973.

——— "Dignity Versus Survival? Reflections on The Moral Philosophy of Social Order." In Richard H. Brown and Stanford M. Lyman, eds. *Structure, Consciousness, and History*. New York and London: Cambridge University Press, 1977.

States, Bert O. *Irony and Drama; A Poetics*. Ithaca: Cornell, 1971.

Staude, John R. *Max Scheler, 1874–1928: An Intellectual Portrait*. New York: Free Press, 1967.

——— "The Theoretical Foundations of Humanistic Sociology." In John F. Glass and John R. Staude, eds. *Humanistic Society: Today's Challenge to Sociology*. Pacific Palisades, Calif.: Goodyear, 1972.

Stein, Maurice. "The Poetic Metaphors of Sociology." In Maurice Stein and Arthur Vidich, eds. *Sociology on Trial*. Englewood Cliffs, N.J.: Prentice-Hall, 1963.

Sterne, Laurence. *The Life and Opinions of Tristram Shandy.* New York: Odyssey, 1940.

Stevens, Wallace. *Collected Poems.* New York: Knopf, 1967.

Stewart, John Quincey. "A Basis for Social Physics." In James Stokley, ed. *Science Marches On.* New York: Washburn, 1951.

Stinchcombe, Arthur L. *Constructing Social Theories.* New York: Harcourt, Brace & World, 1968.

"Bureaucratic and Craft Administration of Production: A Comparative Study." *Administrative Science Quarterly,* 4, 2 (September 1959), 168–187.

Stolnitz, Jerome. "On the Origins of 'Aesthetic Disinterestedness'." *The Journal of Aesthetics and Art Criticism,* 20, 2 (Fall, 1961), 131–143.

Stonequist, Everett V., *The Marginal Man. A Study in Personality and Cultural Conflict.* New York: Russell and Russell, 1937.

Stonier, Alfred, and Bode, Karl, "A New Approach to the Methodology of Social Science." *Economica,* 4, 16 (November 1937), 406–427.

Stouffer, Samuel A. *et al. The American Soldier: Studies in Social Psychology in World War II.* Princeton, N.J.: Princeton, 1949.

Strasser, Stephan. *Phenomenology and the Human Sciences. A Contribution to a New Scientific Ideal.* Pittsburgh: Duquesne University Press, 1963.

Stravinsky, Igor. *Poetics of Music in The Form of Six Lessons.* New York: Vintage, 1956.

Sturtevant, Edgar H. *An Introduction to Linguistic Science.* New Haven: Yale, 1947.

Suchman, Edward A. "Social Patterns of Illness and Medical Care." *Journal of Health and Human Behavior,* 6 (Spring 1965), 2–16.

Sudnow, David. *Passing On: The Social Organization of Dying.* Englewood Cliffs, N.J.: Prentice-Hall, 1967.

Sumner, William Graham. *Folkways.* Boston: Ginn and Company, 1906.

Suppes, Patrick, and Atkinson. R. C. *Markov Learning Models for Multi-Person Interactions.* Stanford: Stanford, 1960.

Surmelian, Leon. *Techniques of Fiction Writing.* New York: Doubleday, 1968.

Sutherland, Edwin H., ed. *The Professional Thief, by a Professional Thief (Chic Conwell).* Chicago: The University of Chicago Press, 1937.

Principles of Criminology. Chicago: Lippincott, 1960.

Sutherland, John W. *A General Systems Philosophy for the Social and Behavioral Sciences.* New York: Brayilber, 1973.

Swabey, Marie C. *The Judgment of History.* New York: Philosophical Society, 1954.

Logic and Nature. New York: New York University Press, 1955.

Comic Laughter. New Haven: Yale University Press, 1961.

Sweeney, James J. "An Interview with Marc Chagall." *Partisan Review,* 11, 1 (Winter 1944), 88–93.

Sweezy, Paul M., ed. *Karl Marx and the Close of his System and Boem-Bawerk's Criticism of Marx.* New York: Kelley, 1949.

Swift, Jonathan. *Works.* London: Henry Bohn, 1859.

Sypher, Wylie. "The Meaning of Comedy." In W. Sypher, ed., *Comedy.* Garder. City, N.Y.: Doubleday, 1956.

Szasz, Thomas S. *The Myth of Mental Illness.* New York: Hoeber-Harper, 1961.

The Manufacture of Madness. New York: Harper & Row, 1970.

Sze, Mai-Mai. *The Tao of Painting: With the Mustard Seed Garden Manual of Painting.* London: Routledge, 1957.

Tagger, Theodor (Ferdinand Bruckner). *Das neue Geschlecht: Programmschrift gegen die Metaphor.* Berlin: Hockstein, 1917.

Taine, Hippolyte Adolphe. *Philosophie de l'art.* Paris: Hachette, 1913.

Tarski, Alfred. *Introduction to Logic.* New York: Oxford 1946.

Tate, Allen. "Tension in Poetry." In *The Man of Letters in the Modern World.* New York: Meridian, 1955.

Taylor, Charles. *The Explanation of Behavior.* New York: Humanities Press, 1964.

Taylor, Paul. *Normative Discourse.* Englewood Cliffs, N.J.: Prentice-Hall, 1961.

Teggert, Frederick J. *Rome and China, A Study of Correlations in Historical Events.* Berkeley: University of California Press, 1939.

Theory and Processes of History. Berkeley: University of California Press, 1941.

Tejera, Victorino. *Art and Human Intelligence.* New York: Appleton-Century-crofts, 1965.

Terman, Lewis Madison. *The Measurement of Intelligence.* Boston: Houghton Mifflin, 1916.

Thomas, William I. *On Social Organization and Social Personality.* Morris Janowitz, ed. Chicago: The University of Chicago Press, 1966.

Thomas, William I., and Znaniecki, Florian. *The Polish Peasant in Europe and America.* New York: Dover, 1958.

Thorner, Isidor. "Sociological Aspects of Affectional Frustration." *Psychiatry,* 6, 2 (May 1943), 157–173.

Thurstone, Louis Leon, and Chave, E. J. *The Measurement of Attitude.* Chicago: The University of Chicago Press, 1929.

Times Literary Supplement. "Dialectical Methodology." March 12, 1970, 269–272.

Tiryakian, Edward, *Sociologism and Existentialism.* Englewood Cliffs, N.J.: Prentice-Hall, 1962.

"Existential Phenomenology and the Sociological Tradition." *American Sociological Review,* 30, 5 (October 1965), 674–688.

Tocqueville, Alexis de. *The Old Regime and the French Revolution.* Stuart Gilbert, trans. Garden City, N.Y.: Doubleday, 1955.

Democracy in America, Richard Heffner, ed. New York: New American Library, 1956.

Todorov, Tsvetan, ed. *Theorie de la Literature. Textes des formalistes russes reunis.* Paris: Seuil, 1965.

Litterature et signification. Paris: Larousse, 1967.

Grammaire de Decameron. The Hague: Mouton, 1969.

Tolman, Edward C. *Purposive Behavior in Animals and Men.* New York: Appleton-Century-Crofts, 1932.

"The Determinants of Behavior at a Choice Point." *Psychological Review,* 45, 1 (January 1938), 1–41.

Tönnies, Ferdinand. *Community and Society* (Gemeinschaft und Gesellschaft), Charles P. Loomis, trans. East Lansing: Michigan State University Press, 1964.

Toulmin, Stephen. *The Philosophy of Science.* New York: Hutchinson, 1953.

Foresight and Understanding, An Enquiry into the Aims of Science. Bloomington: Indiana University Press, 1961.

Tumin, Melvin. "The Functionalist Approach to Social Problems." *Social Problems,* 12, 4 (Spring 1965), 379–388.

Turbayne, C. M. *The Myth of Metaphor.* New Haven: Yale, 1962.

Turgot, A. Robert. *Reflections on the Formation and Distribution of Riches.* New York: A. M. Kelley, 1963.

Turner, Ralph H. "Foci of Discrimination of Non-whites." *American Journal of Sociology,* 58, 3 (November 1952), 247–256.

Turner, V. W. "Symbols in Ndembu Ritual." In Max Gluckman, ed. *Closed Societies and Open Minds.* Chicago: Aldine, 1964.

"Planes of Classification in a Ritual of Life and Death." In *The Ritual Process.* Chicago: Aldine, 1969.

Tussman, Joseph. *Obligation and the Body Politic.* New York: Oxford, 1960.

Tylor, Stephen A. *Cognitive Anthropology.* New York: Holt, 1969.

Urmson, J. O. *Philosophical Analysis.* London: Oxford, 1956.

Vaihinger, H. *The Philosophy of "As If."* London: Routledge, 1924.

Vallier, Ivan, ed. *Comparative Methods in Sociology.* Berkeley: University of California Press, 1971.

Veatch, Henry B. "Alternative Logics: A What-Logic and a Relating-Logic." *Two Logics: The Conflict between Classical and Neo-Analytical Philosophy,* Evanston, Ill.: Northwestern University Press, 1969.

Veblen, Thorstein. *The Theory of the Leisure Class: An Economic Study of Institutions.* New York: New American Library, 1957.

Verlaine, Paul Marie. *Oeuvres completes.* Paris: Club des Libraries, 1960.

Vexliard, Alexandre. "Psychological Theories of P. Sorokin." In Philip Allen, ed. *Pitirim Sorokin in Review.* Durham, N.C.: Duke University Press, 1963.

Vico, Giambattista. *The New Science of Giambattista Vico.* Thomas G. Bergin and Max H. Fisch, trans. Ithaca: Cornell, 1948.

Volosinov, V. N. "Reported Speech." In Ladislav Matejka and Krystyna Pomorska, eds. and trans. *Readings in Russian Poetics: Formalist and Structuralist Views.* Cambridge, Mass.: M.I.T., 1971.

Voltaire. *Micromegas.* Paris: Nilsson, n. d.

Von Bertalanffy, Ludwig. *General Systems Theory.* New York: Braziller, 1968.

von Neumann, John, and Morgenstern, Oscar. *Theory of Games and Economic Behavior.* Princeton, N.J.: Princeton, 1944.

Von Schelting, Alexander. *Max Weber's Eissenschaftslehre; das logiche Problem der historischen Kulturerkenninis: die Grenzen der Soziologie des Wissens.* Tubingen: J. C. B. Mohr, 1934.

"Review of Mannheim's *Ideologie und Utopie,*" *American Sociological Review,* 1, 4 (August 1936), 664–674.

Wald, Abraham. *Statistical Decision Functions.* New York: Wiley, 1950.

Wallace, Walter L. *The Logic of Science in Sociology.* Chicago: Aldine, 1971.

Walzer, Michael Walker. *Obligation: Essays on Civil Disobedience, War, and Citizenship.* Cambridge, Mass.: Harvard, 1970.

Wann, T. W. *Behaviorism and Phenomenology: Contrasting Bases for Modern Psychology.* Chicago: The University of Chicago Press, 1964.

Warner, W. Lloyd. *Yankee City.* New Haven: Yale, 1963.

The Living and the Dead: A Study of the Symbolic Life of Americans. New Haven: Yale, 1959.

Watt, Ian P. "The Ironic Tradition in Augustan Prose from Swift to Johnson." In James R. Sutherland and Ian Watt. *Restoration and Augustan Prose.* Los Angeles: University of California Press, 1957.

Watzlawawick, Paul et al. *The Pragmatics of Human Communication.* New York: Norton, 1967.

Wax, Rosalie. "Reciprocity in Field Work." In Richard Adams and Jack Preiss, eds. *Human Organization Research.* Homewood, Ill.: Dorsey Press, 1960.

Weaver, Robert C. "Integration in Public and Private Housing." *Annals of the American Academy of Political and Social Science,* 304 (March 1956), 86–97.

Webb, Eugene et al. *Unobtrusive Measures: Nonreactive Research in the Social Sciences.* Chicago: Rand McNally, 1972.

Weber, Alfred. "Principielles zur Kultursoziologie: Gesellschafts-prozess: Civilisations-prozess und Kulturbewegung." *Archiv für Sozialwissenschaft und Sozialpolitik.* 47 (1920), 1–49.

Weber, Max. "Science as a Vocation." In Max Weber, *From Max Weber.* Hans Gerth and C. Wright Mills, eds. New York: Oxford, 1946.

The Methodology of the Social Sciences. Edward A. Shils and Henry A. Finch, trans. and eds. Glencoe, Ill.: Free Press, 1949.

"Kategorien der verstehnden Soziologie." In *Gessamelte Aufstaze zur Wissenschaftslehre.* Tubingen: Mohr, 1951.

The Protestant Ethic and the Spirit of Capitalism. New York: Scribner, 1958.

Sociology of Religion. Boston: Beacon Press, 1963.

On Charisma and Institution Building, S. N. Eisenstadt, ed. Chicago: The University of Chicago Press, 1968.

Weinstein, Eugene A. "Toward a Theory of Interpersonal Tactics." In Carl W. Backman and Paul F. Secord, eds. *Problems in Social Psychology.* New York: McGraw-Hill, 1966.

Weiss, Paul. *The Nine Basic Arts.* Carbondale, Ill.: Southern Illinois University Press, 1961.

Wellmer, Albrecht. *Critical Theory of Society.* New York: Herder and Herder, 1971.

Werkmeister, W. H. *The Basis and Structure of Knowledge.* New York: Harper, 1948.

Wertenbaker, L. "The World of Picasso," *Time*. New York: 1957.

Whalley, George. *Poetic Process*. New York: Hillary, 1953.

Wheelock, John Hall. *What is Poetry?* New York: Scribner, 1963.

Wheelwright, Philip Ellis. *Metaphor and Reality*. Bloomington: Indiana University Press, 1954.

    The Burning Fountain: A Study in the Language of Symbolism. Bloomington: Indiana University Press, 1968.

Whitehead, Alfred North, and Russell Bertrand. *Principia Mathematica*. Cambridge, Mass.: Harvard, 1962.

Whorf, Benjamin Lee. *Language, Thought, and Reality*. John Carroll, ed. New York: Wiley, 1956.

Whyte, William F. *Street Corner Society: The Social Structure of an Italian Slum*. Chicago: The University of Chicago Press, 1969.

Wieder, Lawrence D. "The Convict Code: A Study of a Moral Order as a Persuasive Activity." Ph.D. dissertation, University of California at Los Angeles, 1969.

Wildavsky, Aaron. *The Politics of the Budgetary Process*. Boston: Little, Brown, 1964.

Wilden, Anthony G. *The Language of the Self*. Baltimore: Johns Hopkins, 1968.

Will, Frederic. *Intelligible Beauty in Aesthetic Thought*. Tubingen: Max Niemeyer Verlag, 1958.

Willer, David. *Scientific Sociology; Theory and Method*. Englewood Cliffs, N.J.: Prentice-Hall, 1967.

Wilshire, Bruce. *William James and Phenomenology: A Study of The Principles of Psychology*. Bloomington: Indiana University Press, 1968.

Wilson, Brian R., ed. *Rationality*. New York: Harper & Row, 1970.

Wilson, Thomas P. "Conceptions of Interaction and Forms of Sociological Explanation." *American Sociological Review*, 35, 4 (August 1970), 697–710.

Winch, Peter. *The Idea of a Social Science and Its Relation to Philosophy*. New York: Humanities Press, 1958.

Windelband, Wilhelm. *Theories in Logic*. New York: Citadel, 1961.

Wisdom, John. *Paradox and Discovery*. Berkeley: University of California Press, 1970.

Wittgenstein, Ludwig. *Philosophic Investigations*. G. E. M. Anscombe, trans. Oxford: Blackwell, 1953.

Wolff, K. H., ed. *The Sociology of Georg Simmel*. Glencoe, Ill.: Free Press, 1950.

    "The Sociology of Knowledge and Sociological Theory." In Larry T. Reynolds and Janice M. Reynolds, eds. *The Sociology of Sociology*, New York: McKay, 1970.

Wolin, Sheldon S. *Politics and Vision: Continuity and Innovation in Western Political Thought*. Boston: Little, Brown, 1960.

Wollheim, Richard. *Art and Its Objects: An Introduction to Aesthetics*. New York: Harper & Row, 1968.

Woodward, Joan. *Industrial Organizations: Theory and Practice*. London: Oxford, 1965.

Woolf, Virginia. *To the Lighthouse*. New York: Harcourt, Brace & World, 1955.

Wrong, Denis H. "The Oversocialized Conception of Man in Modern Sociology." *American Sociological Review*, 26, 2 (April 1961), 183–193.

Zetterberg, Hans L. *On Theory and Verification in Sociology*. New York: The Tressler Press, 1954.

Ziff, Paul. "Reasons in Art Criticism." In Joseph Margolis, ed. *Philosophy Looks at the Arts*. New York: Scribner, 1962.

Zimmerman, Don H. "Paper Work and People Work: A Study of a Public Assistance Agency." Ph.D. dissertation, University of California at Los Angeles, 1966.

Zimmerman, Don H., and Wieder, Lawrence D. "The Everyday World as a Phenomenon." In Jack D. Douglas, ed. *Understanding Everyday Life*. Chicago: Aldine, 1970.

Zipf, George K. *Human Behavior and the Principle of Least Effort*. Cambridge, Mass.: Addison- Wesley, 1949.

Znaniecki, Florian. *The Method of Sociology*. New York: Octagon, 1968.

Zorbaugh, Harvey. *The Gold Coast and the Slum*. Chicago: The University of Chicago Press, 1929.

Index